Judging Jewish Identity in the United States

Judging Jewish Identity in the United States

Annalise E. Glauz-Todrank

LEXINGTON BOOKS
Lanham • Boulder • New York • London

Published by Lexington Books
An imprint of The Rowman & Littlefield Publishing Group, Inc.
4501 Forbes Boulevard, Suite 200, Lanham, Maryland 20706
www.rowman.com

86-90 Paul Street, London EC2A 4NE

British Library Cataloguing in Publication Information Available

Library of Congress Cataloging-in-Publication Data

Names: Glauz-Todrank, Annalise E., author.
Title: Judging Jewish identity in the United States / Annalise E. Glauz-Todrank.
Description: Lanham : Lexington Books, [2023] | Includes bibliographical references and index.
Identifiers: LCCN 2022031914 (print) | LCCN 2022031915 (ebook) |
   ISBN 9781666923032 (cloth) | ISBN 9781666923056 (paper) | ISBN
   9781666923049 (ebook)
Subjects: LCSH: Jews--Legal status, laws, etc.--United States. | Jews--United States--
   Identity. | Antisemitism--United States. | Whites--Race identity. | Race discrimination--
   United States | United States--Race relations.
Classification: LCC KF4869.J3 G53 2023 (print) | LCC KF4869.J3 (ebook) | DDC
   342.7308/5296–dc23/eng/20220825
LC record available at https://lccn.loc.gov/2022031914
LC ebook record available at https://lccn.loc.gov/2022031915

In loving gratitude for the mentorship of my grandpa,
Gustave Herman Todrank (1924–1982),
whose photo guides me from my desk.
May his memory be for a blessing.

Contents

Acknowledgments

I began this manuscript fifteen years ago. It has been interrupted by brain cancer, from which I lost the ability to speak and write, nevertheless, I have been determined to finish it. If I were to acknowledge all the individuals who have helped me, motivated me, been a friend to me, and prayed for me, it would take a book by itself. I trust that those of you who are not mentioned here know that I have been strengthened by your presence in my life.

Since it began as a dissertation, it is with gratitude that I name the members of my committee: my adviser Richard D. Hecht, Rudy V. Busto, W. Randall Garr, and Lisa Hajjar. I thank the University of California Religious Studies Department and the Law and Society Program, particularly Lisa Hajjar and Eve Darian-Smith.

What became *Judging Jewish Identity in the United States* would never have been possible without the participation and engagement of the Shaare Tefila Congregation, interviews with Jewish Advocacy Centers founders Kevin Lipson and Irvin Shapell, lawyer for the respondents, Deborah Garren, and the Congregation's central lawyer, Patricia Brannan. Special gratitude to my interviewees from Shaare Tefila, many of whom appear throughout the book, and to Rabbi Jonah Layman, Jill Goldwater, Kevin Lipson, and Patricia Brannan for continuing to answer my questions. After meeting with Pat, she sent me an entire box with all the legal materials for the case. Thank you to the Shaare Tefila Congregation for allowing me to access your archives, to Joan Romano and Barbara Kopelman at the *Washington Jewish Week* for giving me access to archived periodicals, to Rockville Memorial Library in Rockville, Maryland, for access to the *Montgomery County Sentinel*, to Principal Historian Mara Cherkasky for being so helpful and providing me with data about the historical segregation of Jews in Washington, DC, to Lauren Strauss for talking with me about her research regarding Neighbors, Inc in the 1950s, to Director Charlotte Bonelli and her assistant, Deisree Guillermo, for their assistance with the archives at for American Jewish Committee, and to Rachel Gordan, for a phone conversation about her article that pertained to the manuscript. For hosting me for several weeks during two summers when I collected much of the above research, my utmost gratitude to my dear friend Lindsay Gonzales, her husband Apollo Gonzales, and their son Corvus. And my sincere appreciation to Harriet Steinhorn Roth, Cantor Gershon Levin, and Martin Roth, who passed away as I prepared the manuscript. May your memories be for a blessing.

I had the pleasure of working in the Religion Department at Wesleyan University. For reading an article that later became a part of this book, I am grateful to Mary-Jane Rubenstein, Attiya Ahmad, Laura Harrington, and Elizabeth McAlister. Thank you to Sam Nelson for inviting me to give a talk related to the article at Yale University for the Religion and Politics Colloquium, sponsored by the MacMillan Center Initiative on Religion, Politics, and Society.

The Department for the Study of Religions at Wake Forest University has been my home for ten years. My colleagues and staff members have been with me through brain cancer and my recovery. I am deeply indebted to all of them for their support. They are Tanisha Ramachandran, Lynn S. Neal, Mary F. Foskett, Nelly Van Doorn-Harder, Ulrike Wiethaus, Stephen Boyd, Simeon Ilesanmi, Lucas Johnston, James Ford, Ron Neal, Ken Hoglund, Leann Pace, Sheila Lockhart, Jeff Nichols, and now Kimberly Wortmann and Tara Baldrick-Morrone.

My doctors saved my life. I would not be here without the radiologist who saw the tumor, Dr. Andrew Evans, my local neurosurgeon who explained it to me, and my Stanford Hospital folks—Dr. Griffith Harsh IV, who performed my open cranial brain surgery; Dr. Richard Jaffe, my anesthesiologist; the many doctors and interns who talked to me while the operation was occurring; and all the medical staff; Dr. Lawrence Recht, my funny and trustworthy neuro-oncologist; and RN Megan Gerson, as well as the doctors and everyone who was with me through the radiation process. Thank you to Dr. Recht's team who answers my medication-related questions. Dr. Harvey Cohen made it all possible by serving on the palliative care committee with my mom, Carolyn Glauz-Todrank. Dr. Jody Noe, my naturopathic doctor, who told me what supplements to take and what to eat, and without whom I would *not* have made it through chemotherapy. My sincere thanks to all the doctors, radiologists, residents, nurses, lab technicians, therapists, and the people who cleaned my hospital room.

I would not have recovered without the amazing support of all the people rooting for me, praying for me in various traditions, and sending all the positive thoughts my way. This included cards, letters, kind gifts, and a meal train. If you have been present with me in my life, please know that I feel the love!

Thank you to the wonderful faculty who covered for me when I could not teach, Andrew Ettin and Barry Trachtenberg.

I am sincerely appreciative to my careful readers: Jarrod Whitaker, Colleen Lerner, Stephen Glauz-Todrank, and Kimberly Wortmann, who read the entire manuscript at various stages; Simeon Ilesanmi, who read three chapters; Silas Allard and Jenna Gray-Hildenbrand, who read various parts of it; and my developmental editors, Emily Mace, who read the introduction and chapter 1, and Ulrike Guthrie, who helped me turn the manuscript into a book. The Jewish Studies Program committee members read and discussed with me what was then my fourth chapter, a big thanks to Dean Franco, Mir Yarfitz, Barry Trachtenberg, and Leann Pace. Steve Boyd has been a confidante. Mary Foskett worked with me to shape the manuscript at a critical point in the process. Lynn S. Neal has been an important mentor.

I could not cite my sources or find necessary data without my reference librarians! Many thanks to Kaeley McMahan, Lance Burke, Rosalind Tedford, and Hu Womack. Special thanks to Kate Irwin-Smiler, legal citation expert extraordinaire, and Kyle Denlinger, who worked with my tight timeline on the bibliography.

For funding this manuscript, thank you to the University of California, Santa Barbara for the Doctoral Student Travel Grant, the Pat and Irving Glazer Jewish Studies Research Fellowship, the Humanities and Social Science Research Grant, the Fee Fellowship, the Graduate Division Dissertation Fellowship, and the Professor Phillip E. Hammond Scholarship. Thank you to the Wake Forest University Humanities Institute for a Book Development Fund and for the Summer Writing Grant. Thank you to the Wake Forest University Research and Development Fund for indexing assistance.

Thank you to the other people who have academically supported me, not listed above, some of whom allowed me to talk to them about this dissertation/manuscript/book: Leonard B. Glick, Alan Hodder, David Cooper, Erica Srinivasan, Jared Lindahl, Megan Adamson Sijapati, Aaron Gross, Aysha Hidayatullah, Patricia Kubala, Sarah Schulman, Greg Prieto, Colleen Windham-Hughes, Howard Winant, Elvin Lim, Mariah Schug, Michelle Zarowitz, Laura Levitt, Sarah Imhoff, Jonathan Crane, Tanisha Ramachandran, Eranda Jayawickreme, Simone M. Caron, Karin Friederic, Brian Burke, Sara Dahill-Brown, Guy Witzel, Bradley Onishi, Sue Rupp, Jeffrey Lerner, Penny Sinanoglou, Ana-Maria González-Wahl, Shana Sippy, Mike Backfield, Lynn Byrd, Elisabeth Maselli, and Neha Ratna Shrestha.

Thank you to Hampshire College, where "knowing" is not enough. Let's get out there and do it!

Many thanks to all my students, current and former.

Special gratitude for the guidance of Donna Hampton and Rabbi Mark Cohn.

And with utmost love to all members of my family, who has always been here for me; notably to my grandparents who have passed, Roy L. Glauz Jr., Elizabeth C. Todrank, Gustave H. Todrank, may your memories be for a blessing; and to Jane W. Glauz, Carolyn Glauz-Todrank, Stephen Glauz-Todrank, Tyler Glauz-Todrank, Bimla Lama Budaprithi Banks, and my dear husband, Surjya Raj Banks.

Many thanks to my editor Judith Lakamper, assistant editor Mark Lopez, and assistant production editor Linda Kessler, without whom this would not be a book.

Introduction

Late in the evening of November 1, 1982, the Board of Trustees at Shaare Tefila Congregation finished their meeting. The synagogue is affiliated with the Conservative movement and was located in Silver Spring, Maryland. It was the Monday before Election Day, and their synagogue was the local polling station. Trustees Jack and Bess Teller walked to their car across the street and immediately noticed spray paint on the front of their sandalwood-colored Oldsmobile. Looking more carefully, they recognized two swastikas. One was a confused mess, the other one was clearly identifiable as the Nazi symbol. Shocked, they took the car and drove home. Jack then called the synagogue's president, Maurice Potosky, and its executive director, Marshall S. Levin, who were still at Shaare Tefila, to inform them about the vandalism. Disturbed, Potosky and Levin headed outside the white building and found antisemitic graffiti spray-painted either in red or black over the synagogue walls: "Death to the Jude," "Death to the Jews, '*Toten Kampf Raband*' (a misspelling and a reference to the Nazi 'death head units').[1] In addition, there was a large image of a flaming cross, a Nazi eagle, several swastikas, and the letters 'SS' on a cement pipe used as playground equipment.[2] The most graphic graffiti was spray-painted over a door: 'In, Take a Shower, Jew.'[3] Horrified, Potosky and Levin called Rabbi Martin S. Halpern, z"l (*zichrono livracha*, may his memory be for a blessing), who had left directly after the meeting ended. He returned to the synagogue, and the three men discussed what to do.

Eliminating antisemitic graffiti and keeping it from the non-Jewish community was a common practice in the 1980s. The prevailing sentiment within the Jewish community was that instances of antisemitic[4] vandalism should be immediately cleaned up and quietly removed. Better if the surrounding community and the press did not find out. Better to keep it quiet so that "copycat" crimes did not occur.[5] The majority of Jewish Americans attempted to assimilate into their predominately White, Christian surroundings by not drawing attention to themselves. Levin noted that many Jewish Americans viewed these instances of defacement as an embarrassment to the Jewish community.[6] As journalist Marjorie Hyer reported in the *Washington Post* three days after the incident: "Jewish leaders say that statistics do not accurately reflect the true extent of such incidents, since there is a great reluctance on the part of many victims to report such acts for fear of encouraging their repetition."[7] There was a long history behind such sentiments, as we shall see in chapter 1.

On that November evening at the synagogue, however, Executive Director Levin, President Potosky, and Rabbi Halpern puzzled over the practicality of removing the paint overnight.[8] The next morning Shaare Tefila would be holding a morning minyan, a group of ten Jews, for morning services, and neighbors would be coming to vote. Rabbi Halpern worried: "How will the survivors of the Holocaust who come to our daily minyan react tomorrow morning?"[9] He himself was a survivor of the Shoah, the Hebrew term for "catastrophe" and for the Holocaust. When the Shaare Tefila members and the voters arrived the next day, they would see the six-foot Nazi eagle and the words painted on the walls. The men would need to hire someone with a sandblaster to remove the paint from the walls.

Levin approached the vandalism as affecting not only Shaare Tefila Congregation itself but also the entire population of Silver Spring. He proposed leaving it *in situ*. He was the youngest of the three men. When the vandalism incident occurred at Shaare Tefila, Levin contextualized it in terms of other violence committed against Jews, and he thought about these acts as *crimes*, emphasizing the role of law.[10] He noted that *Kristallnacht*, beginning the night of November 9–10, 1938, when Nazi soldiers killed nearly one hundred Jews; burned synagogues, homes, businesses, and schools all over Germany; and sent about thirty thousand Jewish men to concentration camps, was not a "crime" when it occurred.[11] With the implementation of the Nuremberg Laws in 1935, Jewish rights to citizenship were revoked.[12] Because Jewish Americans *were* citizens according to US law, Levin believed they should be protected from these crimes.

In contrast to Levin, Potosky and Halpern likely considered the effects of the graffiti if they left it in place. It clearly referenced Nazi and Ku Klux Klan ideologies. What if many non-Jews in Silver Spring secretly agreed with those sentiments? What if they harbored less-extreme racist sentiments? Or what if they simply didn't like Jews?

In the end, Levin convinced them, and they elected to leave the graffiti. Their decision marked a turning point for Jewish responses to antisemitic vandalism in the Washington, DC, area, which eventually spread throughout the United States.[13] Rather than covering the vandalism, Shaare Tefila leaders took a proactive stance to draw attention to it, a move that forced non-Jews to confront the vandalism along with them. Rabbi Halpern later wrote that he "insisted the inscriptions remain on the walls, that the press be notified, that we photograph everything, that we expose everything to the community at large so that they could see what antisemitism and bigotry were capable of perpetrating."[14]

This book examines the civil suit that emerged from the vandalism, *Shaare Tefila Congregation v. Cobb*, and its significance to the Jewish American narrative. The case explores how Jewishness in the United States is dominantly defined according to the legal categories of "religion" and "race," but also according to the experiences of Shaare Tefila synagogue members, both individually and collectively. It grapples with the social and legal definitions of "religion" and "race" as they are represented in different ways and for various reasons in American life and in the lived realities of the congregants who witnessed the vandalism.[15] It draws a distinction between two ideas. First, it acknowledges the dominant socio-legal assumption in the United States that "religion" and "race" have been *functionally* separated in everyday life— even according to many excellent scholars—and secondly, it maintains that they are not separate in embodied experience. For example, an individual can be both Black, considered a "racial" identity, and Jewish, considered a "religious" identity in the United States. These characteristics infuse each other so that one's Blackness and one's Jewishness cannot be parsed out separately.[16]

This case radically challenges the Jewish American narrative because it was the first case to account for racist, antisemitic defacement, and, further, the first example of a race-based case in support of Jewish Americans. Most Jews, in contrast, have conformed to a "religious" identity in the United States, in which "religion" typically derives from Protestant Christian ideals and assumptions that emphasize belief and choice.[17] In the United States, "race" usually refers to skin color and other physical features, such as eyes, nose, stature, hair color, and type, which initially and primarily has targeted Black people.[18] Both of these categories are culturally imposed: often imperfectly and sometimes violently, onto Jewish people and traditions for centuries, in Europe and in what became the United States. Neither of these words properly fit the ways most Jews understand themselves. In the US context, synagogue-going Jewish Americans may describe themselves as "religious," but Jewish Americans also define themselves as "secular" or culturally Jewish.

Laura Levitt, a prominent scholar of Jewish studies, argues that Jewish Americans do not fit the liberal, Protestant religious norm and should not be required to do so.[19] In her chapter in *Secularisms*, "Other Moderns, Other Jews: Revisiting Jewish Secularism in America," she focuses on Eastern European Jewish immigrants who arrived during the turn of the twentieth century and saw themselves as embracing a modern Yiddish "*weltlich*" (secular) identity, which involved Yiddish theater, newspapers, and literature. They were confused when they encountered Jewish Americans who identified themselves as "religious" in accordance with American norms.[20] Jewish Americans of

European origin, especially during the early twenty-first century, distanced themselves from the term "race," because they were concerned about either being grouped with Blacks or—for the Jews in the United States prior to the Eastern European immigration—being understood as "foreigners" and unable to attain citizenship.

Contrary to "religious" identity, defined in Protestant terms, Jewishness, in *Jewish* terms, cannot be defined by choice or belief but rather is identified by birth or conversion. Important to this narrative is that most Jewish Americans have ended up adopting and internalizing the Protestant trope of "religion"[21] and for the European descendants and emigrants among them, internalizing, whenever possible, the identity of Whiteness.[22] This religious, White basis had been the reality for most Jewish American synagogues for about thirty years before our story begins.

This book is about the Shaare Tefila Congregation, a somewhat typical Jewish American Conservative community located in the Washington, DC, area, and its pursuit of a civil suit against the antisemitic vandals who defaced their synagogue. It identifies the Shaare Tefila Congregation as members of a larger, and what Khaled Beydoun describes as an "aspirational," White Jewish community, who are "formally white."[23] Beydoun differentiates between "formal" Whiteness—Jews and Muslims who originated or emigrated from Europe, the Middle East, or North Africa—which does "not always confer the privileges, presumptions, and status theoretically attendant with whiteness,"[24] and "substantive" Whiteness, which he defines as "an experience colored by access to and enjoyment of the slate of privileges and positive presumptions theoretically thought to emanate from whiteness."[25] Shaare Tefila Congregation members were not "substantively" White because their synagogue's walls, some playground equipment, and a car were vandalized by White supremacists, who did not believe that White-perceived Jewish Americans *were* White. "Formally" White Jewish and Muslim Americans are not considered "substantively" White because they are not also *Christian*.

He also considers Whiteness an *experience*.[26] To give a brief example, in one of my interviews, Susan Goldsamt stated that she was the first "open Jew" where she worked. She is "formally" White, but she was not perceived that way by her boss. Due to her "formal" Whiteness, she could visually and performatively *be* "White," if she chose. However, it would require that she conceal her Jewishness, and as an active member of a Conservative synagogue, it would mean not saying blessings over food out loud and not telling her co-workers about her weekend plans, which would include observance of Shabbat at the synagogue, potentially Friday evening, but certainly Saturday morning. It would also include other activities with synagogue members, and if she were to bring coworkers to her house, they would see her mezuzahs, small boxes placed on every major doorpost in the house that encases the

Shema, one of the most important Jewish prayers. She would have to recode herself as White and Christian, the religious identity that White people project and are assumed to entail.[27]

My interviews represent the various voices of twenty-six Shaare Tefila members who discussed their experiences, some of whose conversations resound throughout the book, and the majority of whom were self-selecting. My discussion of particular congregants in this book highlights how these determined individuals saw the civil suit through to the end and sent their leaders to describe to the vandals how it affected them. It also demonstrates how they used the atrocious defacement of their synagogue for educational purposes in their community. In doing so, they were modeling a new role of publicly grappling with their White-perceived, marginalized community identity. This significant role exemplified the synagogue as a catalyst who exposed the racist antisemitic graffiti *not* just to other local Jews but also to the Silver Spring community.

RESPONDING TO THE VANDALISM

Over the next few days, congregation members brought their children to see the graffiti.

Outsiders, including many Christians, saw or learned about the graffiti and sent letters of support, some with money to help pay for repairs, particularly the Colesville Council of Community Congregations, within which Shaare Tefila was the only synagogue. Letters retained by the congregation, all from Christians, show that the people who wrote wanted Shaare Tefila members to know that they were speaking out *as* Christians, and, although the letters did not say this exactly, in opposition to the Christian-derived Nazis and the Christian-proud Ku Klux Klan members. One man wrote as a Catholic on behalf of "almost all Americans," and stated that "even though the Jewish people carry the brunt against bigotry in most instances, yet we Catholics are not very far beyond you, and if anything, this sort of thing brings us all closer together."[28] His position articulates his Catholic identity as a response to the dominant Protestant Christian sentiment. This relationship is outside the scope of this book but reflects his social location as a religious minority in the 1980s and recalls the quotas passed by Congress in the Immigration Act of 1924.[29]

This act of vandalism, to a space sacred to Jews, also significantly affected nonmembers who witnessed or heard about the defacement. Because Silver Spring was not yet religiously diverse, many folks prayed in churches, some in synagogues, and far fewer in mosques, temples, or gurdwaras, but they all recognized these places as "holy," given the context of their own traditions.

Several Jewish-related organizations and synagogues wrote to the synagogue. One was United Synagogue of America: Seaboard Region, whose Executive Director, Donald D. Weisman, wrote to Potosky and Halpern that he had just returned from visiting Shaare Tefila; he reported that it was "a shocking site" [sic] and looked like the work of the Ku Klux Klan. He had spoken with the President-Elect of the Seaboard Region of the Board and invited Potosky and Halpern to their forthcoming board meeting on November 7 to discuss the incident in depth.[30] In a second letter, Sidney Kramer,[31] a state senator affiliated with B'nai Israel Congregation, had handwritten a note that presented a resolution on behalf of the forty-six synagogues in the seaboard region.[32] Robert Abrams, the President of Har Tzeon-Agudath Achim, also wrote the following day to Halpern, expressing his horror at the desecration. The same day Abrams wrote to County Executive Charles W. Gilchrist, urging him to ask the chief of police for Montgomery County to act and seek justice for all involved.[33]

Other significant establishments, such as the Arab-American Anti-Discrimination Committee, Washington, DC, organization Neighbors Inc., and the Judiciary Committee—representing Montgomery-Howard Counties, 14-A, in Annapolis, Maryland—also sent letters.[34] James J. Zogby, of the Arab-American Anti-Discrimination Committee, wrote that they were "outraged by this and all other acts of anti-Semitism, knowing from personal experience the pain and fear such racism inflicts upon its victims."[35] Note that Zogby used the word "racism" in his statement, which he used to define the Shaare Tefila Congregation incident as similar to discrimination against Arab Americans, who are also "formally" White.[36]

After the desecration of Shaare Tefila Congregation, the press came to film, photograph, and talk to congregation members. When they arrived, Levin told them that they must return on the following Sunday, when the members of the Shaare Tefila youth group had organized a cleanup day. Between six hundred and one thousand people, according to different sources, showed up that day to support the congregation. True to Levin's belief, the community embraced rather than abandoned them. Alan P. Dean with the Human Relations Commission of the Montgomery County Government wrote that "the extremely courageous stand taken by the Shaare Tefila Congregation, when their synagogue was desecrated, was an historic turning point in addressing anti-Semitic hate acts."[37] Their story made national and international news.[38] German television as well as "Soviet," French, and Israeli newspapers covered it.[39] Hence, Shaare Tefila's reaction to the vandalism began to shift ideas about the social implications of permitting non-Jews to witness antisemitic graffiti.[40]

Sometime after the defacement, police identified eight White individuals after someone was heard talking about the vandalism in a local store. Prior to their defacement of the synagogue, several of them had spray-painted the back of Drug Fair, a pharmacy at the White Oak Shopping Center about a block away, with a giant Nazi eagle, a burning cross with three "K"'s in it, the words "White Power," the slogan "Aryan Brotherhood," a Confederate flag, a Star of David with an arrow or line running through it, and all their initials. Apparently, after they finished drinking and smoking marijuana, someone said either "Let's go paint a synagogue"[41] or "Somebody should do that on a synagogue."[42] Thus, the location of the defacement mattered: it must be a *Jewish* space, significant and sacred to Jewish Americans. Seven young men were charged in court, and three were found guilty and sentenced to jail: one for three years, one for six months, and one for four months.

For many synagogue members, these convictions were the end of the story. The vandals were accused, tried, and met with justice. The congregation thought the case was solved, but the Jewish Advocacy Center (JAC), a legal organization based in Washington, DC, wished to pursue the vandalism further.

WHY THIS CASE IS IMPORTANT

The JAC, founded by Irvin Shapell and his colleague Kevin Lipson, based its design on the Southern Poverty Law Center (SPLC), which was discussing a key case that would later result in a major financial loss to the Ku Klux Klan.[43] The JAC hoped to do the same, targeting antisemitic lawbreakers to make their offenses federally applicable. Like the SPLC, the JAC aimed to use the law as a tool in the larger social battle to protect civil rights on an everyday basis. At the time, unlike the Anti-Defamation League of B'nai B'rith, the American Jewish Committee, the American Jewish Congress, and the National Jewish Community Relations Council, who at the time offered support, defense, and legal protection to both individuals and groups of Jewish Americans who had experienced antisemitism, the JAC aggressively aimed to take cases to federal court and make them federal legal issues.[44]

The JAC wished to build a new precedent that would protect Jewish Americans from discriminatory vandalism and other actions that referred to their Jewish identities. This legal precedent would protect Jews who would not otherwise have recourse. Shapell and Lipson heard about the criminal case, in which vandals were charged with defacing the Shaare Tefila Congregation. Shapell contacted Marshall Levin and asked if he could address the congregation about filing a civil suit. Levin agreed. Eventually, the synagogue's Board of Trustees voted to approve it. Thereafter, Lipson spoke about it at area synagogues, and then successfully found a law firm, Hogan & Hartson, to support the Congregation pro bono.[45]

Shaare Tefila Congregation v. Cobb figures as an important moment in Jewish American life. It is not a landmark case, because other rulings pertain more broadly to a larger set of racialized groups, but it situates Jewishness at the interface of "religion" and "race" and focuses on the social implications of American Jewishness in the 1980s. First, the book explains why the Jewish American community dealt with antisemitic vandalism at that time by concealing it or covering it up. It then turns to the Shaare Tefila Congregation who shifted those terms dramatically when it left the graffiti and allowed it to be seen by the public.

Prior to *Shaare Tefila*, Jewish American legal cases had invoked laws grounded in religion, such as school prayer, kosher observance, Christmas decorations on public property, and Sunday Laws, which enforced Sunday as the day of rest for all Americans. In many cases, plaintiffs positioned themselves as similar to White Protestants, due to the implicit dependence on a "Christian baseline" in US law, as well as the general reliance on Whiteness as the epitome of legal and political Americanness.[46] In the past, Jewish Americans had almost exclusively used religion-based laws to assert their rights as they assimilated into the category of religion, according to a Protestant Christian framework. In the context that led to the Shaare Tefila case, however, religion-based laws would not succeed because none of them would protect the congregation from the antisemitic racist defacement of the synagogue or any other property. The First Amendment, for instance, which contained the Free Exercise Clause and the Establishment Clause, only could apply to the states, not private parties, and the Civil Rights Acts passed in 1964 and 1968 that protected religion applied only to employment and to "hate crimes" laws that did not pertain to vandalism, respectively. Note that although "hate crimes" became law in 1968, they did not become a social concept until the early 1980s.[47]

Because Hogan & Hartson's lawyers could not cite religion-based laws, they decided to cite sections from the Civil Rights Acts of 1866 and 1871, which further protected the Thirteenth Amendment and focused on formerly enslaved peoples but also included other peoples who were not deemed "White" at the time. These Acts protected Black citizens from *much* more egregious acts than vandalism; however, they could also potentially prevent racist, antisemitic defacement as well. The vandals had spray-painted the synagogue with Nazi and Ku Klux Klan–related words and imagery; these organizations relied on the hierarchy of races for their existence, notably with Aryan, White, Caucasian, and Christian at the top. In sum, the Shaare Tefila Congregation, though perceived as White in the 1980s, was not "*substantively*" White, and therefore faced Jewish American shame as they opposed vandalism that threatened them as *Jews*.

Hogan & Hartson's lawyers planned to argue that the vandals' racist *views* informed their actions. Patricia Brannan, one of these lawyers, met with members of the Board of Trustees to discuss this novel approach. She recalled that "from the start, our approach was that we should argue that the perceptions of the perpetrators . . . [based on their actions] were sufficient to trigger coverage of the Civil Rights Acts,"[48] and she explained that sections from these laws had been used successfully in legal suits by both Black and White people.[49]

When I interviewed congregants in 2008 and 2009, two members of the board of trustees recalled concern at the time about whether or not their use of these sections of law could pin Jews as a "race."[50] Although Jewish Americans had taken pains to ensure they were *not* a race just thirty-seven years prior, Nazis in Germany were murdering Jews in horrific ways due to their supposed racial inferiority.[51] The synagogue's case specifically asserted that the *vandals*, like the Nazis, *viewed* Jews as non-White.

Thus, the Board of Trustees decided to file a civil suit acknowledging their White racial identity but suing the vandals for *perceiving* the synagogue members as an inferior race and defacing the synagogue based on those perceptions. The judges in the Federal District Court of Maryland and the Fourth Circuit Court of Appeals, however, agreed with Brannan's argument that Jews are *White* but rejected her argument related to the vandals' perception of Jews. They sided with the vandals' lawyer Deborah Garren, who asserted that Judaism is a "religion," and argued that because Jews are "white," they could not sue the vandals, who were *also* White.

When the case reached the Supreme Court in 1987, the justices heard the oral argument, along with the arguments for both sides. As they posed hypothetical examples to Brannan and Garren, another feature of Jewish American historical context became apparent: that antisemitism, in some of the ways it operated, functioned *like* racism, given its racialized assumptions. Justices Thurgood Marshall and Antonin Scalia, who represented two racial and religious minorities on the Court, recognized this problem. The other justices seemed to recognize it as well, and, as a result, the Court reversed the ruling of the Fourth Circuit Court of Appeals.

Shaare Tefila established for the first time that Jewish American identification was legally configured in relation to the civil rights category of "race" . . . but as a race in *1866*. The Court used the argument of its companion case, *St. Francis College v. Al-Khazraji*, in which Caroline Mitchell asserted that Majid Ghaidan Al-Khazraji would have been considered a different race in 1866, as an "Arab," because he was a Muslim of Iraqi origin.[52] The Court determined that "Hebrews" would have been viewed that way as well. Companion cases may reach the Supreme Court because a circuit split occurs, which means at the appeals level, two or more courts reach opposite interpretations of federal law.[53]

Jewish Americans could use this case as a precedent for discrimination that had any racial content, opening the floodgates for almost every crime that targeted them. According to journalist Marcie Alvarado of the *Maryland Coast Dispatch*, it "marked one of the first successful prosecutions of an anti-Semitic vandalism case in the country."[54] For the most part, however, Jewish Americans did *not* cite it, because, in the 1980s, Jewish Americans were not usually seeking race-based rights in courts. Occasionally, it was used to press vandalism charges, but, at the time, it did not significantly change how Jewish Americans self-identified.

In the 1980s, in Silver Spring, Maryland, Shaare Tefila Congregation exemplifies the uneasy "different" space that Jewish Americans perceived as White occupy in the United States. This book examines this space from the perspectives of three groups: the congregation members, the vandals, and the judges, focusing mostly on the former and the latter. Shaare Tefila members whom I interviewed discussed their experiences of vandalism and their thoughts about Jewish identities in the United States; in some sense, their conclusions often typified the values and perspectives of other members of the synagogue. In sharp contrast, the vandals and the larger White supremacist movement drew on a colonized narrative of fear that non-White people will "take over" the United States, ruining the mythical image of the Protestant founding fathers and the origins of the United States as a White nation. For the most part, the judges in the first Federal District Court of Maryland and the Fourth Circuit Court of Appeals considered Jews "White," and failed to consider the antisemitism that defaced the outer walls of the Shaare Tefila Congregation as racism due to the congregation's argument that emphasized the vandals' *perception*. Finally, the Supreme Court accounted for historical antisemitism that Jewish Americans have faced and viewed the defacement in race-based terms—partly because Justices Thurgood Marshall and Antonin Scalia identified with the religious and the racial marginalization experienced by the Shaare Tefila members. Hence, in this ethnographic and legal study, *Shaare Tefila Congregation v. Cobb* epitomizes the nuanced and contrasting conceptions of the Jewish experience in the American narrative.

SETTING THE BOOK IN A LARGER CONTEXT

In its broadest analysis, this book considers how the United States has drawn from the concept of "race," as it was historically fabricated in Europe, and how it has been socially and historically constructed in the United States. It also acknowledges the overwhelming impact of "religion" in the American experience, evident in the trope that Americans have the "right to religious freedom," one of the most elevated rights in the US context.[55] Notably, both "religion" and "race" were *produced* by Christian leaders in Europe, yet those dominant discourses have been internalized and accommodated, in different times and in various ways, by Jewish Americans.[56]

This internalization and accommodation have a legal history in the European context that is significant to the White-perceived Jewish Americans at Shaare Tefila Congregation who aimed for federal protection against the racist, antisemitic defacement of their synagogue. It begins with one law that is "sometimes called the earliest act of racist legislation in Europe," and potentially, the defining origin of Jews as a "race."[57] The setting is the fifteenth century, in what was later Spain. Many Jews had been forcibly converted to Christianity, based on the mass riots against Jews in 1391. These conversions caused mass confusion for the already-Christians in Toledo, and they decided they needed to distinguish between themselves and the new Christians, known as *conversos*.[58] This new law, in 1449, called the "*Sentencia-Estatuto* de Toledo," formed the basis of bodily differentiation between already-Christians and *conversos*. It was the first *limpieza de sangre* or "purity of blood" law, and it prevented *conversos* from holding public or private office and from serving as witnesses against "Old Christians."[59] It articulated numerous reasons based on the "Jewish blood" of the conversos that they could not be trusted in the Catholic Toledo.

To contextualize this law, let's turn to Irene Silverblatt, who argues that it formed part of an early version of "race thinking," which emerged beginning with Portugal and Spain in the sixteenth century.[60] "Race thinking" was coined by Hannah Arendt when she sought a precedent in Western history for the origins of fascism, which she applied to nineteenth-century English imperialism.[61] Silverblatt describes Arendt's conceptualizing the origins of fascism as "machinery" "that included an organization for absolute political control and an ideology of social superiority" and notes Arendt's fear that "intertwined 'race thinking' and bureaucratic rule could unleash 'extraordinary power and destruction,' which would be all the more terrible since it was bathed in an aura of rationality and civilization."[62] "Rationality and civilization" are the harbingers of the Enlightenment. Silverblatt asserts that they were enforced in the legal bureaucracy of the Spanish Inquisition, which targeted heretical Christians, *conversos*, and *moriscos*, Muslims who converted to Catholicism.[63] In Silverblatt's terms, "race thinking" refers to "any mode of any mode of engaging social hierarchies through the lens of descent."[64]

Let's bring this concept of race thinking to the American context. Granted, as demonstrated by numerous scholars, European and American Jews have not faced the same degrees of marginalization: for example, Jewish Americans were never emancipated, they were not considered the dominant

Other, and there were no political parties formed to oppress them.[65] This book agrees. It addresses the congregants and the *Shaare Tefila* case; and while it does not examine the Nazi origins or background for the vandals' actions, it's premised on the migration of Nazi ideas and their iteration in the US context, as well as the Ku Klux Klan's view of Blacks, and also Jews, as inferior races. Considering the context, the White vandals not working or working low-paying jobs may have defaced the synagogue because they understood themselves as economically and politically powerless in contrast to Jews.

Sociologists Michael Omi and Howard Winant provide the most useful definition of race in the American environment. They write that race is a "concept which signifies and symbolizes social conflicts and interests by referring to different *types* of *human bodies*."[66] In their argument, race is built into the social structure of the United States. Their definition explains why Jewish racialization does not "make sense" in the United States in the 1980s, where "race" is based on "color." Although they do not focus on Jews in *Racial Formation in the United States from the 1960s to the 1990s* (1994)—since Jews are considered "White"—White-perceived Jewish Americans exemplify their argument about race, because it's not (necessarily) apparent in physical features. Through their lens, race is a concept that can be embodied in a variety of ways, for example, in terms of "blood" lineage, visually, or performatively.

Most judges in *Shaare Tefila Congregation v. Cobb*, however, treated Jewish Americans as a "religion" and could not understand how they might be considered a "race," and, because of its encoding in US law, conceptualized "religion" and "race" as distinct from each other. Most Jewish Americans have internalized these distinctions as well. Recall that prior to *Shaare Tefila*, Jewish American legal cases had invoked laws grounded in religion and that they identified themselves as "religious" in accordance with American norms. Beginning with the G.I. Bill and then with Directive 15 in 1977, which coded Jewish Americans of European origin for the US Census, they were also officially considered "White."[67] Although Shaare Tefila congregants internalized this identification as well—and in the 1980s identified themselves as "Jewish" and "White"—socially, the concepts of "religion" and "race" cannot be distinguished in human bodies. Here, Henry Goldschmidt's assertion that "religion" and "race" are "co-constituted" applies, by which he means that they are "wholly dependent on each other for their social existence and symbolic meanings."[68]

Further, Goldschmidt writes: "In the United States and throughout the Americas, from the fifteenth century through the twenty-first, racial and religious identities (and others) have been inextricably woven together, to such an extent that 'race' and 'religion' have helped define the very nature of the other."[69] Highlighting their symbiosis, Goldschmidt notes: "Race and religion each enter into, while emerging from, a composite identity formation that cannot be defined by either term alone . . . each is shot through with the other, and may thus be found—indeed must be accounted for—at the heart of the other's social existence."[70] Here, he means that "religion" and "race," categories that most people, and even exceptional scholarship, understand as disparate, actually *depend* on each other, and are not, ultimately, separate at all. Goldschmidt makes the insightful point that "However fluidly they may interact in the course of social life, in the eyes of most scholars race and religion manage to maintain their analytical clarity and autonomy."[71] Race and religion are not distinct because different components of embodied selves are not distinct, they are just *treated* separately, and this text engages Goldschmidt's premise which demonstrates how and why they are not.

Recall, however, that neither "religion" nor "race" are concepts associated with Jewish traditions, they are a part of Christian dominant discourse. In that context, this book adopts Daniel I. Rubin's exploration of a concept that he calls HebCrit, a relatively new scholarly arena in which Jews operate in a racialized context.[72] Specifically, *Judging Jewish Identity in the United States* examines White-perceived Jewish American congregation members who experienced racist, antisemitic defacement that covered their synagogue's outer walls.

Rubin maintains that HebCrit includes the following concepts: 1) Jews continue to be discriminated against and persecuted, 2) Jews are a racialized group, 3) Jews, and their perception as White, create invisibility and tension, 4) Jews' political and economic power is hyperbolic, and 5) Jewish personal stories have value.[73]

Having already discussed all the above points in this introduction, allow me to address further the impact of Jewish personal stories. Why is telling the story of these Jewish Americans, Shaare Tefila Congregation members who filed a civil suit, so important? For one, the case, and the legal analysis, cannot be disconnected from the people who brought it. They brought it for a reason, and the reason was that they wanted, and needed, federal protection as a disempowered community. Shaare Tefila members may have been economically well-off and White-perceived, but that quickly changed when their unmarked synagogue was defaced.[74] They did not conceal the vandalism as was the norm at the time: they broke from that norm and moved toward setting a new one—indeed the ADL's recommendation for responding to antisemitic vandalism changed after their response, in which they gathered their neighbors from different backgrounds and cleaned the synagogue together.[75] In this instance, and in many others of lesser magnitude, such as being the first "open Jew" in a workplace, White-perceived Jewish Americans are a largely invisible minority. This book tells their stories and the range of experiences they had and felt: anger, fear, sadness, gratitude for the solidarity of their neighbors, and for justice in the Supreme Court—regardless of how it was configured. Rubin reminds us *why* and *how* their stories are important.

Let's move to *how* they are important. For one, the recording of these interviews contributes to the breadth of stories about White-perceived Jewish Americans. In this case, it not only highlights why racist antisemitism is significant, but it also documents the words of people who experienced these events, and their answers to questions about their own Jewish American identities. These narratives contribute to the overall field of Jewish Studies—the stories of White-perceived Jews in the context of racist antisemitic vandalism—but also to the larger realm of scholarship, so that, like the far more marginalized BIPOC American communities whose stories are told by Critical Race Theorists, others may understand their experiences more clearly.

Rubin, however, does not apply his concept of HebCrit to a legal case that might exemplify his theory. This book does. In fact, it addresses the first case to consider Jewish Americans persecuted on a racial basis.

In sum, *Judging Jewish Identity in the United States* emphasizes how the courts addressed the argument made in *Shaare Tefila Congregation v. Cobb* by Patricia Brannan and Deborah Garren: either that Jewish Americans are White and that the vandals perceived them as a race or that they are White and a religion, therefore not a race. In its ruling, the Supreme Court adopted the decision of the companion case, *St. Francis College v. Al-Khazraji*, and determined that Jews *also* would have been deemed a racial group in 1866.

Meanwhile, this book also examines the efforts of the Shaare Tefila Congregation members to turn the defacement of their synagogue into an experience of solidarity and justice. This entailed a transformation within the Jewish community regarding best practices toward exposure of racist, antisemitic graffiti; an educational program for both Jewish and non-Jewish students at schools in the Montgomery County; a documentary film meant to promote awareness to be shown at schools, and other events; and, in the courts, a federal response to protect synagogues and other buildings from race-based antisemitic vandalism; and finally, the attempt for congregation leaders to speak with the vandals and explain what their defacement meant and how it affected their congregation. The vandals, in this case, aimed to deface a synagogue, which was not only a Jewish location but also a source of sustenance for Jewish life.

The Structure of the Book

Chapter 1 begins at Shaare Tefila Congregation on a Shabbat morning in 2008, when I first met the synagogue members, several of whom significantly influenced the filing of the civil suit in 1985. It situates the random act of vandalism in 1982 within the synagogue's historical context, which began in the 1950s. In doing so, it followed the wave in which Jewish Americans who could be perceived as White were included as White in the G.I. Bill, for instance, but were still victims of redlining and racial covenants.[76] It returns to the 1850s, just before the Civil Rights Act of 1866 was passed, when Jewish Americans *were* considered a racialized group, it continues to follow Jewish racialization and then turns to focus on the Shaare Tefila Congregation at its formation. Like most other White-perceived Jewish Americans at the time, the congregation members conformed to the dominant discourse governing Whiteness, which meant White and *Christian*. Congregants were often, but not always, perceived as White: they were "formally" White, but not necessarily "substantively" White, unless they coded themselves as Christian.

This chapter elaborates on how the congregation members experienced the vandalism as White-perceived Jewish Americans. By letting the vandalism remain as is, the congregation leaders opposed the Anti-Defamation League's prescriptions to remove or conceal antisemitic graffiti, and by doing so they allowed non-Jewish people to witness the vandals' racialization of their synagogue.[77] This action was important, both for the congregation members, to recognize that they were not excluded, at least, from *White* society; and for the community at large, many of whom flocked to Shaare Tefila Congregation to support them and help them clean their synagogue. Congregation members viewed this day with almost as much pride as the legal resolution.

The congregation leaders' decision correlated with the national sentiment in the early 1980s regarding the legal terms "hate violence" and "hate crimes": these terms were a relatively new social concept and explained the violence that targeted people based on their identities. After the criminal case, the congregants filed a civil suit, to tell their story, and for the first time in US history, to seek justice for themselves: Jewish Americans who had experienced race-based antisemitism. One of the aims was to speak to the vandals and explain how their graffiti affected the Shaare Tefila members.

Chapter 2 articulates why the initial criminal case was significant and addresses its content, but the reasons that it did not fulfill the legal goals important to many members of the congregation. At the behest of the Jewish Advocacy Center, the members decided to bring a civil suit grounded in the Civil Rights Acts of 1866 and 1871. The chapter examines their trauma at experiencing the defacement, alongside the vandals' potential motives for committing the antisemitic act. It also historicizes the legal content of race-based US civil rights acts that the lawyers thought could best protect the congregation from the defacement, since the acts had already been cited by Black, Latinx, Asian, and White Americans. In sum, the Shaare Tefila Congregation, though perceived as White, was federally disempowered from preventing vandalism that threatened them as *Jews*.

In 1985 and 1986, all but one of the judges in the Federal District Court of Maryland and the Fourth Circuit Court of Appeals assumed that Jewish Americans were "White" and a "religion," and ruled likewise, based on Deborah Garren's argument. They did so because most Jewish Americans have European ancestry, conform to the (Protestant) American category of "religion," and have been generally accepted as "White" after World War II.

Chapter 3 examines these assumptions in response to the Congregation's argument that emphasized sections of the Civil Rights Act of 1866 and of 1871. Because Jewish Americans had never been legally categorized, the judges might have to determine if Jews were a "religion" or a "race" or some combination of the two. This chapter focuses on how and why the judges of the lower courts chose *not* to adopt these sections and ruled that the vandalism was not enough to trigger the laws pertaining to race.

The fourth chapter addresses the US Supreme Court's oral argument and decision in *Shaare Tefila Congregation v. Cobb*, which overturned the lower courts' decisions. In the oral argument, the outcome depended, to a certain extent, on the congregation's, or the plaintiff's argument that the vandals targeted the synagogue because they *perceived* Jews as an inferior race, versus the defense attorney's assertion that Jews were a religious group and may not claim protection based on race. The justices determined that Jews in the United States had been discriminated against historically and ultimately used Caroline Mitchell's argument for Majid Ghaidan Al-Khazraji in *St. Francis College* that Jewish Americans *would have been understood* as a "race" or a "stock" at the time of the Civil Rights Act of 1866 and 1871. In the unanimous decision, Justice White determined that Jews were included in the Civil Rights Act of 1866 when the 39th Congress had passed it. This chapter concludes with a discussion of the unanimous decision, written by Justice White.

Chapter 5 returns to the congregation and investigates how the members of Shaare Tefila experienced the outcome of the Supreme Court decision at that time and how they spoke about the vandalism and the case years later. It considers how the congregants and their different relationships to the synagogue addressed their perceptions of the vandalism relative to their respective roles. After the case returned to the Federal District Court of Maryland, the congregation opted to settle it. They decided to have their leaders speak with the vandals about how the congregation members had experienced its defacement, instead of pursuing the case for monetary gain. This meeting between Rabbi Halpern, congregation president Shirley Altman, and lawyer Patricia Brannan empowered the congregation and facilitated a legal resolution with the vandals.

The conclusion summarizes how and why *Shaare Tefila Congregation v. Cobb* shifted the Jewish American narrative. The case did not change the national discourse, but it enabled individuals to exercise racial minority status as a matter of personal or communal identity. Although the two lower courts did not rule that antisemitic vandalism was a civil rights abuse, the Supreme Court did. The Supreme Court based its conclusion on the historic racialized antisemitic wrongs that Jewish Americans have experienced. The conclusion revisits how the judges, the lawyers, and the congregation members conceptualized the role of "religion" and "race" in *Shaare Tefila Congregation v. Cobb*. It then describes several legal cases that relied on *Shaare Tefila* and the sections of the law that it cited, demonstrating that the case became, for some other Jewish Americans, a tool for race-based Jewish American justice.

NOTES

1. Oral argument at 673, Shaare Tefila Congregation v. Cobb, 606 F.Supp. 1504 (D. Md. 1985) (No. R-84–880), *rev'd*, 107 S.Ct. 2019 (1987), in *Landmark Briefs and Arguments of the Supreme Court of the United States: Constitutional Law, 1986 Term Supplement* (Frederick, MD: University Publications of America, Inc., 1988), 673.

2. Oral argument at 673, Shaare Tefila Congregation v. Cobb, 606 F.Supp. 1504 (D. Md. 1985) (No. R-84–880), *rev'd*, 107 S.Ct. 2019 (1987), in *Landmark Briefs and Arguments of the Supreme Court of the United States: Constitutional Law, 1986 Term Supplement* (Frederick, MD: University Publications of America, Inc., 1988), 673.

3. Oral argument at 673, Shaare Tefila Congregation v. Cobb, 606 F.Supp. 1504 (D. Md. 1985) (No. R-84–880), *rev'd*, 107 S.Ct. 2019 (1987), in *Landmark Briefs and Arguments of the Supreme Court of the United States: Constitutional Law, 1986 Term Supplement* (Frederick, MD: University Publications of America, Inc., 1988), 673.

4. Note: I use the spelling "antisemitism," rather than the more common "anti-Semitism." See journals in the field such as *Journal of Contemporary Antisemitism* and *Antisemitism Studies* as well as organizations such as the United States Holocaust Memorial Museum, the World Jewish Congress, and Yad Vashem, which have dropped the hyphen.

5. The Anti-Defamation League of B'nai B'rith's policy, sent out to Jewish organizations before High Holidays in 1982, stated: "The defacement of any Jewish site, and especially of a synagogue, should be removed immediately upon its discovery so as not to grant the vandals the publicity they seek by these acts." Marshall Levin, "Desecration in Darkness," in *The Price We Pay: The Case against Hate Speech, Hate Propaganda, and Pornography* Eds. Laura Lederer and Richard Delgado (New York: Hill & Wang, 1995), 40.

6. Marshall Levin, interview by author, New York City, July 10, 2008.

7. Marjorie Hyer, "Jewish Leader Seeks Action on Vandalism," *Washington Post*, 4 November 1982, Metro Section, Final edition.

8. Marshall Levin, interview by author, New York City, July 10, 2008.

9. Rabbi Martin S. Halpern, "The Desecration of a Synagogue," [Unnamed Source], 33.

10. Marshall Levin, interview by author, New York City, July 10, 2008.

11. Marshall Levin, interview by author, New York City, July 10, 2008.

12. See Annalise Glauz-Todrank, "'Race Thinking' and Rights Making," *Critical Research on Religion* 2, no. 2 (August 2014): 191–94.

13. See Naomi Wiener Cohen's argument that the Shaare Tefila Congregation laid a new path for Jewish Americans' public recognition of their Jewishness in her article "*Shaare Tefila Congregation v. Cobb*: A New Departure in American Jewish Defense?" in *Jewish History* 3, no. 1 (1988).

14. Rabbi Martin S. Halpern, "The Desecration of a Synagogue," [Unnamed Source], 34.

15. See Brian Z. Tamanaha, *A General Jurisprudence of Law and Society* (New York: Oxford University Press, 2001).

16. See Bruce D. Haynes, particularly chapter 6. Bruce D. Haynes, *The Soul of Judaism: Jews of African Descent in America* (New York: New York University Press, 2018), 141–66.

17. Historian David Sehat asserts: "Protestant Christian influence in U.S. history was long-standing, widespread, and from the perspective of dissenters, coercive." David Sehat, *The Myth of American Religious Freedom* (New York: Oxford University Press, 2011), 2. See also Leora Batnitzky, *How Judaism Became a Religion: An Introduction to Modern Jewish Thought* (Princeton, NJ: Princeton University Press, 2011), 1.

18. See Neil Gotanda, "A Critique of 'Our Constitution is Color-Blind,'" in *Critical Race Theory: The Key Writings That Formed the Movement*, eds. Kimberlé Crenshaw, Neil Gotanda, Gary Peller, and Kendall Thomas (New York: The New Press, 1995), 258–63.

19. See Laura Levitt's excellent chapter regarding Eastern European immigrants who arrived at the turn of the twentieth century and who attempted to maintain their cultural Yiddish context and did not identify with the American concept of "religion." Laura Levitt, "Other Moderns, Other Jews: Revisiting Jewish Secularism in America," in *Secularisms*, ed. Janet R. Jakobsen and Ann Pellegrini (Durham, NC: Duke University Press, 2008).

20. Laura Levitt, "Other Moderns, Other Jews: Revisiting Jewish Secularism in America," in *Secularisms*, ed. Janet R. Jakobsen and Ann Pellegrini (Durham, NC: Duke University Press, 2008), 118.

21. See Laura Levitt, "Other Moderns, Other Jews: Revisiting Jewish Secularism in America," in *Secularisms*, ed. Janet R. Jakobsen and Ann Pellegrini (Durham, NC: Duke University Press, 2008), 108, 123–24, 131.

22. See Eric L. Goldstein, *The Price of Whiteness: Jews, Race, and American Identity* (Princeton, NJ: Princeton University Press, 2006); Karen Brodkin, *How Jews Became White Folks and What That Says about Race in America* (New Brunswick, NJ: Rutgers University Press, 1999); Matthew Frye Jacobson, *Whiteness of a Different Color: European Immigrants and the Alchemy of Race* (Cambridge, MA: Harvard University Press, 1998).

23. Khaled Beydoun uses both terms in his article: Khaled Beydoun, "Faith in Whiteness: Free Exercise of Religion as Racial Expression" in *Iowa Law Review* 105, no. 4 (May 2020): 1478, 1480.

24. Khaled Beydoun, "Faith in Whiteness: Free Exercise of Religion as Racial Expression" in *Iowa Law Review* 105, no. 4 (May 2020): 1487.

25. Note: I'm guessing the pun is intended. Khaled Beydoun, "Faith in Whiteness: Free Exercise of Religion as Racial Expression" in *Iowa Law Review* 105, no. 4 (May 2020): 1487.

26. Khaled Beydoun, "Faith in Whiteness: Free Exercise of Religion as Racial Expression" in *Iowa Law Review* 105, no. 4 (May 2020): 1487.

27. See also Khaled Beydoun, "Faith in Whiteness: Free Exercise of Religion as Racial Expression" in *Iowa Law Review* 105, no. 4 (May 2020): 1481.

28. Dermot A. Nee, Industrial and Commercial Land Developers and Consultants, November 15, 1982, private collection of Shaare Tefila Congregation.

29. This Act reduced the quota to 3 percent of any nationality in 1910 and 2 percent of the number of foreign-born persons according to the 1890 census. See Major U.S. Immigration Laws, 1790–Present (March 2013) Fact Sheet, *Migration Policy Institute*, accessed February 25, 2021, www.migrationpolicy.org/research/timeline-1790.

30. Donald Weisman, United Synagogue of America: Seaboard Region, November 2, 1982, private collection of Shaare Tefila Congregation.

31. Sidney Kramer, County Executive, 1986–1990, Montgomery County, Maryland, Maryland Manual Online: A Guide to Maryland and Its Government, accessed April 13, 2021, msa.maryland.gov/msa/mdmanual/36loc/mo/former/html/msa02719.html.

32. Sidney Kramer, State Senator, Anti-Semitic Acts at Shaare Tefila, B'nai Israel, November 7, 1982, private collection of Shaare Tefila Congregation

33. Robert Abrams, President, Har Tzeon-Agudath Achim, November 2, 1982, private collection of Shaare Tefila Congregation.

34. Susan Learmonth, Neighbors Inc., November 9, 1982, private collection of Shaare Tefila Congregation. Joel Chasnoff, Montgomery-Howard Counties District 1A, Judiciary Committee, House of Delegates, November 3, 1982, private collection of Shaare Tefila Congregation.

35. James J. Zogby, Anti-American Discrimination Committee, November 4, 1982, private collection of Shaare Tefila Congregation.

36. Khaled Beydoun, "Faith in Whiteness: Free Exercise of Religion as Racial Expression" in *Iowa Law Review* 105, no. 4 (May 2020): 1478, 1480.

37. Alan P. Dean, HRC to Be Recipient in Synagogue Lawsuit, Montgomery County Government, For Immediate Release, March 7, 1984, 1.

38. Synopsis prepared by Marshall S. Levin, Executive Director, "Desecration in Darkness: A Community Fights Back, A Historic Documentary Film," stapled to press release, January 7, 1985, Film Premiere, 3.

39. Marshall Levin, "Desecration in Darkness" in *The Price We Pay: The Case against Hate Speech, Hate Propaganda, and Pornography*. Laura Lederer and Richard Delgado, eds. (New York: Hill & Wang, 1995), 42.

40. See Naomi Wiener Cohen, "*Shaare Tefila Congregation v. Cobb*: A New Departure in American Jewish Defense?" in *Jewish History* 3, no. 1 (1988).

41. Partial trial transcript at 54, Direct examination of William Randall Harris, State of Maryland v. Michael David Remer (Cir. Ct. for Montgomery Cty. July 18, 1983) (No. 29903) (trial proceedings of June 14, 1983).

42. Partial trial transcript at 57, Direct examination of Michael David Remer, State of Maryland v. Michael David Remer (Cir. Ct. for Montgomery Cty. Aug. 11, 1983) (No. 29903) (trial proceedings of June 14, 1983).

43. Kevin Lipson, phone interview by author, May 20, 2009.

44. Naomi Wiener Cohen, "*Shaare Tefila Congregation v. Cobb*: A New Departure in American Jewish Defense?" in *Jewish History* 3, no. 1 (1988): 98.

45. Kevin Lipson, phone interview by author, May 20, 2009.

46. See Varun Soni for "religion," and Nell Irvin Painter for "Whiteness." Varun Soni, "Freedom from Subordination: Race, Religion, and the Struggle for Sacrament," *Temple Political and Civil Rights Law Review* 15, no. 33 (Fall 2005): 33. Nell Irvin Painter, *The History of White People* (New York: W.W. Norton and Co., 2010), 106.

47. Overview of Hate Crime, United States Department of Justice, Office of Justice Programs, accessed September 6, 2021, nij.ojp.gov/topics/articles/overview-hate-crime.

48. Patricia Brannan, email received by author, April 9, 2021.

49. Patricia Brannan, phone interview by author, March 23, 2021.

50. Bess Teller, interview by author, Silver Spring, MD, July 8, 2008; Jack Teller, interview by author, Silver Spring, MD, August 17, 2009.

51. See Robert Proctor, *Racial Hygiene: Medicine under the Nazis* (Cambridge, MA: Harvard University Press, 1988).

52. See Stolzenberg's excellent article that addresses these two cases as well as the relationship between religion and race in law. Nomi Maya Stolzenberg, "Righting the Relationship Between Race and Religion in Law," *Oxford Journal of Legal Studies* 31, no. 3 (2011).

53. Circuit Split, Legal Information Institute, Cornell Law School, accessed June 5, 2022, law.cornell.edu/wex/circuit_split.

54. Marcie Alvarado, "The Trail of Michael D. Remer: Ocean City Robbery Suspect Linked to Several Other Crimes," *Maryland Coast Dispatch*, August 30, 1991, 3.

55. See David Sehat, *The Myth of American Religious Freedom* (New York: Oxford University Press, 2011), 1–10, particularly.

56. For Christian production of "race," see how Irene Silverblatt adopts Hannah Arendt's concept of "race thinking," as the origins of fascism, to describe Catholic Spanish and Portuguese imperialism, colonization, and bureaucracy. Silverblatt refers to "race thinking" throughout the book but defines it more specifically on page 17. Irene Silverblatt, *Modern Inquisitions: Peru and the Colonial Origins of the Civilized World* (Durham, NC: Duke University Press, 2004), 17. For Christian production of "religion," see Daniel Dubuisson, *The Western Construction of Religion: Myths, Knowledge, and Ideology* trans. William Sayers (Baltimore, MD: Johns Hopkins University Press, 2007 [2003]), 9; Daniel Boyarin, *Border Lines: The Partition of Judaeo-Christianity* (Pennsylvania, PA: University of Pennsylvania Press, 2006), 202, 203–4 (disagrees with Asad), 206, 209; Talal Asad, *Genealogies of Religion:*

Discipline and Reasons of Power in Christianity and Islam (Baltimore, MD: Johns Hopkins Press, 1993) 1, 18–24.

57. David Nirenberg, *Anti-Judaism: The Western Tradition* (New York: W.W. Norton and Company, 2013), 239.

58. David Nirenberg, *Anti-Judaism: The Western Tradition* (New York: W.W. Norton and Company, 2013), 238–39.

59. KB Wolf. Texts in Translation. *"Sentencia-Estatuto* de Toledo, 1449." Last modified 2008, accessed November, 21 2013, canilup.googlepages.com. See David Nirenberg, *Anti-Judaism: The Western Tradition* (New York: W.W. Norton and Company, 2013), 238–39. Note that although Nirenberg refers to the leaders enacting this law as "rebels," and as oppositional to the pope, it was still a Christian argument. See also Annalise E. Glauz-Todrank, "'Race Thinking' and Rights Making" *Critical Research on Religion* 2, no. 2 (August 2014): 191–94.

60. Irene Silverblatt, *Modern Inquisitions: Peru and the Colonial Origins of the Civilized World* (Durham, NC: Duke University Press, 2004), 3.

61. Irene Silverblatt, *Modern Inquisitions: Peru and the Colonial Origins of the Civilized World* (Durham, NC: Duke University Press, 2004), 3.

62. Irene Silverblatt, *Modern Inquisitions: Peru and the Colonial Origins of the Civilized World* (Durham, NC: Duke University Press, 2004), 3.

63. Irene Silverblatt, *Modern Inquisitions: Peru and the Colonial Origins of the Civilized World* (Durham, NC: Duke University Press, 2004), 3–8.

64. Irene Silverblatt, *Modern Inquisitions: Peru and the Colonial Origins of the Civilized World* (Durham, NC: Duke University Press, 2004), 3, 17–18.

65. See Naomi Wiener Cohen, *Jews in Christian America: The Pursuit of Religious Equality* (New York: Oxford University Press, 1992); Jonathan D. Sarna and David G. Dalin, *Religion and State in the American Jewish Experience* (Notre Dame, IN: University of Notre Dame Press, 1997).

66. Michael Omi and Howard Winant, *Racial Formation in the United States from the 1960s to the 1990s, Second Edition* (New York: Routledge, 1994), 55, emphasis added.

67. Office of Management and Budget, Directive 15: Race and Ethnic Standards for Federal Statistics and Administrative Reporting (1977) available at https://wonder.cdc.gov/wonder/help/populations/bridged-race/directive15.html [https://perma.cc/FHL3-7C8U].

68. Henry Goldschmidt, *Race and Religion among the Chosen Peoples of Crown Heights* (New Brunswick, NJ: Rutgers University Press, 2006), 26.

69. Henry Goldschmidt, *Race and Religion among the Chosen Peoples of Crown Heights* (New Brunswick, NJ: Rutgers University Press, 2006), 26.

70. Henry Goldschmidt, *Race and Religion among the Chosen Peoples of Crown Heights* (New Brunswick, NJ: Rutgers University Press, 2006), 29.

71. Henry Goldschmidt, *Race and Religion among the Chosen Peoples of Crown Heights* (New Brunswick, NJ: Rutgers University Press, 2006), 28.

72. Daniel Ian Rubin, *The Jewish Struggle in the 21st Century: Conflict, Positionality, and Multiculturalism* (Boston: Brill, 2021). Rubin published an article titled "HebCrit: A New Dimension of Critical Race Theory" in 2020, which answered my

call for more work on the subject in my cited article below. See Daniel Ian Rubin, "HebCrit: A New Dimension of Critical Race Theory," *Social Identities* 26, no. 4 (2020). See Annalise E. Glauz-Todrank, "Jewish Critical Race Theory and Jewish 'Religionization' in *Shaare Tefila Congregation v. Cobb*," in *Judaism, Race, and Ethics: Conversations and Questions*, ed. Jonathan K. Crane (University Park: Pennsylvania State University Press, 2020).

73. Daniel Ian Rubin, *The Jewish Struggle in the 21st Century: Conflict, Positionality, and Multiculturalism* (Boston: Brill, 2021), 20.

74. Rabbi Jonah Layman, email with author, April 23, 2022.

75. Marshall Levin, "Desecration in Darkness," in *The Price We Pay: The Case against Hate Speech, Hate Propaganda, and Pornography.* Laura Lederer and Richard Delgado, eds. (New York: Hill & Wang, 1995), 40.

76. Lisa Tessman, "Jewish Racializations: Revealing the Contingency of Whiteness," in *Jewish Locations: Traversing Racialized Landscapes.* Lisa Tessman and Bat-Ami Bar On, eds. (Lanham, MD: Rowman & Littlefield, 2001), 137.

77. Marshall Levin, "Desecration in Darkness" in *The Price We Pay: The Case against Hate Speech, Hate Propaganda, and Pornography.* Laura Lederer and Richard Delgado, eds. (New York: Hill & Wang, 1995), 40.

Chapter One

"It Was a Crime against the Community"

Before traveling to Silver Spring, Maryland in 2008 to interview members of the Shaare Tefila congregation, I contacted the current rabbi, Jonah Layman.[1] During our phone call, he invited me to talk about my research concerning the congregation's legal journey after a summer Shabbat morning service. Because Shaare Tefila had sold their synagogue building to a Protestant Hispanic Church in 2005 to be closer to more Jewish Americans, services on that day were held in another, more traditional synagogue. Such suburban shifts had been happening for a while, as middle- and upper-class Jewish Americans who were generally perceived as "White" moved farther out into the suburbs. These Jewish Americans identified more with other middle- and upper-class White Americans, choosing to live with them. Over time, as housing prices changed, the majority of Jewish Americans were able to move into tonier suburbs, whereas low- to middle-income racially marginalized peoples from an increasing number of religious traditions came to settle in Silver Spring.[2]

The congregation president, Bess Teller, greeted me warmly at the door. During the service, I sat next to her husband, Jack, whose car had been defaced during the vandalism incident twenty-six years earlier in 1982. The congregation's cantor, Wendy Fried, led the prayers.

After the announcement period at the end of the service, Bess Teller invited me to the front by the *bimah*, a raised platform from which the Torah is read, and I explained my interest in meeting with congregation members to learn more about the defacement and the following court case, as well as how those events had affected them.[3] Though I would be investigating the legal components of the case, presenting the congregation members' perspectives and experiences was formative to my overall argument. This would provide a better sense of what the case revealed about Jewish American identification during the 1980s, and how it would affect Jewish Americans going forward.

At the end of my talk, a handful of members briefly recalled their experiences at the time, and a newer member asked me to explain what had happened. The request surprised me because, at that time, I thought the Supreme Court case had been significant to Shaare Tefila's communal identity; apparently, I was wrong—many congregants had been proud of it at the time, but most of them did not want to continue reliving their response to the defacement. Several congregation members responded to the new member's question, including Maurice Potosky, and I contributed several points that I had learned recently about the case.

Because the congregation *davens minhah* (prays the afternoon service) after *shaharith* (the morning service), the cantor asked that we take a quick break to eat a little and that congregation members speak with me individually. Many of them rushed over immediately, some well-prepared for my visit with photos or newspaper articles that would help me to understand what had happened and how the graffiti had looked on the synagogue's white walls. Sipping on soda in paper cups, and munching on fruit and cookies, they expressed great interest in the project and offered to attempt to recall their experiences. Because it was Shabbat, and writing would be considered work, I could not write down their names, phone numbers, or what they told me. For that reason, I could not set up meetings with them and instead tried to recall everything later when I was able to record it. Particularly memorable conversations included one with a former nursery school teacher who brought me color copies of photos of the vandalism and told me about her many years teaching at the synagogue and her memories of children now grown up and living elsewhere. Then, I spoke with a woman, the only person there in my age bracket, and she told me that although she was only five years old at the time of the defacement in 1982, she still remembers it.

As I departed from the synagogue service, after attempting to engage as many members as possible in conversation, I was struck by the extent to which the congregation had changed over the intervening twenty-six years, losing many of the members who had witnessed the defacement and experienced the legal process, and gaining new members who knew little or nothing about the events of those days. I also pondered the variety of emotions evident in the voices of congregation members who responded to my short talk. They ranged from curiosity to proud recounting of Shaare Tefila's decision to leave the graffiti, to quiet nods, to one person who seemed to respond with suspicion, at first, to my desire to meet with congregation members and write about their stories.

What I found was that while members of Shaare Tefila shared a narrative among themselves about the vandalism, they also had distinct, and at times quite disparate, memories of their experiences. Inspired initially by Executive Director Marshall Levin, congregation leaders responded to the historical method of concealing the vandalism by leaving it *in situ*. In interviews, they express how they understood the vandalism in the 1980s, when "hate violence" and "hate crimes" against non-White, Christian, heterosexual groups were in the process of becoming a national topic, as well as in 2008 and 2009 when I conducted them. It is also evident that White-perceived Jewish American members of Shaare Tefila had adapted their religious identities to fit the White, Christian American norm.

As this chapter tells the story of congregation members and their recollections of the vandalism, it continues to underscore the main objective of the *Shaare Tefila* case. That objective was to federally prohibit race-based actions that target Jewish American citizens. With the exception of one individual, Virgil Philip Marlowe, who in 1973 had sought and received race-based protection under section 1981, which originated in the Civil Rights Act of 1866, no Jewish individual or group had previously sought race-based legal protection from antisemitic vandalism or racialized antisemitic violence in any way.[4] My interviews and analyses of the congregation members' experiences provide insight into their lives as Jewish Americans who were grappling with the antisemitic defacement of their synagogue.

What I recognized in conducting my interviews was that, for some congregation members, the cleanup day, in which the congregation leaders invited the local community to clean the synagogue with them, was almost as important as the case itself. The cleanup day provided them with a sense of solidarity and, also drew public attention to the vandalism. Moreover, it sustained them in the way a legal case could not do: it filled a place inside them that had been empty previously, showing them that their neighbors cared about their Jewishness, which was a core facet of their identities; the neighbors cleaned their Jewish space with them, which was unmarked to conceal the congregants' Jewish identity.[5]

I interviewed congregation members in person as well as over the phone, and via my attendance at several Shabbat services during the summers of 2008 and 2009, beginning with that first visit described above. I also went to New York City to interview former Executive Director Marshall Levin. In total, I conducted thirty interviews, of which twenty-six were with current or former congregation members. The other four interviews were with Kevin Lipson and Irvin Shapell of the Jewish Advocacy Center and with the lawyers who represented the congregation and the vandals, in the US Supreme Court; Patricia Brannan and Deborah Garren, respectively.

Several of the former members had been children or teenagers at the time of the defacement, and their memories added a different vantage point. One former member had survived the Shoah and had then had spent many years teaching and directing Hebrew School at Shaare Tefila before retiring. Even after her retirement and before her passing, she continued to travel and give lectures about her experiences during World War II. A few members, or former members, who had been young during the defacement specifically mentioned the significance of her classes and how her portrayal of the Shoah had helped them to make sense of the meaning of the vandalism and its relevance.

The interviews were, to some extent, a self-selected sample, in that most of the members whom I met in person volunteered to speak with me, and several of them provided me with contact information for their children or other people they knew who had been involved in the congregation at the time of the vandalism but who were no longer affiliated. Not surprisingly, the congregation members were not monolithic. Each person was unique and had an individual history related to their social location, but they were also members of a collective.

In the 1980s, the Shaare Tefila Congregation understood themselves as a religious group and identified themselves as White even though they were also Jewish. Although they were "formally" White, they navigated their Jewishness with care. For example, as mentioned previously, one congregation member told me that she was the first "open Jew" where she worked.[6] After the antisemitic vandalism to their synagogue in 1982, however, the Shaare Tefila leadership and Board of Trustees acknowledged the racialized perception of their Jewish identity more publicly.

The chapter continues with a history of Jewish racialization in the United States to contextualize the Whiteness of Shaare Tefila Congregation members when it first formed in 1951. It discusses Jewish American racialization in the 1850s, prior to the Civil Rights Acts of 1866 and 1871, sections of which were later used by Shaare Tefila Congregation's lawyers. This is a crucial issue debated at the end of the next chapter. In the process, it highlights the anti-Jewish environment of the past and notes its continued presence, in various forms, in the Washington, DC, area and Montgomery County, Maryland. It emphasizes that Jews of European origin became passably White given their White privileges regarding the G.I. Bill, which passed after World War II, and then "formally" White after the enactment of Directive 15 in 1977. It then focuses on its members' participation in the congregation from its founding until November 1, 1982, when vandals defaced it. At that point, the chapter turns to interviews that recount recollections of the vandalism and various congregants' responses to it—in some cases—in the context of other antisemitic vandalism they had experienced. The decision of the congregation leaders to leave it in place dramatically differed from the Jewish American norm. Marshall Levin called it a "crime against the community," and, afterward, members of the local population stood with the congregation and cleaned the synagogue with them.[7] Hence, the criminal and then civil suit fulfilled the congregation's legal pursuit of justice, and the cleanup day fulfilled their need for social solidarity with their neighbors.

A BRIEF HISTORY OF JEWISH RACIALIZATION
IN THE UNITED STATES

Let's turn to Jewish racialization in the United States. Racialized identities were not always negative for Jews. For example, most Jewish Americans in the 1850s had originally immigrated from various German regions, were financially stable, associated mostly with each other, and identified as a "race."[8] In the 1854 edition of *Encyclopedia Americana*, Jews were described as "Hebrews."[9] At this time, the "Know-Nothing" Party responded to the large number of Irish and German Catholics who immigrated in the 1840s with a staunch nativist, populist mentality, which sometimes led to violence. They did not direct their attention toward Jews, however; in fact, some Jews were even members of the party.[10] Nonetheless, extreme xenophobia remained dominant but rarely targeted Jews, even as the US Congress passed the Reconstruction Amendments and then the first Civil Rights Acts.[11]

Previously, the United States had been divided between enslaved Blacks, and free, yet racialized groups in a hierarchy based on their nationalities of origin. So, Jewish Americans who originated in Europe continued to understand themselves as a racial group but were not concerned, pre-twentieth century, that it might eventually become problematic in the United States. They continued to employ racial language during the 1870s, when many of them increasingly engaged with the economically stable dominant Anglo-Saxon group, due to their recently attained wealth and social prominence.[12] As the century came to an end, however, American Jewish historian Eric L. Goldstein maintains that "Jews became linked in the popular imagination with many of the destabilizing changes that Americans were confronting."[13] At that time, most Jews were solidly Americanized, economically secure, and socially stable, but they would soon witness an influx of mostly impoverished Jewish immigrants from Eastern Europe, who would bring their racial identity into doubt.[14]

In 1909, Jewish American organizations were worried about the popular use of the word "Hebrews," which they believed had a racial connotation that might jeopardize their citizenship. Legally, some thought that it might prevent Jews and Jewish immigrants from accessing rights given to White Americans.[15] Key leader Louis Marshall, attorney for the American Jewish Committee, was concerned about Jewish Congressman Henry Goldfogle's bill, which proposed that "Asiatics who are Armenians, Syrians, or Jews" were free to become naturalized citizens. Marshall was disturbed that asserting all Jews were "Asiatic" could lead to uncertainty about whether Jews were citizens.[16] He had been arguing a case for Syrian clients in a Circuit Court of Appeals and convinced the Court to approve his position that Syrians were "free white persons," thereby preventing the question from reaching the halls of Congress.[17] Even though many Jewish Americans understood themselves as "Hebrews" in the early years of the twentieth century and as racially separate from others, they never desired to be *legally* distinct from White Americans.

During this time, Simon Wolf, a longtime attorney for the Union of American Hebrew Congregations, campaigned to reverse the Bureau of Immigration's description of Jews as "Hebrews," and configured it as a "religious" liberty issue.[18] Wolf presented his case to the US Immigration Commission, in which he emphasized the religious component of Judaism without addressing its cultural components or the importance of Jewish peoplehood.[19] This argument was likely necessary at that time. It was remarkably similar, however, to lawyer Deborah Garren's assertion in *Shaare Tefila*. She denied Jewish Americans race-related rights because, she claimed, Jews are *only* a religion, reinforcing the dominant American view in the 1980s.

A more significant racialized law targeting Jews, among other Eastern and Southern Europeans, was the aforementioned Immigration Act of 1924 or the Johnson-Reed Act. This Act cited the 1890 census before massive numbers of immigrants arrived from those parts of Europe and kept the incoming quota at 2 percent. Beginning in 1880, about two and a half million Jews from Eastern Europe arrived in the United States, this Act significantly impeded their access, slowing their immigration to almost a standstill. The Act federally advocated the rise of xenophobia and antisemitism, encouraging pride in "Anglo-Saxon" self-identification, and resulting in a massive increase in Ku Klux Klan membership.

Beginning in the 1920s and escalating through the 1950s, two other forms of legalized racialization were occurring in the housing market: redlining[20] and racial covenants. Jewish Americans had been restricted from buying or renting in wealthier White areas.[21] Deeds from that time in the Washington, DC, area, including one from W.C. and A.N. Miller Development Company— which remains open for business—is worth quoting at length:

> TWELFTH. No part of the land hereby conveyed shall ever be used, or occupied by, or sold, demised, transferred, conveyed unto, or in trust for, leased, or rented, or given, to negroes, or any person or persons, of negro blood or extraction, or to any person of the Semitic Race, blood, or origin, which racial description shall be deemed to include Armenians, Jews, Hebrews, Persians, and Syrians, except that; this paragraph shall not be held to exclude partial occupancy of the

premises by domestic servants of the said parties of the second part, their successors and assigns.[22]

Some developers also excluded Jews by refusing to sell to them. For example, although Morris Cafritz was himself Jewish, he would not sell his row houses in Brightwood Park to other Jews. Some real estate advertisements specified "gentiles only."[23] Such discrimination and division were not isolated to real estate sales but also pervaded social norms.

During World War II, as racial discrimination against European communities became identified with the war aims, government agencies such as the Immigration and Naturalization Service constructed new naturalization forms for emigrants from Europe, including a special exception in 1943 for Jews, who ceased being described as "Hebrews."[24] Goldstein notes that the wartime policies of the government meant that it redrew its position on racial boundaries, enforcing the increased division between European groups and Blacks.[25]

One of the first major examples of public policy linking Jewish Americans and Americans already perceived as White was the G.I. Bill. The G.I. Bill—formally known as the Servicemen's Readjustment Act of 1944—differentiated Black veterans from White veterans due to what the Bill availed to them. White veterans, at this point, included Jewish veterans. One of the most important benefits for veterans was receiving funds for higher education, which Black veterans rarely received.[26] This shift also diminished the racial power of the term "Hebrew" and brought assimilated Jews who were perceived as mostly White into similar spaces already occupied by Italian and Irish immigrants.

As Shaare Tefila Congregation was founded in November 1951, only several years after World War II ended, these racial sentiments were already in place. Shaare Tefila began as a small congregation in Riggs Park, located in the northeast corner of Washington, DC, at 405 Riggs Road. In the early 1950s, Riggs Park, sometimes called "Little Tel Aviv," was predominately inhabited by Jewish Americans due to its affordable housing.[27] According to *Washington Jewish Week* writer Merry Madway Eisenstadt: as a "small, down to earth shul [synagogue]," Shaare Tefila "served as the center of its members' universe."[28] Florence Lipsky, a synagogue charter member, recalled: "People were looking for a place for their kids to grow up in a Jewish area."[29] Lipsky noted that it "became our circle right away . . . it was our outlet. We would go there for lectures, meetings on how to educate our children, and scouts."[30] The synagogue quickly established a Hebrew school, hired a cantor, and founded an organization called the Sisterhood that remains to this day.[31] During that period, the congregation held services in a rented space, and in 1953, the members hired Rabbi Raphael Gold.

Several years later, members who preferred not to have mixed-gender seating and to preserve other forms of Orthodox observance left the Shaare Tefila and founded an Orthodox synagogue on Eastern Ave NE in Riggs Park, named Shomrai Emunah.[32] Thanks to one of its founders, its website provides evidence of its early separation in the late 1950s from Shaare Tefila Congregation—although Shaare Tefila is not named. One of these founders, Dr. Lee Spetner, described the separation of the two synagogues: Shomrai Emunah represented "Torah-true Judaism" and the "other one" represented "community centerites."[33]

In 1954, Shaare Tefila bought its own building and hired Rabbi Martin Halpern as an additional leader in 1956. Three years later, however, there was a "mass exodus" of Jewish residents from Riggs Park. After the G.I. Bill, Meriam Williamowsky noted that "As people started becoming more prosperous, they wanted larger homes and started moving away."[34]

Shaare Tefila eventually decided to follow its congregants into Silver Spring, Maryland in 1961. Shomrai Emunah moved around the same time to the same city. Why did both synagogues decide to move at the same time to the same place? The simple answer is "White flight" . . . or, perhaps, a more complex descriptor is "White *Jewish* flight."[35] Because Jewish Americans had been restricted from living in certain areas, they wanted to move—if they had the means—to nicer properties. Shul-attending Jews like to be with other shul-attending Jews, because typically their "second home" is the synagogue. So, if many or most of the members left, likely the synagogue would move with them. For *Shomer Shabbes* Jews—those who observe the commandments to keep Shabbat—it's essential to live close to the synagogue because it's forbidden to drive on the sabbath. This restriction would apply certainly to Shomrai Emunah members, and perhaps to some or most Shaare Tefila members.

The congregation's former website noted that by 1976, Shaare Tefila had 850 families listed in its phone directory, an all-time record[36] that revealed the growth of Jewish Americans in Silver Spring. In Montgomery County, where the synagogue was located, not only had the Black population more than doubled between 1970 and 1980, from 4.1 percent to 8.7 percent, which was about 55,000 people, but tens of thousands of people from abroad had moved to Silver Spring from their countries of origin, especially countries in Southeast Asia, the Caribbean, and Central America.[37]

Significantly, on May 12, 1977, Jewish Americans became defined as "White" for census purposes. That day, the Office of Management and Budget, part of the Executive Branch of the government, issued Directive No. 15, Race and Ethnic Standards for Federal Statistics and Administrative Reporting, which defined Jews with origins in Europe as "White."[38] It was not particularly notable in social terms because, typically, White-perceived Jewish

Americans *already* considered themselves "White." They "looked" White, but to varying extents, had to perform Whiteness.[39] In Khaled Beydoun's terms, they were "formally" White, but not "substantively" White.[40]

Montgomery County in 1980 became about one-sixth Jewish and one-fifth Black, Asian, and Hispanic.[41] In the early 1980s, therefore, Shaare Tefila's buildings were expanded to seat about one thousand people and remained the location of Shaare Tefila until 2005.[42]

As the population of Montgomery County, particularly in the Silver Spring area, shifted from predominately White and Christian to far less so, race-based and antisemitic incidents began to increase. One of the primary causes was the Ku Klux Klan, which specifically targeted Blacks and, to a lesser extent, Jews. In that atmosphere, Shaare Tefila members were concerned about their social location as Jewish Americans who were only "formally" White.[43] Although the Klan was again on the rise in Maryland, in large part due to the economic fallout of the early 1980s, it was far from the only problem.

The congregants had reason for alarm: as a January 1981 study demonstrated, antisemitic beliefs were far from uncommon in the United States, and indeed some of them were on the rise. The 1981 study, conducted by Gregory Martire and Ruth Clark, relied on a national survey directed by Gertrude Selznick and Steven Steinberg in 1964 and published in 1969 as *The Tenacity of Prejudice*.[44] The Anti-Defamation League of B'nai B'rith funded the Selznick and Steinberg study, which was conducted at the University of California, Berkeley. In 1981, Martire and Clark's investigation, which followed up on that research, reported that a minority of non-Jewish individuals held antisemitic beliefs, but it still represented a significant social problem in the United States."[45] A sampling from the data revealed: that 40 percent of non-Jews in 1981 believed that "Jews should stop complaining about what happened to them in Nazi Germany" down from 51 percent in 1964, and 53 percent of non-Jews in 1981 believed that "Jews stick together too much," down from 58 percent in 1964, and 22 percent of non-Jews in 1981 believed that "Jews don't care what happens to anyone but their own kind" down from 30 percent in 1964.[46] Certain percentages, in terms of what non-Jews believed about Jews, however, were higher in 1981. These included: 14 percent of non-Jews believed that "Jews are stirring up trouble with their ideas" up from 13 percent in 1964, and 37 percent of non-Jews believed that "Jews have too much power in the business world" up from 33 percent in 1964, 48 percent of non-Jews in 1981 believed that "Jews are more loyal to Israel than to America" up from 39 percent in 1964, and 23 percent of non-Jews in 1981 believed that "Jews have too much power in the United States" up from 13 percent in 1964.[47] These higher percentages may be attributed, in part, to the relationships between Jewish Americans and Israel in the 1970s leading up to 1981.[48]

Due to the continuation of antisemitic stereotypes, antisemitic vandalism, and more violent antisemitism, Jewish Americans were concerned that they could not entirely trust the public. By living their everyday lives, Shaare Tefila congregants understood these stereotypes well. In fact, the issues addressed above refer to those raised in the introduction regarding the Jewish American hesitancy to share what they viewed as Jewish American problems with outsiders.

In 1982, for instance, a comparison of the local county newspaper, the *Montgomery County Sentinel*, and the Washington, DC, area Jewish newspaper, the *Washington Jewish Week*, illustrated that Jewish Americans communicated privately to other Jewish Americans about antisemitic attacks rather than exposing them to the wider world. Whereas the county paper had few reports of vandalism targeting Jews, the Jewish paper regularly provided information about defacement incidents. Statements in the *Washington Jewish Week* implied that perhaps many of the incidents were not reported to the police and that the local Jewish communities shared the information only via the Jewish newspaper.[49]

The *Washington Jewish Week* reported the following antisemitic incidents in 1982 alone. In January, the letters "KKK" were painted on a Silver Spring synagogue; a swastika was painted on a Rockville elementary school and on Shapiro's Foodtown grocery store in Silver Spring in February. Three incidents occurred in March: a window was smashed (supposedly with antisemitic intent), a synagogue received a bomb threat on its answering machine, and a female Jewish student at the University of Maryland was shot with a BB gun.[50] Four instances of graffiti were found each in April and May. In July, there were two (supposedly antisemitic) cross-burnings. Antisemitic graffiti occurred once in August and twice in September. Additionally, in September, someone left an antisemitic message on a synagogue answering machine. In November, three instances of defacement were reported, and by mid-November, the Anti-Defamation League (ADL) decided to allocate one full-time expert for terrorist and extremist activity.[51]

Responses to the Defacement: It Was a "Crime Against the Community"

With this racist and antisemitic context in mind, let's turn our attention to how it affected Shaare Tefila Congregation. Prior to the events at Shaare Tefila, no synagogue within memory had made the decision to let vandalism remain on its building. Most Jewish American communities were accustomed to blending into American norms.

Before the High Holidays in 1982, Marshall Levin wrote in a published chapter about the vandalism, "The Anti-Defamation League sent a formal, though thoroughly unpublicized,[52] set of instructions advising that if there were any crimes against property (as distinct from crimes against persons) such as incidents of defacement or other vandalism to buildings, the graffiti should be removed immediately."[53] It said: "The defacement of any Jewish site, and especially of a synagogue, should be removed immediately upon its discovery so as not to grant the vandals the publicity they seek by these acts."[54] The ADL believed that other prospective vandals could be motivated to commit similar crimes, as Marshall Levin had mentioned in the introduction.

Levin and other Shaare Tefila leaders disagreed with this policy: he asserted that such desecration was a crime against the *entire* community, not just Shaare Tefila, or even the whole Jewish community. This defacement, Levin argued, would morally offend every human being, and instead of being embarrassed about it, the synagogue should make the wider community aware of it and ask for its help. Although the ADL believed that if the antisemitic acts were publicized, more of them would likely occur both locally and nationally, Levin noted that in the Washington metropolitan area alone, an increasing number of synagogues had been defaced, had erased, or covered, and not reported them to the local media. Levin asserted that Shaare Tefila decided that "it was time to take a stand," bring attention to the desecration that happened there, and raise awareness among the community. This stance would lead Shaare Tefila to eventually file a civil suit.

When Levin later reflected on the defacement of Shaare Tefila, he told me: "It was a crime against the community, not a crime against the congregation."[55] And he pushed the local community to grapple with it alongside the congregation. Because Levin believed that the community would rally around Shaare Tefila, he took a risk that not only resulted in community support, but also in local recognition of antisemitism and its detrimental effects on Jewish residents.

"Once we decided to press charges, we were surprised to find that actions like this had never been successfully litigated before in this country," he noted.[56] "Apparently, Jewish people had turned to the courts before for protection, but because Judaism is, strictly speaking, a religion and not a race, we are not covered under general civil rights legislation."[57] Like other Jewish and non-Jewish Americans, he had internalized the American norm that Jews are a "religion."

In September 1982, two months before the vandalism occurred, Shaare Tefila had recruited Marshall Levin to serve as executive director for the congregation. He had moved with his wife to the Washington, DC, area so that she could pursue a doctoral degree. For his own doctoral work, his studies had focused on Jewish identity and the Shoah, and particularly the effects of the Shoah on female survivors. Prior to this position, he had worked as a lecturer at Haifa University and as the head of crisis intervention in northern Israel. Levin grew up in a family of lawyers, and his father had clerked for the US Supreme Court. Levin's philosophy regarding how to respond to this antisemitism played a central role in the congregation's decision to leave the graffiti on the synagogue walls for the public to see.[58]

Levin did more, however, than persuade the congregation to leave the graffiti to elicit the community's solidarity. He also organized meetings and discussion groups at Shaare Tefila the week after the incident so that congregation members understood the reasons for the plan to leave the graffiti up.[59] Bill Harkaway, a board member who was later critical to convincing other board members to support the civil suit, remembered Levin's broader role in bringing local attention to the problem of the vandalism:

> Marshall took the bull by the horns and quickly notified other [Jewish and non-Jewish] congregations in the area, and they were most supportive. I think that was helpful for everybody feeling better by letting us make this an open display. This sort of thing had happened in some other synagogues. And they hushed it up. But we played it to the public because we thought the public ought to know about it. And the public by and large was very supportive.[60]

Harkaway referenced the positive ramifications for the congregation in making the defacement public.[61] Leaving the graffiti allowed the congregation to confront publicly the intensity of the antisemitism that the graffiti displayed and to seek solace within the larger community rather than suffering in silence and on their own. Harkaway further explained: "Some people I know that I talked to wanted to get out there and wash this off as quickly as they can. Marshall and the Rabbi said, no, let people see it so they know what it's about."[62]

Many congregation members described to me their responses to the incident: several of them expressed anger, whereas others felt shock, sadness, and fear.[63] They recalled various instances of anti-Judaism before their synagogue was defaced, including one congregant whose classmate had relentlessly insulted him with statements about Jews killing Jesus,[64] a confrontation with a swastika tattoo at a baseball game,[65] or the expectations from a shopkeeper that an employee had secret knowledge about Israel.[66] These incidents illustrated religious anti-Judaism, as well as racial and political antisemitism,[67] which counter the prevailing narrative that Jewish Americans are "White."

The day of the election was a school holiday. Students who were members of Shaare Tefila knew or had heard about the vandalism and asked to be taken or themselves drove to see it. Levin recounted: "Waves of young people circled the building, confronting the reality of antisemitism in their midst. Their response ranged from raw 'gut anger' to disgust to confused yet palpable fear. They struggled to find appropriate channels for venting their intense feelings."[68] That Saturday, the local community believed that the KKK would be marching in Montgomery County, and some of the young people considered counterprotesting. But that seemed "too indirect," according to Levin. He noted, "Each of them felt personally attacked, personally violated. As was true for the adult members of the Congregation, each of them identified as a 'victim' in the legal sense of the term." "One of the young people," Levin continued, "asked if he and his friends would be permitted to take that graffiti off that afternoon."[69] Levin told him that it would need to remain until the weekend and that the means of removal had not been determined, but he promised him an answer soon.

Some adult synagogue members, such as board member Jack Teller, were angry about the vandalism. Recall his experience of finding two black swastikas on the hood of his car. In a calm voice, he recollected:

> I do remember at the very beginning seeing that and thinking, "ooo!" anger, you know. Anger at these parties unknown, you know, the anonymous cowards that spread this kind of filth around. . . . You have to understand—the car was light-colored . . . pale, brownish gray. It was almost like [what] they called sandalwood at the time. I don't really remember exactly. But it was an Omega, an Oldsmobile Omega of that vintage, something in the '80s . . . but it was in good, good condition. And here's this expanse of the windshield—you could see it through the windshield—this big expanse of the hood. And on this side was a botched-up swastika. The guy with the spray paint—whichever one of those bums that it was—got it wrong and was making like a Z or something. And then on the other side, he got it right, and there was a swastika inside of a big circle just like they put on the Nazi flags.[70]

The next day, Teller took pictures of the graffiti and bought a cleaning agent to repair his car. In a measured, thoughtful tone, he conveyed how he felt about the vandalism of his car:

> I cleaned off the car, because I just couldn't stand the thought that this was on my car. And I was angry every minute, it was like about two days, a day and a half, ok? So, if you want to know what I thought, I thought, boy, if I could get a hold of that nasty whatever, I'd throttle him.[71]

Congregation member Susan Goldsamt remembered the defacement of the Tellers' car as well:

> I think seeing my friend Bess's car was one of the first things. Just seeing that it had the black *thing*. And then I looked around, and it [my anger] grew and it

grew. And even the children's equipment in the playground was defaced. And you know it wasn't always, it wasn't all out front . . . you went further and further and in the back with the eagle and the 'In, Jew, take a shower.' And I don't know whether I'm normal or not, but I don't feel fear. I was *furious*. And just enraged . . . I thought: How could they do this? We didn't do anything to deserve this![72]

Susan's husband, Milton Goldsamt, commented: "I think I was amazed and shocked that our synagogue had been desecrated. I wasn't there that day, but I saw pictures of it. . . . I was amazed that someone had decided to do that. It took my breath away, and it made me nervous too."[73]

Shaare Tefila members who had lived through the Shoah experienced the vandalism in the context of their former lives in Europe, in which they had survived horrible antisemitic persecution and the deaths of family members, friends, and other loved ones.[74] Jack Teller sent me a deposition in which he recalled how close he was to the Shoah. His mother came from a family of eleven children. She communicated regularly with her brothers and sisters as well as her parents. The brothers and sisters were all married and had "three to five children apiece."[75] He told the lawyers: "I mean, I didn't even know how many there were. And she was communicating with them until about the first year of the war and then there was no more communication."[76] What a shock the Shoah must have been for his mother's family, for her—and for Jack—especially when she did not receive any more letters.

The content of the defacement evoked palpable memories of tragedy. Holocaust survivor and former Hebrew School principal Harriet Steinhorn Roth remembered her reaction to the defacement vividly: "First of all, total shock. It was very difficult to believe that it would happen here in Silver Spring, it's such a nice, quiet community."[77] The White vandals, however, happened to live in the same town. She recalled:

The first moments I remember just being numb. And then I cried. And I won-dered, how could anybody be so cruel? But then I thought that if it's young people, young kids then they just don't really understand. They don't know what they're doing. I felt very sad, but I asked the teachers to discuss it in class. And, of course, the students were brought down to see what happened. . . . It was pretty badly defaced, and bold colors, strong colors. They had showers, and "Jew, that's where you belong," and gas chambers, that kind of thing. It was terrible. It was very vivid. And it just brought [back] so many horrible, horrible memories. And the problem is that especially survivors, friends of mine, thought that if it happened once, it will happen again.[78]

Steinhorn Roth lost her father and two younger sisters in concentration camps and survived a year in a camp on her own without family members when she was thirteen, before reuniting with her mother.

She decided that she firmly supported the decision to leave the defacement in place after initially thinking that the graffiti should be removed immediately:

> I'm sure there were some people who'd rather they be quiet, and [that] no one knew about it, but Rabbi Halpern was very determined that this was not going to be shoved under the rug, so to speak. And he was right. He was really right. He proved that he was right. . . . I mean, he believed it was wrong what happened and that we had to speak up. So often, I mean, the Jewish people are so afraid of spreading antisemitism. That's why they would be very quiet about things.[79]

This comment reveals the reasoning behind the dominant response of the Jewish American community to antisemitism in the 1980s: that allowing the public to witness antisemitic crimes and pursuing legal consequences for the perpetrators of these crimes would result in the exponential spread of such incidents. In contrast, once the vandals were found and charged and three convicted, the JAC convinced the congregation to move forward with the civil suit, in part because members were so gratified by the community's response.

The Anti-Defamation League and Media Responses to the Defacement

To situate the response to the antisemitic defacement, it's important to contextualize the situation. Following the November 1 defacement of the walls, playground equipment, and car at Shaare Tefila Congregation, on November 4, Edward N. Leavy, the director of the Anti-Defamation League of B'nai B'rith, appealed in the *Washington Post* to Mayor Marion Barry of Washington, DC, the governors of Maryland and Virginia, and leaders of religious bodies to "protect area places of worship, especially those which seem to be targets of extremist attacks, like synagogues."[80] According to Leavy, the Shaare Tefila vandalism was the fourth incident in the past month.[81] Leavy "keeps his home phone and address unlisted, and when he leaves the office after a day of taking calls and reading the mail, he doesn't waste any time getting to his car."[82]

In another article, *Montgomery County Sentinel* staff reporter Christian Ward wrote on November 4 that the KKK "Support Your Police" rally was planned for Saturday, November 6. Because of the proximity of the events, Shaare Tefila members and others in the local community believed that the KKK could have committed the defacement.[83] With this theme, the KKK allied themselves with the police as though they were *also* an arm of the law.

The Klan leader lived in Rohrersville, about nineteen miles west of Frederick, and had applied for the necessary permit on October 26. Since he did not live within the county, legal rules dictated that the march was necessarily postponed for a month after that date; however, the public was not aware that this was the case. When asked about the theme for the event, he declared, "Certainly all the police in the state of Maryland support the Ku Klux Klan."[84] Corporal Phillip Caswell, on behalf of Montgomery County Police Chief Bernard Crooke, responded "We don't support the activities of the Klan," and that the County Police would be "coordinating all activities" with the park police and the state police if the rally occurred. Caswell continued: Crooke is "not in favor of them coming here at all but they have a constitutional right to hold a peaceful rally."[85] Organizations opposed to the Klan, such as the All-People's Congress, a coalition of civic activists, and the Montgomery County Citizens United Against Hate (MCCUAH) applied to hold a rally the same day.[86] MCCUAH included members of both county Republican and Democratic central committees, the local NAACP, the Montgomery County Education Association, AFL-CIO Committee on Political Action, and some elected officials.[87]

Then, on November 6, the date that the public thought the KKK would rally, Marjorie Hyer reported for the *Washington Post*, at 6 p.m. on the same evening, that the Ad Hoc Coalition for Community Unity would sponsor the Service of Prayer and Justice event on the steps of the National City Christian Church. This group entailed an organization of thirty-four religious, civil rights, labor, community, and business organizations constructed the previous month in opposition to the planned insurgence of KKK rallies. Jewish and Christian leaders along with the District of Columbia and Montgomery County officials would attend.

Hyer also noted that Shaare Tefila Congregation was a member of an interreligious group in Montgomery County called the Colesville Council of Community Congregations and that Reverend Bordner, from one of the congregations, immediately sent a letter to all the others, advising them of the attack. Due to the support and visibility of the vandalism, Marshall Levin said he had "been flooded with calls" by people asking what they can do to help.[88] Other church leaders, including Roman Catholic Archbishop James A. Hickey, joined with two auxiliary bishops in a statement "condemning anti-Semitism and racism as sinful and calling membership in the KKK 'incompatible with the teaching of the Catholic Church.'"[89] Episcopal Bishop John T. Walker also condemned the KKK and said it was "appalling" "that people who 'call themselves Christian" are part of the Klan.[90]

The Importance of the Cleanup
Day to the Congregation

Now, let's return to Shaare Tefila Congregation to understand why the cleanup day mattered to them: it was through this day that the congregation and larger community contested the authority of the racist antisemitic vandalism and helped them clean their synagogue.[91] The solidarity expressed by the wider community caused congregation members to feel that they were valued and equal inhabitants of their locale. This feeling of inclusion seemed to supply exactly what many congregation members sought in response to the anti-Jewish vandalism that had shocked, angered, and dismayed them. The hundreds of locals who attended the cleanup day demonstrated symbolically and literally that they did not support the vandals' beliefs that Jews are an inferior race. Whereas the later Supreme Court decision changed the dominant narrative about Jewish identity in the legal sense, providing expanded civil rights for Jews, the cleanup day changed the discourse for Shaare Tefila members regarding their sense of social interconnection with their neighbors. Both shifts were significant, fulfilling different identification-related needs.[92]

How exactly did this cleanup day come about? The night after the defacement, Rabbi Halpern, President Potosky, and Executive Director Levin met to discuss the congregational and community reactions to the defacement. The three of them quickly realized that even members of the town who did *not* belong to Shaare Tefila experienced it as a personal affront, for many of these folks had expressed empathy and horror. Consequently, they decided to invite the local community along with Shaare Tefila members who would participate together in a youth-led form of activism to resist the defacement by cleaning the walls of the synagogue. This would occur at 1 p.m. the following Sunday after the Annual Shaare Tefila Youth Breakfast and was led by the United Synagogue Youth and the Kadima (USY's program for preteens) members. They decided that the statement to the media should emphasize the synagogue's "willingness to include the community in a joint statement of revulsion and condemnation of this hate-inspired vandalism," and to "broadcast our message to the media that the leading story at Shaare Tefila was not 'Synagogue Hit by Hate Group' but rather 'Congregation and Community Unite in Response to Hate Group.'"[93]

"We assembled on Sunday," Cantor Gershon Levin, z"l, remembered": Over six hundred people were in the auditorium. We had speakers, members of the clergy [Jewish and non-Jewish]."[94] That morning, Rabbi Halpern had presented powerful remarks. "After the assembly, we went outside, and we started the cleanup. Many photographs were taken, which later were used in the case at the Supreme Court."[95] He scrubbed the wall, with his son on his arm.[96]

Rabbi Halpern later spoke with reporter Janice Kaplan from the *Washington Jewish Week* and told her: "the congregation's young people were 'very upset about the defamation and were looking for outlets to express it. When they saw all the people coming and offering their assistance, this was a positive influence.'" Halpern "pointed to the fact that the congregation had made the decision to publicize the desecration, adding that 'what we have done has affected people in terms of demanding more publicity against racist groups.'"[97] His message cited two reasons why publicizing the event helped the synagogue to heal in response to the defacement that he, Potosky, and Marshall Levin had already discussed: the community responded to the young people's dismay with its assistance, and it recognized the need to acknowledge and condemn racist organizations openly.

More than two hundred teenagers attended the Annual Youth Breakfast, the theme of which was "Anti-Semitism and Jewish Identity, or Who Cares If I'm Jewish?"[98] Afterward, according to Marshall Levin, eight hundred people came together to clean the outer walls of the synagogue.[99] At one point during the afternoon, Levin noted that "spontaneous singing and dancing erupted when, after several minutes of scrubbing the walls with Ajax and water, the first blood-red symbol began to fade."[100] More than half of the eight hundred people were not synagogue members but locals and others who wanted to express their support for the synagogue and their shock that this vandalism had happened in their community.[101]

For two congregation members, whom I interviewed simultaneously, the significance of the cleanup day was particularly memorable; and in several other interviews, interviewees returned to the topic after we had already discussed it and reiterated how wonderful it was that so many people from local churches and the wider community had come to help them. The recurring theme was that the cleanup day made congregation members feel that they were an accepted and valued part of the wider community where they lived, a feeling that many of them had not necessarily experienced before the event. It became clear that although many of the congregants did not participate in the civil suit that the congregation later filed, the cleanup day had an especially deep and lasting impact: it transformed an experience of devastating alienation as a racialized target into an experience of profound solidarity and unity with members of the community. One congregant after another remembered the wide span of ages, religious institutions, and racial diversity represented among the townspeople who came to scrub the walls with them.[102]

For Harriet Steinhorn Roth, z"l (zichronah livracha, may her memory be for a blessing) who survived the Holocaust, the cleanup day demonstrated that the wider community cared about the synagogue members and would not abandon them. She confided:

And then when the day arrived, and I saw so many people came. Ministers, priests, neighbors, White, Black, Muslim, Jewish, Christian, I mean every walk of life, people came. And they were terribly upset over it. And I thought what a wonderful learning experience this provided, and the camaraderie, the people that were there, it was wonderful to see that. Especially for me or for any Holocaust survivor to see the anxiety and the desire to help. To be there. Just by their presence being there. It meant so much. Because I felt totally abandoned, as I mentioned before. Totally abandoned. And no one cared. And this was just the opposite. Just what I would have wished.[103]

She continued:

I'm so glad that this hard thing helped to teach the right thing. That's the way I looked at it. It brought the community together, and that was a wonderful thing to see, especially for me to see: other people gathered together and tried to scrub the stuff off the walls, angry at those who had committed these crimes. And you could see the love and affection. When I came they would help me and say comforting words. It was good to know how much people can care. Very good. It was a good experience for me, in that respect, and it showed that people do care.[104]

This public expression of support brought her relief and countered the experiences she had faced in Poland during the war. "Because when it [the Shoah] happened to us, nobody reached out to us, no one," she told me. "We felt totally forgotten by the world, and by God."[105]

Jack Teller expressed his recollections of the cleanup day as a very positive experience for the congregation because it brought members together and it incorporated the larger community:

When we decided we wanted to go public, and then we finally did, the community was wonderful. They rallied around us. It was just a beautiful thing. The churches, in particular. I can't say the same for our Jewish institutions that were close by. The other Jewish institutions, other Jewish synagogues, ones not so close to us, were really terrific. They came, and they helped and supported us. They brought kids, you know, volunteers, teenagers, and they helped to clean up, and some people who had little businesses to do painting . . . you know, cleaning supplies, they came and supported it. And that was like very warming, you know. . . . So it was really great, I mean the whole community was involved. It was terrific. . . . I mean, that made me prouder of the community than anything. I mean, I really felt good about being a part of this community. . . . Thinking back on that time, I get a little misty-eyed about us.[106]

Teller's statement reveals the emotional impact for him of the cleanup day and the meaningful sense of community that resulted. He indicated his pride in the efforts of local inhabitants to offer physical and emotional support, especially in churches and synagogues a bit farther away. The less-supportive, closer Orthodox synagogues might not have wanted to be grouped with Shaare Tefila; perhaps they would have made a different decision about the graffiti if it had happened to their synagogue. Many other congregants noted the contributions of this variety of institutions as well. The cleanup day involved significant interfaith action.

Several congregation members specifically mentioned Shaare Tefila's involvement in the Colesville Council of Community Congregations. This council consists of churches along the Colesville Corridor, a thoroughfare that runs through Silver Spring, and Shaare Tefila. At the time of the vandalism incident, Shaare Tefila was the only synagogue and the only non-Christian congregation in the organization. Bill Harkaway explained:

> There's the Colesville Council of Community Congregations that had been formed and we were the Jewish member of it. And all up and down Hampshire Avenue there were churches that belonged. It was a good organization and I was a member of the synagogue representatives. I was one of the synagogue's representatives for a long time. And we did a lot of good things at Colesville, 'Four Cs' we referred to them [the Council]. . . . They have a clothes closet: people donate clothing and other people can come and take them without charge. . . . Barbara [his wife] and I work there usually in December before Christmas, so that the non-Jews can do the things they do at Christmas. . . . They have a board, which meets regularly, and they have an annual meeting, and they have a unit that delivers meals on wheels, and Barbara did that for almost thirty years, and once I retired I joined her doing it once a week.

The congregation members' references to their involvement in this organization demonstrate that they valued interfaith social action, that they were identifying as a *religion* here, and that their collaboration with local churches on issues of local poverty was meaningful to their own religious identities and to their values as Jews.

When the vandalism incident occurred, the other congregations in the council were instrumental in offering support, on the cleanup day itself and more generally. Harkaway's words above immediately followed his discussion of the community response to the vandalism. Milt and Susan Goldsamt also referred to the council and their relationship to it before mentioning the empathetic reactions to the vandalism from members of the churches that were part of the council.[107]

Arguably, the church members' involvement in the cleanup day reflected the same type of service to the Council: their condemnation of the antisemitic vandalism invoked their religious identities and values *as* Christians.[108] Robert Wuthnow's book on the restructuring of American religiosity since

World War II notes the significance of values to the dominant American culture and the role of values in connecting religiosity and public life:

> If values were the cornerstone of culture, they were also thought to be the pivotal connection between personal faith and the larger society. The reasoning went somewhat as follows: the good society depends on individuals acting responsibly to uphold moral and democratic values, but a sense of personal responsibility is best supported by conceptions of individual accountability to the sacred; and this sense of accountability requires acknowledging the higher authority of the divine.[109]

Congregants repeatedly mentioned the presence of church members at the cleanup day, arguably illustrating the significance, for them, of Christian support but also the fact that church members *identified* themselves as such at the event. This identification seems to highlight Wuthnow's point above, that the churchgoers felt a moral responsibility to enact their values publicly as religious individuals, due in part, perhaps, to American discourse about what a "good society" entails.[110] They must also have felt the weight of Christian anti-Jewish history.

That nearly all interviewees mentioned the cleanup day or returned to it in our conversations, and that they mentioned how meaningful it was that such a varied group of community members arrived to demonstrate solidarity suggests that the cleanup day served as a counterpoint to the defacement. It provided emotional solace through the affirmation of Jewish identification and Jewish presence in the public culture. It also functioned to denounce the hatred exhibited in the vandalism. Thus, it elevated a certain type of thinking about Jewish identity in the United States—that Jews are equal members of (at least White) American society—and it rejected another type of thinking—that Jews constitute an inferior race.

At Shaare Tefila Congregation, Marshall Levin wrote to the Chief of Police, Bernard Crooke, in Rockville, several weeks after the cleanup day, thanking him, on behalf of the entire congregation and himself, for the Montgomery County Police Department's systematic investigation of the defacement of the synagogue. He particularly thanked Detective Andrew Pecorarou for his continued investigation that led to the apprehension of five suspects in the crime. Conveying what seemed like renewed confidence in the police department, Levin expressed his gratitude to the detective for his persistent "dedication to furthering justice in our community and his tenacity in pursuing the perpetrators of this 'hate vandalism.'"[111] He thanked the police department "from the approximately 600 families of Shaare Tefila Congregation, from the hundreds of non-Jewish members of our community who have expressed their sympathy and support to us," and himself.[112] Levin's letter implied that he had not expected the County Police Department's response to the crime and to finding its perpetrators.

In the weeks that followed, before the Klan rally actually occurred, on November 27, Judy Green from the *Montgomery County Sentinel* spoke with six White sophomore high school students at MacGruder High School who had viewed a documentary about the KKK in their social studies classes.[113] One of those students, Hillary Glatt, told Ms. Green that she's Jewish and that prior to living in Montgomery County, she was the only Jew in a "really red-neck" part of New Jersey. Other kids there used to tell her sometimes what they heard at home—that Jews are dirty people and take all your money. She told them, "We don't do that. I'm just a person," but she said she saw more prejudice in Montgomery County, given the planned KKK rally and the defacement of the synagogue.[114] Another student, Spencer Meader, had lived in California and Georgia before coming to Montgomery County and said that California was less prejudiced but in Georgia, bigotry was widely accepted. Other students theorized about the nature of KKK beliefs; Glatt noted: "they want to belong to something—they want to be something, and they feel like they aren't anything. Putting down others makes them feel better."

In the early 1980s, national discourse began to focus on crimes committed against racially marginalized peoples, such as Jews, Blacks, Asians, Latinxs, and Indigenous peoples, and the legal term "hate crime" became commonly used.[115] Likewise, police reports began to separately track "hate violence" in Montgomery County. The *Washington Post* reported on November 22, 1982, that "race" and "religion" were two key factors in hate violence.[116] John Furman, research director for the Southern Poverty Law Center's Klan Watch, based in Montgomery, Alabama noted that "It's a widespread problem, not confined to any one region. There is a definite rise in anti-Semitic activity, and of course, the Klan has always been antiblack."[117]

Locally, Montgomery County led the state of Maryland in terms of recorded incidents of hate violence. The *Post* article also noted that in the twenty-one days *since* the Shaare Tefila Congregation attack, the county police received twelve reports of race-based and antisemitic events, which were aimed almost evenly against Blacks and Jews.[118] To explain the rise in hate violence, the *Post* looked to the changing religious and racial demographics mentioned earlier in the chapter.

In the months following the defacement, the references to the cleanup day were essential to the solidarity that Shaare Tefila Congregation experienced with their neighbors, and from there, enabled them to feel more confident about educating the non-Jewish American public. Many interviewees also mentioned the documentary film that they had made about the defacement, called *Desecration in Darkness*, which won an international award.[119] It included interviews with congregation members, community members,

County Council members, clergy, police officers, congressional representatives, and children.[120] Milt Goldsamt proudly recounted that he narrated the film.[121] The Sensitivity Awareness Symposium (SAS) Day was another educational effect that resulted from the defacement. It was launched by the congregation's leadership, in association with the Human Relations Commission (HRC), and put into every Montgomery County public school by the HRC and the Montgomery County Council.[122] Congregation members also spoke at local community meetings.[123]

In response to the Shaare Tefila defacement, as well as the rash of incidents that plagued the county at large, on November 30, 1982, the Council of Montgomery County adopted two penalties for racial violence: first, to make cross-burnings, which occurred without the consent of the owner on whose property it took place, a civil offense; and second, to establish a $50,000 fund, called the "anti-hate violence fund." Cross-burning offenses would result in up to $1,000 paid to the victim and damages of up to $1,000 paid to the county "for 'damage to the peace and the peace of mind to the victims.'"[124] Clearly, these acts were occurring, otherwise, there would be no need to construct a penalty. After the bill had been passed, council member Esther Gelman said "she hoped the bills 'will restore Montgomery County to its rightful place where people won't live in fear of these acts.'"[125]

For the first time in US history, attorneys began to build the case that "hate violence"—attacks that focused on the religion or race of the victim(s)—could be categorized separately in the State of Maryland. This new categorization did not mean that crimes or civil rights suits were being *added*, only that they were being identified separately. It meant that the defacement Shaare Tefila members had experienced could become a civil suit, due to its racial basis. The Congregation still had to argue for the vandalism's racist antisemitic distinction in the courts, however, because it was not defined *legally* as racist.

In this vein, some of the members wanted to tell their story and express to the vandals how they experienced the defacement. Linguistic and legal anthropologist Elizabeth Mertz calls this a form of "narrative control": "The voice in the case of the individual litigant is that of the individual, and narrative control means that the individual has had the opportunity to tell her or his story with minimal constraint or structuring by legal authorities."[126] For the congregants, it would involve their leaders speaking to the vandals in the courtroom about why the desecration of their synagogue caused them trauma.[127] This opportunity was not fulfilled, however, until the case wound its way from the Federal District Court of Maryland to the Fourth Circuit Court of Appeals, to the Supreme Court decision, and finally back to Federal District Court.

Taking a step back from their experience of the vandalism, how did Shaare Tefila members understand their relationships with non-Jewish Americans, in the 1980s? The following paragraph is mostly based on speculation. They enjoyed their participation in the Colesville Council of Community of Congregations. They also lived in a time in which the KKK was rampant and antisemitism was ever-present. Congregant Sid Schwartz mentioned that they had tried to blend in—not mentioning because it seemed obvious—with other White people.[128] The scenario was "racialized" even if they might not have thought of it in quite those terms. When they imagined an external community, congregants might have assumed that it was non-Jews, in *general*, likely not thinking about all the types of conscripted racialized identities or the racialized hierarchies that existed. In other words, Shaare Tefila members, among other Jewish Americans perceived as White, understood themselves as marginalized, given their own experiences and the vandalism that defaced their synagogue; but non-"formally" White Jewish Americans would not see them that way due to the color of their skin, the fact that they and their ancestors had benefited from the G.I. Bill, and their relative wealth in relation to other racialized minorities, among other examples. On the street, unless they were wearing a kippah, they would not likely be pegged as Jewish. In terms of the material world, the space of their synagogue was one among other Jewish places that could be attacked. For this reason and others, such as discrimination based on their last names, Shaare Tefila members *may* have believed that they were equally marginalized. This might be attributed partly to long-held historical and "mythical" experiences of exile, expulsion, and identification as slaves in the Land of Egypt. Historian of religions scholar Bruce Lincoln describes "myth" as "the small class of stories that possess both credibility and authority" in a particular society.[129] His classification of myth can be applied to the Torah, the origin narrative for Jews. Every year at Passover, for example, Shaare Tefila congregants told the *magid* (story), recounted the exodus from *Mitzrayim* (Egypt or a "narrow place"), and remembered *themselves* as having been slaves in the Land of Egypt. These are the stories that Jews hold dear, they possess credibility, even if Jews do not believe them literally. Even secular Jews trace their lineage to the Torah.[130] In the United States, however, "formally" White Jews were *White*, even though they were not "*substantively*" White. Therefore, Shaare Tefila congregants were *both* marginalized *and* perceived as White, and these two qualifiers factored into how they were racialized.

In the 1980s, Jewish Americans, in general, were perceived as White. "Formally" White Jewish Americans thus may have appeared more economically, politically, and materially powerful to other marginalized groups than they believed they were. "Formally" White Jewish Americans automatically accrue White privilege[131] unless the observer knows that they are Jewish. In that case, whatever automatic thoughts the observer holds about Jews or Jewish Americans become projected onto the way the observer thinks, feels, or experiences who that Jewish person is. An individual Jew may become, for a non-Jew, the personification of *all* Jews.[132]

The antisemitic, racist young men who defaced the synagogue on November 1, 1982, held precisely such assumptions but in a very negative way. Such images derive from stereotypes, but many non-Jewish Americans, and even some Jewish Americans, may think these stereotypes are valid or jokingly refer to them as such. Whereas these non-Jewish Americans may see such stereotypes as evidence of Jewish *advantages* over non-Jews, the same Jewish Americans may be proud of those same situations. Some White non-Jewish Americans, particularly those who view Jewish Americans as racially inferior, such as the vandals, may believe that they have a right to this economic, political, and material power.[133]

Given the supposed linkage between Jews and race, both Jews and non-Jews also base their thinking about Jews on the assumption that people cannot *convert* to Judaism.[134] Many Jews and non-Jews think that "Jewish" means a lineage or even a "bloodline," and conversion complicates that belief. Texts that describe Jewish identities often forget that people *do* convert to Judaism, among them books that discuss "Jewish genes," such as Jon Entine's *Abraham's Children: Race, Identity, and the DNA of the Chosen People*.[135] Such books prevent Americans from getting an accurate story about the significance of converts to Judaism. All of the lineage and bloodline stories distract from what's actually occurring: by 2015, one in six Jewish Americans were Jews *by choice*.[136] Neglecting the topic of conversion means that both Jewish and non-Jewish Americans may have a very different concept of what "being Jewish" means: it does not require lineage, it does not entail a bloodline, and it certainly does not refer to inherent qualities that are similar among all Jews.

This same narrative suggests that if one converts to Judaism, one should behave "like a Jew." Likewise, if one marries someone who is not Jewish, that same Jewish person should conduct herself "like a Jew." If a Jewish person "passes" as White or as BIPOC, they are still "a Jew underneath." In other words, this narrative of Jews as a racial group insists that there must be some *Jewishness* that shows up in all these people. Taking these racial divisions to heart, White supremacists, such as the vandals that defaced Shaare Tefila Congregation, are troubled by the fluidity of racialized shifting because it complicates their conception of what a "Jew" is.

CONCLUSION

Returning to the synagogue, let's summarize the discussion in this chapter. It begins with my presentation to the Shaare Tefila Congregation members one Shabbat morning in July 2008, and my individual conversations with them that day. The congregation clearly had changed over the years since the vandalism occurred and newer members were not aware that it had won a Supreme Court case. It is evident that the important daily and yearly functions of Shaare Tefila take precedence over that memory.

To highlight the fluidity of Jewish racialization in the United States and to point out that Jewish Americans are now considered "White," it continues with a brief history of Jewish racialization, beginning in the 1850s, before the Civil Rights Acts of 1866 and 1871. This history provides context for the third chapter, in which the lower court judges deemed Jews "White" and a "religion," and the fourth chapter, in which the Supreme Court determined that Jews were "not white" in 1866.

Next, it focuses on Jews whose Whiteness was in jeopardy and describes their history through World War II and then concentrates specifically on the Shaare Tefila Congregation. It explains how despite redlining and racial covenants, the White-perceived Jewish American community would come to be perceived as "White" due to the G.I. Bill and other changes in the US government around the end of World War II. After 1977, the Shaare Tefila Congregation would be perceived as "formally" White but never "substantively" White. For instance, vandals could deface their synagogue in 1982. This distinction contextualizes the defacement in the racialized environment of Montgomery County and the Washington, DC, area in the early 1980s.

Finally, it turns to interviews with the Shaare Tefila Congregation members regarding their responses to the vandalism and their reactions to their leaders' decisions to leave it *in situ*. They felt empowered by standing in solidarity with their neighbors on the cleanup day, which allowed them to emerge from their previously coded identity as "formally" White Americans. This cleanup day ultimately bolstered their motivation to pursue a civil suit. As a result of the cleanup day, the Anti-Defamation League of B'nai B'rith significantly altered its official policy regarding antisemitic vandalism at Jewish sites: they now recommend that Jewish organizations include the wider community in denouncing antisemitic behavior.[137]

Two main views on how to proceed with the civil suit emerged in my conversations with Shaare Tefila members, views based on alternate approaches to antisemitism. Recall that Maryland did not have a law that would account for antisemitic vandalism. Also, remember that the dominant discourse about Jews had changed since the end of World War II such that in the 1980s these Jewish synagogue members who passed as White were able to *appear* and *function* as White in non-Jewish social settings and could attempt to conceal their Jewishness if they so desired.

The first approach emerged from the discourse that discouraged Jewish Americans from revealing their Jewish identities and obscuring or removing any anti-Jewish vandalism without publicizing it. This was also the message that the Anti-Defamation League of B'nai B'rith announced to all Jewish organizations before the High Holidays in 1982. Such an approach asserts that antisemitism is prevalent but usually hidden. From this view, publicity of an antisemitic attack may or will result in similar actions by others, and, therefore, that evidence of such attacks should be kept secret or at least shielded from the wider, non-Jewish community.

The second approach emphasizes that contemporary antisemitic incidents recall a long history of anti-Judaism and antisemitism; it considers how Jewish responses to anti-Judaism and antisemitism have functioned negatively in the past and what types of responses might result in an improved situation for Jews. In this case, Marshall Levin, who studied the Shoah, as well as Shirley Altman, who survived World War II, viewed the desecration of Shaare Tefila in the context of the war and the Shoah. Rabbi Halpern, also a survivor, seemed to disagree with them at first—reflecting the dominant view of Jewish Americans of the time—before Levin changed the Rabbi's mind. Halpern then changed Harriet Steinhorn Roth's perception of the defacement. All of them came to support the decision to leave the graffiti in place and to file the civil suit because of their knowledge and/or experience of the extreme antisemitism perpetrated by the Nazis.[138]

In the end, the Shaare Tefila congregation chose the second narrative as their response to the defacement, and they were gratified by the solidarity they felt from their neighbors. Decades later, they remembered this community support, many of them returning to memories of it during my interviews with them. This solidarity signified that they did not need to fear the recourse of other potential criminals because their community stood with them. Before their neighbors came to the cleanup day, they took a risk. They confronted the defacement and did not cover it up. The next chapter describes how the vandals were found, charged, and convicted, and then why the Shaare Tefila Board of Trustees chose to pursue it as a civil suit.

NOTES

1. Rabbi Jonah Layman, phone call with author, June 20, 2008.

2. See Religious Bodies, 1980 Report, Montgomery County (Maryland), County Membership Report, Association of Religion Data Archives, accessed September 29, 2021, www.thearda.com/rcms2010/rcms2010a.asp?U=24031&T=county&S=Name &Y=1980. Contrast with Religious Bodies, 1990 Report, Montgomery County (Maryland), County Membership Report, Association of Religion Data Archives www.thearda.com/rcms2010/rcms2010a.asp?U=24031&T=county&S=Name&Y =1990, accessed September 29, 2021. For race-based data, see Department of

Planning Maryland State Data Center, Historical Census, Census 1980, 1990 and 2000 Profile of General Demographic Characteristics (PDF Formant), Montgomery County, accessed June 20, 2002, planning.maryland.gov/MSDC/Pages/census/censushHistorical.aspx.

3. Eric L. Goldstein, *The Price of Whiteness: Jews, Race, and American Identity* (Princeton, NJ: Princeton University Press, 2006) 225, 305.

4. Marlowe v. Fisher Body 489 F.2d 1057 (1973). Section 1981 states: "All persons within the jurisdiction of the United States shall have the same right in every State and Territory to make and enforce contracts, to sue, be parties, give evidence, and to the full and equal benefit of all laws and proceedings as is enjoyed by white citizens." 42 U.S.C. Section 1981. See Joseph Avanzato, "Section 1982 and Discrimination against Jews: Shaare Tefila Congregation v. Cobb," *American University Law Review* 37, no. 1 (1987): 237.

5. Rabbi Jonah Layman, email with author, April 23, 2022.

6. Susan Goldsamt, interview by author, Silver Spring, MD, July 7, 2008.

7. Marshall Levin, interview by author, New York, NY, July 10, 2008.

8. *Decision: St. Francis College v. Al-Khazraji*, 481 U.S. 604 (May 19, 1987) Philip Kurland and Gerhard Casper, *Landmark Briefs and Arguments of the Supreme Court of the United States: Constitutional Law, 1986 Term Supplement* (Frederick, MD: University Publications of America, Inc., 1988), 251–54.

9. *Decision: St. Francis College v. Al-Khazraji*, 481 U.S. 604 (May 19, 1987) Philip Kurland and Gerhard Casper, *Landmark Briefs and Arguments of the Supreme Court of the United States: Constitutional Law, 1986 Term Supplement* (Frederick, MD: University Publications of America, Inc., 1988), 253. My assumption is that Jewish Americans identified as a "race" in the 1850s, because Goldstein mentions that it was significant to their identity in the 1860s. Eric L. Goldstein, *The Price of Whiteness: Jews, Race, and American Identity* (Princeton, NJ: Princeton University Press, 2006), 15–16.

10. Hasia R. Diner, *The Jews of the United States, 1654 to 2000* (Berkeley, CA: University of California Press, 2006), 158.

11. U.S. Const. amend. XIII; U.S. Const. amend. XIV; U.S. Const. amend XV; United States. Civil Rights Acts of 1866, 1871.

12. Eric L. Goldstein, *The Price of Whiteness: Jews, Race, and American Identity* (Princeton, NJ: Princeton University Press, 2006), 13.

13. Eric L. Goldstein, *The Price of Whiteness: Jews, Race, and American Identity* (Princeton, NJ: Princeton University Press, 2006), 31.

14. Eric L. Goldstein, *The Price of Whiteness: Jews, Race, and American Identity* (Princeton, NJ: Princeton University Press, 2006), 31.

15. Eric L. Goldstein, *The Price of Whiteness: Jews, Race, and American Identity* (Princeton, NJ: Princeton University Press, 2006), 102–7.

16. Eric L. Goldstein, *The Price of Whiteness: Jews, Race, and American Identity* (Princeton, NJ: Princeton University Press, 2006), 103.

17. Eric L. Goldstein, *The Price of Whiteness: Jews, Race, and American Identity* (Princeton, NJ: Princeton University Press, 2006), 104.

18. Eric L. Goldstein, *The Price of Whiteness: Jews, Race, and American Identity* (Princeton, NJ: Princeton University Press, 2006), 105. See also Victoria Hattam, *In the Shadow of Race: Jews, Latinos, and Immigrant Politics in the United States* (Chicago, IL: University of Chicago Press, 2007), 86–91.

19. See Noam Pianko, *Jewish Peoplehood: An American Innovation* (New Brunswick, NJ: Rutgers University Press, 2015).

20. Daniel Schere, "Researchers Look at Where Jews and Blacks Weren't Allowed to Go," *Washington Jewish Week*, May 10, 2017, accessed July 2, 2020, www.washingtonjewishweek.com/38483/researchers-look-at-where-jews-and -blacks-werent-allowed-to-go/news/.

21. According to Mara Cherkasky's email: Jews were restricted in the areas around American University; upper 16th Street; and a few in Crestwood. December 30, 2020. She is the Principal Historian of Prologue DC, LLC, Mapping Segregation in Washington DC.

22. Deed for 4920 Upton Street NW, in DC's Spring Valley neighborhood, recorded March 14, 1958. DC Recorder of Deeds. "Legal Challenges to Racially Restrictive Covenants," Mapping Segregation in Washington D.C., accessed January 5, 2021, mappingsegregationdc.org/index.html#mapping.

23. My thanks to Mara Cherkasky for her email detailing this information. December 30, 2020. She is the Principal Historian of Prologue DC, LLC, Mapping Segregation in Washington, DC.

24. Eric L. Goldstein, *The Price of Whiteness: Jews, Race, and American Identity* (Princeton, NJ: Princeton University Press, 2006), 192.

25. Eric L. Goldstein, *The Price of Whiteness: Jews, Race, and American Identity* (Princeton, NJ: Princeton University Press, 2006), 192.

26. See Hilary Herbold, "Never a Level Playing Field: Blacks and the GI Bill," *The Journal of Blacks in Higher Education*, no. 6 (Winter 1994–1995): 104–8. Joseph Thompson, "The GI Bill Should've Been Race Neutral, Politicos Made Sure It Wasn't," *MilitaryTimes*, November 9, 2019, accessed January 5, 2021. www .militarytimes.com/military-honor/salute-veterans/2019/11/10/the-gi-bill-shouldve -been-race-neutral-politicos-made-sure-it-wasnt/

27. Thank you to Mara Cherkasky, Principal Historian of Prologue DC, LLC, Mapping Segregation in Washington DC, for providing me with a helpful interview that she had done with Francine Berkowitz, who grew up in Riggs Park. Francine Berkowitz, interview by Mara Cherkasky and Sarah Shoenfeld, Oral History Interview, *DC Oral History Collaborative*, Petworth Public Library, Washington DC, July 18, 2017.

28. Merry Madway Eisenstadt, "Golden Anniversary Shaare Tefila Celebrates 50 Years of Touching Lives," *Washington Jewish Week*, February 1, 2001: 1.

29. Merry Madway Eisenstadt, "Golden Anniversary Shaare Tefila Celebrates 50 Years of Touching Lives," *Washington Jewish Week*, February 1, 2001: 1.

30. Merry Madway Eisenstadt, "Golden Anniversary Shaare Tefila Celebrates 50 Years of Touching Lives," *Washington Jewish Week*, February 1, 2001: 2.

31. www.shaaretefila.org/page/history, cited April 22, 2010.

32. "Who's Who," Young Israel Shomrai Emunah of Greater Washington, accessed December 29, 2020, wp.yise.org/about/whos-who/ (in comparison with the

information I had accessed earlier from Shaare Tefila's old website, accessed on April 22, 2010, www.shaaretefila.org/page/history.

33. Lee Spetner, "A History of Young Israel Shomrai Emunah Genesis of a Washington Synagogue" in Young Israel Shomrai Emunah of Greater Washington, Silver Spring, MD 20902, accessed December 18, 2020, wp.yise.org/about/.

34. Merry Madway Eisenstadt, "Golden Anniversary Shaare Tefila Celebrates 50 Years of Touching Lives," *Washington Jewish Week*, February 1, 2001: 3.

35. For an analysis of "White flight," see David L. Chappell, "Review: Did Racists Create the Suburban Nation?" *Reviews in American History* 35, no. 1 (March 2007): 89–97. With thanks to Lauren Strauss for telling me about her early research of Jewish civil rights activists in a Washington, DC, in the 1950s, conversation held December 24, 2020.

36. www.shaaretefila.org/page/history, Accessed April 22, 2010.

37. See Unnamed author, "Cross burnings, Anti-Semitic Incidents Increase in Montgomery," *Washington Post*, November 22, 1982, A11.

38. Office of Management and Budget, Directive 15: Race and Ethnic Standards for Federal Statistics and Administrative Reporting (1977) available at wonder.cdc.gov/wonder/help/populations/bridged-race/directive15.html [perma.cc/FHL3–7C8U].

39. For "performing Whiteness," see John Tehranian,"Performing Whiteness: Naturalization Litigation and the Construction of Racial Identity in America" in *Yale Law Journal* 109, no. 4 (Jan. 2000): 817–48.

40. Khaled Beydoun, "Faith in Whiteness: Free Exercise of Religion as Racial Expression" in *Iowa Law Review* 105, no. 4 (May 2020): 1487.

41. Unnamed author, "Cross burnings, Anti-Semitic Incidents Increase in Montgomery," *Washington Post*, November 22, 1982, A11. For race-based data, which does not identify Jews separately, see Department of Planning Maryland State Data Center, Historical Census, Census 1980, 1990 and 2000 Profile of General Demographic Characteristics (PDF Formant), Montgomery County, accessed June 20, 2002, planning.maryland.gov/MSDC/Pages/census/censusHistorical.aspx

42. Jeremy Goldberg's Washington, Shaare Tefila Congregation, Through the Lens, Photographic Histories, accessed December 20, 2020, www.jhsgw.org/exhibitions/online/goldberg/photographs/shaare-tefila.

43. Khaled Beydoun, "Faith in Whiteness: Free Exercise of Religion as Racial Expression," *Iowa Law Review* 105, no. 4 (May 2020).

44. Gregory Martire and Ruth Clark, *Anti-Semitism in the United States: A Study of Prejudice in the 1980s* (New York: Praeger, 1982), 3.

45. Gregory Martire and Ruth Clark, *Anti-Semitism in the United States: A Study of Prejudice in the 1980s* (New York: Praeger, 1982), 4.

46. Gregory Martire and Ruth Clark, *Anti-Semitism in the United States: A Study of Prejudice in the 1980s* (New York: Praeger, 1982), 19.

47. Gregory Martire and Ruth Clark, *Anti-Semitism in the United States: A Study of Prejudice in the 1980s* (New York: Praeger, 1982), 19.

48. Michael Kernan, "The Specter of Anti-Semitism, The Unending Web of Fear," *Washington Post*, December 1, 1982.

49. Unnamed author, "Synagogue Defaced as Board Meets Inside," *Washington Jewish Week*, November 4–10, 1982, 14.

50. A Statement of the United States Commission on Civil Rights, *Intimidation and Violence: Racial and Religious Bigotry* (Clearinghouse Publication 77, January 1983), 2, citing the *Baltimore Sun*, May 18, 1982, p. 1. One of the five instances mentioned on the second page as "problems" is the following quote: "On March 10, 1982, a Jewish female student was shot five times with a BB gun on the University of Maryland college campus at College Park, Maryland. The attacker shouted "Heil Hitler" as he fired and used other epithets that indicated anti-Jewish feelings. An underground campus newspaper hailed the assailant as a hero and suggested that next time he use a flamethrower on the victim.

51. Unnamed author, "Publicity Led to Arrest," *Washington Jewish Week*, November 18–24, 1982, 1.

52. Author has made multiple attempts to corroborate this account with the Anti-Defamation League but has failed to receive a reply.

53. See Marshall Levin "Desecration in Darkness" in *The Price We Pay: The Case against Racist Speech, Hate Propaganda, and Pornography*, eds. Laura J. Lederer and Richard Delgado (New York: Hill & Wang, 1995), 40.

54. Synopsis prepared by Marshall S. Levin, Executive Director, "Desecration in Darkness: A Community Fights Back, A Historic Documentary Film," stapled to press release, January 7, 1985, Film Premiere, pp. 1–2.

55. Marshall Levin, interview by author, New York City, July 10, 2008.

56. Levin, "Desecration in Darkness," 43.

57. Levin, "Desecration in Darkness," 43.

58. The paragraph describes a conversation I had with Marshall Levin in his New York City office. Marshall Levin, interview by author, New York City, July 10, 2008.

59. Levin, "Desecration in Darkness," 41.

60. Bill Harkaway, interview by author, Bethesda, MD, August 19, 2009.

61. Bill Harkaway, interview by author, Bethesda, MD, August 19, 2009.

62. Bill Harkaway, interview by author, Bethesda, MD, August 19, 2009.

63. One mother told me that her child experienced fear upon seeing the words and images, and that she was upset about it and had not wanted him to react in that way. Matsuda notes that "Patricia Williams has called the blow of racist messages 'spirit murder' in recognition of the psychic destructions victims' experience." Mari Matsuda, "Public Response to Racist Speech: Considering the Victim's Story" in *Words That Wound: Critical Race Theory, Assaultive Speech, and the First Amendment* eds. Mari Matsuda et al. (Boulder, CO: Westview Press, 1993), 24. She cites Williams, *supra* note 8, at 129.

64. Michael Holmes, phone interview by author, July 2, 2009.

65. Milton and Susan Goldsamt, interview by author, Silver Spring, MD, July 7, 2008.

66. Susan Goldsamt, interview by author, Silver Spring, MD, July 7, 2008.

67. Although the Anti-Defamation League kept statistics regarding the frequency of such incidents, it would be difficult to assess the relationship between the number of them and the perception of community members, because most of this vandalism

was quickly erased. The *Washington Jewish Week* reported some cases of antisemitic vandalism, but it is impossible to know how many cases were unreported or whether the congregation members I interviewed were regularly reading the paper or discussing such incidents within the community. In the issue published the week after the Shaare Tefila defacement, the *Washington Jewish Week* stated that four other area congregations had been the sites of "anti-Jewish daubings" since January. See Unnamed author, "Interfaith Service," the *Washington Jewish Week* 18, no. 43 (11--17 November 1982): 11. A *Washington Post* article noted, however, that director of the DC-Maryland area regional office of the Anti-Defamation League reported that four synagogues in the Washington DC area had been targeted in the past *month*. See Marjorie Hyer, "Jewish Leader Seeks Action on Vandalism," *Washington Post*, 4 November 1982, sec. B, p. 1.

68. Synopsis prepared by Marshall S. Levin, Executive Director, "Desecration in Darkness: A Community Fights Back, A Historic Documentary Film," stapled to press release, January 7, 1985, Film Premiere, p. 2.

69. Synopsis prepared by Marshall S. Levin, Executive Director, "Desecration in Darkness: A Community Fights Back, A Historic Documentary Film," stapled to press release, January 7, 1985 Film Premiere, p. 2.

70. Jack Teller, interview by author, Silver Spring, MD, August 17, 2009.

71. Jack Teller, interview by author, Silver Spring, MD, August 17, 2009.

72. Susan Goldsamt, interview by author, Silver Spring, MD, July 7, 2008.

73. Milton Goldsamt, interview by author, Silver Spring, MD, July 7, 2008.

74. Congregation members told me that a number of survivors had been members of the congregation at that time. When I conducted the interviews, however, most of them had passed away. I spoke with two current members besides Harriet Steinhorn Roth who had escaped World War II but who were not survivors of the concentration camps. One was Shirley Altman, president at the time that the congregation decided to bring the civil suit, who had lived in England, and the other was Frances Berger, who had fled Poland, and who said that the defacement reminded her of events that happened regularly when she lived there.

75. Deposition of Jacob A. Teller at 14, Shaare Tefila Congregation v. Cobb, 606 F.Supp. 1504 (D. Md. 1985), *rev'd*, 107 S.Ct. 2019 (1987) (deposition of Aug 3, 1988).

76. Deposition of Jacob A. Teller at 14, Shaare Tefila Congregation v. Cobb, 606 F.Supp. 1504 (D. Md. 1985), *rev'd*, 107 S.Ct. 2019 (1987) (deposition of Aug 3, 1988).

77. Harriet Steinhorn Roth, interview by author, Silver Spring, MD, August 17, 2009.

78. Harriet Steinhorn Roth, interview by author, Silver Spring, MD, August 17, 2009.

79. Harriet Steinhorn Roth, interview by author, Silver Spring, MD, August 17, 2009.

80. Marjorie Hyer, "Jewish Leader Seeks Action on Vandalism," *Washington Post*, November 4, 1982.

81. Marjorie Hyer, "Jewish Leader Seeks Action on Vandalism," *Washington Post*, November 4, 1982.

82. Michael Kernan, "The Specter of Anti-Semitism, The Unending Web of Fear," *Washington Post*, December 1, 1982.

83. Christian Ward, "KKK, Anti-KKK Groups Head for Confrontation," *Montgomery County Sentinel*, November 4, 1982, A3.

84. Christian Ward, "KKK, Anti-KKK Groups Head for Confrontation," *Montgomery County Sentinel*, November 4, 1982, A3.

85. Christian Ward, "KKK, Anti-KKK Groups Head for Confrontation," *Montgomery County Sentinel*, November 4, 1982, A3.

86. Christian Ward, "KKK, Anti-KKK Groups Head for Confrontation," *Montgomery County Sentinel*, November 4, 1982, A3.

87. Christian Ward, "KKK, Anti-KKK Groups Head for Confrontation," *Montgomery County Sentinel*, November 4, 1982, A3.

88. Marjorie Hyer, "KKK, Desecration Strengthen Resolve to Combat Bigotry," *Washington Post*, November 6, 1982.

89. Marjorie Hyer "KKK, Desecration Strengthen Resolve to Combat Bigotry," *Washington Post*, November 6, 1982. The KKK would not want to be associated with the Catholic Church either.

90. Marjorie Hyer, "KKK, Desecration Strengthen Resolve to Combat Bigotry," *Washington Post*, November 6, 1982.

91. Bruce Lincoln argues that a "myth" is a narrative that is true and authoritative to a certain society. He also asserts that contesting the *authority* of a myth is a way to detract from its power. See Bruce Lincoln, *Discourse and the Construction of Society: Comparative Studies of Myth, Ritual, and Classification* (New York: Oxford University Press, 1989), 25.

92. From my interviews, it seemed that congregation members viewed non-Jews as a *singular* group because they experienced collective alienation in the same way that other marginalized groups did who wanted to be accepted as "equal" to their vision of a society that *should* exist. From their own marginalized position, however, of people who "pass" as White, it *could* seem like all other minority communities experience the same inequalities, which is not the case.

93. Synopsis prepared by Marshall S. Levin, Executive Director, "Desecration in Darkness: A Community Fights Back, A Historic Documentary Film," stapled to press release, January 7, 1985, Film Premiere, 3.

94. Cantor Gershon Levin, written responses to interview questions by author, submitted via email, August 26, 2009.

95. Cantor Gershon Levin, written responses to interview questions by author, submitted via email, August 26, 2009.

96. Cantor Gershon Levin, written responses to interview questions by author, submitted via email, August 26, 2009.

97. Janice L. Kaplan, "Halpern sees good from evil in reaction to synagogue vandalism," *Washington Jewish Week* 18, no. 43 (November 1982): 11–17, p. 1.

98. Synopsis prepared by Marshall S. Levin, Executive Director, "Desecration in Darkness: A Community Fights Back, A Historic Documentary Film," stapled to press release, January 7, 1985, Film Premiere, p. 3.

99. Synopsis prepared by Marshall S. Levin, Executive Director, "Desecration in Darkness: A Community Fights Back, A Historic Documentary Film," stapled to press release, January 7, 1985, Film Premiere, p. 3.

100. Synopsis prepared by Marshall S. Levin, Executive Director, "Desecration in Darkness: A Community Fights Back, A Historic Documentary Film," stapled to press release, January 7, 1985, Film Premiere, p. 3.

101. Synopsis prepared by Marshall S. Levin, Executive Director, "Desecration in Darkness: A Community Fights Back, A Historic Documentary Film," stapled to press release, January 7, 1985, Film Premiere, p. 3.

102. A number of interviewees also mentioned their intense disappointment that their nearest "co-religionists," as one congregation member said—an Orthodox synagogue—failed to support them.

103. Harriet Steinhorn Roth, interview by author, Silver Spring, MD, August 17, 2009.

104. Harriet Steinhorn Roth, interview by author, Silver Spring, MD, August 17, 2009.

105. Harriet Steinhorn Roth, interview by author, Silver Spring, MD, August 17, 2009.

106. Jack Teller, interview by author, Silver Spring, MD, August 17, 2009.

107. Milton and Susan Goldsamt, interview by author, Silver Spring, MD, July 7, 2008.

108. A letter from S. Henry Harris to Rabbi Halpern states: "Please accept this token of disgust at what happened to your house of worship this week. Use this for cleaning . . . [the last word is illegible]" It is signed "A Christian friend, S. Henry Harris." A note written at the top of the letter indicates that Harris had included a check for $25. The congregation's file on the case also contains a number of other letters to Rabbi Halpern from local citizens and religious leaders who identify themselves as Christians. They include: a handwritten letter from Rev. Harwood C. Bowman Jr., rector of the Episcopal Church of Our Savior in Silver Spring on November 12, 1982; a letter from Dermot A. Nee, who identifies himself as "an American and a Catholic" and who enclosed a check to help with the cleaning costs on November 15, 1982; and an undated letter from Marianne Van Fossen, the Interim Worship Coordinator at the Universal Fellowship of Metropolitan Community Churches in Washington DC.

109. Robert Wuthnow, *The Restructuring of American Religion: Society and Faith Since World War II* (Princeton, NJ: Princeton University Press, 1988), 58.

110. Prevailing narratives in the United States during the 1980s condemned antisemitic acts, such as the defacement of Shaare Tefila, even as many such acts occurred. Thus, the presence of religious organizations at the cleanup reflected the publicly accepted sentiment of the times and arguably represented Wuthnow's agreed upon "moral value."

111. Marshall Levin, Letter to Chief of Police Bernard Crooke, November 22, 1982.

112. Marshall Levin, Letter to Chief of Police Bernard Crooke, November 22, 1982.

113. Judy Green, "High School Students Kick the Klan," *Montgomery County Sentinel*, November 11, 1982, A7.

114. Judy Green, "High School Students Kick the Klan," *Montgomery County Sentinel*, November 11, 1982, A7.

115. Overview of Hate Crime, United States Department of Justice, Office of Justice Programs, accessed September 6, 2021, nij.ojp.gov/topics/articles/overview-hate-crime.

116. Unnamed author, "Cross burnings, Anti-Semitic Incidents Increase in Montgomery," *Washington Post*, November 22, 1982, A11.

117. Unnamed author, "Cross burnings, Anti-Semitic Incidents Increase in Montgomery," *Washington Post*, November 22, 1982, A11.

118. Unnamed author, "Cross burnings, Anti-Semitic Incidents Increase in Montgomery," *Washington Post*, November 22, 1982, A11.

119. Marshall Levin, "Desecration in Darkness," in *The Price We Pay: The Case against Hate Speech, Hate Propaganda, and Pornography*, eds. Laura Lederer and Richard Delgado (New York, NY: Hill & Wang, 1995), 43.

120. Marshall Levin, "Desecration in Darkness," in *The Price We Pay: The Case against Hate Speech, Hate Propaganda, and Pornography*, eds. Laura Lederer and Richard Delgado (New York, NY: Hill & Wang, 1995), 43.

121. Milton Goldsamt, interview by author, Silver Spring, MD, July 7, 2008.

122. Marshall Levin, "Desecration in Darkness," in *The Price We Pay: The Case against Hate Speech, Hate Propaganda, and Pornography*, eds. Laura Lederer and Richard Delgado (New York, NY: Hill & Wang, 1995), 42.

123. Marshall Levin, "Desecration in Darkness," in *The Price We Pay: The Case against Hate Speech, Hate Propaganda, and Pornography*, eds. Laura Lederer and Richard Delgado (New York, NY: Hill and Wang, 1995), 42.

124. "Hate: Council Adopts Penalties for Racial Violence," *Montgomery County Sentinel*, December 2, 1982, A3.

125. "Hate: Council Adopts Penalties for Racial Violence," *Montgomery County Sentinel*, December 2, 1982, A3.

126. Elizabeth Mertz, "Consensus and Dissent in U.S. Legal Opinions: Narrative Structure and Social Voices" in *Disorderly Discourse*, ed. Charles Briggs (New York: Oxford University Press, 1996), 140.

127. Elizabeth Mertz, "Consensus and Dissent in U.S. Legal Opinions: Narrative Structure and Social Voices" in *Disorderly Discourse*, ed. Charles Briggs (New York: Oxford University Press, 1996), 137.

128. Sid Schwartz, interview by author, Silver Spring, MD, July 7, 2008.

129. Bruce Lincoln, *Discourse and the Construction of Society: Comparative Studies of Myth, Ritual, and Classification* (New York: Oxford University Press, 1989), 24.

130. David Biale, *Not in the Heavens: The Tradition of Jewish Secular Thought* (Princeton, NJ: Princeton University Press, 2010), 1.

131. David Schraub, "White Jews: An Intersectional Approach," *AJS Review* 43, no. 2 (2019): 407.

132. Cohen writes: "The word 'Jew' was less likely to connote an individual than a stereotypical figure upon whom Christian society foisted its images of the entire religious out-group." See Naomi Wiener Cohen, *Jews in Christian America: The Pursuit of Religious Equality* (New York: Oxford, 1992), 13.

133. See Joe R. Feagin's concept of the "white racial frame" as it applies to Jews in *The White Racial Frame: Centuries of Racial Framing and Counter-Framing* (New York: Routledge, 2010), 8–13.

134. The requirements for conversion have changed over time, even in the *Tanakh*— different in Moses's day when he married a Midianite, then in the books of Ezra and Nehemiah when marriage to foreigners was forbidden. For Moses, see Exodus, 2:21. For no marriage to foreigners, see Ezra 10:1–8 and Nehemiah 13:1–3. See Dr. Jacob L. Wright, and Prof. Rabbi Tamara Eskanzi, "Contrasting Pictures of Intermarriage in Ruth and Nehemiah," *The Torah.com: A Historical and Contextual Approach*, thetorah.com/contrasting-pictures-of-intermarriage-in-ruth-and-nehemiah/ Also see Rabbi Emily Korzenik, "Letter to the Editor," *New York Times*, Nov. 5, 1992, www.nytimes.com/1992/11/05/opinion/l-remember-moses-married-a-midianite-563692.html.

135. See Jon Entine, *Abraham's Children: Race, Identity, and the DNA of the Chosen People* (New York: Grand Central Publishing, 2007).

136. Drew Himmelstein, "One in Six American Jews Are Converts and Nine Other Findings in Pew Study" *The Jewish News of Northern California*, jweekly.com, March 15, 2015.

137. Submitted by Marshall Levin: "Application for a 1983 Solomon Schecter Award: United Synagogue of America," Presented by Shaare Tefila Congregation: 11120 Lockwood Drive, Silver Spring, Maryland 20901, Category: Unique Programs, p. 5.

138. Harriet Steinhorn Roth, interview by author, Silver Spring, MD, August 17, 2009.

Chapter Two

Preparing to Take Legal Action

Shaare Tefila members were relieved when the police arrested the young White men responsible for defacing their synagogue. As mentioned in the previous chapter, Montgomery County established a "tipster fund," which rewarded anyone who reported information about "hate crimes," a new term in the early 1980s.[1] Someone heard a person boasting about the synagogue defacement in a store, and it was through this tip that the police identified the vandals.[2] These arrests marked the beginning of the process to attain justice for Shaare Tefila Congregation. About a year later, three men were found guilty of the vandalism.[3] The Jewish Advocacy Center then approached the synagogue because they hoped that the congregation would file a civil suit. Eventually, the Shaare Tefila leaders and the Board of Trustees decided to take legal action, based on their understanding of what was best for the synagogue and, they hoped, for other Jewish Americans.

This chapter articulates how the criminal case unfolded and why the Shaare Tefila members ultimately decided to bring the civil suit. It examines the vandals' defacement of the synagogue, antisemitic graffiti within a broader historical context, and the fact that racist antisemitic narratives form part of racist narratives more generally. Likewise, it continues to highlight the "formal" Whiteness of the Shaare Tefila congregants yet emphasizes their experiences as marginalized and "substantively" White in the United States. With that distinction in mind, the chapter addresses and historicizes the race-based US civil rights laws that the lawyers thought could best protect the Shaare Tefila Congregation from the defacement, and in doing so, it considers the role of White-perceived Jewish Americans in the 1980s using the Civil Rights Acts of 1866 and 1871.

When the Shaare Tefila Congregation members filed the civil suit, with the aid of the Jewish Advocacy Center,[4] they achieved what previously would have been impossible in the early twentieth century, when Jewish Americans were more concerned about being identified as a "race."[5] Recall that previously they were worried about the racialized term "Hebrews." The congregation still took a risk, but they could position themselves differently in the early 1980s, in large part because they were now included among people classified as "White."

In their civil suit, the congregation's lawyers claimed that the Shaare Tefila members *were* White. Again, the lawyers were able to identify them as White because Jews were now imagined as White in the US context. Hence, the lawyers' adopted this racialized narrative in their legal argument.

In 1982, Shaare Tefila Congregation had internalized the norms of Whiteness, which often included White privilege, and unlike most other marginal racialized groups, they, and most Jewish Americans, had the immense benefit of social, material, and financial resources. The congregation's and the Jewish community's larger social connections with White people, as well as their respective wealth, offered possibilities to which most other marginalized peoples did not have access. Shaare Tefila Congregation members were mostly middle- to upper-class, there were many lawyers among them, and there were also lawyers in the wider Jewish community who worked for big law firms that did pro bono work. By the 1980s, many Jewish Americans had long been among the corporate and social elite.[6]

During the late 1970s and 1980s on a broader scale, the United States was beset with numerous antisemitic events, some of them violent. These instances of racist antisemitism recall the implicit discourse that the United States is a White, Christian nation.[7] One of the most well-known events, which led to a legal case, was the 1977 Chicago-based Nationalist Socialist Party of America's (NSPA) attempt to demonstrate in Marquette Park in Chicago. They were prevented from doing so by Chicago authorities. They then requested permission to hold a march in Skokie, Illinois, where five- to seven-thousand survivors of the Shoah lived, in a larger community of 40,500 Jews.[8] The Jewish community leaders there sought to reject the neo-Nazi march, the case went back to the court, and the NSPA were allowed, in the end, to march in Chicago.

In the case of neo-Nazi parades, speech, or vandalism, racialized legal victims are forced to endure verbal and visual expressions of race-based hatred. Critical race theorist Mari Matsuda examines the speech that legal victims experience, and in response, she advances an anti-subordination approach to the Free Exercise Clause.[9] The Free Exercise Clause provides several rights, and among them is that the government "shall make no law . . . prohibiting the free exercise [of religion] . . . or abridging the freedom of speech." An anti-subordination approach, Matsuda explains, "determines when hate speech is antithetical to the underlying democratic principles that inform both the First Amendment and the equal protection clause [of the Fourteenth Amendment]."[10] The Fourteenth Amendment took effect in 1868, and it maintains that no state should deny "the equal protection" of the First Amendment laws to any person within the state's jurisdiction. This approach should, she argues, substantially inform how and why the First Amendment protects speech. In other words, it should not protect or enable a *dominant* group more than *marginalized* groups to speak "freely." By adopting Matsuda's approach, the Equal Protection Clause should have protected Jewish Americans from neo-Nazi slogans and the swastikas defacing the Shaare Tefila synagogue.

Although racism pervades the United States, its acceptability differs according to where one lives, as Spencer Meader noted in the article describing high school students' responses to the KKK mentioned in the previous chapter. Montgomery County is part of Maryland, which is in the South, below the Mason-Dixon Line. White people who have lived there even for a short time, but certainly for a long time, may identify with the Confederacy or may have had ancestors who fought for the South in the Civil War. Regardless, the ideology of White supremacy had infected Montgomery County, Maryland, since 1664 with the first slave law, which ordered that "all Negroes and other slaves within the Province And all Negroes and other slaves to bee hereafter imported into the Province shall serve Durante Vita,"[11] as well as the Maryland Act concerning Religion in 1649, which promised religious freedom only to people who believed in "Jesus Christ."[12] Until 1826, the Maryland "Jew Bill" prevented Jewish Americans from serving in public office because they would have had to swear on a Christian Bible.[13] The vandals who defaced Shaare Tefila likely had no knowledge of these laws, but certainly, they were influenced by the anti-Black and anti-Jewish legacy of the state, as well as by the recent economic downturn.

From 1980 to early 1983, the US economy experienced two deep recessions, the worst, at that time, since the Great Depression.[14] Recessions, especially ones this significant, inflict economic trauma on those who experience them, and especially on people who do not have many resources. In 1982, Dr. Philip Glasner, a Baltimore child psychiatrist, explained why non-Jewish high school students might resort to antisemitism: "These are angry kids. . . . Their life is rough, they're angry at the society and the system. Their unemployment rate is terrific. Anti-Semitism arises only in bad, bad times. People look for a scapegoat, and it's apt to be the Jews, historically, since they are viewed as having money. . . . It's economics. That's what it's all about. The economic situation."[15] In Washington, DC, in December of the same year, Michael Berenbaum, of the Jewish Community Council, noted a pattern that had recently appeared and was felt by many Jewish Americans: "It started in the '70s. . . . A new language came to be, the language of anti-Israel and anti-Zionist." Berenbaum continued: "Of course, you can't say every criticism of Israel is anti-Semitic, but some definitely is."[16] This perception, likewise, had entered prevailing narratives about Jewish Americans, and it also permeated schools as well as other areas of public life. Therefore, it likely played a role in the vandals' behavior.

The economic and political historical context, thus, influenced the deface-ment of Shaare Tefila Congregation. After it occurred, the Montgomery County Police Department worked with the Shaare Tefila Congregation leaders.[17] Detective Barry Litsky, assigned to the Silver Spring Investigative Section, arrested twenty-three-year-old Michael D. Remer at the White Oak Shopping Center and interviewed him at the police station on the evening of November 14, 1982.[18] Other young men were arrested later, including Thomas Heine, William Randall Harris Jr., John William Cobb, Dominic Maurice Queen, and Thomas Joseph Hunt Jr., all eighteen years old; and the police expected to arrest a fifteen-year-old boy as well.[19] After initial inter-views, William Randall Harris Jr. was served with a warrant for two charges of destruction of property and one charge of theft on November 19, 1982.[20]

According to accounts in most of the depositions, Michael Remer had led the one nineteen-year-old, five eighteen-year-olds, and one fifteen-year-old young man in the vandalism. He had met some of them for the first time only that evening. Initially, they had been lounging and drinking alcohol behind Drug Fair, and then began defacing the back of it with a burning cross, the slogans "White Power" and "Arian [*sic*] Brotherhood," a Confederate flag, the initials KKK, an eagle with a swastika, a Star of David with an arrow through it, and their initials.[21] Remer stated that Dominic Queen said, "somebody should do that on a synagogue,"[22] and they all knew where to find Shaare Tefila, even though it gave no evidence of being one,[23] because they lived locally and it was just across the road. There, some of them had spray-painted what Potosky and Levin had found during their chilling walk around the synagogue.

In the August 11, 1983, criminal trial, Remer had exclaimed: "I'm so ashamed—and my family—my family is Jewish. It made me talk to my mother, my mother talks to me. It took me 23 years to tell her that I love her. Look at the situation I had to be in to tell her that."[24] Remer's stepfather and stepbrothers are Jewish—a family situation that he did not choose. Note that he said that his "*family* is Jewish," as if he had no place in his own family. It seems very possible, therefore, that his antisemitic behavior resulted from his home life. To reconcile his act of defacement, he was compelled to express his love to his mother.

Some of the vandals may have also known the congregants personally. Michael Remer certainly did. He had attended the bar mitzvah of his cousin at Shaare Tefila Congregation several years earlier. Alma Guillermoprieto from the *Washington Post* interviewed Michael Remer's stepfather, who explained that Michael had not lived at his parents' house in Wheaton, a town close to Shaare Tefila, since he was eighteen.[25] He thought that Michael resided in an apartment complex in Silver Spring and that he might have worked at a fast-food restaurant in Ocean City the previous summer, but he had not been in touch with him for years. He told her that Michael had not "displayed anti-semitic or bigoted behavior in front of him" and noted that if he desecrated the synagogue, it was probably an "act of ignorance" rather than one of anti-semitism.[26] This disconnection between Michael Remer and his stepfather provides more evidence that his family situation, at least in part, sparked his motivation to deface the synagogue.

During the criminal trial, William Randall Harris, or Randy, as he was called, testified against Michael Remer, maintaining that Remer alone had painted much of the graffiti at the synagogue, except for one side of it, because he did not see him paint that one.[27] Remer was represented in court by Robert Jacques, who attempted to find out if Harris was being granted a plea bargain to testify against Remer. Early in the second day of testimony, Harris pled guilty to physically destroying property at the synagogue, but he did not claim to have any part in the defacement when he described the van-dalism the previous day. This cued Jacques to question Harris directly about his willingness to testify against Remer. After some back-and-forth, in which Harris did not *say* that he agreed to a plea bargain in exchange for reduced jail time, Jacques asked Harris: "And you volunteered to come forward as a public-spirited citizen in a mood of remorse, and that is the only reason you are here."[28] "Yes, sir," replied Harris. "And you don't think that your testi-mony against Mr. Remer had anything to do with the plea bargain that was offered to you or to your sentence on July 18th?"[29] Jacques inquired. "No, sir," responded Harris. Later in the interrogation, Jacques asked Harris if the State's attorney ever asked him to testify at Remer's trial. Harris answered that he did. Jacques dryly remarked: "Well, then you are not here voluntarily, are you?"[30] Harris said that he had "a choice of either coming here or not."[31] Jacques wanted to know if there was any condition placed on him, but Harris said pleading guilty was the only requirement.

Then, Michael Remer was called up to the witness stand and gave a very different story. He admitted to painting, as he calls it, the "steel eagle" on the back of Drug Fair, and on the sides of it the words "Arian [sic] Brotherhood," and his initials. According to him, Tommy Hunt told him to write it because "It sounds really cool."[32]

Later during the questioning, Jacques asked Remer why John Cobb or William Hess put swastikas up on the Drug Fair wall, and Remer responded: "Well, they liked my drawing of the eagle, and they said it resembled a Nazi eagle, and then when John put the swastika down there—"[33] "Did you resent him putting the swastika there?" Jacques asked. "Yes," responded Remer. He claimed that he minded "very much." And when Jacques asked why, Remer said: "Because it is not a Nazi eagle in my opinion. It is a *steel* eagle."[34]

Remer stated that he watched Cobb and Hess painting swastikas and observed Hess spraying a Star of David with an arrow going through it, who told them it meant "death to the Jews."[35]

By the time Remer arrived at Shaare Tefila synagogue, apparently with Dominic Queen, he claimed that two swastikas had already been painted by Luke Gordon and John Cobb. Then Cobb also spray-painted one of the cars at the synagogue.[36] Afterward, Remer reported that "a guy had come out and gotten into his car, and he saw some people. That is what I figure. He saw some people, and we all ran."[37] According to Remer, everyone dispersed except for Luke Gordon and Randy Harris; they returned to the synagogue, and Gordon spray-painted a swastika, and skull with crossbones, "and a bunch of lettering and stuff."[38] Remer said he was drunk and laughing "because they [Gordon and Harris] kept falling down."[39] He asked Luke what the lettering meant, and Luke said: "Death head unit," which he explained meant "the guards or something at the concentration camp."[40] Remer told the court that Luke Gordon knew German and that Gordon and William Hess knew a lot about "Nazi stuff."[41]

Back at White Oak, where the Drug Fair was, Remer said that he and many of the other defendants, along with some new people, were talking. Gordon was telling Remer about what he had painted on the synagogue, including the swastika "and the lettering and whatnot."[42]

Although Randy Harris had testified that Michael Remer did all the painting at the synagogue and that Harris had watched him do it, when questioned about it, Remer said he recalled him saying that, but it was not true. When asked why Harris would come into the courtroom and report that, Remer said: "He has his own reasons. I don't know if he is being paid or whatnot, but he came in here and he did it. I couldn't believe it."[43]

Remer's testimony in court was different from what he told Detective Litsky when he was arrested; at that time, he knew many people in the community were outraged about it. In his interview, he claimed that Luke Gordon, the fifteen-year-old, was the only one who painted graffiti at the synagogue, and he did not mention that Harris was there. Apparently, Litsky was not aware Remer was drunk when he interviewed him. In court, Remer stated that Tommy Hunt painted the flaming cross and that Harris was present, along with Luke Gordon, but Remer denied painting anything on the synagogue.

A jury of ten women and two men deliberated for two hours before finding Michael Remer guilty of painting a swastika, a flaming cross, a skull-and-crossbones, the words "KKK," and a Nazi eagle on Shaare Tefila synagogue. At three different trials, Judge Rosalyn Bell[44] convicted Michael Remer, William Randall Harris, and John Cobb for the defacement. Remer served the maximum sentence—three years in prison and three hundred hours of community service, upon release, preferably to a Jewish charity.[45] Harris, who pled guilty and testified against Remer, received a four-month sentence, and John William Cobb received six months for painting a swastika on the Tellers' car. Thomas Joseph Hunt Jr. and Dominic Queen received probation for stealing a van from Hardware City, another crime committed on the same evening. The jury did not have enough evidence to charge anyone else, but they believed that the others had participated.[46]

According to Parole Officer Scott Gunnison, Remer continued to have an antisemitic mindset during his confinement at the Department of Corrections. At one point, Remer was expected to engage in outside counseling with a therapist, Ron Levin, for drug treatment and urine surveillance, but he was not interested in seeing him because Levin is Jewish. Gunnison reluctantly allowed him to see another therapist.[47] Later, Remer wrote a letter to Judge David K. Cahoon, the new administrative judge of the circuit court, to request permission to perform the community service hours at a non-Jewish organization or charity.[48] He acknowledged: "Because of some of the charges of my convictions, it gave a great negative impact to the Jewish Community, and due to the fact that I have learned through experience the ideas of sensitivity, I too have felt a great negative impact," and in another part of the letter he confirmed: "I feel that I am using good grounds and judgment in wanting to eliminate the special conditions on my probation, and I feel it would be a positive move for the benefit of both parties so as to help with the idea that the said situation will never occur again."[49] Gunnison's summation of Remer's open hostility to these "special conditions," and his refusal to see Levin after serving his time in the Department of Corrections, tell another story. After receiving Remer's letter, Judge Cahoon wrote to Rabbi Halpern about his request. Rabbi Halpern thanked Judge Cahoon for the opportunity to respond to Remer's letter, discussed it with the congregation members, and reported, that "almost uniformly," they decided that "we would prefer not to impose a condition of serving the Jewish community if Michael Remer retains hostility toward the Jewish People."[50]

Throughout his five years of probation, Michael Remer continually tested positive for marijuana, and during the first two analyses, for cocaine as well. In 1986, he was evicted from his residence in Montgomery County; he told Gunnison he hated that county and wanted to move to the Ocean City area. For a while, he worked for the Quality Inn before he was fired because he was late too frequently. Although he claimed to be volunteering at the local Humane Society, when it was contacted, they had never heard of him. Near Ocean City, he was arrested by the Maryland State Police for breaking and entering and theft.[51] Gunnison wrote in his evaluation and recommendation of Remer that he "has been quite openly hostile and negative about his probation," "he views himself as a white socialist and is verbally critical of all other races"; he "cannot live by society's rules and he could pose a danger to the community if he fails to control his anger and temper."[52] Also, Gunnison warned, he "has proven to be an excellent manipulator."[53] Gunnison then requested that a bench warrant should be issued that charged Remer with the violation of probation.[54]

BRINGING THE CIVIL SUIT

The criminal charges for the defacement of Shaare Tefila Congregation appeared in many local papers. Irvin Shapell and Kevin Lipson of the Jewish Advocacy Center took note. As mentioned previously, their goal was to bring anti-Jewish crimes to federal court as civil suits and they decided to litigate antisemitic violence, in the hopes that the violent actors would be severely financially impaired.

Shapell and Lipson were best friends. They had attended law school together at Washington University in St. Louis. Shapell had substantial financial resources from his family, who did a great deal of philanthropic work, and they were both committed to advocacy for Jews who had been targeted because of their Jewish identification.

As mentioned earlier, they modeled their actions on the Southern Poverty Law Center's (SPLC) case that eventually caused the bankruptcy of the Ku Klux Klan. Among the JAC's Board of Directors were Morris Dees, former Director of the SPLC; Martin Mendelsohn, attorney for the Office of Special Investigations, who received the American Association of Jewish Lawyers and Jurists Pursuit of Justice Award in 2009;[55] and Jerold Solovy, who was a distinguished attorney in Chicago, and remembered as "a fierce litigator with the heart of a public servant."[56]

The SPLC case responded to a horrific lynching that occurred on March 21, 1981, and went to court as *Donald v. United Klans of America* in 1984. In 1987, Beulah Mae Donald finally won a historic $7 million for the lynching of her son, Michael Donald, which in effect, bankrupted the entire KKK. The United Klans were responsible, according to the SPLC, for beating the Freedom Riders in 1961, murdering civil rights worker Viola Liuzzo in 1965, bombing Birmingham's 16th Street Baptist Church in 1963, and, in the process, killing four young girls: Addie Mae Collins, Denise McNair, Carole Robertson, and Cynthia Wesley.

As noted, the Jewish Advocacy Center's motive was markedly different from other established Jewish organizations, such as the Anti-Defamation League of B'nai B'rith, the American Jewish Committee, the American Jewish Congress, and the National Jewish Committee Relations Council because they wanted to aggressively litigate antisemitic violence and construct a new civil rights law that could then be used as precedent. Naomi

W. Cohen, who wrote about the case after the Supreme Court verdict, noted that there could have been competition or professional jealousy between the organizations.[57]

The JAC would have liked the other established Jewish organizations to support them, but Lipson recalls that he and Shapell were "dissatisfied with some of the more tepid responses to antisemitism that existed at the organized Jewish community."[58] When Lipson attempted to discuss the suit with Ed Leavy, the director of the Anti-Defamation League of B'nai B'rith, Lipson said that Leavy "essentially threw me out of his office."[59] He did not remember much about his other visits, but he recalls that he was not welcomed at the American Jewish Committee's office either.[60]

After the Shaare Tefila criminal case had gone to the District Court, Lipson recalled that he "used to run around and give speeches at synagogues, and the reaction among lay Jewish leaders was quite the opposite" of the organizations' leaders.[61] Consistently, members of the Jewish community agreed with Lipson's rationale. "There was an understanding of what our motive was . . . and there was a very positive reaction," he recalled. He was a featured speaker during a service at a synagogue in Arlington, Virginia, and at the end, Robert Waldman, who was a partner at Hogan & Hartson, came up to talk with him and said this case would be perfect for them.[62] That sounded great to Lipson, who told me: "Irv and I decided that we would let Hogan & Hartson handle it pro bono."[63]

Shapell and Lipson met with Executive Director Marshall Levin and proposed the civil suit to him. Then they met with the Board of Directors, which included the president, treasurer, secretary, and directors of specific groups within the synagogue. They had several meetings with the Board to convince them of the value of pursuing the strategy.[64] The Board finally passed a unanimous motion in which they agreed that the JAC should be authorized to act on behalf of the congregation as legal representative for the synagogue.[65]

Shapell spoke with the congregation at the Friday evening Shabbat service on January 7, 1983, and he reminded them of the long history of attacks on Jews and then noted their substantial increase in the local area during the previous three years.[66] He recalled the response of the rabbis in the Talmud to that week's Torah portion, in which Moses had slain an Egyptian, in violation of "God's law."[67] As the rabbis explained, he stated, "Justice—*tzedek*—not more violence is the required response when justice is available."[68] In Mosaic law, he continued, compensation rather than literal revenge is required as a response to crimes. Legal remedies exist in the United States and therefore, he argued, Jews must use the law. Shapell then explained the necessity of civil lawsuits as a response to antisemitic crimes:

The need for civil lawsuits, in addition to criminal prosecution, lies in the difference between criminal and civil law. . . . Criminal law is designed to punish illegal actions. In most cases anti-semitic acts are classified as misdemeanors, carrying with them minor penalties. With the overcrowded dockets, plea bargaining and discretionary sentencing, the necessary sentences have not been imposed. More importantly, criminal courts try *only* an individual's actions, not his motivation. Thus, the criminal justice system cannot take into account the anti-semitic nature of attacks against Jews. For example, criminal law views the defacement of a synagogue like the defacement of any building. Consequently, the particular damage suffered by Jews from anti-semitic acts is simply not part of the criminal case.[69]

In effect, the congregation would highlight the damage the vandals caused in the civil suit to provide "formally" White Jewish Americans with the same rights that White Christian Americans unconsciously experience.

In sum, Shapell identified two accomplishments that he expected would result from the civil suit he proposed that the JAC would file. First, the congregation would send a "clear and emphatic message that the Jewish community will not tolerate this type of conduct."[70] Meanwhile, the new law would deter future antisemitic acts. Second, the suit would signify the significance of antisemitic violence and the community's response to it.

The Board of Trustees and the congregation responded positively to Shapell's remarks, but it took its time to decide what to do. It would require Shaare Tefila Congregation to make a *legal* statement with their civil suit. This presented a conundrum.

Social Locations of the Shaare Tefila Congregation Members and the Vandals

Let's pause and consider a variety of factors, including the very different social locations of the Shaare Tefila congregants and the vandals. Note that some discussion of the vandals' experiences will necessarily be speculative.

The congregants understood themselves as a marginalized group, a nation that had been expelled from the Land of Israel beginning with the Babylonian exile. Shaare Tefila members, like other Jews, revere the Torah by placing it in an ark, and by chanting a weekly parashah (section) or a megillah (scroll related to a holiday), they articulate its sacredness to them. Bruce Lincoln affirms: "when one feels pride in [a] story, in that very moment, one *(re-)becomes*" Jewish.[71] By this statement, he means that every time one practices an act, one embodies it. In doing so, congregants recall over two thousand years of exile in the diaspora, pervaded by religious anti-Judaism, later co-constituted with racist antisemitism, and the recent horror of over six million Jews being murdered in the Shoah.

Shaare Tefila members were well aware of their status as a minority community and perhaps less so of their Whiteness. In the civil suit, congregants argued that they were White because, most of the time, they were socially accepted as White. Recall that in 1977, they were officially coded as White by the Executive Branch's Office of Management and Budget Directive 15.[72] This Directive determined how Jewish Americans of European, North African, or Middle Eastern origin would be defined on the US Census. The Directive was at least partially a result of racial prerequisite cases, through which judges, in individual cases, decided that North African and Middle Eastern Christian and Muslim immigrants counted as "White." This wide variety of individuals was typically prevented from becoming citizens by the Naturalization Act of 1790, which granted citizenship only to "free white persons."[73] The Immigration and Nationality Act of 1952, also known as the McCarran-Walter Act, officially ended the quota system and lifted all restrictions regulated by the Immigration Act of 1924. However, in their everyday life, Shaare Tefila members potentially could experience antisemitism if they looked stereotypically Jewish, had a Jewish last name, were open about their Jewishness, *or* were at their synagogue.

In Montgomery County particularly, antisemitism pervaded the underbelly of Whiteness.

The vandals likely thought of Jewish Americans as economically successful and themselves as already excluded from those professions. They may have expected that their Whiteness should afford them more social and economic privilege than it did. In their depositions, some of them had responded to the lawyer's questioning and said that they had gotten their GEDs, or General Education Diplomas, and were not working, or were working at jobs that might lead to blue-collar careers, such as painting parts at Precision Spray Painting, apprenticing to an electrician, or monitoring mentally disabled people at a mental health facility.[74] Their rage echoes that of many other White supremacists: desperate for the privileges they expected from Whiteness, but financially dependent, for now, on low-wage positions. Perhaps they merely wanted to express that they were still there, for people to notice they existed. The vandals possibly aimed to disprove Jewish Whiteness, reinforce the view that they were superior to the Jewish congregants, and—although they probably did not think of it in these terms—define the synagogue as a "non-White" space. They turned to the white walls of Shaare Tefila Congregation, which served as a "screen" for them to voice their anger about their own positionality and where they could express the frustration they felt about their expectations of themselves as White men.[75]

Psychologist and law professor Phyllis Gerstenfeld notes that humans are extremely influenced by social situations, and lists several important contributing factors that determine how humans function, including deindividuation, identification, internalization, and "groupthink."[76] In her view, "Many hate crime offenders may be led to commit their crimes not primarily out of bias, but rather out of pressure or a desire to follow their group."[77] "Deindividuation" may occur when a person thinks they're anonymous, for instance, bullying that occurs online. She cites Zimbardo's experiment (1969) in which students who were the subject of the study and who were wearing large hoods gave longer shocks to people than those who did not.[78]

"Identification," she notes, occurs when a person wants to be like the members of a group, and as a result, behaves like them. When the views of the group seem credible, individual members are likely to "internalize" them. Then the attitudes of this community become very important to the members. Gerstenfeld observes that I. L. Janis invented the term "groupthink" in 1972, which he applied to errors among policymakers and business leaders, but she applies it to criminal offenders, who make poor decisions *because* of the group that they may not have made based on their own ideas.[79]

Applying Gerstenfeld's theory, let's consider some reasons the vandals defaced Shaare Tefila Congregation. According to Randy Harris, somebody stated: "Let's go paint the synagogue."[80] Thus, the other defendants "identified" with that statement, and many of them followed along. Even if he did not say that there could have been a "groupthink" mentality, in which they made bad decisions for antisemitic racist reasons.[81] In Tommy Hunt's deposition, he recalled: "It just was not me. I guess we were influenced by this Remer, the oldest guy there. You sort of followed-the-leader type thing."[82] Antisemitic and racist reasons privileged their Whiteness and, thus, their actions became "rebellious."

Other scholars note that White male group situations result in "rebellious" behavior that involves racism and antisemitism. In his book, *The White Racial Frame: Centuries of Framing and Counter-Framing* (2010), Joe R. Feagin reports on a nationwide study of college students who journaled about their activities regarding racial issues.[83] He was surprised to note that they included antisemitism in their notes. Most likely he was confused because most scholars who write about "race" think about it in terms of skin color and assume that Jews are White.[84] He mentions a White student at a Midwestern college who reported on a scene that he witnessed among other White male students:

> When any two of us are together, no racial comments or jokes are ever made. However, with the full group membership present, anti-Semitic statements abound, as do racial slurs and vastly derogatory statements. . . . Various jokes concerning stereotypes were also swapped around the gaming table, everything

from 'How many Hebes fit in a VW Beetle?' to 'Why did Jews wander in the desert for forty years?' . . . The answers were 'One million in the ashtray and four in the seats' and "because somebody dropped a quarter,' respectively.[85]

Not only does this example show that antisemitism has not disappeared, but it also demonstrates that expressing racism, more specifically antisemitism, as a form of rebellion is a viable option for young White, Christian men.

To deflect attention from their racist, antisemitic behavior at the synagogue, the vandals claimed in their depositions that they were ill-informed about racial differences. For example, Tommy Hunt mentioned that he had wanted his flaming cross removed because he said that he had Black friends, and he told the lawyers: "somebody brought it to my attention that the burning cross is against black people."[86] In an apology letter that Michael Remer wrote in 1988 to the congregation, he said that he and the other vandals conceived of the graffiti on the synagogue more as a "rebellious" act rather than one of directed anti-Judaism. From a White, Christian perspective, this is certainly plausible.

Although they were almost certainly not aware of it, Michael Remer, Tommy Hunt, and the others who joined them in their defacement drew from the longtime "rebellious" trope of the Christian masses who targeted Jewish "heretics" in the European medieval period for having killed their Savior. The Christian masses, likewise understood themselves as wrongly oppressed in opposition to the Jews' privileged status, since some Jews worked directly for their feudal lords as financial advisers. Over time, as mentioned earlier, the religious component became "co-constituted" with racial narratives that drew from Jewish lineage and emphasize Jewish blood, due to the Spanish fifteenth- and sixteenth-century *limpieza de sangre* (blood purity) laws.[87] Further iterations of this "co-constitution" in Europe consist of seventeenth- through twentieth-century race science; nineteenth- and twentieth-century reappearance of medieval "blood libel" cases—based on the false assumption that Jews killed Christian children for blood and used it for ritual purposes;[88] and the 1933–1935 Nazi Nuremberg Laws, three of which differentiated Jews from "citizens of Germans or kindred blood."[89]

From their positions as young White (plausibly) Christian men, they could not possibly relate to Jewish experiences of exile, narratives of trauma, and memories of marginalization. Linda Martín Alcoff explains: "to claim that some perceptual facts are visible from some locations is correlative to claim that they are *hard* to see from others." Given that concept, she notes, "Social identity operates then as a rough and fallible but useful indicator of differences in perceptual access."[90] In this case, the vandals who had defaced the walls and playground equipment of Shaare Tefila Congregation out of drunken rebelliousness and anger were not competent to comprehend the

vandalism from a different position. It seems likely that they had no awareness that their vandalism would stay with the congregation members for a
very long time. They had no idea that Cantor Gershon Levin, z"l, would still
be able to see the defacement on a part of the wall that he had scrubbed with
his son on his arm during the cleanup day until the synagogue members sold
the building.[91] They could not possibly have experienced the same *Jewish*
marginalization, ancestral—and even personal—memories of exile, or have
felt the anger, pain, and sorrow in the same way as the Shaare Tefila members
did. These were the narratives and the emotions that factored into Shaare
Tefila's decision to file a civil suit.

THE CONGREGATION'S DEBATE AND
THE DECISION TO FILE THE CIVIL SUIT

A year after the congregation had agreed that the JAC could support them
legally, the civil suit was still being debated in the Board of Trustees. The
lawyers also were considering their legal argument. In conversations with
the other Hogan & Hartson lawyers and the JAC, Patricia Brannan and Joe
Hassett[92] determined that they would advocate for the congregation based
on three statutes from two civil rights acts passed to protect the rights of the
Thirteenth Amendment. During one of her visits, Patricia Brannan talked with
a small group of Board members about these sections in terms of what they
involved and noted that the vandals' actions were enough to trigger coverage
of these statutes.[93]

The Civil Rights Act of 1866 includes people who were not deemed
"White citizens" and the Civil Rights Act of 1871 emphasizes equal protection. Three of the statutes the lawyers would use included the 42 U.S.C. sections 1981 and 1982 from the Civil Rights Act of 1866 and 42 U.S.C. section
1985(3) from the Civil Rights Act of 1871. Section 1981 states: "All persons
within the jurisdiction of the United States shall have the same right in every
State and Territory to make and enforce contracts, to sue, be parties, give
evidence, and to the full and equal benefit of all laws and proceedings as is
enjoyed by White citizens." Section 1982 entails: "All citizens of the United
States shall have the same right, in every State and Territory, as is enjoyed by
White citizens thereof to inherit, purchase, lease, sell, hold, and convey real
and personal property."[94] Finally, section 1985(3) affirms the "equal protection" of "any person or class of persons" and "any citizen who is lawfully
entitled to vote."[95]

Her explanation resulted in an intense debate that occurred later at another
Board meeting about whether Jews could be pinned as a "race." Bess and Jack
Teller, both board members at the time, recalled that it was hotly contested.

Finally, after much further discussion, on February 23, 1984, the Board voted to file a civil suit. It transpired in the following way. Marshall Levin presented a proposal in which he reviewed the statutes that Patricia Brannan would cite in her representation of Shaare Tefila Congregation and noted that she would also seek a small monetary compensation for the vandalism, which the congregation would then donate, possibly to a national interfaith organization, such as the National Council of Christians and Jews.

After Levin's speech, a board member rejected his plan. This person argued that the congregation should not pursue the suit because it stood a good chance of defeat, it would not be worthwhile monetarily, and it might "touch off resentment among the public."[96] This reasoning refers to the first approach to antisemitism described before: that Jewish Americans should conform to White Christian norms. Because, stereotypically, Jews are "in it for the money" that was not an option that Shaare Tefila members should pursue, said this board member. The first approach also would mean assimilating by *not* bringing a civil suit, in other words, they should not make it a big issue. Another board member noted that Levin's motion was out of order since he was "not a dues-paying member of our congregation, [and was] therefore unable to bring a motion before the floor."[97] Then a third board member stated that members of the National Council for Christians and Jews had recently visited Israel and neighboring Arab countries and had returned with "much PLO and anti-semitic propaganda," and this negated the possibility of the Board donating to that organization.[98] Finally, a fourth board member entered a motion to file the civil suit, with the representation of Hogan & Hartson, and to donate any monetary awards to the Montgomery County Human Rights Commission, which both Hogan & Hartson and the congregational advisory committee had recommended as the recipient. The motion was seconded, and a majority passed the measure, with only one person dissenting.

Shirley Altman was a board member at the time of the incident and president at the time that the Supreme Court heard the congregation's case. She heartily supported pursuing the civil suit, and she cited her childhood in England during World War II as significant to her belief that the vandalism was a serious offense and should be treated as such: "Some people said they didn't feel threatened by it. I said absolutely, yes. I lived in England during the war. At this age [referring to the vandals], it's not playful and it's not a prank. The paintings were so professional, and it wasn't kids . . . When you lived as close as I did to WWII, then you feel a shadow go down your spine."[99]

Throughout my conversation with Shirley, she discussed the defacement in the context of a history of antisemitism, and she reiterated her belief in the importance of openly resisting it. She mentioned certain congregation members who did not initially support the civil suit. She remembered one person saying: "if you go raking up coals, then they can burn you."[100] Altman advocated for the civil suit due to her beliefs about how to respond to anti-semitism. She asserted: "If you let the bastards get away with it, you encourage it to go further and further. The next time they may come in and attack you."[101] Here, she noted how the antisemitic beliefs of the vandals could continue to grow if left unchecked. And for this reason, bringing the civil suit was a means of advancing their aims as a congregation. In opposition to the Nazis' concerted effort to kill Jews, Shaare Tefila meant to protect themselves from any instances of antisemitic behavior. Altman understood it as a continuum: antisemitic vandalism could lead to antisemitic attacks could lead to killing Jews. If these young vandals believed that their acts were acceptable among the American public, in her view, it could lead to violence, such as the previously mentioned attack on a female Jewish student at the University of Maryland with a BB gun.

The JAC brought the suit against all eight young men, not alleging that they all participated, but that they all were "equally responsible because they were present."[102] "It is the congregation's intent," one congregation member stated, "not only to apply the civil rights law to this desecration but also to set a moral example."[103] Representative Michael D. Barnes, D-Md-8th, the congressperson from Montgomery County's District noted that "This suit will educate the public that these acts involve more than just property damage. People and communities suffer. This lawsuit will send the clear message that attacks on religious groups and institutions will not be tolerated."[104] Note that Barnes mentioned "religious groups and institutions," because the prevailing narrative determined that Jews were a "religious" group in the 1980s, not a "racial" one.

So, with the aid of Hogan & Hartson, the JAC brought the case to the Federal District Court of Maryland in Baltimore. On April 22, 1985, the Court dismissed it based on Deborah Garren's argument that Jews are a "religion" and are "white." As a result, the Shaare Tefila Congregation could not bring a suit derived from sections of the Civil Rights Act of 1866 or that of 1871 because they protected against racial acts, not religious ones and because they and the vandals were both "white."

At the May 6, 1985 board meeting, the Board of Trustees discussed the Federal District Court of Maryland's dismissal of the civil suit. Board member Gerald Sommer reminded the board that the ruling was based on an interpretation of the Civil Rights Acts that applied only to *racial* and not to *religious* persecution. The minutes state that the "Board discussion raised questions about potentially undesirable implications that could arise depending on the outcome of the appeal. Further, the outcome could very well impact the entire Jewish community, not just Shaare Tefila."[105] Nevertheless, Jack Teller moved that the board direct the congregational legal advisory panel to file a motion to appeal the case, which then occurred.[106] Teller recalled:

There was a lot of concern. I remember a couple of meetings in a row . . . and we were concerned about the definition of Jews, as people, as a race, as a community, as a religion. And what the courts would do with those, how we would be defined by law. And we decided that that was a risk we were willing to take, but there was a lot of debate about that. Because you see we're not a race. We are a religion, we are a culture. We are a people, and we are a community. . . . Yeah, there was a lot of debate, pros, and cons, about it, but in the end, I don't know if you want to call them the hotheads, but the determined among us won out, and we did decide to pursue it. We pursued it all the way to the Supreme Court. . . . I do remember people worried about us getting pigeonholed. That if a new law were made that we shouldn't be treated as a race because we're not. And you know of course the lawyers among us, and there were several on the board, really started setting forth all of these possibilities about this could be good for us and this could be bad for us. What would be good for us as Jews as opposed to what's good for us as a synagogue. . . . I just remember that overwhelmingly we wanted to go after them, especially after we had had such a positive community response with the cleanup. So, we went after them.[107]

He noted that Jews are *not* a race, instead, he described Jews as a "religion," a "culture," a "people," and a "community." He then pointed to the significance of the community's response to the cleanup day, which was a central reason that the Shaare Tefila Board of Trustees progressed forward with the civil suit.

Bess Teller, the synagogue president at the time, remembered how her opinion about the legal argument shifted when she attended one of the board meetings at which it was discussed:

So, the question came to us as to whether we should consider ourselves a race and get protection as a race. That was one path we could have taken. And the discussion that was held about it was very interesting. And in some ways, there is a part of me that says yes, we are a race, because we've interbred so much in a way, in some manner of speaking. You know, I mean Groucho Marx *looks* Jewish. Racial features, there's something there that says that that's one way to go, but it isn't, it's a choice. It's an intellectual decision or an emotional decision to be Jewish. It was—it made me think about what it is to be Jewish, and Judaism, and Jews as a people, which was very interesting.[108]

For her, the question of which legal argument to pursue regarding Jewish identification provided an opportunity for reflection and a consideration of different possibilities that might describe Jewishness. Her statement about Groucho Marx reveals the impact that racial narratives had on her immediate thoughts about Jewish physicality. She then considers Jewish identity a "choice."

Teller's statement describes the prevailing American concept that religious identity is a "choice." For Jews "by *choice*," it certainly is. This concept underlies the First Amendment, which asserts, in part, that "Congress shall make no law respecting an establishment of religion, or prohibiting the free exercise thereof."[109] *Legal* freedom for religious choice theoretically exists. However, it's not a *choice* for Jews in the United States who have Jewish last names, are known to be Jewish, or wear ritual clothing, for example, as long as antisemitism exists. These Jews cannot detach themselves from Jewishness so long as people hate them because they are Jews. If Jewish identification is not a *choice*, then what is it? It must not be a "religion," as it's defined in the American legal context. Here, it seems more like a "race," as it's defined in the United States.

Antisemitic behavior disempowers Jewish Americans. During the 1980s in the Washington, DC, area, two conflicting responses to this behavior existed; both appear to be from "formally" White Jews. One consisted of the general habit of synagogues concealing antisemitic vandalism, which was validated by the ADL's best practice announced to the Jewish community before High Holidays in 1982. The second consisted of Shaare Tefila leaders inviting their community to clean the antisemitic vandalism with them.

When the Shaare Tefila leaders and the Board of Trustees decided to file a civil suit, Patricia Brannan and Joe Hassett recognized that the congregation needed a legal solution that no religion-based laws would supply and knew that the Board of Trustees was not keen on arguing that they were a "race," because it recalled most recently the Shoah, but also the long history of Jewish racialization. Here, it's important to note that because race is divisive and, more importantly, hierarchical, *no* group enjoys being classified as a "race." Hence, Brannan and Hassett constructed their legal argument to focus on the *perception* of the vandals.[110] Their argument would be that because the vandals perceived the congregants as an inferior race, that perception was the basis for their actions.

WHY *SHAARE TEFILA* DECIDED TO EMPLOY SECTIONS FROM THE CIVIL RIGHTS ACTS OF 1866 AND 1871

To explain why Shaare Tefila decided to cite these sections, let's briefly discuss the historical context for the Civil Rights Acts and which various racialized groups used them, beginning with Black Americans. The Civil Rights Act of 1866 was the first civil rights act in U.S history: it defined American citizenship, which excluded "Indians not taxed," provided the rights of citizenship, and prohibited the denial of citizenship rights based on color, race, or prior condition of slavery or involuntary servitude, with the exception for the conviction of any crime.[111] One of the primary reasons for the Act was to integrate formerly enslaved Blacks, who became citizens by this Act. It was passed by the US Senate and the House, but vetoed by President Andrew Johnson; finally, it was overridden with a 2/3 vote by the Senate and the House and was enacted by the 39th Congress on April 9, 1866. The Act further specified the rights afforded by the Thirteenth Amendment by including rights to employment and housing protections. These rights eventually became part of the US legal code as 42 U.S.C. § 1981 and § 1982. The Civil Rights Act of 1871, also called the "Ku Klux Klan Act," enforced the rights of the Fourteenth Amendment. It targeted the KKK, in that it detailed the "penalty for conspiring or going in disguise upon the public highway."[112] This language became codified as 42 U.S.C. § 1985(3).

The sections that derive from the Civil Rights Act of 1866, sections 1981 and 1982, and the Civil Rights Act of 1871, section 1985(3), were rarely applied before the Civil Rights Act of 1964. A legal loophole in the Thirteenth Amendment, which has not been addressed in *any* Civil Rights Act, allows those convicted of crimes to be *re*-enslaved. This loophole sanctioned Black Codes, beginning in Mississippi and South Carolina, which forced formerly enslaved people to sign labor contracts paying them a pittance, prevented them from "loitering or vagrancy," along with many other prohibitions, or be arrested.[113] In states where Black Codes did not exist, the horrors of lynching, constant oppression, and lack of financial resources made it nearly impossible for Black people to use these supposed "rights" in court, where they would not be tried by a jury of their peers anyway. Anti-Black discrimination continued with Jim Crow laws, which consisted of discriminatory state and local laws that were federally upheld in the 1896 case of *Plessy v. Ferguson*. This case was famous for its "separate but equal" legal doctrine that applied to Black Americans and sanctioned the "neutral," color-blind approach that still legally applies today in private institutions.[114]

After World War II, Black soldiers hoped they would have the same access to the G.I. Bill as White soldiers, including White-perceived Jewish soldiers, but they faced local and state-based racialized restrictions to the Bill in terms of access to education, housing, and reentering the workforce.[115] Based on expectations due to funding from the G.I. Bill, some Black Americans, not necessarily former soldiers, began to use Sections 1981, 1982, and 1985(3). *Shelley v. Kraemer* (1948)[116] was the landmark Supreme Court case that prevented public racially restrictive housing covenants as a violation of the Fourteenth Amendment Equal Protection Clause. In the same year, *Hurd v. Hodge* (1948)[117] held that the District of Columbia, like states, forbids similarly restrictive covenants. These cases were strengthened by *Jones v. Alfred H. Mayer Co.* (1968), in which Joseph Lee Jones, a Black man, charged that a real estate company in St. Louis County, Missouri, refused to sell him a home in a certain neighborhood because of his race.[118] Jones based his case on section 1982, and it played a major role in *Shaare Tefila Congregation v. Cobb*.

The Civil Rights Act of 1964 enormously impacted racial equality. Asian and Latinx Americans joined Black Americans in citing these sections of law in civil suits beginning in the 1970s, and *Shaare Tefila* drew from these precedents. In *López v. Sears, Roebuck and Co.* (1980), significant to Judge Ramsey in his ruling for *Shaare Tefila* in the Federal District Court of Maryland, Ramon López filed a suit against Sears because he was fired due to his race, color, and national origin. López is Malaysian American and his skin color is Brown. Judge Ramsey used López's skin color against the members of Shaare Tefila because the congregation identified as White. According to Ramsey, one must *look* a certain way and have a non-White skin color to be considered a "race," and to successfully cite this section. In the Fourth Circuit Court of Appeals, *Shaare Tefila* cited *Manzanares v. Safeway Stores, Inc.* (1979) of the Tenth Circuit, which held that Anthony Manzanares and other people of Mexican American descent are "of such an undeniable nature that the treatment afforded its members may be measured against that afforded against Anglos" because they are Mexican American, or Spanish American, or have Spanish surnames.[119] But Judge Hall rejected *Shaare Tefila*'s use of the case because he viewed Mexican Americans and Jewish Americans as groups that were "not . . . analogous."[120]

In the 1970s, one could argue that White Americans either employed protections initially intended for racially marginalized peoples or fought against these same protections as they claimed access to seats set aside for these same peoples as affirmative action.[121] For example, in 1976, White employees filed *McDonald v. Santa Fe Trail Transportation Co.* because they were discharged for misappropriating cargo from one of the company's shipments, but a Black employee was not discharged.[122] The White employees won the case. Throughout *Shaare Tefila*, however, Patricia Brannan cited *McDonald* to support the congregation's claim, which was an important precedent from a *legal* standpoint.

Given all the precedents addressed in the section above, *Shaare Tefila* raises an important question: how appropriate is it for Jews who are "formally" White to cite from these two Civil Rights Acts?[123] For critical race theorists and for scholars who are invested in legal interpretations of race more broadly, this is a significant issue. These Civil Rights Acts were passed to provide emancipatory rights in employment and housing to recently enslaved peoples. Why, then, was a middle- to upper-socioeconomic status Jewish synagogue citing these sections to outlaw vandalism on their synagogue?

Consider the argument above, however, that Jewish Americans are disempowered by antisemitic behavior. This puts Shaare Tefila congregants in a position in which the vandals racially dominate them. From this perspective, it's clear that they should have access to these statutes. They may have been able to assume individually the privileges of Whiteness, as long as they did not reveal their Jewishness, but, as a group, they were subject to racist antisemitic behavior.[124] Here, the problem is not the Shaare Tefila Congregation members who misused a law meant for formerly enslaved peoples, it is *US law itself* for not protecting Jewish Americans from racist antisemitic vandalism.

CONCLUSION

This chapter has examined the criminal trial and considered the depositions that occurred after the vandals' defacement of the synagogue. Their antisemitism, in the broader historical context of antisemitism in the United States, formed part of a larger racist trope. Some of the vandals explained this experience as "rebellious" behavior. The Jewish American members of Shaare Tefila, in contrast, had their own experience of the vandalism as racist antisemitism, grounded in their historic marginalization, iterated in the Torah, their consequent exile, and pursuit at the hands of "rebellious" Christian masses in European and American contexts. These depictions of the two groups are very general, but they clearly highlight the disparate experiences of the vandals and the congregants.

From the beginning, the Shaare Tefila Congregation decided to pursue the civil suit after they were approached by the JAC because they were heartened and relieved by their community's support. It was a process for them because after the JAC discussed their legal argument with the Board of Trustees, the Board had to consider their opinions about being situated in relation to the category of "race." As Jack Teller indicated above, the board eventually concluded that pursuing the suit, with the aim of gaining civil rights protection against antisemitic vandalism outweighed the potential identification of Jews as a race.

Nevertheless, the decision was challenging. Many board members wanted to avoid either a social or a legal linkage between Jews and race because that would associate them with Nazi ideology and with a long history of Jewish racialization. In the United States, "formally" White Shaare Tefila members were able to draw on their White privilege and could disassociate themselves from this racialization. For that reason, especially in the 1980s, some congregation members might not have wished to associate too closely with Black and Brown individuals.

Given, however, that Shaare Tefila members were disempowered by antisemitic behavior, they were racialized by these actions, and they did not "fit" the American conception of religion. As a scholar invested in legal interpretations of race that are empowering, I argue that it was permissible to use these statutes. Although Brannan continually cites *McDonald*, she tries to illuminate for the judges that even as the White employees in *McDonald* won their case, the Shaare Tefila members should also win.

In considering how to legally respond to the vandalism, the Board of Trustees eventually adopted their lawyers' argument, which would draw on sections of the Civil Rights Act of 1866 and 1871. This was not what the Board of Trustees had planned, but they had to make an important decision. They elected to go forward.

However, as noted above, on April 22, 1985, the Federal District Court of Maryland determined that Jewish Americans were a "religion" and "white," but that the vandals were *also* White. This was a problem, given this particular interpretation, because a "white citizen" could not sue another "white citizen" under the statutes that originated in the Civil Rights Act of 1866. As the following chapters demonstrate, Jewish Americans had *always*, with one exception, brought religion-based cases, but this case would shift how the courts, based on the lawyers' arguments, would come to consider the broad scope of Jewish identity.

NOTES

1. Marshall Levin, "Desecration in Darkness" in Laura J. Lederer and Richard Delgado, eds. *The Price We Pay: The Case against Racist Speech, Hate Propaganda, and Pornography* (New York: Hill & Wang, 1995), 42. *Washington Jewish Week* reported in its December 9–15, 1982 issue: "Council Member David Scull proposed a second bill which creates a $50,000 'tipster fund' designed to retrieve evidence from anonymous sources, much like the current successful crime-solvers program which provides rewards for information on serious crimes. As the police report that they have great difficulty in obtaining enough evidence to prosecute, Scull said the Council has decided to 'put our money where it counts.' Tipsters who provide information leading to an arrest could receive up to $1,000. The new laws were approved unanimously and have become effective immediately." See Lisa Schneider, "New Anti-Hate Laws in Montgomery County" *Washington Jewish Week* 18, no. 47 (December 9–15, 1982): 1.

2. *Washington Jewish Week* reported in its December 9–15, 1982 issue: "Council Member David Scull proposed a second bill which creates a $50,000 'tipster fund' designed to retrieve evidence from anonymous sources, much like the current successful crime-solvers program which provides rewards for information on serious crimes. As the police report that they have great difficulty in obtaining enough evidence to prosecute, Scull said the Council has decided to 'put our money where it counts.' Tipsters who provide information leading to an arrest could receive up to $1,000. The new laws were approved unanimously and have become effective

immediately." See Lisa Schneider, "New Anti-Hate Laws in Montgomery County" *Washington Jewish Week* 18, no. 47 (December 9–15, 1982): 1.

3. Michael Remer's case was decided on August 11, 1983. William Randall Harris's court date was July 18, 1983, and I do not have a date for John Cobb's decision.

4. "The congregation is seeking compensatory and punitive damages, according to Irvin Shapell, an attorney with the Jewish Advocacy Center. The center, a national non-profit that represents victims of anti-semitic violence, is representing Shaare Tefila. The Washington D.C. law firm of Hogan and Hartson is also representing the congregation." Steve Arabia, "Congregants Sue over Defaced Synagogue," *Montgomery County Sentinel*, March 9, 1984, p. 3.

5. See Naomi Wiener Cohen, "Shaare Tefila Congregation v. Cobb: A New Departure in American Defense," in *Jewish History* 3, no. 1 (1988).

6. Richard L. Zweigenhaft and G. William Domhoff, *Jews in the Protestant Establishment* (New York City: Praeger Special Studies, 1982), vii.

7. Khaled Beydoun, "Faith in Whiteness: Free Exercise of Religion as Racial Expression" in *Iowa Law Review* 105, no. 4 (May 2020).

8. Chris Demaske, *"Village of Skokie v. Nationalist Socialist Party of America (Ill)* (1978)" The First Amendment Encyclopedia, 2009. Accessed January 14, 2021. www .mtsu.edu/first-amendment/article/728/village-of-skokie-v-national-socialist-party-of -america-ill.

9. Mari Matsuda, "Introduction" in *Words That Wound: Critical Race Theory, Assaultive Speech, and the First Amendment* eds. Mari Matsuda et al. (Boulder, CO: Westview Press, 1993), 9.

10. Mari Matsuda, "Introduction" in *Words That Wound: Critical Race Theory, Assaultive Speech, and the First Amendment* eds. Mari Matsuda et al. (Boulder, CO: Westview Press, 1993), 9.

11. Archives of Maryland, ed. William Hand Browne et al. (in progress; Baltimore, 1883 to date), I, 520 cited in Ross M. Kimmel, "Chapter IV: Freedom or Bondage" in *Blacks before the Law in Colonial Maryland*, Master's Thesis, January 24, 1974. For excellent analysis of this point and a much broader historical analysis of race and the law in the United States, see Ariela J. Gross, *What Blood Won't Tell: A History of Race on Trial in America* (Cambridge, MA: Harvard University Press, 2008).

12. Jonathan D. Sarna and David G. Dalin, *Religion and State in the American Jewish Experience* (Notre Dame, Indiana: University of Notre Dame Press, 1997), 48–50.

13. Jonathan D. Sarna and David G. Dalin, *Religion and State in the American Jewish Experience* (Notre Dame, Indiana: University of Notre Dame Press, 1997), 48–50, 94–97.

14. 1980–1982 Early 1980s Recession, Timeline, *Slaying the Dragon of Debt: Fiscal Politics from the 1970s to the Present*, Regional Oral History Office, The Bancroft Library, University of California, Berkeley. accessed January 31, 2021. bancroft. berkeley.edu/ROHO/projects/debt/1980srecession.html.

15. Michael Kernan, "The Specter of Anti-Semitism, The Unending Web of Fear," *Washington Post*, December 1, 1982.

16. Michael Kernan, "The Specter of Anti-Semitism, The Unending Web of Fear," *Washington Post*, December 1, 1982.

17. Marshall Levin, Letter to Chief of Police Bernard Crooke, November 22, 1982.

18. Partial transcript at 34, 37, State of Maryland v. Michael D. Remer (Cir. Ct. Montgomery Cty. Aug. 13, 1983) (No. 29903) (trial proceedings of June 14, 1983).

19. "Six Arrested in Defacing," *Montgomery County Sentinel*, November 25, 1982, B-18. See the following quote: "In fact, a tipster fund helped police arrest six men involved in defacing Shaare Tefila Synagogue in Silver Spring last November." Frank Jossi, "Symposium Focuses County's Attention on Racial Violence," Montgomery County Sentinel, October 28, 1983, p. 7.

20. Partial transcript at 21, State of Maryland v. Michael D. Remer (Cir. Ct. Montgomery Cty. Aug. 11, 1983) (No. 29903) (trial proceedings of June 14, 1983).

21. Transcript at 1, Shaare Tefila Congregation v. Cobb, 481 US 615 S.Ct.

22. Partial transcript at 57, Direct examination of Michael D. Remer, State of Maryland v. Michael D. Remer (Cir. Ct. Montgomery Cty. Aug. 11, 1983) (No. 29903) (trial proceedings of Aug. 11, 1983).

23. Rabbi Jonah Layman, email to author, April 23, 2022.

24. Partial transcript at 12, Direct examination of Michael D. Remer, State of Maryland v. Michael D. Remer (Cir. Ct. Montgomery Cty. Aug. 11, 1983) (No. 29903) (trial proceedings of Aug. 11, 1983).

25. Alma Guillermoprieto, "23-Year-Old Charged in Desecration of Synagogue in Montgomery County," *Washington Post*, November 16, 1982.

26. Alma Guillermoprieto, "23-Year-Old Charged in Desecration of Synagogue in Montgomery County," *Washington Post*, November 16, 1982.

27. Partial transcript at 59–66, Direct examination of William Randall Harris, State of Maryland v. Michael D. Remer (Cir. Ct. for Montgomery Cty. July 18, 1983) (No. 29903) (trial proceedings of June 14, 1983).

28. Partial transcript at 9, Direct examination of William Randall Harris, State of Maryland v. Michael D. Remer (Cir. Ct. for Montgomery Cty. July 18, 1983) (No. 29903) (trial proceedings of June 15, 1983).

29. Partial transcript at 10, Direct examination of William Randall Harris, State of Maryland v. Michael D. Remer (Cir. Ct. for Montgomery Cty. July 18, 1983) (No. 29903) (trial proceedings of June 15, 1983).

30. Partial transcript at 10, Direct examination of William Randall Harris, State of Maryland v. Michael D. Remer (Cir. Ct. for Montgomery Cty. July 18, 1983) (No. 29903) (trial proceedings of June 15, 1983).

31. Partial transcript at 10, Direct examination of William Randall Harris, State of Maryland v. Michael D. Remer (Cir. Ct. for Montgomery Cty. July 18, 1983) (No. 29903) (trial proceedings of June 15, 1983).

32. Partial transcript at 48, Direct examination of Michael D. Remer, State of Maryland v. Michael D. Remer (Cir. Ct. for Montgomery Cty. Aug. 13, 1983) (No. 29903) (trial proceedings of June 15, 1983).

33. Partial transcript at 54, Direct examination of Michael D. Remer, State of Maryland v. Michael D. Remer (Cir. Ct. for Montgomery Cty. Aug. 13, 1983) (No. 29903) (trial proceedings of June 15, 1983).

34. Partial transcript at 54, Direct examination of Michael D. Remer, State of Maryland v. Michael D. Remer (Cir. Ct. for Montgomery Cty. Aug. 13, 1983) (No. 29903) (trial proceedings of June 15, 1983) (emphasis added).

35. Partial transcript at 55, Direct examination of Michael D. Remer, State of Maryland v. Michael D. Remer (Cir. Ct. for Montgomery Cty. Aug. 13, 1983) (No. 29903) (trial proceedings of June 15, 1983).

36. Partial transcript at 64, Direct examination of Michael D. Remer, State of Maryland v. Michael D. Remer (Cir. Ct. for Montgomery Cty. Aug. 13, 1983) (No. 29903) (trial proceedings of June 15, 1983).

37. Partial transcript at 64, Direct examination of Michael D. Remer, State of Maryland v. Michael D. Remer (Cir. Ct. for Montgomery Cty. Aug. 13, 1983) (No. 29903) (trial proceedings of June 15, 1983).

38. Partial transcript at 65, Direct examination of Michael D. Remer, State of Maryland v. Michael D. Remer (Cir. Ct. for Montgomery Cty. Aug. 13, 1983) (No. 29903) (trial proceedings of June 15, 1983).

39. Partial transcript at 66, Direct examination of Michael D. Remer, State of Maryland v. Michael D. Remer (Cir. Ct. for Montgomery Cty. Aug. 13, 1983) (No. 29903) (trial proceedings of June 15, 1983).

40. Partial transcript at 66, Direct examination of Michael D. Remer, State of Maryland v. Michael D. Remer (Cir. Ct. for Montgomery Cty. Aug. 13, 1983) (No. 29903) (trial proceedings of June 15, 1983).

41. Partial transcript at 69, Direct examination of Michael D. Remer, State of Maryland v. Michael D. Remer (Cir. Ct. for Montgomery Cty. Aug. 13, 1983) (No. 29903) (trial proceedings of June 15, 1983).

42. Partial transcript at 75, Direct examination of Michael D. Remer, State of Maryland v. Michael D. Remer (Cir. Ct. for Montgomery Cty. Aug. 13, 1983) (No. 29903) (trial proceedings of June 15, 1983).

43. Partial transcript at 75, Direct examination of Michael D. Remer, State of Maryland v. Michael D. Remer (Cir. Ct. for Montgomery Cty. Aug. 13, 1983) (No. 29903) (trial proceedings of June 15, 1983).

44. Judge Rosalyn B. Bell was commemorated, in memoriam, as the first woman to serve on the Montgomery County District Court and the second woman to be appointed to the Maryland Court of Special Appeals. For more on her amazing accomplishments, please see "The Honorable Rosalyn B. Bell, Date of Death: August 17, 2016," *The Bar Association of Montgomery County, MD Newsletter* 64, no 4 (October 2016): 7, accessed January 21, 2021. cdn.ymaws.com/www.barmont.org/resource/resmgr/newsletters/complete-october16.pdf.

45. "Vandals Sentenced for Graffiti," *Montgomery County Sentinel*, August 19, 1983, 4.

46. Tom Vesey, "Synagogue in Md. Files Rights Suit in Defacement Case," *Washington Post*, March 4, 1984.

47. The report was written by Scott L. Gunnison, who was the Senior Agent at the Division of Parole and Probation.

48. Request for Warrant at 2, State of Maryland v. Michael D. Remer (Cir. Ct. Montgomery Cty. Aug. 11, 1983) (No. 29903) (warrant request dated Oct. 6, 1986)

49. Request for Warrant at 2, State of Maryland v. Michael D. Remer (Cir. Ct. Montgomery Cty. Aug. 11, 1983) (No. 29903) (warrant request dated Oct. 6, 1986).

50. Rabbi Martin S. Halpern, Shaare Tefila Congregation, Letter to Judge David L. Cahoon, Montgomery County Circuit Court, Judicial Center, Rockville, Maryland 20850, April 15, 1986.

51. Request for Warrant at 4–5, State of Maryland v. Michael D. Remer (Cir. Ct. Montgomery Cty. Aug. 11, 1983) (No. 29903) (warrant request dated Oct. 6, 1986).

52. Request for Warrant at 4–5, State of Maryland v. Michael D. Remer (Cir. Ct. Montgomery Cty. Aug. 11, 1983) (No. 29903) (warrant request dated Oct. 6, 1986).

53. Request for Warrant at 5, State of Maryland v. Michael D. Remer (Cir. Ct. Montgomery Cty. Aug. 11, 1983) (No. 29903) (warrant request dated Oct. 6, 1986).

54. Request for Warrant at 5, State of Maryland v. Michael D. Remer (Cir. Ct. Montgomery Cty. Aug. 11, 1983) (No. 29903) (warrant request dated Oct. 6, 1986).

55. Schnader, "Former Managing Partner of Schnader's Washington Office Honored by the American Association of Jewish Lawyers and Jurists," *Schnader: the Higher Calling of Law*, December 3, 2009, accessed April 12, 2021, www.schnader.com/event/former-managing-partner-of-schnaders-washington-office-honored-by-the-american-association-of-jewish-lawyers-and-jurists/.

56. See citation of Anton R. Valukas, former US attorney and chair of Jenner & Block, in Margaret Ramirez and Ameet Sachdev, "Jerold S. Solovy, 1930–2011," *Chicago Tribune*, January 19, 2011, accessed April 12, 2021, www.chicagotribune.com/lifestyles/ct-xpm-2011-01-19-ct-met-solovy-obit-0120-20110119-story.html.

57. Naomi Wiener Cohen, "Shaare Tefila Congregation v. Cobb: A New Departure in American Defense," in *Jewish History* 3, No.1 (1988), 98.

58. Kevin Lipson, phone interview by author, January 13, 2021.

59. Kevin Lipson, phone interview by author, January 13, 2021.

60. This is in concert from what I learned from the American Jewish Committee's archive. I wrote to Charlotte Bonelli, the Director of the American Jewish Committee's Archive and Records Center, and she responded with the suggestion that I search the digitized archives, which I had already done—finding three documents, but nothing of compelling interest. She responded a day later, telling me that her assistant, Deisree Guillermo, had been able to find a little bit more information about the case, which is copied here: "From 1986 October BOG Minutes:

REPORT OF THE NATIONAL LEGAL COMMITTEE Mr. NEVAS next asked Carl Koch to report on the activities of the National Legal Committee.

Mr. KOCH stated that the Governors will soon be receiving the latest summary of the activities of the National Legal Committee. He referred to a specific case that the committee is currently debating — Shaare Tefila Congregation vs. Cobb. This case involves a Maryland congregation which is seeking damages from vandals who defaced their synagogue and were convicted of their crime. Instead of using existing state laws to support their claim, they are invoking the old Federal law which protects races from discrimination. The Legal Committee originally voted not to get involved in this case, since AJC has always maintained that Jewishness is not a distinct race, but this decision is now being reconsidered by the Committee since the case will be heard by the Supreme Court. (The Committee subsequently decided to intervene.)

Bruce RAMER mentioned that the Shaare Tefila case and the Important issues involved would be discussed further at the meeting of the National Affairs Commission."

61. Kevin Lipson, phone interview by author, January 13, 2021.

62. Kevin Lipson, phone interview by author, May 20, 2009.

63. Kevin Lipson, phone interview by author, May 20, 2009.

64. Kevin Lipson, phone interview by author, May 20, 2009.

65. Shaare Tefila Congregation Board of Trustees Meeting, December 6, 1982, 3.

66. In my interview with Irvin Shapell, he did not recall giving this speech and posited that perhaps his codirector Kevin Lipson had done so instead, although he also said that he might have given it. It seems likely that he was indeed the one who spoke, since the document from Shaare Tefila's file on the vandalism incident begins with this statement: "At services on Friday, January 7, 1983, Irvin Shapell, President of the Jewish Advocacy Center, spoke to the congregation about the problem of anti-semitic acts and about the legal responses to the problem."

Phone interview with Irvin Shapell, May 11, 2009.

67. Speech given by Irvin Shapell, Shaare Tefila Congregation, January 7, 1983, 4.

68. Speech given by Irvin Shapell, Shaare Tefila Congregation, January 7, 1983, 4.

69. Speech given by Irvin Shapell, Shaare Tefila Congregation, January 7, 1983, 6–7.

70. Speech given by Irvin Shapell, Shaare Tefila Congregation, January 7, 1983, 7.

71. Bruce Lincoln, *Discourse and the Construction of Society: Comparative Studies of Myth, Ritual, and Classification* (New York: Oxford University Press, 1989), 23.

72. Office of Management and Budget, Directive 15: Race and Ethnic Standards for Federal Statistics and Administrative Reporting (1977) available at wonder.cdc. gov/wonder/help/populations/bridged-race/directive15.html [perma.cc/FHL3–7C8U]

73. Immigration and Nationality Act of 1952, Pub. L. No. 82–414, 66 Stat. 163 (1952).

74. Deposition of John W. Cobb at 5, Shaare Tefila Congregation v. Cobb, 606 F.Supp. 1504 (D. Md. 1985) (No. R-84–880), *rev'd*, 107 S.Ct. 2019 (1987), (deposition of Sept. 6, 1984); Deposition of Thomas Joseph Hunt, Jr. at 9, Shaare Tefila Congregation v. Cobb, 606 F.Supp. 1504 (D. Md. 1985) (No. R-84–880), *rev'd*, 107 S.Ct. 2019 (1987), (deposition of Nov. 1, 1984); Deposition of Thomas Lloyd Heine at 7, Shaare Tefila Congregation v. Cobb, 606 F.Supp. 1504 (D. Md. 1985) (No. R-84–880), *rev'd*, 107 S.Ct. 2019 (1987) (deposition of Oct. 18, 1984).

75. Thank you to my friend and colleague Dean Franco for this image. See his book on space, particularly chapter 3: Dean Franco, *The Border and The Line: Race, Literature, and Los Angeles* (Stanford, CA: Stanford University Press, 2019), 111–52.

76. Phyllis B. Gerstenfeld, *Hate Crimes: Causes, Controls, and Controversies* (Thousand Oaks: Sage Publications, 2004), 87–88.

77. Phyllis B. Gerstenfeld, *Hate Crimes: Causes, Controls, and Controversies* (Thousand Oaks: Sage Publications, 2004), 87.

78. Phyllis B. Gerstenfeld, *Hate Crimes: Causes, Controls, and Controversies* (Thousand Oaks: Sage Publications, 2004), 87.

79. Phyllis B. Gerstenfeld, *Hate Crimes: Causes, Controls, and Controversies* (Thousand Oaks: Sage Publications, 2004), 88.

80. Partial trial transcript at 54, Direct examination of Randy Harris, State of Maryland v. Michael David Remer (Cir. Ct. Montgomery County July 18, 1983) (No. 29903) (trial proceedings June 14, 1983).

81. I differentiate between "antisemitic" and "racist" in this sentence, because the vandals could have understood *Jews* as a separate and inferior group, or they could have viewed *all* "minority" groups not their own as lesser than they were.

82. Deposition of Michael Remer at 118, Shaare Tefila Congregation v. Cobb (Cir. Ct. Montgomery County) (No. R84-880) 606 F.Supp. 1504 (D. Md. 1985), *rev'd*, 107 S.Ct. 2019 (1987) (deposition of June 21, 1988).

83. Joe R. Feagin, *The White Racial Frame: Centuries of Racial Framing and Counter-Framing* (New York: Routledge, 2010). See also Annalise E. Glauz-Todrank, "Jewish Critical Race Theory and Jewish 'Religionization' in *Shaare Tefila Congregation v. Cobb*" in *Judaism, Race, and Ethics: Approaches and Conversations*, ed. Jonathan Crane (University Park, Pennsylvania University Press, 2020), 191–216.

84. Joe R. Feagin, *The White Racial Frame: Centuries of Racial Framing and Counter-Framing* (New York: Routledge, 2010), 12.

85. Joe R. Feagin, *The White Racial Frame: Centuries of Racial Framing and Counter-Framing* (New York: Routledge, 2010), 11.

86. Deposition of Thomas Joseph Hunt, Jr. at 73, Shaare Tefila Congregation v. Cobb (Cir. Ct. Montgomery County) (No. R84-880), 606 F.Supp. 1504 (D. Md. 1985), *rev'd*, 107 S.Ct. 2019 (1987) (deposition of Nov. 1, 1984).

87. I use this word, "co-constituted," which was previously used by Henry Goldschmidt, *Race and Religion among the Chosen Peoples of Crown Heights* (New Brunswick, NJ: Rutgers University Press, 2006), 26.

88. David Biale, *Blood and Belief, The Circulation of a Symbol Between Jews and Christians* (Berkeley: University of California Press, 2007), 126.

89. See "The Nuremberg Laws: The Reich Citizenship Law" (September 15, 1935), Article 2, Sources: Jeremy Noakes and Geoffrey Pridham. Documents on Nazism 1919–1945. New York: Viking Press, 1974, pp. 463–467, and The Nizkor Project. Jewish Virtual Library. www.jewishvirtuallibrary.org/the-reich-citizenship-law.

90. Linda Martín Alcoff, *Visible Identities: Race, Gender, and the Self* (New York: Oxford, 2006), 44.

91. Cantor Gershon Levin, written responses to interview questions by author, submitted via email, August 26, 2009.

92. Patricia Brannan, phone interview by author, March 23, 2021.

93. Interviews revealed some debate on this topic. While Patricia Brannan noted that it was important to her to represent the congregation as it wanted to be represented, and while Jack and Bess Teller remembered the discussion about the legal argument, Kevin Lipson told me that the congregation had not been consulted for its opinion on the argument.

94. 42 U.S.C. §§ 1981 and 1982.

95. The full statute for 42 U.S.C. 1985(3) states: "DEPRIVING PERSONS OF RIGHTS OR PRIVILEGES: If two or more persons in any State or Territory conspire or go in

disguise on the highway or on the premises of another, for the purpose of depriving, either directly or indirectly, any person or class of persons of the equal protection of the laws, or of equal privileges and immunities under the laws; or for the purpose of preventing or hindering the constituted authorities of any State or Territory from giving or securing to all persons within such State or Territory the equal protection of the laws; or if two or more persons conspire to prevent by force, intimidation, or threat, any citizen who is lawfully entitled to vote, from giving his support or advocacy in a legal manner, toward or in favor of the election of any lawfully qualified person as an elector for President or Vice President, or as a Member of Congress of the United States; or to injure any citizen in person or property on account of such support or advocacy; in any case of conspiracy set forth in this section, if one or more persons engaged therein do, or cause to be done, any act in furtherance of the object of such conspiracy, whereby another is injured in his person or property, or deprived of having and exercising any right or privilege of a citizen of the United States, the party so injured or deprived may have an action for the recovery of damages occasioned by such injury or deprivation, against any one or more of the conspirators."

96. Shaare Tefila Congregation Board of Trustees Meeting, February 23, 1984, 2.

97. Shaare Tefila Congregation Board of Trustees Meeting, February 23, 1984, 2.

98. Shaare Tefila Congregation Board of Trustees Meeting, February 23, 1984, 2.

99. Shirley Altman, phone interview by author, June 1, 2009.

100. Shirley Altman, phone interview by author, June 1, 2009.

101. Shirley Altman, phone interview by author, June 1, 2009. See also Mari Matsuda, "Public Response to Racist Speech: Considering the Victim's Story" in *Words That Wound: Critical Race Theory, Assaultive Speech, and the First Amendment*, eds. Mari Matsuda et al. (Boulder, CO: Westview Press, 1993), 22.

102. Steve Arabia, "Congregants Sue Over Defaced Synagogue," *Montgomery County Sentinel*, March 9, 1984, p. 3.

103. Steve Arabia, "Congregants Sue Over Defaced Synagogue," *Montgomery County Sentinel*, March 9, 1984, p. 3.

104. Steve Arabia, "Congregants Sue Over Defaced Synagogue," *Montgomery County Sentinel*, March 9, 1984, p. 3.

105. Shaare Tefila Congregation Board Meeting, May 6, 1985, 2.

106. Unfortunately, the minutes from the board meeting are not forthcoming about the details of this discussion.

107. Jack Teller, interview by author, Silver Spring, MD, August 17, 2009.

108. Bess Teller, interview by author, Silver Spring, MD, July 8, 2008.

109. U.S. Const. amend. I

110. Patricia Brannan, phone interview by author, March 23, 2021.

111. An Act to protect all Persons in the United States in their Civil Rights, and furnish the Means of their Vindication [Civil Rights Act of 1866]; Laws of 1866, ch. 31; 14 Stat. 27 (1866) (codified in Rev. Stat. §§ 1982–1989 (1875)).

112. An Act to enforce the Provisions of the Fourteenth Amendment to the Constitution of the United States, and for other Purposes; Laws of 1871, ch. 22; 17 Stat. 13 (1871) (codified in Rev. Stat. §§ 1979–1981 (1875)).

113. Nadra Kareem Nittle, "How the Black Codes Limited African American Progress After the Civil War," History.com, updated January 28, 2021, original October 1, 2020, accessed February 4, 2022, www.history.com/news/black-codes-reconstruction-slavery

114. Neil Gotanda, "A Critique of 'Our Constitution is Color-Blind,'" in *Critical Race Theory: The Key Writings that Formed the Movement*, eds. Kimberlé Crenshaw, Neil Gotanda, Gary Peller, and Kendall Thomas (New York: The New Press, 1995), 263.

115. See Ira Katznelson, *When Affirmative Action Was White: An Untold Story of Racial Inequality in Twentieth-Century America* (New York, NY: W.W. Norton and Co., 2006 [2005]).

116. Shelley v. Kraemer, 334 U.S. 1 (1948).

117. Hurd v. Hodge, 334 U.S. 24 (1948).

118. Jones v. Alfred H. Mayer Co., 392 U.S. 409 (1968).

119. From the case summary of Manzanares v. Safeway Stores, Inc. 593 F.2d 968 (10th Cir. 1979) casetext.com/case/manzanares-v-safeway-stores-inc/case-summaries?PHONE_NUMBER_GROUP=C Accessed February 2, 2021.

120. Shaare Tefila Congregation v. Cobb, 785 F.2d 523, 527 (1986).

121. See Regents of the University of California v. Bakke, 438 U.S. 265 (1978) and Marco DeFunis Jr. v. Odegaard 416 U.S. 312 (1974).

122. McDonald v. Santa Fe Trail Transportation Co., 427 U.S. 273 (1976).

123. Khaled A. Beydoun, "Faith in Whiteness: Free Exercise of Religion as Racial Expression," *Iowa Law Review* 105, no. 4 (May 2020): 1481, 1483.

124. Khaled A. Beydoun, "Faith in Whiteness: Free Exercise of Religion as Racial Expression," *Iowa Law Review* 105, no. 4 (May 2020): 1529.

Chapter Three

Judging Religion and Race in the Federal District Court of Maryland and the Fourth Circuit Court of Appeals

Most Jewish Americans have assumed that they are "religiously" Jewish, and they have also assumed these norms in the courts. Until the 1980s, Jewish Americans who had filed lawsuits had done so based on the "Free Exercise" Clause and the "Establishment" Clause of the First Amendment; the category of religion in Title VII of the Civil Rights Act of 1964, which refers to employment;[1] or the category of religion in the Civil Rights Act of 1968, which concerns "hate crimes" law that did *not* pertain to vandalism, and to the sale, rental, and financing of housing.[2] Because no religion-based laws applied to their civil suit, the lawyers for Shaare Tefila Congregation elected to try a different route: they would argue it based on race. This would require the judges from the Federal District Court of Maryland and the Fourth Circuit Court of Appeals to determine whether the members of Shaare Tefila Congregation, who stated that they were "White," could claim race-based rights under Sections 1981, 1982, and 1985(3), along with Maryland state laws.

First, let's examine the reasons that Shaare Tefila Congregation could not pursue religion-based laws to file their civil suit. The First Amendment, due to the "incorporation doctrine," requires "*state action*," which means that a plaintiff—a person who files a claim—must demonstrate that the local, state, or federal government was responsible for the violation, rather than a private actor. The state action *also* must raise a constitutional issue.[3] Recall that the First Amendment maintains: "Congress shall make no law respecting an establishment of religion, or prohibiting the free exercise thereof." In the past, most Jews had brought lawsuits under the Free Exercise Clause, which protects the freedom of Americans to "accept any religious belief," "to engage in religious rituals" without the federal government's interference, and to participate in "actions made on behalf of those beliefs."[4]

The religion-based laws of the rights of the First Amendment were "incorporated" along with the other nine amendments within the Bill of Rights on July 9, 1868, with the Due Process Clause of the Fourteenth Amendment. The "incorporation doctrine" would selectively apply these amendments to the state governments, but a plaintiff, or plaintiffs, would have to bring a legal case that would make these laws applicable. The Free Exercise Clause was first applied to the states in 1940, when the U.S. Supreme Court sided unanimously with Cantwell, in *Cantwell v. Connecticut*.[5] From that point onward, citizens could bring lawsuits against states and local laws under the Free Exercise Clause. The other part of the First Amendment that pertains to religion is the Establishment Clause, which stipulates that the federal government cannot make any law respecting an establishment of religion. In the 1947 case *Everson v. Board of Education*, the Supreme Court sided with the Board of Education in a 5–4 decision.[6] Afterward, citizens were able to bring lawsuits against local and state laws under the Establishment Clause.

Outlining how "religion" is realized in US law enables us to think about the role that it plays in American life. In US law, the concept of "religion" is imbedded in Christian and specifically Protestant, discourse, with its mythical origins derived from the arrival of English, Pilgrim colonists in 1620.[7] The dominance of Protestantism occurred not only in social discourse but in judicial rulings. From the US Supreme Court's origin in 1790, all the Supreme Court justices were Protestant until the first Catholic justice, Roger B. Taney, was appointed in 1836. We will see this division emerge later as important to *Shaare Tefila*, in which Catholic Judge Murnaghan and Justice Antonin Scalia identified with the Jewish community because at the time, they were minority judges. We also can consider Catholics a minority based on the English settlement of what became the United States. Of the initial thirteen colonies, Maryland, founded in 1632, was the only one set aside for persecuted English Catholics. Puritans, however, claimed it in 1654.[8] A long history of assumed Protestant discourse pervades the United States to this day.[9]

The conception of "religion," in Protestant terms and in US laws, prioritizes beliefs,[10] which may then result in actions, such as rituals or other behavior. In US law, religious *actions* based on beliefs may be proscribed in US courts. As religious studies scholar Eric Michael Mazur explains: "The ability to limit the actions of the believers in the realm of religious participation, is the ability to limit their religion in a very tangible way. An Orthodox Jew will find little comfort, for example, in being told she may believe in the dietary laws but that no kosher food is available."[11]

With the distinction between "belief" and "action" in mind, let's briefly examine one US Supreme Court issue that has long heralded Christian ideals:

Sunday Laws. One of the most important forms of Jewish observance is the ability to rest on Shabbat, or Saturday, and, in the American context—because the weekend is the busiest day for sales—to work on Sunday. Due to the Sunday Laws, however, significant to long-standing Christian principles of not working on the Lord's Day, Jews were prevented from doing business. Not only did these laws bring religion into the public sphere, many Jews understood them as a form of economic discrimination.[12] Even after the Due Process Clause incorporated the Free Exercise Clause, opponents to Sunday laws lost in courts because they did not demonstrate a burden on the free exercise of religion that was substantial *enough* for the majority Christian judges.[13] The Supreme Court heard and rejected four cases pertaining to Sunday laws on May 29, 1961.[14] In one of them, *McGowan v. Maryland*, Chief Justice Warren concluded that despite origination in Sunday blue laws, the law now had "sufficient 'secular justifications.'"[15]

Immediate public opposition to the Supreme Court's decision in all four cases caused states to repeal many of their Sunday laws. Observant Jewish shopkeepers were now allowed to sell any item permissible within what remained of the Sunday laws in their states. This opposition, potentially more than other factors, led to the Court's strict scrutiny determination of *Sherbert v. Verner* in 1963.[16] Strict scrutiny is a form of judicial review that requires "compelling government interest," and the constructed law must be narrowly tailored to achieve that interest.[17] The case, based on the Free Exercise Clause, provided a day of rest for Adele Sherbert, a Seventh Day Adventist, after she was fired because she refused to work on Saturday, her religious day of rest. The case also provided accommodations for individuals, including Jews, who made their day of rest known to their workplace, unless it caused "undue hardship."

As Shaare Tefila Congregation took its case to the Federal District Court of Maryland, the Supreme Court was tightening the boundaries of what the Free Exercise Clause could entail and was beginning to limit state-based religious laws applicable to Jews. After ruling expansively in *Wisconsin v. Yoder* in 1972, supporting the Old Order Amish dedication to their traditional way of life by allowing them to take their children out of school as teenagers, the Court would reject later cases that pertained to Jewish and Native American community religious practices.[18] For example, it ruled in *Goldman v. Weinberger* (1986) that a rabbi who served as a psychologist in a mental health clinic at a military base could not wear a yarmulke, otherwise known as a kippah, when wearing his military uniform. Although the military code had exemptions for other religious items, such as crucifixes, his yarmulke was not allowed. In *Employment v. Smith* (1990), the Court prohibited two counselors from obtaining unemployment benefits because they had ingested peyote, a hallucinogenic drug important to their membership in the Native

American Church. Other factors are also significant in these civil suits, but because these were landmark cases, the Court could be read as preferencing Christian actions over Jewish and Native American ones.

Now, let's return our attention to *Shaare Tefila*. Importantly, Jewish identification has never been legally categorized in terms of either "religion" or "race." Yet, at stake in the civil suit was the legitimacy of Jewish claims to race-based protection.[19] Deborah Garren, the lawyer defending Michael Remer, had successfully argued for the dismissal of the case in district court by arguing that Jews are members of a religion and "white," and thus cannot cite the Civil Rights Act of 1866, which covers racial, not religious, discrimination.[20] This argument draws on the fact that most Jewish Americans have attempted to ascribe to "religious" norms[21] in what became the United States, as well as become "white," if they could, in the years after World War II.[22] Legal protection thus depended on the ability of the congregation's lawyer, Patricia Brannan, to convince the judges that the congregation was entitled to race-based protection due to the perspective of the antisemitic vandals. Thus, the legal definition of Jewish identification *itself* was on trial.

Broadly, the suit—perhaps inadvertently—tested how US law would identify Jewish Americans. Specifically, it revealed how the boundaries of the social concepts "religion" and "race" would be used to categorize Jewish identification. These forms of religious and racial categorization have informed the history of Jewish American social location, which underpins legal history and continually figures into legal decisions about Jewish civil rights.

As we will see, the judges' arguments and conclusions in *Shaare Tefila* reflect conceptions of "religion" and "race"[23] operative in the dominant discourse of US society, during the 1980s. These qualifiers likewise have been significant throughout American legal history, particularly because the judicial impact of "Caucasian" and "White" Christianity had informed US policy internally in practices exclusive of non-White, Christian peoples. As we have seen, for example, male, White, Protestant, and Christian political leaders had intentionally tried to prevent non-"Caucasian" and non-"Anglo-Saxon" peoples from immigrating to the United States.

In the 1980s, however, burgeoning attention to what were called "hate crimes" became part of the dominant socio-legal conversation. As it extended race-based civil rights to Jews for the first time, *Shaare Tefila Congregation v. Cobb* contributed to the genealogy of "hate crime" laws. Although it was not a criminal case, and it did not engage the language of "hate crimes," nor did it explicitly provide "penalty enhancement," which are increased penalties for committing a "hate crime," as later laws did, *Shaare Tefila* expanded protection for civil suits committed based on "bias," sharing the same *concepts* as hate crimes legislation. "Bias" is not only a social term but also a legal term.

In legal language, it refers to "the predisposition of . . . anyone making a judicial decision against or in favor of one of the parties or a class of persons," which "can be shown by remarks, decisions contrary to the fact, reason or law, or other unfair conduct."[24]

The objective of a "hate crime" and a "bias" is the same. The Congregation argued that the vandals *viewed* Jews as a "race," and cited the protections of the Civil Rights Act of 1866 and 1871.[25] Specifically, it expanded federal civil rights laws to Jews, especially federal civil damage cases. It shared the same goals with the general trend of the decades that followed, in which both popular and legal discourse increasingly engaged the *idea* of "hate crimes"—as well as the term—to describe illegal incidents based on "bias."Although this case does not describe a "hate crime," the logic is largely the same.

As we move through the chapter, first, we will examine the legal process undertaken by lower courts in the civil suit—the Federal District Court of Maryland and the Fourth Circuit Court of Appeals. Next, we will address the judges' interpretations and decisions regarding the legal category of "race" and their socio-legal assumption that Jews are a "religion." In the District Court, Judge Ramsey determined first that Jews are a religious group and not a racial group, and second, refuted the congregation's argument that the vandals were "irrational" in their view that Jews are a race. Ramsey understood race as based on skin color and asserted that the congregation members were not "brown." The congregation appealed to the Fourth Circuit Court of Appeals, in which Judge Hall affirmed Judge Ramsey's decision. In addition, we will analyze the socio-legal location of Jewish identification in both courts.[26] As a part of that analysis, we will focus in-depth on Judge Wilkinson's partial dissent from the ruling in the Fourth Circuit Court of Appeals. In Wilkinson's lengthy commentary, he asserted that the Court was perpetuating the racial prejudice that the civil rights laws were designed to protect.

Before addressing the courts' decisions, let's focus briefly on this book's legal approach to race. This judicial analysis of *Shaare Tefila Congregation v. Cobb* acknowledges two methods of interpreting race: as a structural inequality or as a "neutral" quality.[27] Whereas the first method concentrates on the inequities inherent in its' functionality, the second method treats race impartially and does not take the concept of race into consideration when making legal decisions. An example of the first method is racial profiling. Some judges do consider racial discrepancies a pervasive issue, but it has not yet become the mainstream US judicial approach. Rather, the assumption that the US "Constitution is color-blind" provides the basis for a "race neutral" method in making legal decisions.[28] Based on this second method, affirmative action may seem unfair by giving privileges to racially marginalized people.[29] In the first method, race is important to decision-making in American life.

For example, consider Critical Race Theorist Neil Gotanda's critique of color-blindness, in that it "fosters White racial domination."[30]

If we consider the dominant view of Jewish Americans in the 1980s as unequivocally White, then Neil Gotanda's critique that colorblindness "fosters White racial domination" applies to *all* Jewish Americans. Although this is not accurate, because "formally" White Jews are not "substantively" White, and because many Jews are BIPOC, let's pursue this idea.[31] Jewish Americans perceived as White also often perceive *themselves* as White, just as the legal victims did in this civil suit. They may use their assumed Whiteness to use "race-neutral" laws, such as opposition to affirmative action. This may be in part because they, their families, or other Jews historically *also* had suffered from quotas in colleges and universities from at least 1918 to 1947.[32] One example of a Jewish American who pursued a "race neutral" law is Marco Defunis in *DeFunis v. Odegaard* (1971), who filed a civil suit against the University of Washington Law School because he argued that it employed "preferential admissions policies" that admitted "unqualified minorities" over him.[33]

Nevertheless, Jewish Americans, even those perceived as White, are consistently spatially disenfranchised, based on a history of exclusion that determines how space is *produced*. Given this framework, spatial divisions *prefer* peoples considered socially dominant and *target* peoples considered socially excluded. Here, we're differentiating Jews and Jewish Americans from Caucasian, Anglo-Saxon, White, Christians, or Americans within the umbrella of "Whiteness." These divisions, for example, include race-based immigration laws, rejection from certain types of employment, quotas at colleges or universities, and prohibitions from country clubs, fraternities, or sororities. They also *target* certain places spatially associated with Jews and Jewish Americans, such as synagogues, Holocaust or Shoah memorial museums, and kosher delis, to perpetuate vandalism, take hostages, or commit murders.[34] These forms of spatial difference demarcate Jewish space from White, Christian space. This is one reason that although the Jewish Americans who were members of Shaare Tefila Congregation were perceived and perceived themselves as White, their synagogue still could be the site of an antisemitic racist attack. Let's turn now to the initial hearing of their case.

THE FEDERAL DISTRICT COURT DECISION

The Federal District Court of Maryland in Baltimore was the first court that heard Shaare Tefila Congregation's complaint. Plaintiffs included Rabbi Martin Halpern, Shirley Altman, William Harkaway, Marshall Levin, Maurice Potosky, and Dr. Jacob Teller. They brought the civil suit against the White defendants, John William Cobb; William Randall Harris, Jr.; Thomas Lloyd Heine; William Hess; Thomas Hunt, Jr; Raymond Lee Jordan; Dominic Queen; and Michael D. Remer. As previously noted, Judge Norman Park Ramsey determined the outcome on April 22, 1985.

Judge Ramsey was a liberal White judge appointed by President Jimmy Carter in 1980. Born in Fairchance, Pennsylvania on September 1, 1922, Ramsey received his B.A. at Loyola College in 1941 and enrolled the same year at the University of Maryland School of Law. He began law school six years after Black students were finally allowed to register. In 1936, lawyer and later Supreme Court Justice Thurgood Marshall had represented Donald Gaines Murray, in *Murray v. Pearson*, who was prohibited from enrolling at the University of Maryland School of Law because he was Black.

Marshall argued the case alongside Charles Hamilton Houston on behalf of the National Association for the Advancement of Colored People (NAACP). The School of Law had cited *Plessy v. Ferguson*'s doctrine of "separate but equal," but Marshall and Houston prevailed in the Maryland Court of Appeals. This was the first test case that paved the way for other cases contesting the "separate but equal" clause that finally led to *Brown v. Board of Education*. Judge Ramsey must have known about these cases, and they informed his thinking, in line with US norms, in which "race" distinguished between Black and White based on the "color line."[35]

By the early 1980s, White support for the government to implement legal changes that would provide Blacks equal access to housing, the same schools, jobs, and accommodations for hotels and restaurants had declined in most arenas. The only area in which government intervention had increased was housing.[36] In fact, the Civil Rights Act of 1964 likely would not have passed if put to a popular vote during the early 1980s.[37] Even as a liberal White Democrat, Ramsey was necessarily shaped by these socio-legal factors.

Thus, on April 22, 1985, Judge Ramsey ruled in favor of defendant Michael Remer, who had argued that Jews, as a religious group, could not be protected under the Civil Rights Act of 1866. Based on Remer's argument, Ramsey did not recognize that Jewish Americans face racial discrimination in the United States. Because of this ruling, the cases against the other defendants were also dismissed.

Notably, from January 1, 1980 until December 31, 1986, Ramsey had ruled on only one other racial discrimination case, *Equal Employment Opportunity Commission (EEOC) v. International Business Machines Corporation (IBM)*,[38] which pertained to Black employees who argued that IBM had discriminated against them, as well as their whole "racial class," in violation of Title VII of the Civil Rights Act of 1964, specifically 42 U.S.C. Sec. 2000e-3, in terms of promotion, pay, and appraisals. The inclusion of this case does not necessarily illustrate or support what Ramsey ruled in *Shaare Tefila*, but it's important to consider it for the basis of comparison. Here, Ramsey used the precedent *McDonnell Douglas Corp. v. Green* (1973), which required that only if complainants prove to the *judge* that racial discrimination is, on its face, "sufficient to establish a fact or raise a presumption unless disproved or rebutted," would the onus shift to the employer to rebut the claim. *McConnell Douglas Corp.* may have been controlling for claims filed under 42 U.S.C. section 2000e-3. If so, it prioritized the judge's discretion in a time when nearly all judges were White men and were not required or trained to reflect on the United States as a patriarchal, colonial White society. In this case, the Black employees of IBM could not prove that they had been discriminated against as a "class," because, according to Ramsey, the plaintiffs could not demonstrate that the discriminatory behavior applied to *all* Black employees. In making this determination, the judge relied on *Griggs v. Duke Power Co.*(1971), which referred to a discriminatory height requirement that would adversely affect all females. In other words, the Black employees of IBM could not prove that IBM had the same type of requirement for them as an entire class. Thus, in the only other racial discrimination case that he heard, Ramsey dismissed the charges, as he did in *Shaare Tefila*.

Recall that the issue at stake in the *Shaare Tefila* was not whether the vandalism occurred since criminal trials had already found several of the defendants guilty. In civil suits, however, the court is instructed to view the complaint in the way that was most favorable to the plaintiffs. The plaintiffs constructed their argument based on three sections of the US civil code, and on Maryland state law regarding trespass, nuisance, and intentional affliction of emotional distress. The three sections of federal law they invoked included sections 1981 and 1982, and section 1985(3). Remember that they were passed to further protect the rights of the Thirteenth Amendment, and to prevent discrimination according to Black Codes operative at the time of the two Civil Rights Acts. Given the almost entirely White, Protestant, and male members of every branch of government in the 1980s, however, "discrimination" was a term that most of them had a difficult time comprehending from personal experience. Personal experience, however, is key to the ideological underpinnings supporting judges' beliefs, which inform their thoughts and necessarily shape their rulings in court.

The plaintiffs alleged under section 1981, the first count submitted, that the defendants had deprived them of the right to the "full and equal" benefits of property. Recall that this statute states: "All persons within the jurisdiction of the United States shall have the same right in every State and Territory to make and enforce contracts, to sue, be parties, give evidence, and to the full and equal benefit of all laws and proceedings as is enjoyed by *white* citizens."[39] Shaare Tefila members also asserted that the defendants' conduct was "motivated by racial prejudice in that the defendants perceive [the] plaintiffs as racially distinct because they are Jews."[40]

Michael Remer argued for the dismissal of this count on the basis that the plaintiffs' claim constitutes religious rather than racial discrimination and that section 1981 covers only the latter. He also maintained that state action was required for this claim and that no state action had occurred. Judge Ramsey agreed with Remer based on the second claim and therefore found no need to examine the first argument.

The plaintiffs asserted that although no state action occurred in this situation, state action was not required under the statute due to the precedent of a prior case, *Mahone v. Waddle*.[41] Judge Ramsey, however, did not find the earlier decision binding as precedent in this case. Rather, he determined that the statute was split so that while state action was not necessary for the contract clause of section 1981, it *was* required for the equal benefits clause of 1981, which was at stake in the plaintiffs' argument. Again, because Judge Ramsey dismissed the first count based on the plaintiffs' second argument—that state action was required but not present in the congregation's situation—the issue of religious versus racial discrimination became irrelevant.

In the second count, the congregation's members claimed that the defendants' defacement had deprived the congregation of the right to "hold real and personal property," as provided under section 1982. Recall that it states: "All citizens of the United States shall have the same right, in every State and Territory, as is enjoyed by white citizens thereof to inherit, purchase, lease, sell, hold, and convey real and personal property."[42] Once more, the plaintiffs asserted that the defendants' conduct was "motivated by racial prejudice in that defendants perceive plaintiffs as racially distinct because they are Jews."[43] In his request for dismissal, Remer again argued that although the plaintiffs claimed that racial discrimination occurred, it was in fact religious discrimination and that section 1982 does not cover the latter.

Judge Ramsey noted that the Civil Rights Act of 1866—from which these sections of law derive—was intended to protect a "limited category of rights, specifically defined in terms of racial equality"; he also pointed out that the Supreme Court had determined that this Act does not apply to religious discrimination, which would include Jews.[44] The plaintiffs, Ramsey stated, did not ask for a broad interpretation of the statute that would cover religious discrimination, nor did they ask for judicial recognition of Jewish identification as a "race" so that the act would be applicable. Instead, Judge Ramsey concluded, Shaare Tefila Congregation based its argument on the perception of the defendants[45] despite "whatever the reality may be."[46] Here, the Shaare Tefila Congregation argued that the vandals *viewed* them as a race because of their racist graffiti, which emblazoned the Nazi and KKK slogans, words, and symbols on the synagogue walls, its playground, and on Jack and Bess

Teller's nearby car. Ramsey asserted: "As defendant notes, such an approach would have the practical effect of extending section 1981 and section 1982 to apply to any group, however, defined, merely by virtue of alleging that an individual defendant *perceived* the group as racially inferior, however irrational that perception might be."[47]

Because, in Ramsey's decision, views of race were based on the American dominant discourse of the "color line," a defendant's mental state in targeting members of a group who claimed to be White could thus be deemed "irrational." His statement presumed that a commonly identifiable categorization of race *exists*, such that the determination in a case like this one would rely on an agreed-upon definition of race. In the absence of those definitional terms, actions conducted for "irrational" reasons would not be eligible for a civil rights claim. The Congregation's argument, based on the racialized *perception* of the vandals, for him, fit this description.

Judge Ramsey proceeded to state that the court was "sympathetic" to the plaintiffs' "outrage" and "sorrow" over the desecration of the synagogue and that it "recognized" the history of discrimination against Jews. Despite these sentiments, however, he insisted that because Jews do not constitute a "distinct or recognizable 'race'" and are not "*commonly identified* as such,"[48] the discrimination, in this case, does not fall under the discrimination covered in the statute, despite the "distorted beliefs" of "deviant groups."

In his main argument, he cited two cases in support of this decision. In one of these cases, *Budinsky v. Corning Glass Works* (1977), the court found that persons of Slavic, Italian, or Jewish origin "are not so commonly identified as 'races' or so frequently subject to that 'racial' discrimination which is the specific and exclusive target of section 1981."[49] In the second case, *Wald v. International Brotherhood of Teamsters* (1980), the court determined that claims of discrimination against Jews are not covered by section 1981.[50] Finally, Judge Ramsey cited a third case, *Marlowe v. Fisher Body Division* (1973), in which the court determined that *some* discrimination against Jews could constitute racial discrimination under section 1981 but only discrimination based on employment.[51]

The last argument that the Shaare Tefila members made relied on section 1985(3). They contended that it applied because the defendants conspired to prevent them from traveling across state lines to their synagogue.[52] Ramsey determined that because he had already dismissed counts one and two of the suit, and because the plaintiffs agreed that section 1985(3) did not apply to the First Amendment in the absence of state action, the remaining issues included only the federal right to travel and the state rights mentioned above. Judge Ramsey found the congregation members' claim insubstantial regarding the right to travel: they maintained that the defendants conspired to prohibit their access to the synagogue, given that it is located close to the state line.

Members who lived in Washington, DC, would be required to cross the line to access it. In *Griffin v. Breckenridge* (1971), the case that the plaintiffs cited as precedent for their claim, the plaintiffs' passage was physically blocked on a state highway.[53] Judge Ramsey found the two situations incommensurable. In that instance as well, he rejected the plaintiffs' claim that section 1985(3) applies to state laws as well as federal laws. Therefore, he concluded that count three was invalid and that state laws do not apply at all in the case.

ANALYSIS OF JUDGE RAMSEY'S DECISION
IN THE FEDERAL DISTRICT COURT

Let's return to Judge Ramsey's analysis in the second count and delve more deeply into his logic. The language of the statutes ascribes the same rights to "all citizens" as they are accorded to "whites." He assumed, along with usual legal presumptions that the color line, specifically regarding the relationship between Black and White people, applied to the precedents he engaged. Two precedents were most significant for his decision in *Shaare Tefila*.

In the first case, *Martinez v. Hazelton Research Animals* (1977), the plaintiff, Edgardo Serpas Martinez, alleged discrimination due to his identity as "Hispanic" under section 1981.[54] In this case, Judge Murray determined first that some Hispanic individuals "may suffer discrimination closely akin to that experienced by members of the black race," but that the plaintiff's legal counsel must demonstrate sufficiently the "alleged racial background of the plaintiff in order to support an allegation of racial discrimination" under the statute.[55] In other words, a Hispanic plaintiff may cite the statute but must prove that he or she is of a "racial background" other than White. Judge Murray did not view "Hispanic" as a racial category but as a "national origin."[56]

Second, Judge Ramsey cited *López v. Sears, Roebuck and Co.* (1980), which relied on *Martinez* as precedent. Ramsey made his determination in *Shaare Tefila* based on the ruling in *López v. Sears*. In the *López* case, Judge Miller adopted Judge Murray's language in *Martinez*, but concluded that in *López* the plaintiff had "clearly stated that the alleged discrimination is based both on nationality (Hispanic) *and* race (brown)."[57] In *Shaare Tefila*, Judge Ramsey focused on the latter basis for the "alleged discrimination": "race (brown)."[58] He writes: "Again, it is, to use Judge Murray's term, the 'racial background' of the plaintiff ('race (brown)') that was found to support a cause of action under the statute. Applying this principle to the instant case, the Court finds that the plaintiffs' allegation that defendants perceive them as racially distinct fails to establish a cause of action under § 1982."[59]

Thus, Ramsey concluded that "Hispanic" does not refer to a racial category, but that "brown" does. Let's consider the origins of "race" within the realm of colonialism and its subsequent hierarchy. Racial categories developed in western European as a means of cataloging geographic regions and people who live in them as embodying certain characteristics.[60] "Hispanic" is a colonial, linguistic term that Spaniards brought to what they called the "New World." In the regions the Spaniards colonized, the Spanish language became dominant, and people in these countries continue to speak it.

As Judge Ramsey noted, "Hispanic" is not considered a racial term in the United States, because it refers to "national origin." But "Hispanic" also may mean much more. It's an identifying feature that *matters* to Americans' racial identity. It figures into the ways one views oneself racially as well as the ways one is viewed racially by others. Anthropologist Jonathan Rosa asserts that the "co-naturalization of language and race," regarding "Hispanic" identity, functions as a "key feature of modern *governance*" in the United States, which means that "languages are perceived as racially embodied and race is perceived as linguistically intelligible."[61] In other words, language and race cannot be separated and are indelible components of dominant discourse as it engages the law.

At some point, US law and government policies may recognize the racial factors of Hispanic identity. In 1985, however, Judge Ramsey determined that race must mean "brown." Therefore, the defendants could not have perceived Shaare Tefila congregation members as a "race," because they are not "brown." For that reason, the plaintiffs could not cite section 1982.

In sum, Judge Ramsey concluded that *Shaare Tefila* could not cite section 1982 for two reasons: first, because Jews are not a distinct race, as the congregation's lawyer stated, and, second because they are not "commonly identified" as a race.[62] He wrote: "as plaintiffs themselves affirm, Jews do not constitute a distinct or recognizable 'race' and are not commonly identified as such."[63] Although it is not clear whether both of these reasons hold individually, it *is* apparent that dominant narratives regarding race play a significant role in Ramsey's ruling. His statement reinforced the concept of race as a socially constructed category, even if that was not his intent, because it demonstrated that the necessary quality for being considered a member of a race is "common" identification. He relied on society at large to determine what race *is* and secondarily, what the subcategories of races are. Although he pointed to precedent to construct his ruling, the cases that he cited also do not clarify how anyone would know what "commonly identified" might mean.[64]

Judge Ramsey's decision, in this case, affirms the significance of "myths" about race. As already noted, Bruce Lincoln defines "myth" as a narrative that is considered "true" and "authoritative" in a particular society.[65] In this case, the "myth," in question, equates either to the dominant discourse and the people who internalize it *or* to some other narrative, such as White supremacy, that people collectively believe. Because they believe it's true, it becomes true for them. Thus, it's socially constructed.

Legal studies scholar Robert Cover describes the role of "myth" as it functions in law. He writes:

> A legal tradition is hence part and parcel of a complex world. The tradition includes not only a *corpus juris* [a body of law], but also a language and a mythos—narratives in which the *corpus juris* is located by those who will act upon it. These myths establish paradigms for behavior. . . . These myths establish a repertoire of moves—a lexicon of normative action—that may be combined into meaningful patterns culled from the meaningful patterns of the past.[66]

In other words, prevailing myths establish precedents, which are dependent on the temporal situation. The myths invoke actions that inform how and why precedents *become* established.

According to the racial myths operative at the time of Judge Ramsey's decision, and substantiated by the congregation's argument—Jews, in the Shaare Tefila case, are "white" and not "brown," and are therefore *not a race*. The predominant view was, and is, that White people are not racialized. Because Jews were not "commonly identified" as a race in the 1980s, they could not claim protection under the Act even though the vandalism itself clearly invoked hatred based on race.

Recall Judge Ramsey's distinction between "rational" and "irrational" perceptions of race. An "irrational" perception would use a logic other than the American emphasis on the color line. "Irrational" perceptions might rely on other bases of supposedly embodied difference, such as the Christian European domination marginalizing Jews throughout the centuries, or caste in South Asia. Embodied distinctions serve bureaucratic leaders, who isolate *which* differences are significant to racialized functions. Judge Ramsey ignored the content of the graffiti when he determined that the discrimination was not based on race but rather on religion. Both the Nazis and the Ku Klux Klan, some of whose ideologies were emblazoned on the synagogue walls, expressed and perform acts of hatred against Jews due to their supposed physical, immutable characteristics: characteristics associated with race rather than religion.

Judge Ramsey's conclusion in *Shaare Tefila* determined how Jewish Americans are defined as subjects before the law. His ruling reified the categorization of Jews as a "religious" group and not as a "racial" group. He determined that Shaare Tefila members experienced discrimination, but also that the discrimination *must* be based on religion since that is the broader category in which Jews were socially located in the 1980s.

The ruling in the civil suit resembled the legal approach to the graffiti that had occurred in the criminal trials of the vandals, in which the *content* of the graffiti had no impact on the ruling. Judge Ramsey's assessment followed a similar process in that he did not address the substance of the graffiti. This decision denied Shaare Tefila members protection from their *experience* of race-based antisemitism resulting from the vandals' acts of graffiti, which drew from an "irrational" conception of race. This understanding of race, however, was not so "irrational," it engaged the blood lineage language of race important to the Nazis and the KKK but was not far removed from the color line, "commonly conceived" as the dominant narrative in the United States.

THE FOURTH CIRCUIT COURT OF APPEALS DECISION

After this decision, Shaare Tefila Congregation members wanted to further pursue the case, so they brought it to the Fourth Circuit Court of Appeals. This Circuit Court has jurisdiction over Maryland and the Eastern Seaboard stretching south to South Carolina. The Court agreed to hear Shaare Tefila's appeal.

Patricia Brannan appealed the case on November 5, 1985, and the Court ruled on the case on March 7, 1986. In appeals court cases, three judges hear cases and a majority decision determines the outcome. In this instance, Judge Kenneth Keller Hall, Judge Francis Dominic Murnaghan Jr., and Judge Harvie Wilkinson III heard the case. They ruled in favor of the defendants for reasons resembling Judge Ramsey's conclusion. Judge Hall wrote the decision, Judge Murnaghan concurred, and Judge Wilkinson concurred in part and dissented in part.

The judges came to the bench with unique and disparate identities based on their childhoods, their religious traditions, and their attitudes toward religion and race, which, to some extent, influenced their decisions in *Shaare Tefila*. Judge Hall came from a working-class background and had a judicial tendency to side with the underdog or underdogs in opposition to large, profitable companies.[67] Because Jewish Americans were perceived as White in the 1980s, however, that may have shaped his perception of the middle- to upper-socioeconomic status of the Shaare Tefila Congregation members. Judge Wilkinson was born to wealthy, conservative parents who approved of integrated schools, which likely guided him to perceive "race" from a White, elite but progressive perspective. Hall and Wilkinson were both raised as Protestants, but Judge Murnaghan was Catholic. His father was an Irish immigrant, so he was second-generation Irish. In *Shaare Tefila*, he referred to his "Hibernian" background as a way of relating to the Jewish synagogue members. He agreed with Hall, however, that the defendants' *perception* of Jews should not be viewed as "fact," and, therefore, he concurred with Hall completely.[68]

The judges' rulings indicate important characteristics of their decision-making based on how they understood the world, which relied, to a large degree, on their upbringing. Their lived experiences informed their political ideology, which aligned with the parties of the presidents who nominated them. All these components, along with the dominant social discourse of the 1980s, informed their decisions in *Shaare Tefila*.

Judge Hall, who wrote the decision, was born as Kenneth Keller "K.K." Hall on February 24, 1918, in Greenview—a community named after his grandfather, V. B. Green—located in Boone County, West Virginia on the Spruce Fork of the Little Coal River.[69] His father died when he was young, and, following his death, his mother married Clarence Charles Hopkins, who later became the sheriff in Boone County. In high school, K.K. was captain of the football team, and he attended college at New River State, which is now West Virginia University Institute of Technology, where he also worked as a janitor.[70] He then transferred to Morris Harvey College in Charleston and then to another college in Washington, DC, at which point he married Gerry Tabor, his high school sweetheart. He enlisted in the Navy in 1942, earned nine battle stars, and was discharged in 1945 with the rank of Lieutenant. Following World War II, he enrolled in law school at West Virginia University and earned his JD in 1948.

Afterward, he went home to Boone County, worked in private practice, and served two terms as mayor of Madison, West Virginia; he then became a candidate for judge of Boone and Lincoln counties, which he won at thirty-four years old, the youngest judge on the circuit.[71] During this time, he allowed Blacks and women to serve as jurors for the first time, giving the defendants, to some degree, a jury of their peers.[72] Although in 1968 he filed for the Democratic nomination for Congress from the Third Congressional District, he later withdrew, and ran for the Supreme Court of Appeals of West Virginia, but was defeated by the incumbent, Fred H. Kaplan. Following the race, he worked for the Social Security Administration as a hearing examiner.

He was nominated to the Southern District of West Virginia by President Nixon on November 22, 1971, in which he assumed the role vacated by John Field and was confirmed by the Senate on December 1, 1971. Following confirmation, he received commission, which means that he began work at the Court. On the one hand, he was a strict constructionist in court, articulating that "judges should only referee the law."[73] But on the other hand, he also identified with the individual, making clear that the Miranda decision, which required police to tell suspects of their constitutional rights, must be upheld.

During this time, he banned West Virginia's outdated abortion law. He also ruled on one of the most famous disasters in coal mining history. In February 1972, a coal-waste refuse pile, deposited by the Buffalo Mining Company, had dammed a stream in Middle Fork Hollow in Logan County, and when it burst, it sent a huge wave down the river to Buffalo Creek Valley, where it killed over 125 people and caused massive property damage.[74] Under Judge Hall's supervision, it was brought to a settlement, with $13.5 million going to the plaintiffs.[75] Perhaps partly because of that settlement, President Gerald Ford nominated Judge Hall to the Fourth Circuit Court of Appeals on August 26, 1976, and he was confirmed by the Senate on September 1, 1976. Two days later he received commission.

In his response to the *Shaare Tefila* case, Judge Hall stated that the court affirmed, on all counts, the district court's decision to dismiss the action. The Circuit Court of Appeals agreed with the District Court that no state action had occurred in the vandalism incident, beginning with the assertion that none was necessary to bring a "full and equal benefit" action under section 1981,[76] citing *Mahone v. Waddle* from the Third Circuit.[77] Hall also upheld the district court's ruling regarding "racial motivation" in the context of section 1981, determining that it was lacking. In response, the congregation argued that because the defendants viewed the congregation as members of an inferior race, their actions constituted racial discrimination and violated section 1982, and cited *Manzanares v. Safeway Stores, Inc.* as an important precedent.[78]

In *Manzanares*, the Mexican American plaintiff claimed that he had been discriminated against in his place of employment due to "race and/or national origin" and that he was "treated differently from Anglo-Americans."[79] The Tenth Circuit Court agreed in with him in an opinion written by Judge Oliver Seth. Incidentally, President John F. Kennedy nominated Judge Seth for this position, and he received commission on June 20, 1962, just a year before the President proposed an extensive civil rights act, and a few months before the president died. What became the Civil Rights Act of 1964 under President Lyndon B. Johnson was a response to White police brutality, including the use of vicious dogs, clubs, and high-pressure fire hoses, against non-violent, mostly Black protesters throughout the South. The intense focus on racial issues, including the Black Power movement and the Brown Berets during the mid-1960s through the 1970s influenced Judge Seth's decision in *Manzanares* that Spanish-speaking or Spanish surnames differentiate Mexican Americans from "Anglos."[80]

In *Manzanares*, Judge Seth stated that "section 1981 makes no mention of race, national origin, or alienage. The only reference is that 'all persons' shall have described rights and benefits of 'white citizens.'"[81] He pointed out that "the measure is group to group, and plaintiff has alleged that the 'group' to which he belongs—those he describes as of Mexican American descent—is to be measured against Anglos as the standard."[82] Judge Seth noted that Manzanares identified as an individual among the Mexican American "group," and that this group may be "measured against that afforded to Anglos."[83] Here, Judge Seth asserted that other judges may have incorrectly understood this issue as "national origin" *alone*; however, he determined that "prejudice is as irrational as is the selection of groups against whom it is directed," and thus, it is "a matter of practice or attitude in the community, it is usage or image based on all mistaken concepts of 'race.'"[84] In other words, even if there is a real category of race, defendants may have also constructed their outlooks from other forms of prejudice that do not coincide with that category, but nevertheless would fit within the classification of section 1981. To defend this statement, he cited the definition of race from Webster's Third New International Dictionary, which includes, in his own writing, "a class of individuals with common characteristics, appearance, or habits." The definition also notes that "RACE is anthropological . . . implying a distinct physical type."[85] So, he argued that the defendants might be "poor anthropologists" but despite that, did not base their judgments on their "mistaken" conceptions.[86] The defendants' prejudice could have included a "real" basis in race, a false one, or any number of other false impressions. Judge Seth asserted that "it would not seem to serve a useful purpose to analyze the *reasons* for the acts of prejudice, as that can be left to the sociologists. We are not considering prejudice based on sex or religion, as those are wholly outside the basic framework of section 1981 as above indicated."[87] He determined that persons with Spanish surnames "is a group who can be measured against the standard group or control group referred to in section 1981."[88] For this reason, Judge Seth ruled that Safeway Stores, Inc. treated Manzanares differently from "Anglos."

Judge Hall, however, found that *Manzanares* did not support the congregation's claim. He emphasized, in his decision, that *Manzanares* differed from *Shaare Tefila*, in that the Tenth Circuit had stated that "Mexican-Americans" as a group are often treated differently from "Anglo-Americans" as a group. Hall argued that the position of Jewish Americans is not "analogous to that of Mexican Americans or others commonly considered to be non-whites."[89]

Because Jewish Americans are not commonly treated differently from other Whites, according to Hall, the claim of racial discrimination rested solely on the argument about the defendants' conception of Jewish Americans. He noted: "*Manzanares* did not hold that a defendant's mere perception of a plaintiff as racially distinct is sufficient to constitute racial discrimination in violation of section 1981."[90] Therefore, he found the plaintiffs' claim inviable. Hall stated that he "sympathize[d]" with Shaare Tefila's position, but to agree with the congregation's claim, in his opinion, "would permit charges of racial discrimination to arise out of nothing more than the subjective, irrational perceptions of defendants."[91] In other words, he understood the dominant view of "race" as "rational" and the defendants' view as "irrational." This statement implied that some types of racial discrimination *are* rational and objective, and some types are not. It reflected the prevailing discourse about race in the 1980s: the categorical differences between races are obvious and normative, and deviating from the standard interpretation of them constitutes irrationality. At stake, however, is who *makes* the decision about racial categorization, and the prospect of people with disreputable and hateful beliefs doing so greatly worried Judge Hall.

In further support of his position, Judge Hall noted the Supreme Court's decision in *Jones v. Alfred H. Mayer Co.* (1968),[92] in which it determined that section 1982 does not cover discrimination based on national origin or religion. Here, he thought of Jews as *only* a religious group.[93] Therefore, he agreed with the district court's ruling on sections 1981 and 1982. Finally, he found that because the congregation claimed protection under section 1985(3) based on sections 1981 and 1982, which he rejected, its last claim was also invalid. Finally, he denied the congregation's claims under the statute regarding state law.

Although anti-Jewish vandalism was a common occurrence in the United States in the mid-1980s, Jewish Americans were simultaneously understood to be White and to have assimilated. Thus, how did the disjuncture between Judge Hall's assumption of Jewish American Whiteness and the vandals' angry insistence on Jewish racial inferiority occur? Because many Jews have appeared to assimilate into the White culture, the vandals defaced Shaare Tefila Congregation to reveal publicly their view that Jews are "different" from "real" White Americans.

Even though Jewish Americans have never been defined legally as non-White, they have been denied the right to exist in certain spaces. Jews were rejected from hotels and faced quotas at colleges and universities.[94] For instance, President Abbott Lawrence Lowell, President of Harvard University from 1909 to1933, was concerned about the "Judaizing" of Ivy Leagues; he then struggled to figure out how to prevent it and did so by changing the definition of "merit" to limit "Hebrews."[95] The historical trope of restricting Jews from certain spaces played a large factor in Jewish decisions to construct their own fraternities as well as country clubs.[96]

Synagogues, kosher markets, and Jewish neighborhoods are all places that embrace Jewish life and continuity. Holocaust memorial museums vow that Jews murdered in the Shoah must be remembered. Both Jews and non-Jews identify these spaces as Jewish ones. But all of them, in various locations throughout the United States, have been defaced, hostages were taken, or people were murdered. Typically, synagogues provide a safe space for Jewish gatherings, learning, and prayer. Thus, when Dominic Queen allegedly stated:

"let's go paint the synagogue," it highlighted the significance of its elevated and *Jewish* space.[97] His alleged statement employs spatial disenfranchisement because, among other factors, it marked Shaare Tefila, otherwise a secure space for Jews, as harmful and dangerous to them in its evocation of long-standing antisemitic racist tropes.

Because Jews historically have assimilated to religious norms in the United States, synagogues have become *religious* spaces. Therefore, Judge Hall automatically could categorize Jews as a "religion," even though the content of the graffiti and the statements made by the defendants were racist. As a result, he deemed all their legal claims invalid.

Let us turn to Judge Murnaghan's concurring opinion, but before doing so, let us consider his life in more detail. On June 20, 1920, Francis Dominic Murnaghan Jr., who became Judge Murnaghan Jr., was born in Baltimore. He grew up in the Pinehurst community and graduated from City College.[98] Afterward, he earned a degree from Johns Hopkins University in 1941, where he played lacrosse and was elected to Phi Beta Kappa. He went on to Harvard Law School and was a member of the Harvard Law Review and graduated in 1948. Throughout World War II, he worked for naval intelligence to break the Japanese code. Between 1950 and 1952, Murnaghan served as a lawyer for the US Office of the High Commissioner for Germany and worked to disassemble Germany's industrial power center.[99] He married Jane Hughes in 1949, an assistant professor at the Hopkins School of Hygiene and Public Health, but they divorced in 1972. In 1984, he married Diana Lee Edwards, an author, art historian, and Smithsonian teacher.[100] Later, he joined the Venable, Baetjer and Howard law firm in 1954 and then became a senior partner. There, he represented the *Baltimore Sun* on First Amendment issues for almost twenty-five years.[101]

His father, a famous mathematician, was born in Ireland as a Catholic. His uncle, whom he met often as a child, lived in Dublin, Ireland, and served as an Irish Supreme Court justice. This relationship inspired Murnaghan Jr. to enter the field of law.[102] Partly because of his trips to his father's home country, he also felt a close connection with his Irish Catholic ancestry.

Their family certainly identified with John F. Kennedy (JFK)—the first Irish American, Catholic president. When Kennedy was elected in November 1960, Judge Murnaghan was forty years old. Three years later, JFK was assassinated. This was devastating for all Americans, but even more so for Catholics and particularly for *Irish* Catholics. Kennedy had proposed a sweeping Civil Rights Act as a formative part of his presidency, which originally outlawed segregation in public places, and prohibited discrimination in employment based on race, color, religion, sex, and national origin, and later based on gender and sexual identity. Finally, it was passed by President Lyndon B. Johnson in 1964 as a tribute to him after his assassination.

Murnaghan was an advocate for equality, particularly in terms of race and gender, and he ran for mayor, in 1967, on a ticket that included Black and Jewish candidates.[103] He defended civil rights activists in the 1960s, who attempted to integrate the Gwynn Oak amusement park in Baltimore County. In 1968, he became the school board president of Baltimore before he resigned in response to a policy dispute over acts of violence at Eastern High School; when civil rights protestors disturbed several board meetings, he refused to call the police.[104] President Jimmy Carter nominated him to the Fourth US Circuit of Appeals on May 8, 1979.[105] During his tenure, Murnaghan wrote more than five hundred opinions and more than 250 concurrences and dissents. His rulings widely impacted civil rights, labor rights, and First Amendment law.[106]

In his concurring opinion for *Shaare Tefila*, Murnaghan made three key points. First, he addressed the behavior of the defendants and deemed it "execrable," then he emphasized how sympathetic he was toward the congregation members regarding the "regrettable indignities" they endured as a result of the defacement.[107] Finally, he noted that he has often sympathized with Jews, more generally, and on previous occasions "as bad as or far worse than the instant one."[108]

Initially, he addressed the congregation's legal arguments, and attested that "the law is grounded on facts, not on misperceptions of fact."[109] Here, he referred to the plaintiffs' argument as "misperceptions of fact." He observed: "For persons of the ilk which the defendants . . . are revealed to be, to have the power to confer jurisdiction on the federal courts would, in all probability, lead to very regrettable consequences."[110] Clearly, like Judge Hall, he thought that the law should not be determined based on the defendants' supposed misperceptions of Jewish racial identification. Specifically, he asserted that "persons" of their "ilk" should not have the power to determine which narratives about identity should reign in the courts and that only certain types of people should decide how racism operates. Murnaghan did not consider the nuance involved in terms of who defines the "facts," which "facts" matter, and for what purpose.

Then, Murnaghan stated that "fracases" such as these belong in the state courts and should not be accorded the "dignity of status of civil rights controversies."[111] In doing so, he reflected on his own identity and his regret over quarrels between Catholics and Protestants in Ireland. Apparently, he conceived of the Shaare Tefila defacement and Protestant/Catholic violence as comparable. He also seemed to understand the defacement as an incident of religiously-based anger. In *Shaare Tefila*, however, no "fracas" existed between the synagogue and a group of local youth and young men; rather it was a one-sided attack with no history of mutual violence.

On the one hand, Murnaghan thought that he understood Jewish experiences of marginalization, acknowledged the history of anti-Judaism, and referenced a personal connection to the events; but on the other hand, he did not find it worthy of the federal court system. Evidently, he interpreted the vandalism of Shaare Tefila as an affront, but not as a "real" civil rights violation. Thus, Judge Murnaghan reiterated Judge Hall's conclusion that the defendants' misperception of a Jewish racial identification did not provide enough basis for the congregation's claim. Perhaps, as a liberal during that time, he had internalized narratives that Catholic and Jewish civil rights were not *as* important as what *he* perceived were racialized ones.

One of the most important factors, however, in the *Shaare Tefila* case at the Fourth Circuit Court of Appeals level was Judge J. Harvie Wilkinson III's dissent, specifically, the language he used to piece apart the concepts of race and racism. For a conservative judge in the 1980s, Judge Wilkinson held some remarkably progressive opinions about how to understand race and ethnicity.[112] It's possible that he drew in part on the logic underlying *Manzanares v. Safeway Stores, Inc.*, in which Judge Seth concluded that "prejudice is as irrational as is the selection of groups against whom it is directed."[113] Wilkinson's view of race followed a similar trajectory, in that he conceived of "all racial prejudice" as "the result" of "irrational perceptions."[114]

Before becoming a judge, he earned his undergraduate degree with honors from Yale University in 1967, during which time he served as chairman of the Conservative Party of the Yale Political Union. After graduating, he published his first book in 1968, about the political scene in Virginia when he was growing up, titled *Harry Byrd and the Changing Face of Virginia Politics*. He joined the army for two years, from the beginning of 1968 to the end of 1969. Then he began law school at the University of Virginia but quit to run for the US Congress, attempting to beat a three-term incumbent Democrat. He lost, so he went back to the law school, graduating with a Juris Doctor in 1972. He then clerked for US Supreme Court Justice Lewis F. Powell Jr. for one year, and joined his former law school as an associate professor. Eventually, he earned full professor status.[115]

Judge Wilkinson was forty-one years old and twenty-four and twenty-six years younger than his compatriots on the US Court of Appeals for the Fourth Circuit when they heard *Shaare Tefila*. President Ronald Reagan nominated him on January 30, 1984, to replace Judge John D. Butzner Jr. Eight months later, on August 13, 1984, he was confirmed by the Senate and received commission.[116] His rulings as a judge were consistently conservative, including a controversial case, *Richmond Medical Center for Women v. Hicks* (2005), in which he upheld a partial-birth abortion ban for the Commonwealth of Virginia.[117]

What would become his firmly integrationist beliefs were based, in large part, on his upbringing in Richmond, Virginia. During the time of the state's Massive Resistance crisis, the desegregation of state schools was blocked by Virginia's state government in 1956. He observed his father, a prominent banker, discussing this with his equally prominent friends, including Lewis Powell, who quietly supported integration. As Governor J. Lindsay Almond closed several public schools in 1958 specifically to prevent desegregation, Wilkinson attended the private St. Christopher's School. Despite his son's attendance at a private school, his father organized business executives who then encouraged Governor Almond to bring the Massive Resistance to an end.[118] His father and friends informed Wilkinson's ideological support of integration, nevertheless, he also referred to them as the "old guard."[119]

Wilkinson wrote about memories of these years that eventually led to his rulings on this topic in his fourth out of six books, published in 1997, *One Nation Indivisible: How Ethnic Separatism Threatens America.*[120] His main concern in this book was civil rights in the context of a national unity that connects peoples of all "ethnic" backgrounds. Wilkinson noted in the preface that the book "reflects his professional outlook" and cited his background as a judge and law professor as important. He acknowledged that "the separatist threat to our country is larger than the law alone."[121] But—and this quote reflected his view about what law *is* and *does*—it "can affect our behavior . . . it can bridge differences or it can open chasms that we cannot close."[122] "Americans," he continued, "have the potential for profound racial fellowship and for intense racial animosity. The law," he then argued, "will have much to say about which side of our country's personality prevails."[123] Wilkinson then explained: "Indeed, it is the function of the law to punish *prejudiced conduct* rather than legitimize the barriers that prejudice attempts to create."[124] This quote directly referenced his dissent in the Shaare Tefila case. What he meant was that the members of the congregation did not have to *consider* themselves a race, or even argue that they were, because the racialized conduct of those who vandalized their synagogue was a crime.

The crux of Judge Wilkinson's response, in which he concurred in part and dissented in part, was his dismay at his fellow judges' reasoning regarding racial discrimination and how it should be determined. He critiqued them for ruling that a case cannot be made based on "nothing more than the subjective, irrational perceptions of defendants."[125] Rather, Judge Wilkinson countered: "*All* racial prejudice is the result of subjective, irrational perceptions, which drain individuals of their dignity because of their perceived equivalence as members of a racial group."[126] He then referred specifically to the Civil Rights Act of 1866, the basis for the legal statutes cited by the congregation, as well as the Civil Rights Act of 1871, as acts passed to "halt the spread of violence and hatred by those motivated by such perceptions."[127] He found the "erroneous" but "all too sincere view" of the defendants that Jews are a race to be sufficient for the congregation's claims under sections 1982 and 1985(3), in particular.[128] In a footnote, he elaborated that while he agreed with his fellow judges that state action is required to cite the "full and equal benefit" clause in 1981, the claim to racial discrimination under section 1982 applies equally to 1981.[129] He also agreed with the court that section 1985(3) claims could not rely solely on the basis of violations of state law, such as the violations that the congregation claimed. Because he thought that the plaintiffs had legitimate cause to claim section 1982, however, he concluded that they could also use this argument to support a conspiracy claim under section 1985(3).

Judge Wilkinson examined the context of the evening in which the deface-ment occurred to understand the behavior of the defendants, and he noted the depositions, unlike the other judges. He mentioned the vandalism of the nearby drugstore with the following phrases and drawings: "Arian [sic] Brotherhood," "White Power," "KKK," an eagle with a swastika, and a Star of David with an arrow through it, and their initials.[130] He addressed the transition from the drugstore to the synagogue and focused on their actions, as well as the evidence that supported their understanding of those actions, rather than the perceptions of the defendants. By interpreting the congrega-tion's argument as he did, and by shifting the focus from *perception* to *action*, he avoided the quandary that the other judges cited as the reason for find-ing on behalf of the defendants—that "perception" alone could potentially qualify as racism.

Wilkinson noted that federal civil rights laws *do* protect citizens from actions based on discriminatory intent. Because all discrimination is based on misperception, the discrimination, in this case, is no different. He concluded: "There is simply no good reason why we should interpret this statute to pro-tect against some forms of racial animus but not others."[131] He maintained that the Civil Rights Act of 1866, the source of sections 1981 and 1982, was "aimed at the evil fostered by racially discriminatory animus."[132] Although Supreme Court cases had determined that the sections deriving from the act do not apply to discrimination based on religion or national origin, Wilkinson argued that the act was intended to be interpreted broadly and to apply to "all persons" in the case of section 1981 and to "all citizens" in section 1982, and not just to freed slaves. For example, he cited *McDonald v. Santa Fe Trail Transportation Co.*, which found that section 1981 is also available to White people.[133] As Wilkinson understood it, the laws "established the right of every person to be free of enumerated deprivations motivated by racial animus."[134]

To support his assertion that racial animus is a legitimate cause for bring-ing a suit based on the statutes found in the Civil Rights Act of 1866, Judge Wilkinson examined the nature of racial prejudice itself. Discrimination and prejudice, he noted, are based on "erroneous perceptions" and on the "misperception of the relevance of racial identity."[135] "Broad, stereotypical assumptions about race" form the basis for both "private" and "official" acts of discrimination.[136] Significantly, he argued that it would be a mistake and even "preposterous" for the courts to require that these beliefs about race be "objectively true" in order to gain protection under the law.[137] In fact, civil rights laws were constructed in the first place to address discriminatory actions based on such "false and reprehensible" beliefs. Wilkinson clarified his position: "It is, of course, clear to this court, the district court, and counsel that Jews are not, under any legitimate view, a distinct race, but are in fact members of a religious community with a rich cultural heritage."[138] Although Wilkinson described Jewish Americans as a religious group, he *also* found the racial attitudes demonstrated by the defendants "clearly within the scope of [Section] 1982."[139]

Judge Wilkinson then situated the racial attitudes of the defendants in the context of historical repression of Jews based on race. He focused on the fallacy of Hitler's belief that Jews are a separate and inferior race and the "vicious mythology" of Nazi race theories.[140] In a footnote, he emphasized the racial character of Nazi ideology and distinguished it from hatred based on national origin to insist that *Shaare Tefila* should not be dismissed as a "national origin" case.[141] Moreover, he noted that "the warped racial classification of Jews" remained a contemporary problem. He cited quotations from neo-Nazi literature to prove that Hitler's racial classification schema regarding Jews remains central to the ideology of US organizations, such as Aryan Nations and the National Socialist Party of America. Furthermore, he noted that racist views of Jews are a "major tenet" of the Ku Klux Klan, as an affidavit for the plaintiff states.[142] Due to these views, Wilkinson emphasized, numerous acts of violence against Jews have occurred. He cited statistics published by the Anti-Defamation League in 1985 regarding 638 anti-Jewish incidents in that year alone as evidence for the prevalence of vandalism attacks and the pressing nature of the problem.[143] Although the Civil Rights Act of 1866 would not cover every crime against Jews, he acknowledged that the ideologies referenced in this particular case were "avowedly racial."[144] He also pointed out that the Ku Klux Klan was one of the same organizations operative in the Reconstruction era, and that its members were among the foremost agents of crimes that the Civil Rights Acts of 1866 and 1871 were passed to prevent.

Wilkinson critiqued the majority for basing its decision on an unworkable argument that relied on the existence of objective racial categories. Not only is the majority's argument inconsistent with the intent of the protection provided by the Civil Rights Acts, Wilkinson asserted, but the court's ruling also resulted in the adoption of the "inappropriate burden of delineating racial distinctions in a context where they are irrelevant and unnecessary."[145] The majority's decision to base its rejection of the plaintiffs' case on the fact that Jewish Americans are not, in fact, a distinct racial group requires the court to support the argument that an objective method of determining racial identification exists and is a prerequisite for coverage under the act.

Applying Robert Cover's argument provides helpful insight here. Cover writes: "Law may be viewed as a system of tension or a bridge linking a concept of reality to an imagined alternative—that is, as a connective between two states of affairs, both of which can be represented in their normative significance only through the devices of narrative."[146] In other words, Wilkinson asserts an approach quite disparate from Judges Ramsey and Murnaghan: one in which "race" is perceived rather than actuated. These views of "race" imagine very different conceptions of what it means, and they describe and represent "race" in separate ways.

Wilkinson admonished the court for constructing this argument and for not providing any guidance about how courts would undertake the task of objectively determining racial identification. He offered, instead, a critique of existing legal methods used to understand what constitutes race. First, he argued that scientific and anthropological methods are insufficient. He maintained: "Scientists engaged in racial classification recognize that the choice of characteristics used to determine racial groups is arbitrary and depends upon the reason for classification rather than objective reality."[147] In addition, he asserted that such classifications are not fixed but fluid, reaffirming the inexact nature of the classification in the first place. Second, he argued that scientific categories are inappropriate and "irrelevant to the determination of the protection of a statute addressed to a social phenomenon."[148] He noted that it is not the scientific classifications but "distorted social perceptions" that form the basis for acts of racial violence. Wilkinson cited scholars of race, such as Ashley Montagu and Gunnar Myrdal, as well as the UNESCO statement on race from 1950, to emphasize the significance of social over scientific conceptions of race.[149] He concluded that because social perceptions of race are ultimately the reigning factor in cases of discrimination, "To limit [section] 1982 to discrimination against scientifically established racial groups would deprive the remedy of its force in an artificial and disingenuous manner."[150]

After Wilkinson rejected the feasibility of the scientific test in race discrimination cases, he assessed the other main legal approach to cases regarding race: the "common perception" test. The court majority determined that sections 1981 and 1982 do not apply to Jews because "the position of Jews in this society [is not] analogous to that of Mexican-Americans or others commonly considered to be non-white."[151] The majority opinion held that Jews are not a race because they are not commonly perceived to be one; hence, the common perception test does not result in legal protection under the statutes.

Wilkinson faulted this argument on several counts. First, he pointed out that the misperception that Jews are a race is shared by a much larger number of individuals than the court considered. Therefore, the plaintiffs should be allowed to prove the extent of this misperception before the court determines that it is not widely shared. Second, the extent and breadth of racial misperception are not a controlling factor in whether the congregation merits protection. As Wilkinson wrote: "The very purpose of the Civil Rights Acts was to ensure that the most bigoted people are not permitted to translate their impulses into tangible harms. Protection against the acts of racial prejudice is necessary whether the views are widely held or idiosyncratic."[152] The fact that courts find "common perception" tests convenient, he concluded, should not prevent the plaintiffs from demonstrating the racial character of the discrimination. Finally, Wilkinson insisted that the plaintiffs must be permitted to make the argument they did because otherwise, the court is in the position of having to determine racial boundaries, thus perpetuating the racial prejudice that the civil rights laws were designed to protect.[153]

Wilkinson determined that the majority's approach required the construction of a "list" of races according to common perception, which he found objectionable on two counts. First, such a classification system would serve only to continue practices of racial prejudice. Second, because the racial nature of the acts, in this case, was "clear and compelling," the court's approach was especially disturbing. He noted that it was only due to the court's requirement for racial distinction that it rejected the plaintiffs' argument since in *McDonald v. Santa Fe Trail Transportation Co.* the Supreme Court assessed the legislative history of the Civil Rights Act of 1866 and determined that it can apply to White people as well.

Finally, Wilkinson disputed the majority's argument that the "plaintiffs are limited to some unidentified state law remedy."[154] To insist the plaintiffs rely on state courts belies the reasoning behind civil rights acts in the first place, he argued. He asserted that when Congress passed the Civil Rights Act of 1866, it "intended at the very least to supplement state laws."[155] Furthermore, he stated, that the Civil Rights Act of 1871 "was designed precisely to provide a federal remedy for activities such as those found in this case."[156] Therefore, he emphasized: "To now relegate these matters exclusively to state law simply disregards the nature and scope of federal remedies provided by Congress and the unique capacity of federal law to voice a strong and uniform commitment to the eradication of discrimination in our midst."[157]

Judge Wilkinson concluded by stating that he would reverse the judgment of the court and find the plaintiffs' claims sufficient to seek protection under sections 1982 and 1985(3).[158] He wrote:

As the property, indeed the place of worship, of this community was desecrated for reasons and with symbols that resorted unabashedly to race, I would hold the congregation of Shaare Tefila Synagogue entitled to the protection of our civil rights laws. To do otherwise is to blind ourselves as a nation to the real nature of race prejudice, and to leave American citizens open to the depredations of racial violence—the very acts against which Congress more than a century ago had sought to protect them.[159]

In other words, Wilkinson reported that not to hold the defendants accountable was to fail to see what racial prejudice is and how it works. Race is not marked or defined by "color," necessarily, as the prevailing discourse concludes; but, as sociologists, Michael Omi and Howard Winant posit, it is due to "the social conflicts and interests" that refer to "different types of human bodies."[160]

Judge Wilkinson's response is notably distinct from those of the other judges for his views on race and discrimination. He rejected Judges Hall's and Murnaghan's interpretations of racial discrimination as necessarily "logical" and based on factual racial categories. Further, he argued that all racial discrimination is based on misperception—the misperception that certain groups of people are inherently better or worse than others. Hence, Wilkinson did not dispute race *itself* as misperception, only the negative stereotypes that some individuals make on a racial basis. Wilkinson's approach to race disregarded the pattern exhibited by Judges Ramsey and Hall, who insisted that some proof that Jews are a race or are commonly perceived as such must exist for the court to grant the congregation protection under the statutes it claims. For Wilkinson, although racial categories inform social life, they are not "objective" or "factual"; and he noted that scientific claims depend on scientists' objectives, inferring that no one scientific "answer" to race exists.

Wilkinson's reasoning was informed by his attention not just to the synagogue's argument but also to the incident that occurred which led to the civil suit in the first place. He examined the content of the graffiti, the defendants' vandalism earlier that evening, and the depositions in support of his position that the defendants' actions were indeed based on racism. He noted the history of the Nazis and the Ku Klux Klan as two groups that have targeted Jews for racial reasons, and he reminded the court that the Civil Rights Acts of 1866 and 1871 were designed to prevent, in part, crimes committed by the Klan. The other judges, in contrast, while claiming that the case belonged in the state court, affirmed the legitimacy of the only option available in the state court, which was to treat this vandalism case—replete with its racist imagery—the same as any other vandalism incident.

Judge Wilkinson's partial dissent deeply impressed some of the congregation members who were involved in the case, surprised and heartened Shaare

Tefila's lawyers—namely Patricia Brannan—and ultimately seemed to be expedient to Shaare Tefila's case in the Supreme Court.[161] Indeed, Brannan noted in an interview that Wilkinson's dissent read like a letter to the Supreme Court on behalf of the congregation.[162] In his ruling, Judge Wilkinson acknowledged the contingency of racial divisions as based on social constructions, as Judge Ramsey did, but he took the logical step of decrying *all* racism as misconstrued and faulty, rather than requiring that the vandals' actions *rationally* conform to contemporary dominant attitudes about Jews.

CONCLUSION

The disparate approaches among the Fourth Circuit Court of Appeals judges are striking because they highlight different legal interpretations of discrimination and of race, demonstrating the lack of legal consistency in handling cases of racism, especially, in this case—racial antisemitism—and the lack of a standard legal definition of "race."

In *Shaare Tefila*, Judge Wilkinson posed the first of two unexpected outcomes regarding the dominant American discourse in the 1980s. Unlike Judge Murnaghan who identified with the congregation members as a marginalized person yet concurred with Judge Hall, he did not agree entirely with Judge Ramsey's ruling. Whereas all three of the other judges interpreted the case similarly and without much demonstrated need to defend their determinations, Judge Wilkinson questioned the very foundations of their claims. For him, "race" is not limited to the narrow discourse of acknowledged and acceptable contemporary perceptions but encompasses other notions of seemingly inherent difference that continue to permeate American culture in generally unacknowledged and, therefore, less easily perceptible ways. And for Judge Wilkinson, "discrimination" is *not* limited to bounded civil rights categories that are detached from histories of marginalization but reflect misperceptions of all kinds that are historically grounded in the terrorization, oppression, and murder of specific groups. He noted that some forms of racial discrimination, such as Nazism, have traversed oceans and have become implanted on American soil, albeit without the same widespread support.

For Judge Wilkinson, the defacement of Shaare Tefila did not occur in a vacuum, devoid of discursive frameworks or historical connections. Racism does not involve only the socially acknowledged divisions of race based on color or "common perception." He understood and appreciated the broad spectrum of historical narratives that inform identity-based crimes. His conception of Jewish identification, in terms of civil rights categories and legal protection, accounted for a larger picture than the dominant American discourse of the 1980s, in which Jews were defined as a "religious group" and as "white." At the same time, he ultimately did not attempt to define Jewish identification in *legal* terms, because he understood that a variety of qualifiers can inform (mis)perceptions of Jewish identification, as a whole.

Judges Ramsey, Hall, and Murnaghan were all persuaded by the prevailing American discourse about race—that the color line governs all race-related issues.[163] Likewise, they were certain that race is an objective "fact" that can be argued, and that Jewish Americans do *not* experience race-related forms of marginalization. The neo-Nazi and Ku Klux Klan–related vandalism did not convince them that race might be a factor, despite the history of racialization that Jews have endured since the first race-based law governing the *limpieza de sangre* of *conversos* in 1449 in Toledo, Spain.[164] At the conclusion of the lower courts' decisions, Jewish Americans were identified only as a "religion," and that status remained until the Shaare Tefila synagogue had the opportunity to appeal to the US Supreme Court in 1987. Given the Fourth Circuit Court judges' decisions on the three statutes, Patricia Brannan and her legal team narrowed their focus to section 1982.

NOTES

1. One exception is Virgil Philip Marlowe, who sued under the race-based section 1981 along with his other legal claims in Marlowe v. Fisher Body 489 F.2d 1057 (1973). Judge Pierce Lively determined that recovery based on acts in violation of Section 1981 after September 29, 1968, were allowed.

2. Title VII of the Civil Rights Act of 1964 "prohibits discrimination by covered employers on the basis of race, color, religion, or national origin," and Title VIII of the Civil Rights Act of 1968 "prohibits discrimination in the sale, rental and financing of dwellings based on race, color, religion, sex or national origin."

3. "State Action Requirement," Legal Information Institute, Cornell University Law School, accessed August 18, 2021, www.law.cornell.edu/wex/state_action _requirement.

4. "Free Exercise Clause," Legal Information Institute, Cornell University Law School, accessed June 6, 2016, www.law.cornell.edu/wex/free_exercise_clause. See also John Witte, Jr. and Joel A. Nichols, *Religion and the American Constitutional Experiment, Third Edition*, (Boulder, CO: Westview Press, 2011), 118.

5. "Cantwell v. Connecticut." *Oyez*, accessed August 18, 2021, www.oyez.org/ cases/1940-1955/310us296.

6. "Everson v. Board of Education of the Township of Ewing," *Oyez*, accessed August 18, 2021. www.oyez.org/cases/1940-1955/330us1.The question at stake was whether the New Jersey law should authorize reimbursement for transportation costs by local school boards. Ninety-six percent of the private schools that benefited were Catholic. Arch R. Everson, taxpayer in Ewing Township, argued that this indirect aid to religion violated both the New Jersey state Constitution and the First Amendment.

The Court held that the law did not violate the Constitution because, according to Justice Black, it did not pay money to parochial schools and it did not assist them directly in any way.

7. John Witte Jr. and Joel A. Nichols, *Religion and the American Constitutional Experiment* (New York: Oxford, 2016 [fourth edition]), 26.

8. History.com Editors, "The Settlement of Maryland," History (A&E Television Networks, March 23, 2021 [February 9, 2010]), accessed December 30, 2021, www .history.com/this-day-in-history/the-settlement-of-maryland.

9. Historian David Sehat asserts: "Protestant Christian influence in U.S. history was long-standing, widespread, and from the perspective of dissenters, coercive," and he concludes, "Religious views pervaded law at all levels." David Sehat, *The Myth of American Religious Freedom* (New York: Oxford University Press, 2011), 2. Historian of religions Daniel Dubuisson rightly asserts that the origin of "religion" is inherently Christian, because it was bound up with construction of the Enlightenment, and it was the co-creation of the "West." Daniel Dubuisson, *The Western Construction of Religion: Myths, Knowledge, and Ideology* trans. William Sayers (Baltimore, MD: Johns Hopkins University Press, 2007 [2003]), 9.

10. John Witte Jr. and Joel A. Nichols, *Religion and the American Constitutional Experiment* (New York: Oxford, 2016 [fourth edition]), 45. These authors focus on the role of religious belief in legal rulings.

11. Eric Michael Mazur, *The Americanization of Religious Minorities: Confronting the Constitutional Order* (Baltimore, MD: Johns Hopkins University Press, 1999), 9.

12. Jonathan D. Sarna and David G. Dalin, *Religion and State in the American Jewish Experience* (Notre Dame, Indiana: University of Notre Dame Press, 1997), 9, 139–65. Jews and Christians wrote important letters and judicial statements regarding Sunday laws in 1838, 1845, 1848, 1893, 1908, 1915, and 1961.

13. John Witte Jr. and Joel A. Nichols, *Religion and the American Constitutional Experiment* (Boulder, CO: Westview Press, 2011), 133.

14. Jonathan D. Sarna and David G. Dalin, *Religion and State in the American Jewish Experience* (Notre Dame, Indiana: University of Notre Dame Press, 1997), 159. They note that *Braunfield v. Brown* and *Gallagher v. Crown Kosher Super Market*, both Jewish plaintiffs, challenged state laws via the Free Exercise Clause and argued that they were prevented from exercising their religion because they had to close their stores on both Saturday and Sunday; and *McGowan v. Maryland* and *Two Guys from Harrison-Allentown, Inc. v. McGinley* both involved people selling merchandise banned by state laws on Sunday, such as floor wax and loose-leaf notebooks, and a long list of prohibitions, respectively. The sellers brought their claims to court via the Establishment Clause.

15. John Witte Jr. and Joel A. Nichols, *Religion and the American Constitutional Experiment* (New York: Oxford, 2016 [fourth edition]), 205.

16. John Witte Jr. and Joel A. Nichols, *Religion and the American Constitutional Experiment* (New York: Oxford, 2016 [fourth edition]), 206.

17. Strict scrutiny, Legal Information Institute, Cornell Law School, accessed January 24, 2022. www.law.cornell.edu/wex/strict_scrutiny.

18. John Witte Jr. and Joel A. Nichols, *Religion and the American Constitutional Experiment* (New York: Oxford, 2016 [fourth edition]), 142.

19. For a discussion of race as a legal concept, see Sharona Hoffman, "Is There a Place for 'Race' as a Legal Concept?," *Arizona State Law Journal* 36 (2004): 1093–1159.

20. For an informative article on the limits of religion-based protection in civil rights laws, see Kenneth L. Marcus, "The Most Important Right We Think We Have but Don't—Freedom from Religious Discrimination in Education," *Nevada Law Journal* 7 (2006): 171–81.

21. See Laura Levitt, "Other Moderns, Other Jews: Revisiting Jewish Secularism in American," in *Secularisms*, ed. Janet R. Jakobsen and Ann Pellegrini (Durham, NC: Duke University Press, 2008).

22. See Eric L. Goldstein, *The Price of Whiteness: Jews, Race, and American Identity* (Princeton, NJ: Princeton University Press, 2006); Karen Brodkin, *How Jews Became White Folks and What That Says about Race in America* (New Brunswick, NJ: Rutgers University Press, 1999); Matthew Frye Jacobson, *Whiteness of a Different Color: European Immigrants and the Alchemy of Race* (Cambridge, MA: Harvard, 1998).

23. For a detailed discussion of race in significant Supreme Court decisions during the Rehnquist years, see Brian K. Landsberg, "Race and the Rehnquist Court," *Tulane Law Review* 66 (1992): 1267–1340.

24. "Bias," Legal Dictionary, Law.com, dictionary.law.com/Default. aspx?selected=61

25. For a discussion of the judicial and legislative enforcement of the Civil Rights Act of 1866 prior to 1989, see Robert J. Kaczorowski, "The Enforcement of the Civil Rights Act of 1866: A Legislative History in Light of *Runyon v. McCrary*," *The Yale Law Journal* 98 (1989): 565–95. For a focused analysis of the Supreme Court's distinction between economic liberty cases and equal rights cases between 1886 and 1908, see David Bernstein, "The Supreme Court and Civil Rights, 1886–1908," *The Yale Law Journal* (1990): 725–44.

26. Note: This book uses the terms "socio-legal location" and "social location" to discuss how the judges attempted to situate Jewish identification in relation to the legal categories of religion and race, since those are the civil rights categories relevant to the argument at stake.

27. Thank you to my colleague and friend, Silas Allard, for explaining the necessity of clearly highlighting the structural relationship between race and social resources.

28. Plessy v. Ferguson, 163 U.S. 537, 559 (1896). Neil Gotanda, "A Critique of 'Our Constitution is Color-Blind,'" in *Critical Race Theory: The Key Writings that Formed the Movement* eds. Kimberlé Crenshaw, Neil Gotanda, Gary Peller, and Kendall Thomas (New York: The New Press, 1995), 257.

29. Cedric Merlin Powell, "How Race-Neutral Rulings by the Supreme Court Perpetuate Inequalities," *Scholars Strategy Network*, August 8, 2019, accessed August 25, 2021, scholars.org/contribution/how-race-neutral-rulings-supreme-court-perpetuate-inequalities. Eight states, including California, Michigan, Nebraska, Arizona,

Oklahoma, Florida, Washington, and New Hampshire, to date, have abolished race-based affirmative action in colleges and universities.

30. Neil Gotanda, "A Critique of 'Our Constitution is Color-Blind,'" in *Critical Race Theory: The Key Writings that Formed the Movement* eds. Kimberlé Crenshaw, Neil Gotanda, Gary Peller, and Kendall Thomas (New York: The New Press, 1995), 257.

31. Khaled Beydoun, "Faith in Whiteness: Free Exercise of Religion as Racial Expression" in *Iowa Law Review* 105, no. 4 (May 2020): 1487.

32. Marcia Graham Synott, "Anti-Semitism and American Universities: Did Quotas Follow the Jews?" in *Anti-Semitism in American History*, ed. David A. Gerber (Urbana: University of Illinois Press, 1986), 234.

33. Sharae Wheeler, "DeFunis v. Odegaard: Another Kind of "Jewish Problem," Seattle Civil Rights and Labor History Project, accessed December 23, 2021, depts.washington.edu/civilr/DeFunis.htm.

34. For examples of antisemitic murders, see the following: on April 13, 2014, at a Jewish Community Center of Greater Kansas City in Overland Park, Kansas, seventy-three-year-old Frazier Glenn Miller, Jr. opened fire and shot three people: Reat Underwood, fourteen, his grandfather, William Corporon, sixty-nine, and Terri LaManno, who were actually Christians. Due to the prevalence, these days, of Christians, some of whom are White and are indistinguishable from Jews who pass as White, some antisemitic killers mistake them for Jews. The center had been providing space for the performance of *To Kill a Mockingbird*, a play based on a novel dealing with racial issues. Laura Bauer, Dave Helling, and Brian Burnes, "Man with History of Anti-Semitism Jailed in Fatal Shooting of Three at Johnson County Jewish Centers," *Kansas City Star*, April 13, 2014, www.kansascity.com/news/local/article344979/Man-with-history-of-anti-Semitism-jailed-in-fatal-shooting-of-three-at-Johnson-County-Jewish-centers.html, accessed April 5, 2018. *Jerusalem Post* notes: "None of the victims was Jewish, but Miller assumed they were when he shot them." JTA, "Kansas City JCC Shooter Sentenced to Death," *Jerusalem Post*, Diaspora, November 11, 2015, www.jpost.com/Diaspora/Kansas-City-JCC-shooter-sentenced-to-death-432637, accessed April 5, 2018. In another example, this time a shooting targeting a kosher grocery store, two assailants killed a police detective at Bayview Cemetery and three people, including store-owner Mindy Ferencz, male employee Douglas Miguel Rodriguez, and rabbinical student Moshe Deutsch, at the JC Kosher Supermarket in Jersey City, New Jersey. In the gun battle that followed, the assailants were also killed. In this instance, the perpetrators were Black Israelites. Ali Gold and Michael Watkins, "Suspect in Jersey City Linked to Black Hebrew Israelite Group," *New York Times*, December 11, 2019, www.nytimes.com/2019/12/11/nyregion/jersey-city-shooting.html, accessed January 31, 2020. On July 10, 2009, eighty-nine-year-old James Wenneker von Brunn killed a security guard, Stephen Tyrone Johns, who was Black; he had spent six years protecting the Holocaust museum in Washington, DC. Von Brunn attacked Johns on the day that the museum was supposed to present a play based on the life of Anne Frank, which he had repeatedly denounced as a hoax. Author unknown, "Guard Killed During Shooting at

Holocaust Museum," Washington CNN, June 10, 2009, www.cnn.com/2009/CRIME /06/10/museum.shooting/, accessed April 5, 2018.

35. See W. E. B. Du Bois, *The Souls of Black Folk* (New York: Dover Publications, 1994 [1903]), 9, 111–12.

36. Krysan, M., and Moberg, S. Trends in Racial Attitudes. University of Illinois Institute of Government and Public Affairs, accessed August 26, 2016, igpa.uillinois. edu/programs/racial-attitudes.

37. Krysan, M., & Moberg, S. Trends in Racial Attitudes. University of Illinois Institute of Government and Public Affairs, accessed August 26, 2016, igpa.uillinois. edu/programs/racial-attitudes.

38. *Equal Employment Opportunity Commission v. International Business Machines Corporation*, 583 F. Supp. 875 (D. Md. 1984).

39. 42 U.S.C. 1981, emphasis mine.

40. Shaare Tefila Congregation v. Cobb, 606 F. Supp. 1504 (1985).

41. Mahone v. Waddle, 564 F.2d 1018 (3d Cir.1977).

42. 42 U.S.C. 1982.

43. Shaare Tefila Congregation v. Cobb, 606 F. Supp. 1504, 1506 (1985). Note: In Judge Ramsey's conception of "reality," he relies on "scientific evidence" as one of the bases in his approach—one which arguably went out of date with the *U.S. v. Thind* case in 1922.45. In this case, an Indian man, Bhagat Singh Thind, claimed "scientific evidence," citing that because he is "Aryan," therefore he is "white." Thind pointed to this evidence in order to claim US citizenship, but the judge denied his claim for the same reason, marking the end of "scientific evidence" as the basis for racial pre-requisite cases. Not only does Ramsey utilize this schema, but in the Fourth Circuit Court of Appeals, Judge Hall and Judge Murnaghan seem to do so as well. Ian Haney Lopez (1996) and John Tehranian (2000), among others, have discussed such cases as (what Lopez deems) "racial prerequisite" cases, in which immigrants to the US attempted to claim the status of "white" people so that they could become citizens. This is Lopez's term for suits in which noncitizens attempted to become citizens on the basis of claiming to be "white." See Ian Haney Lopez, *White by Law: The Legal Construction of Race, Tenth Anniversary Edition* (New York: New York University Press, 2006) and John Tehranian, "Performing Whiteness: Naturalization Litigation and the Construction of Racial Identity in America" in *The Yale Law Journal* 109, no. 4 (January 2000).

44. Shaare Tefila Congregation v. Cobb, 606 F. Supp. 1508 (1985).

45. Shaare Tefila Congregation v. Cobb, 606 F. Supp. 1508 (1985).

46. Shaare Tefila Congregation v. Cobb, 606 F. Supp. 1508 (1985).

47. Shaare Tefila Congregation v. Cobb, 606 F. Supp. 1508 (1985), (emphasis added).

48. Ian Haney Lopez, *White by Law: The Legal Construction of Race, Tenth Anniversary Edition* (New York: New York University Press, 2006), 6.

49. Budinsky v. Corning Glass Works, 425 F. Supp. 786 (W.D. Pa. 1977).

50. Wald v. International Brotherhood of Teamsters, 104 U.S. 503 (1983).

51. Marlowe v. Fisher Body, 489 F.2d 1057 (1973).

52. Many members lived across state lines.

53. Griffin v. Breckenridge, 403 U.S. 88 (1971).

54. Martinez v. Hazelton Research Animals, 430 F. Supp. 186 (D. Md. 1977).

55. Martinez v. Hazelton Research Animals, 430 F. Supp. 186 (D. Md. 1977).

56. Martinez v. Hazelton Research Animals, 430 F. Supp. 186 (D. Md. 1977).

57. Lopez v. Sears, Roebuck and Co., 493 F. Supp. 801 (D. Md. 1980). (emphasis added)

58. Shaare Tefila Congregation v. Cobb, 606 F. Supp. 1504, 1508 (1985).

59. Shaare Tefila Congregation v. Cobb, 606 F. Supp. 1504, 1508 (1985).

60. See, descriptions of race in these early texts from the 1634 and 1795, respectively: François Bernier, "A New Division of the Earth" in *The Idea of Race*, eds. Robert Bernasconi and Tommy L. Lott (Indianapolis, IN: Hackett Publishing Company, Inc., 2000 [1965]), 1–4; Johann Friedrich Blumenbach, "On the Natural Variety of Mankind" in *The Idea of Race*, eds. Robert Bernasconi and Tommy L. Lott (Indianapolis, IN: Hackett Publishing Company, Inc., 2000 [1965]), 27–37. See also, Irene Silverblatt, *Modern Inquisitions: Peru and the Colonial Origins of the Civilized World* (Durham, NC: Duke University Press, 2004), 3–5. And Michael Omi and Howard Winant, *Racial Formation in the United States from the 1960s to the 1990s, Second Edition* (New York: Routledge, 1994), 66.

61. Jonathan Rosa, *Looking Like a Language, Sounding Like a Race: Raciolinguistic Ideologies and the Learning of Latinidad* (New York: Oxford University Press, 2019), 2, emphasis added.

62. The "common knowledge" test has a legal history in "racial prerequisite" cases beginning almost as early as the Civil Rights Act of 1866, sections of which Shaare Tefila Congregation cited for civil rights protection. Racial prerequisite cases were brought by US inhabitants hoping to gain citizenship despite the racially restrictive naturalization law imposed by Laws of 1790 (Act of March 26, 1790, ch. 3. I Stat. 103). The first of the cases to rely at least partially on "common knowledge" occurred in 1878: In re Ah Yup, I F.Cas. 223 (C.C.D.Cal. 1878).

63. Shaare Tefila Congregation v. Cobb, 606 F. Supp. 1504, 1508 (1985).

64. See extensive coverage of the "common knowledge" test in the following texts: Ian Haney Lopez, *White by Law: The Legal Construction of Race, Tenth Anniversary Edition* (New York: New York University Press, 2006), 66–72; John Tehranian, *Whitewashed: America's Invisible Middle Eastern Minority* (New York: New York University Press, 2009), 43–63.

65. Bruce Lincoln, *Discourse and the Construction of Society: Comparative Studies of Myth, Ritual, and Classification* (New York: Oxford University Press, 1989), 24.

66. Robert Cover, "Nomos and Narrative," in *Narrative, Violence, and the Law: The Essays of Robert Cover*, eds. Martha Minow, Michael Ryan, and Austin Sarat (Ann Arbor: University of Michigan Press, 1993), 101.

67. Forest J. Bowman, Esq., The History of the United States District Court for the Southern District of West Virginia, 109 *W. Va. L. Rev.*, 725 (2007), 771. Available at: researchrepository.wvu.edu/wvlr/vol109/iss3/8

68. *Shaare Tefila Congregation v. Cobb*, 785 F.2d 523, 528 (1986).

69. Forest J. Bowman, Esq., *The History of the United States District Court for the Southern District of West Virginia*, pp. 768–69, accessed February 8, 2021, www .wvsd.uscourts.gov/pdfs/historysdwv.pdf.

70. Forest J. Bowman, Esq., *The History of the United States District Court for the Southern District of West Virginia*, p. 769, accessed February 8, 2021, www.wvsd .uscourts.gov/pdfs/historysdwv.pdf.

71. Forest J. Bowman, Esq., *The History of the United States District Court for the Southern District of West Virginia*, p. 769, accessed February 8, 2021, www.wvsd .uscourts.gov/pdfs/historysdwv.pdf.

72. Maryclaire Dale, "Longtime Judge Kenneth K. Hall Dies at 81," *Charleston Gazette*, July 9, 1999, at 1A in Forest J. Bowman, Esq., *The History of the United States District Court for the Southern District of West Virginia*, p. 770, accessed February 8, 2021, www.wvsd.uscourts.gov/pdfs/historysdwv.pdf.

73. Forest J. Bowman, Esq., *The History of the United States District Court for the Southern District of West Virginia*, p. 771, accessed February 8, 2021, www.wvsd .uscourts.gov/pdfs/historysdwv.pdf.

74. Gerald M. Stern, *The Buffalo Creek Disaster: How the Survivors of One of The Worst Disasters in Coal-Mining History Brought Suit Against the Coal Company— And Won Second Edition* (New York: Vintage Books, 2008 [1976]).

75. Forest J. Bowman, Esq., *The History of the United States District Court for the Southern District of West Virginia*, p. 772, accessed February 8, 2021, www.wvsd .uscourts.gov/pdfs/historysdwv.pdf.

76. Section 1981 protects the following rights: "to make and enforce contracts, to sue, be parties, give evidence, and to [access to] the full and equal benefit of all laws and proceedings for the security of persons and property as is enjoyed by white citizens." 42 U.S.C. 1981.

77. Mahone v. Waddle, 564 F.2d 1018 (3d Cir. 1977).

78. 593 F.2d 968 (10th Cir. 1979). Note: For further discussion of the significance of the *Manzanares* ruling, see Joseph Avanzato, "Section 1982 and Discrimination against Jews: *Shaare Tefila Congregation v. Cobb*," *American University Law Review* 37, no. 1 (1987): 238.

79. The quotations here are from Judge Hall's decision, not the *Manzanares* case itself.

80. Manzanares v. Safeway Stores, Inc. 593 F.2d 968 (10th Cir. 1979).

81. Manzanares v. Safeway Stores, Inc. 593 F.2d 968 (10th Cir. 1979).

82. Manzanares v. Safeway Stores, Inc. 593 F.2d 968 (10th Cir. 1979).

83. Manzanares v. Safeway Stores, Inc. 593 F.2d 968 (10th Cir. 1979).

84. Manzanares v. Safeway Stores, Inc. 593 F.2d 968 (10th Cir. 1979).

85. Manzanares v. Safeway Stores, Inc. 593 F.2d 968 (10th Cir. 1979).

86. Manzanares v. Safeway Stores, Inc. 593 F.2d 968 (10th Cir. 1979).

87. Manzanares v. Safeway Stores, Inc. 593 F.2d 968 (10th Cir. 1979).

88. Manzanares v. Safeway Stores, Inc. 593 F.2d 968 (10th Cir. 1979).

89. Shaare Tefila Congregation v. Cobb, 785 F.2d 523, 527 (1986).

90. Shaare Tefila Congregation v. Cobb, 785 F.2d 523, 526 (1986).

91. Shaare Tefila Congregation v. Cobb, 785 F.2d 523, 527 (1986).

92. In this case, the Supreme Court determined that 42 U.S.C. § 1982 was intended to prohibit *private* acts of discrimination which violate property rights.

93. Jones v. Alfred H. Mayer Co., 392 U.S. 409 (1968).

94. For discrimination against Jews at hotels, see "60% Drop in Anti-Jewish Bias Since 1957 Noted in Hotel Study," *New York Times*, January 31, 1964, www.nytimes.com/1964/01/31/archives/60-drop-in-antijewish-bias-since-1957-noted-in-hotel-study.html; "Anti-Jewish Discrimination in American Hotels Declines Sharply," *Jewish Telegraphic Agency*, accessed June 21, 2022, www.jta.org/archive/anti-jewish-discrimination-in-american-hotels-declines-sharply; "Not So Grand: Discrimination at the Hotels, Museum of the White Mountains," *Plymouth State University*, accessed June 21, 2022, www.plymouth.edu/mwm/exhibitions/the-grand-hotels-of-the-white-mountains-online-exhibition/not-so-grand/; For quotas at colleges and universities, see Marcia Graham Synott, "Anti-Semitism and American Universities: Did Quotas Follow the Jews?" in *Anti-Semitism in American History*, ed. David A. Gerber (Urbana, IL: University of Illinois Press, 1986).

95. See Annalise E. Glauz-Todrank, " 'Good Schools' and Jewish Americans: The Racialization of Prestige in the Early Twentieth Century,'" American Academy of Religion, 2016, Unpublished paper. "Beginning in 1922, investigation into the personal lives of students came to the forefront. At Harvard, this meant that a letter of reference became mandatory, students were asked to provide a photograph, and 'applicants were required to answer questions on 'Race and Color,' 'Religious Preference,' 'Maiden name of Mother,' 'What change, if any, has been made since birth in your own name, or that of your father. (Explain fully).' The high school principal was supposed to fill out 'religious preference' form for the students, which included the options of 'Protestant,' 'Catholic,' 'Hebrew,' and 'Unknown.' The concept of 'merit,' therefore, meant that particular components of the students' *identities*—their name changes and their 'religions'—could govern their acceptance into Ivy League universities, because they would be disqualified based on these attributes." (4) For further information, see Jerome Karabel, *The Chosen: The Hidden History of Admission and Exclusion at Harvard, Yale, and Princeton* (Boston, MA: Houghton Mifflin Company, 2005).

96. For Jewish fraternities, see Marianne R. Sanua, "Jewish College Fraternities in the United States, 1895–1968: An Overview," *Journal of American Ethnic History* 19, no. 2 (2000); for Jewish country clubs, see "Demise of the Jewish Club," Golfweek, June 22, 2009, golfweek.usatoday.com/2009/06/22/demise-jewish-club/.

97. Petition for Writ of Certiorari to the United States Court of Appeals for the Fourth District, Shaare Tefila Congregation v. Cobb (No. A-876), *rev'd*, 107 S.Ct. 2019 (1987), Philip Kurland and Gerhard Casper, *Landmark Briefs and Arguments of the Supreme Court of the United States: Constitutional Law, 1986 Term Supplement* (Frederick, MD: University Publications of America, Inc., 1988), 417.

98. Jacques Kelly, "Balto. Jurist Murnaghan Dies at 80," *Baltimore Sun*, September 1, 2000. www.baltimoresun.com/news/bs-xpm-2000-09-01-0009010211-story.html Accessed February 10, 2021.

99. Jacques Kelly, "Balto. Jurist Murnaghan Dies at 80," *Baltimore Sun*, September 1, 2000. www.baltimoresun.com/news/bs-xpm-2000-09-01-0009010211-story.html Accessed February 10, 2021.

100. Jacques Kelly, "Balto. Jurist Murnaghan Dies at 80," *Baltimore Sun*, September 1, 2000. www.baltimoresun.com/news/bs-xpm-2000-09-01-0009010211-story .html Accessed February 10, 2021.

101. Jacques Kelly, "Balto. Jurist Murnaghan Dies at 80," *Baltimore Sun*, September 1, 2000. www.baltimoresun.com/news/bs-xpm-2000-09-01-0009010211-story .html Accessed February 10, 2021.

102. Jacques Kelly, "Balto. Jurist Murnaghan Dies at 80," *Baltimore Sun*, September 1, 2000. www.baltimoresun.com/news/bs-xpm-2000-09-01-0009010211-story .html Accessed February 10, 2021.

103. Jacques Kelly, "Balto. Jurist Murnaghan Dies at 80," *Baltimore Sun*, September 1, 2000. www.baltimoresun.com/news/bs-xpm-2000-09-01-0009010211-story .html Accessed February 10, 2021.

104. Jacques Kelly, "Balto. Jurist Murnaghan Dies at 80," *Baltimore Sun*, September 1, 2000. www.baltimoresun.com/news/bs-xpm-2000-09-01-0009010211-story .html Accessed February 10, 2021.

105. Jason Wiener, "Judges of the Fourth Circuit—Hon. Francis D. Murnaghan Jr." *Wake Forest Law Review*, Oct. 17, 2018. wakeforestlawreview.com/2018/10/judges-of-the-fourth-circuit-hon-francis-d-murnaghan-jr/ Accessed February 10, 2021.

106. Jason Wiener, "Judges of the Fourth Circuit—Hon. Francis D. Murnaghan Jr." *Wake Forest Law Review*, Oct. 17, 2018. wakeforestlawreview.com/2018/10/judges-of-the-fourth-circuit-hon-francis-d-murnaghan-jr/ Accessed February 10, 2021.

107. Shaare Tefila Congregation v. Cobb, 785 F.2d, 523, 528 (1986).

108. Shaare Tefila Congregation v. Cobb, 785 F.2d 523, 528 (1986).

109. David Faigman comments: "Fact-finding is one of the great silences in constitutional law. However large a role of facts may play in actual constitutional cases, they have received little attention in constitutional jurisprudence" (156). Later on in the chapter, he remarks, (and please focus on the second sentence): "A more salutary approach is to determine who within the judiciary will be the principal decision makers, who will be the ultimate decision makers, and most important, the dynamic between them. *This dynamic, in turn, depends on the kinds of factual matters that the Constitution makes relevant*" (162, my emphasis). See David L. Faigman, "Fact-finding in Constitutional Cases," in *How Law Knows*, eds. Austin Sarat, Lawrence Douglas, Martha Merrill Umphrey (Stanford, CA: Stanford University Press, 2007).

110. See David L. Faigman, "Factfinding in Constitutional Cases," in *How Law Knows*, eds. Austin Sarat, Lawrence Douglas, Martha Merrill Umphrey (Stanford, CA: Stanford University Press, 2007).

111. Shaare Tefila Congregation v. Cobb, 785 F.2d 523, 528 (1986).

112. He didn't like this term.

113. Manzanares v. Safeway Stores, Inc. 593 F.2d 968, 971 (10th Cir. 1979).

114. Shaare Tefila Congregation v. Cobb, 785 F.2d 523, 528 (1986).

115. Ryan Meier and Jacqueline Canzoneri, "Judges of the Fourth Circuit—Hon. J. Harvie Wilkinson III," *Wake Forest Law Review*, January 29, 2019.

wakeforestlawreview.com/2019/01/honorable-j-harvie-wilkinson-iii/ Accessed February 10, 2021.

116. Ryan Meier and Jacqueline Canzoneri, "Judges of the Fourth Circuit—Hon. J. Harvie Wilkinson III," *Wake Forest Law Review*, January 29, 2019. wakeforestlawreview.com/2019/01/honorable-j-harvie-wilkinson-iii/ Accessed February 10, 2021.

117. Ryan Meier and Jacqueline Canzoneri, "Judges of the Fourth Circuit—Hon. J. Harvie Wilkinson III," *Wake Forest Law Review*, January 29, 2019. wakeforestlawreview.com/2019/01/honorable-j-harvie-wilkinson-iii/ Accessed February 10, 2021.

118. P. Harvie Wilkinson III, *One Nation Indivisible: How Ethnic Separatism Threatens America* (New York: Basic Books, 1997), 69.

119. P. Harvie Wilkinson III, *One Nation Indivisible: How Ethnic Separatism Threatens America* (New York: Basic Books, 1997).

120. P. Harvie Wilkinson III, *One Nation Indivisible: How Ethnic Separatism Threatens America* (New York: Basic Books, 1997).

121. P. Harvie Wilkinson III, *One Nation Indivisible: How Ethnic Separatism Threatens America* (New York: Basic Books, 1997), viii.

122. P. Harvie Wilkinson III, *One Nation Indivisible: How Ethnic Separatism Threatens America* (New York: Basic Books, 1997), viii.

123. P. Harvie Wilkinson III, *One Nation Indivisible: How Ethnic Separatism Threatens America* (New York: Basic Books, 1997), viii.

124. P. Harvie Wilkinson III, *One Nation Indivisible: How Ethnic Separatism Threatens America* (New York: Basic Books, 1997), 89–90, emphasis mine.

125. Shaare Tefila Congregation v. Cobb, 785 F.2d 523, 528 (1986). See also Joseph Avanzato, "Section 1982 and Discrimination against Jews: Shaare Tefila Congregation v. Cobb," *American University Law Review* 37, no. 1 (1987): 243.

126. Shaare Tefila Congregation v. Cobb, 785 F.2d 523, 528 (1986), emphasis mine.

127. Shaare Tefila Congregation v. Cobb, 785 F.2d 523, 528 (1986).

128. Shaare Tefila Congregation v. Cobb, 785 F.2d 523, 528 (1986).

129. *Shaare Tefila Congregation v. Cobb,* 785 F.2d 523, 534 (1986).

130. Shaare Tefila Congregation v. Cobb, 785 F.2d 523, 529 (1986).

131. Shaare Tefila Congregation v. Cobb, 785 F.2d 523, 529 (1986).

132. Shaare Tefila Congregation v. Cobb, 785 F.2d 523, 529 (1986).

133. McDonald v. Santa Fe Trail Transportation Co., 427 U.S. 273 (1976).

134. Shaare Tefila Congregation v. Cobb, 785 F.2d 523, 530 (1986).

135. Shaare Tefila Congregation v. Cobb, 785 F.2d 523, 530 (1986).

136. Shaare Tefila Congregation v. Cobb, 785 F.2d 523, 530 (1986).

137. Shaare Tefila Congregation v. Cobb, 785 F.2d 523, 530 (1986).

138. Shaare Tefila Congregation v. Cobb, 785 F.2d 523, 530 (1986).

139. Shaare Tefila Congregation v. Cobb, 785 F.2d 523, 530 (1986).

140. Shaare Tefila Congregation v. Cobb, 785 F.2d 523, 531 (1986).

141. As noted above, the Supreme Court had excluded the category of national origin from the coverage provided by section 1981.

142. Shaare Tefila Congregation v. Cobb, 785 F.2d 523, 531 (1986).

143. Shaare Tefila Congregation v. Cobb 785 F.2d 523, 531 (1986). Cited from Judge Wilkinson: Anti-Defamation League of B'nai B'rith, 1985 Annual Audit of Anti-Semitic Incidents 1 (1986).

144. Shaare Tefila Congregation v. Cobb, 785 F.2d 523, 531 (1986).

145. Shaare Tefila Congregation v. Cobb, 785 F.2d 523, 532 (1986).

146. Robert Cover, "Nomos and Narrative," in *Narrative, Violence, and the Law: The Essays of Robert Cover*, eds. Martha Minow, Michael Ryan, and Austin Sarat (Ann Arbor: University of Michigan Press, 1993), 101.

147. Shaare Tefila Congregation v. Cobb, 785 F.2d 523, 532 (1986).

148. Shaare Tefila Congregation v. Cobb, 785 F.2d 523, 532 (1986).

149. Shaare Tefila Congregation v. Cobb, 785 F.2d 523, 532 (1986).

150. Shaare Tefila Congregation v. Cobb, 785 F.2d 523, 532 (1986).

151. Shaare Tefila Congregation v. Cobb, 785 F.2d 523, 533 (1986).

152. Shaare Tefila Congregation v. Cobb, 785 F.2d 523, 533 (1986).

153. In making this point, Judge Wilkinson cites the ruling in *Khawaja v. Wyatt*, 494 F. Supp. 302, 304 (W.D.N.Y. 1980).

154. Shaare Tefila Congregation v. Cobb, 785 F.2d 523, 534 (1986).

155. Shaare Tefila Congregation v. Cobb, 785 F.2d 523, 534 (1986).

156. Shaare Tefila Congregation v. Cobb, 785 F.2d 523, 534 (1986).

157. Shaare Tefila Congregation v. Cobb, 785 F.2d 523, 534 (1986).

158. 785 F.2d 534 (1986). Section 1982 protects the right to "hold real and personal property" and section 1985(3) protects from conspiracy to prevent the enjoyment of equal protection under federal laws. 42 U.S.C. 1982; 42 U.S.C. 1985(3).

159. Shaare Tefila Congregation v. Cobb, 785 F.2d 523, 534 (1986).

160. Michael Omi and Howard Winant, *Racial Formation in the United States: From the 1960s to the 1990s, Second Edition* (New York: Routledge, 1994), 55.

161. Patricia Brannan, interview by author, Washington, DC, July 14, 2008.

162. Patricia Brannan, interview by author, Washington, DC, July 14, 2008. She also told me that she was very surprised that the opinion came from this particular judge, who was known for his conservative views.

163. See W. E. B. Du Bois, *The Souls of Black Folk* (New York: Barnes & Noble Classics, 2003 [1903]), 34. Michael Omi and Howard Winant, *Racial Formation in the United States from the 1960s to the 1990s, Second Edition* (New York: Routledge, 1994), 66.

164. KB Wolf. Texts in Translation. "*Sentencia-Estatuto* de Toledo, 1449." Last modified 2008. Available at: canilup.googlepages.com (accessed 21 November 2013). Also see Amos Funkenstein, *Perceptions of Jewish History* (Berkeley: University of California Press, 1993), 320.

Chapter Four

Judging Religion and Race
in the Supreme Court

The *Shaare Tefila* case eventually met with surprising success in the US
Supreme Court because the suit was filed with a companion case. This case,
St. Francis College v. Al-Khazraji,[1] drew upon statutes that were also based on
the Civil Rights Act of 1866. Majid Ghaidan Al-Khazraji, an Iraqi American,
won in the Third Circuit Court of Appeals, proving that he was denied tenure
because of his race, which resulted in a conflicting ruling between his case
and the Shaare Tefila case, called a circuit split. The Supreme Court needed to
resolve the discrepancy between the two cases. Were it not for the conflicting
ruling in *St. Francis College, Shaare Tefila* probably would never have been
heard beyond the Fourth Circuit Court of Appeals.[2]

The oral argument in *St. Francis College* was significant to the Supreme
Court ruling for *Shaare Tefila*, in that the court adopted the assertions of
Caroline Mitchell, the lawyer for Al-Khazraji. She contended that, in 1866,
Al-Khazraji would not have been viewed as a "white citizen," but would have
been considered an "Arab." Mitchell cited dictionaries and encyclopedias
during that time, in which "Arab" was considered a race, and cited evidence
from the 39th Congress, which passed the Act. Based on her argument, the
Supreme Court determined on May 18, 1987, that Jews were *also* viewed as
a race in 1866, and that the Act covered Jewish Americans in 1987 as well.

This chapter discusses the Supreme Court's oral argument and decision in
Shaare Tefila, and the ambiguity among the justices about Jewish identification as a legal concept. It highlights Patricia Brannan and Deborah Garren's
oral argument in which they variously consider "race" and "religion" as applicable to Jewish Americans and specifically to the vandalism at Shaare Tefila
Congregation. The Supreme Court justices responded to their arguments and
interpreted them according to their image of Jewish American racial identification in the 1980s as "White." They are gradually convinced that the predominant conception of Jewish Americans has not always been thus.

The actions of the vandals, the argument for the congregation, and the justices' engagement with the legal assertions on both sides of the civil suit illuminate the multiple and, also often antisemitic narratives that continue to inform and construct Jewish identification. These narratives include Reconstruction-era and Nazi racialized views of Jews, post–World War II assertions of Jewish Whiteness, prevailing discourse regarding the definitional socio-legal boundaries of "religion" and "race" in the 1980s, conceptions of race as it was construed in 1866 by the 39th Congress, and historically pervasive ideas of Jewish "difference," which resulted in both institutional[3] and unofficial discrimination against Jews in pre-American and American history.

In the Supreme Court, oral arguments consist of a legal hearing in which one lawyer for each side of the case presents arguments to all the justices. In this case, the petitioners, Shaare Tefila Congregation, and the respondents, those convicted and those suspected of vandalizing the synagogue, each presented a short argument summarizing the materials already submitted to the justices in the briefs and then responded to questions and hypothetical examples posed by the justices. Although the final decision rested, in large part, on which side constructed the most compelling legal argument, the justices were concerned about the legal ramifications of their decision. The hypothetical examples they posed were particularly significant because they aimed to ascertain how their decision, in the future, could be interpreted as precedent.

The ambiguity of the legal categories "religion" and "race" was noteworthy because the justices' interpretations of these terms informed the background with which the statutes in question could apply to Jewish Americans and provide protection against race-based attacks. The outcome depended on Patricia Brannan's ability to argue that the synagogue was targeted because the vandals perceived Jews as an inferior race and that the deeds could be understood as racial bias because of the vandals' actions, versus Deborah Garren's argument that Jews were a religious group and may not claim protection based on race. The legal boundaries of Jewish American identification were at stake in the case. Although, as already noted, Jewish Americans had never been legally defined as either a "religion" or a "race," they had gained protection in many earlier cases based on religion.

In sum, the justices had to make a few important decisions: were White-perceived Jewish Americans able to cite section 1982, particularly given that the vandals who defaced their synagogue *were also White*?[4] In their response to *Shaare Tefila Congregation v. Cobb*, how would they justify that decision? Would they decide to use Caroline Mitchell's argument regarding Al-Khazraji, that as an Arab, he would have been viewed as a "race" at the time the Civil Rights Act of 1866 was passed by the 39th Congress and then apply the same argument to Jews, who were also viewed as a "race" at the time, to *Shaare Tefila*? The answer to these questions is affirmative. The chapter will discuss the differences between White-perceived Jewish and Iraqi self-perception and a brief history of immigrant Arab race prerequisite cases to emphasize that Iraqis had not always been perceived as "White." Then it will address the amicus curiae briefs and the role of *St. Francis College v. Al-Khazraji* to *Shaare Tefila*. In the context of *Shaare Tefila*, it examines two justices perceived as minorities on the Supreme Court, Justice Thurgood Marshall, and Justice Antonin Scalia, who understood Jewish Americans as more than solely a religious group and illuminated the historical antisemitism they have faced in this country. Most of the chapter, however, engages the process of the oral argument, analyzes it, and then considers Justice White's decision as it focuses on the "race" of Jews in 1866. Let's investigate how it all transpired.

White-perceived Jewish and Iraqi Americans generally had different understandings of what it meant to be viewed as a "race." In the 1980s, these Jewish Americans were extremely uncomfortable identifying as a race because Adolf Hitler and the Nazi regime had murdered over six million Jews on the basis that they were an *inferior* race in the Shoah. Their prevailing fear was that Jews could potentially be differently *embodied*, in biological terms. In the 1980s, however, Jews, in general, would be imagined as "White" by the broader American public. Even when the legality of Hebrew "Whiteness" was most contested during the first twenty or so years of the twentieth century, Jewish senators and political leaders were able to prevent legal cases questioning that Jews were White to reach Congress. Iraqi Americans, however, are grouped legally with other Arabs, who do not typically perceive *themselves* as White.[5]

Caroline Mitchell, who represented Al-Khazraji, had to research and prove to the Court that Iraqis have not always been considered "White." Cultural historians interested only in Jewish socio-legal identification might be surprised by the relevance of this information because it explains why the Court decided *Shaare Tefila* the way it did. Arab qualification as "White" was not always taken for granted. Recall that the Nationality Act of 1790 granted citizenship only to "free white persons." This Act was followed by many other immigration acts, but most notably, the Naturalization Act of 1870, which provided citizenship rights to "aliens of African nativity and to persons of African descent."[6] Individuals making such appeals opted to become White citizens because anti-Black laws and extreme sentiments embraced by much of the White American majority made the decision obvious. In 1922 and 1923, respectively, Takao Ozawa and Bhagat Singh Thind brought cases requesting to become White citizens to the Supreme Court, but it denied both of them because they were not deemed "Caucasian."[7] In *Ozawa v. United*

States, the court refused citizenship to a Japanese man who had been living in the United States for twenty years on the basis of both "common knowledge" and science.[8] The concept of "common knowledge" originated in an 1878 naturalization case, *In re Ah Yup*, in which the court denied citizenship to a Chinese applicant because, at the time, he was not considered "White" to ordinary (White) citizens.[9] Bhagat Singh Thind used a different tactic, identifying himself as Aryan and classifying himself as a "free white person."[10] The court rejected his case as well relying on "familiar observation and knowledge."[11] At one point in his decision for the court, Justice Sutherland asserted:

> It may be true that the blond Scandinavian and the brown Hindu have a common ancestor in the dim reaches of antiquity, but the average man knows perfectly well that there are unmistakable and profound differences between them today, and it is not impossible, if that common ancestor could be materialized in the flesh, we should discover that he was himself sufficiently differentiated from both of his descendants to preclude his racial classification with either.[12]

Here, Sutherland justified the distinction between the "blond Scandinavian and the brown Hindu" on the basis of skin color, and geographic origin, in the Scandinavian example, and precluded Thind's naturalization because he was not White nor European. Arab immigrants, however, continued to seek naturalization because they had not yet been refused.

Ex Parte Mohriez in 1944, brought by a Saudi named Mohamed Mohriez, marked the first time that Arabs were legally considered White.[13] In his description of the case, Critical Race Theorist John Tehranian, who focuses on the performance of Whiteness, cites the court document to demonstrate how Judge Charles Wyzanski viewed Arabs as a class. Wyzanski writes: "The names of Avicenna and Averroes, the sciences of algebra and medicine, the population and the architecture of Spain and of Sicily, the very words of the English language, remind us as they would have reminded the Founding Fathers of the action and interaction of Arabic and non-Arabic elements of our culture."[14] Because men who were (later) defined as "White" are "like" Arabs, Mohriez could become a citizen. From the viewpoint of this judge in 1944, White Americans have benefited from Arab skills and language. Hence, Mohriez, as an individual, might somehow bring these qualities to the United States by becoming a citizen.

Due to *Ex Parte Mohriez*, Arabs were able to "become" White, and hence gain citizenship. For this reason, Caroline Mitchell had to prove that Arabs had not *always* been White. Jewish Americans, however, had never proven one way or the other that they had been legally racialized.

To make sure they would not be mistaken for a non-White race, Shaare Tefila Congregation maintained that they were White, which Beydoun calls "formal whiteness."[15] Recall that, in his language, Jewish Americans who originated in Europe are "White," according to government rules, and deemed White on the census, but are members of a "stigmatized religion," so they are not "substantively" White. In other words, other people do not necessarily consider them White once it's known that they are Jewish. Beydoun highlights this gap between Jewish Americans, in this case, Shaare Tefila congregants, as a "stigmatized religion" but "formally white."

Remember that because they could not claim "difference" legally on a religious basis in this situation, Shaare Tefila's lawyers had to search for race-based laws that could conceivably protect them from the vandalism, in that "race" is the only other legal category that could define Jewish difference. That Shaare Tefila Congregation chose to stake its claim via racial means was important to mainstream Jewish organizations, who rejected the idea that Jews could be considered a "race" due to their long, racialized history, which culminated in the Shoah. Some of these organizations chose not to legally support the Congregation, as is evident below.

THE SIGNIFICANCE OF THE AMICUS BRIEFS

Let's turn now to the *amici curiae* (the plural of "friend of the court") briefs filed on behalf of Shaare Tefila Congregation and Majid Ghaidan Al-Khazraji by numerous organizations, of which the most important are highlighted here. First, the Arab-American Anti-Discrimination Committee (ADC) filed a joint motion of *amicus curiae* briefs for both Al-Khazraji in *St. Francis College* and *Shaare Tefila*. It was especially significant because the brief addressed both cases and made an argument, divided into three parts, that accounted for the ways in which Arabs and Jews were perceived in the United States. It reads: "Arabs, Jews and other groups not defined in terms of skin color taxonomically classified as Caucasian, but subject to discrimination on the basis that they are racially distinct groups, are protected under sections 1981 and 1982, two civil rights statutes derived from the 1866 Civil Rights Act."[16] The ADC also asserted that the term "Caucasian" does not cover all groups who experience racial marginalization, it claimed that there is no "static" interpretation of the Act, and it stressed that the purpose of the Act ensures "equal civil rights to all persons regardless of race or color."[17] The sub-arguments emphasized, first, that dark skin color or scientific classification as "Caucasian" should not prevent claim to these two sections; second, that Arab or Jewish plaintiffs should not be forced to claim national origin or religion, respectively, rather than race; and third, that Arabs and Jews are perceived by some people—and *it does not matter how many*—as "'racially' distinct," and that they "have been the object of racial caricatures and stereotypes, which have been used to justify discrimination."[18] "Race," as the ADC defines it, is more than skin color or scientific classification.

In their third argument, the ADC referred to Patricia Brannan's assertion for the Shaare Tefila case. They reminded the Supreme Court that the Fourth Circuit Court of Appeals did not validate her contention that the vandals perceived Jews as a "race." The ADC stated, in response, "the racial animus in discriminating against Arabs and Jews is not derived from some unique notion concocted by defendants" and that "the subjective belief of defendants is connected to an external racist ideology."[19] They argued that the KKK and neo-Nazis were not unknown ideas or organizations, nor are mainstream assumptions of Arabs as foreigners or even terrorists. These are well-known antisemitic tropes, in the broader, linguistic meaning of the word.[20]

The ADC concluded by emphasizing that at the current time—in 1985 and 1986—violent attacks on Arabs and Jews occurred regularly and argued that both groups should be protected by the Civil Rights Act. However, even if these violent actions did not happen regularly, the victims should be protected by law. Finally, the ADC insisted that it did not matter if Jews were "commonly perceived" to be a racially marginalized group or if they were "frequently expressed openly."[21]

The Anti-Defamation League of B'nai B'rith (ADL) dramatically changed its policy toward *Shaare Tefila* when the Supreme Court granted certiorari and decided that race-based discrimination against property should be illegal.[22] The more conservative American Jewish Committee (AJCommittee) joined the ADL.[23] Two months later, the ADL filed a second brief[24] again with the AJCommittee, along with the National Association for the Advancement of Colored People (NAACP), the Lawyers' Committee for Civil Rights Under Law, the American Civil Liberties Union (ACLU), the International Network of Children of Holocaust Survivors, the American Gathering and Federation of Jewish Holocaust Survivors, the Jewish War Veterans, the Institute of Jewish Law, and the Capital Legal Counsel of B'nai B'rith.[25]

This brief advised the Court not to neglect "minority and ethnic groups who do not belong to distinct 'non-white' races, but who allege discrimination of a racial or racist character."[26] It emphasized that the statutes from the Civil Rights Act of 1866 should not be limited "by narrow and arbitrary definitions of 'race.'"[27] It stressed that the plaintiffs should have the option of continuing with their claims unless they were "clearly inconsistent with the possibility that they were . . . victims of racial discrimination."[28] Throughout the *amicus* brief, the organizations argue that these sections from the Act were meant to protect *every* person, and it quoted from members of the 39th Congress to prove this point.

Two other significant entities sent amicus briefs to the Court. The State of Maryland filed one in support of *Shaare Tefila* because the State did not have any legal recourse for the antisemitic nature of the defacement. The Mexican American Legal Defense and Educational Fund and the Puerto Rican Legal Defense and Education Fund also filed one for *St. Francis College* because they had benefited from the legal usage of sections 1981 and 1982 and wanted to support him and Arabs, more generally.

Certain Jewish organizations, however, such as the American Jewish Congress, which is one of the other big three national Jewish organizations, decided not to back *Shaare Tefila*, because the Third Circuit Court of Appeals' decision in *Al-Khazraji* identified him as "physiognomically distinctive," which referred to his embodied difference, presumably from individuals categorized as "White citizens."[29] The National Jewish Community Relations Council (NJCRC), agreed. It asserted in a vote, passed with only one dissent, "that there ought not to be the suggestion that the Jewish community in any way gives sanction to the notion that Jews constitute a race."[30] State remedies were adequate, and these rights should be sought via legislative means, the NJCRC determined.[31]

Together, the briefs, written by a wide variety of groups some of which were defined in terms of their "race," made an important statement to the Supreme Court. Many of these racialized communities—such as the NAACP, the Mexican American Legal Defense and Educational Fund, and the Puerto Rican Legal Defense and Education Fund, not specifically associated with Arabs or Jews—filed briefs on their behalf. The Supreme Court considered these briefs, along with the organizations more closely affiliated with Jewish and Arab organizations when it decided both cases.

How *St. Francis College v. Majid Ghaidan Al-Khazraji* Informed Both Cases

People do not choose in advance what will happen to them or how they will respond. Such is the case with the racist antisemitic defacement of the Shaare Tefila Congregation and with the racist anti-Muslim discrimination of Majid Ghaidan Al-Khazraji. They both, however, eventually decided to bring lawsuits against the discriminating parties. Let's examine key components of Al-Khazraji's life in the United States, because, as a marginalized person, his "race," and well as his "religion," form the basis of his case.

Majid Ghaidan Al-Khazraji was born on April 15, 1933, in the small town of Ali Gharbi, by the Tigris river in Iraq. He grew up "poor but happy," but his father urged him to study hard and work toward a better life.[32] Winning a scholarship at age twenty-one to study rural sociology at Cornell University, he earned his Bachelor of Science in 1958 and his master's degree in 1959. It was around this time that he met his wife, Emilie Andersen Allan. She recalled, in her tribute to him after he passed away, that she arrived at her friend's party and saw, "on the other side of the room," "positively the most handsome man I had ever seen."[33] "When we were introduced, 'Emilie, I'd like you to meet Majid . . . ,' I must have been blushing like mad. I tried to maintain my cool, while inside I was shaken, thinking to myself that there was no way I could seem attractive to such a man."[34] For the rest of the party, they hardly spoke; she was shy. The group surrounding him on the floor, she wrote, was largely female, and she wished she had had the nerve to join them. The next day, she remembered, they encountered each other in a student hangout, and he invited her to join him for coffee. Then he surprised her by asking her for dinner and a movie the next evening. A few months later, they got married, and thus, according to Allan, "began our lifelong love."[35]

They both earned their Doctorate in Philosophy at the University of Wisconsin–Madison in the same field. After Majid taught at Holy Cross in Worcester, Massachusetts, both of them were hired at St. Francis College. When he failed to earn tenure, he brought a lawsuit against the College.

Al-Khazraji was well-qualified for tenure; he had worked for five years at St. Francis College, in Loretto, Pennsylvania. On February 10, 1978, the Tenure Committee voted to recommend that he not be granted tenure, and he was notified of that decision. He received a one-year written contract for the 1978–1979 year, which was not renewable beyond May 26, 1979. After requesting an internal review of his tenure status, he met with the president of the college and his department chairperson, and they advised him to wait until the review that he had requested had taken its course. On February 26, the Tenure Committee decided again not to reconsider his application for tenure. Al-Khazraji filed a suit on May 10, 1979, against St. Francis College for violating its own tenure guidelines, which, he asserted, were motivated by "bias, prejudice, and discrimination" against his "ethnic (Arab) and religious (Muslim)" background, in the Court of Common Pleas of Cambria County, Pennsylvania.[36] It was finally dismissed on October 26, 1983, and he did not appeal the dismissal.

After learning about his tenure rejection in September of 1978, Al-Khazraji had communicated with the Pennsylvania Human Relations Commission (PHRC) to ask about his rights, given his situation. The EEOC finally issued him a right to sue on August 6, 1980, and he filed a complaint against St. Francis College on October 30, 1980, in the United States District Court for the Western District of Pennsylvania. His complaint alleged that the college had violated Title VII of the Civil Rights Act of 1964, 42 U.S.C. § 2000e et seq. Afterward, he secured a lawyer and filed amended complaints that named the members of the Tenure Committee as additional defendants in their individual and official capacities. These amended complaints added allegations that the defendants had violated 42 U.S.C. §§ 1981, 1983, 1985(3), 1986, as well as the Pennsylvania Human Relations Act, 43 P.S. Sec. 951 et seq. He also alleged breach of contract and intentional infliction of emotional distress under Pennsylvania law.[37] The number of statutes reveals the breadth of his concerns but only one of them is significant to the outcome of the case: 42 U.S.C. § 1981.

In the United States District Court for the Western District of Pennsylvania, Judge Glenn Everell Mencer determined that Al-Khazraji could not claim section 1981, in this case, because the only other person to have received tenure in the Department of Behavioral Science since 1978 was his wife, Emilie Allan. Presumably, she is White. In response, Al-Khazraji appealed the decision to the Third Circuit Court of Appeals, which has appellate jurisdiction over the districts of Delaware, New Jersey, the Eastern, Middle, and Western Districts of Pennsylvania, and the Virgin Islands.

The Third Circuit Court disagreed with the District Court's ruling and argued that "ethnic Arabs" may rely upon section 1981 to respond to racial discrimination against them. The defendants, St. Francis College, had asserted that Al-Khazraji was "taxonomically a Caucasian" and, as such, "not a protected person under Section 1981 when he is presumably claiming other Caucasians or whites were improperly favored over him."[38] To make his determination, Judge Stapleton examined the legislative history, assessed comments that senators and representatives made before the passage of the Act, and found that they supported his claim. Judge Arlin M. Adams concurred, although Adams was concerned initially, that the purpose of the sections that originated in the Civil Rights Act of 1866, was to support the rights of recently freed enslaved Blacks. He noted, however, that the Supreme Court had made several decisions in the 1970s, after the passage of the Civil Rights Act of 1964, that expanded the Act to include other peoples. In the end, the vote was unanimous in Al-Khazraji's case: he won based on section 1981. Judge Walter King Stapleton wrote the decision, and Judge Adams, along with Judge John Joseph Gibbons, concurred.[39]

That Majid Al-Khazraji, an Iraqi American who was considered an Arab "Caucasian," could win his case based on Section 1981, was significant to the Shaare Tefila Congregation.[40] The Congregation identified as White; they were perceived as White by the judges and the dominant discourse at the time, but they had lost their case in the Fourth Circuit Court of Appeals against the vandals, who were also unquestionably White, according to the origins of race science. We will discover that the Supreme Court would use Caroline Mitchell's argument based on dictionaries and encyclopedias to determine that Jews would have been considered a separate "race" in 1866 as well.

The Importance of Two Justices to Shaare Tefila Congregation's Win in the Supreme Court

In November 1982, when the vandalism occurred, the Supreme Court was predominately male and Protestant. The American public viewed several justices on the Court as "minorities," and two of them were Thurgood Marshall and Antonin Scalia. These two justices related to the Shaare Tefila Congregation members' Jewishness and the marginal status of their synagogue.

Both were the first of their "type" of justice: Justice Marshall was the first Black American justice, and Justice Scalia was the first Catholic Italian American justice. Obviously, Justice Marshall suffered from intense structural and interpersonal racism that Justice Scalia did not experience. Law was Marshall's tool to right the wrongs of racial injustice. Justice Scalia's Italianness was an inextricable part of him, and he understood that Jewishness is not defined *only* as a "religion." Their empathy for the Shaare Tefila Congregation was one of their few ideological similarities. Let's go into more detail about their experiences and how they came to serve on the US Supreme Court because it impacts their hypotheticals and their decision in the case.

Justice Marshall was a Black man. This was, and is, important in the United States not only because many Americans "became White," like Justice Scalia's Italian family, but because Black people remain the dominant racial target in the United States. This occurred as the first slave codes were established in late seventeenth-century Virginia. Many enslaved African peoples converted to Christianity to gain freedom, but a law prohibited that in 1667, instantiating that "baptisme of slaves doth not exempt them from bondage."[41] This law differentiates between skin color, which, in large part, *defined* "race" in what became the United States, and conversion to Christianity. Note that in what became the United States, Christianity was the assumed norm.[42] Skin color, and later hypodescent, a percentage of one's "blood" as "Negro," "African," or "Black," has targeted and racialized Black people ever since. At that time, most Christian missionaries' aim undergirds the prior statement: if one has been saved by Jesus Christ, one is accepted in the kingdom of heaven. On earth, however, pro-enslavement Christian leaders argued that Black people could be enslaved.[43] The slave owners, and other members of the dominant community who identified as "Anglo-Saxon," "Caucasian," and "White," gradually tried to clarify what being White *meant*, for themselves and for others.[44] To legalize the continuity of Whiteness, Congress, and various presidents passed one immigration act after another that prevented people who were deemed "not Caucasian," or "not White," from obtaining citizenship in the United States, or even from immigrating altogether, until 1952.[45]

So, when Italian Americans "became" White, Justice Scalia's family was included among them; however, in direct contrast, many of Justice Marshall's ancestors came on slave ships through the Middle Passage,[46] and although his family tried to shield him from racism in Baltimore where he grew up, he faced it every day. He was born on July 2, 1908, to Norma Arica, a kindergarten teacher, and William Canfield Marshall, a writer, who also worked on passenger trains as a dining-car waiter, and then became a chief steward at a ritzy club.[47] Due to school segregation, Marshall was forced to attend all-Black schools, but because his parents were able to afford it, he was able to attend an excellent high school. He was a mischievous student, and, when he was sent out of class, he was made to read the Constitution. When he graduated in 1925, he knew every article and every amendment. Early experiences with his father, who sometimes took Marshall and his brother to court when he had days off, along with his knowledge of the Constitution, contributed to his passion for civil rights and his desire to become a lawyer. He attended Lincoln University, in Oxford, Pennsylvania, where he joined the debate club, helped to desegregate a theater, and met his wife, Vivian Burey. Because he was Black, he could not attend the University of Maryland Law School, his first choice, so he went to Howard University Law School.[48] There, he began to focus on civil rights, was mentored by the first special counsel for the NAACP, Charles Houston, and came to think of the Constitution as a living document, unlike Justice Scalia, who understood it in its original form. Marshall began learning from the NAACP and began to understand US law, which was established originally by mostly slave-owners, as a means to undo racism. Marshall graduated valedictorian, rejected a postgraduate scholarship at Harvard, and set up his own practice in East Baltimore. There, he worked with anyone who needed legal help or advice, even if they could not pay. Focusing on the issues faced by his clients—police brutality, evictions, and racism—he became a confident lawyer.

After working with increasingly powerful clients, he started to volunteer with the NAACP and soon came to work for them, joining his mentor Houston.[49] Marshall's first major victory, as discussed in chapter 2, was in *Murray v. Pearson* (1935), in which he and Houston sued the University of Maryland Law School for not allowing a Black applicant admission due to his race. Marshall became established as one of the top attorneys in the United States during the 1940s and 1950s. He won twenty-nine of thirty-two cases he argued before the Supreme Court, including the previously mentioned *Shelley v. Kraemer* (1948), in which the Court struck down the legality of racially restrictive covenants. Following *Shelley v. Kramer*, he won *Sweatt v. Painter* (1950), which challenged the "separate but equal" doctrine established in *Plessy v. Ferguson* (1896). In this case, he argued that Heman Marion Sweatt should have been granted admission to the University of Texas Law School even though he was not White and had been given the option of attending the "separate but equal" facilities. Following *Sweatt*, Marshall eventually won the landmark case *Brown v. Board of Education* (1954), in which Black parents filed a lawsuit because their children were required to attend "separate but equal" schools, leading the Supreme Court to rule that "separate educational facilities are inherently unequal."[50] After this achievement, President John F. Kennedy appointed him as a federal judge on the Second Circuit Court of Appeals in New York City, and then in 1967, President Lyndon B. Johnson appointed him to be an Associate Justice on the Supreme Court. He served until 1991 when President H.W. Bush named Clarence Thomas to replace him. Justice Marshall passed away due to heart failure in 1993.

During his time serving on the Supreme Court, he voted his conscience for individual rights, the expansion of civil rights, and limits on criminal punishment. He often voted with Justice William Brennan because they had similar legal opinions. Opposed to the death penalty, he voted for *Furman v. Georgia* (1972), which outlawed it, and dissented from *Gregg v. Georgia* (1976), which reinstituted it. Strongly in favor of affirmative action, he contributed significantly to constitutional decisions that supported it.[51] In almost all respects, he voted completely opposite to Justice Scalia.

Antonin Scalia was born on March 11, 1936, in Trenton, New Jersey, the only child of Catherine Panaro and Salvadore Eugene Scalia. His father became a professor of Romance languages at Brooklyn College after emigrating from Sicily and coming through Ellis Island. His mother's parents came from Italy, but she was born in the United States and worked as an elementary school teacher until her son was born. "Nino" was happily the only child in his immediate family, but he was instilled with the discipline and conservatism that would remain important to him throughout his life.[52] The Scalias moved to Queens, New York City, when he was young, and he grew up with children of other recent immigrants. He attended Xavier High School in Manhattan, a military school run by the Jesuit order of the Catholic Church. While at Xavier, he became increasingly religious and conservative and was the first in his class. After high school, he enrolled at Georgetown University, became a debater, and then graduated valedictorian, with a bachelor's degree in history. From there, he attended Harvard Law School, and again, graduated valedictorian. At Harvard, he was the notes editor for the *Law Review*. In his final year, he met his wife, Maureen McCarthy, an undergraduate at Radcliffe College. They were married on September 10, 1960. After law school, he became the Sheldon Fellow at Harvard Law School. Then he entered private practice in 1961, decided he would rather return to the academy, and became an administrative law professor at the University of Virginia in 1967. President Richard Nixon appointed him to serve as general counsel for the Office of Telecommunications Policy in 1971. Among other positions he held during the Nixon presidency, he served as Assistant Attorney General for the Office of Legal Counsel. President Gerald Ford sustained his nomination after Nixon resigned, and he was confirmed by the Senate in 1974. After grappling with various issues related to Watergate, Scalia resumed teaching and joined the faculty at the University of Chicago Law School in 1977. President Ronald Reagan nominated him for the US Circuit Court of Appeals for the District of Columbia Circuit, and he was sworn in on August 17, 1982. After Chief Justice Warren Burger retired, Reagan nominated Associate Justice William Rehnquist to succeed him and named Scalia for Rehnquist's seat. With a unanimous confirmation from the Senate, he took his seat as Associate Justice on September 26, 1986.[53]

Scalia was firmly a Constitutional "originalist," meaning he believed the Constitution could not be changed. He viewed this position as key to his vision for what a Supreme Court Justice must do. His Catholic faith also guided him, such that he held views that were anti-choice, he dissented in *Roe v. Wade* (1973), as well as anti-gay, he voted for *Bowers v. Hardwick* (1986), which was a Georgia sodomy law criminalizing oral and anal sex between consenting adults, and he dissented in *Lawrence v. Texas* (2003), which reversed *Bowers* and legalized homosexual activity between consensual adults. He was also pro–death penalty, beginning with his dissent in *Thompson v. Oklahoma* (1988), which allowed the death penalty for those who were under the age of fifteen at the time of their offense, dissented in *Miranda v. Arizona* (1966), which prevented testimony without the protection of a lawyer, and was pro-gun in *District of Columbia v. Heller* (2008), which allowed individuals in the District of Columbia the right to own a gun.[54]

Due to the ways in which both Justice Marshall, as a Black American man, and Justice Scalia, as an Italian American, had grown up, they understood what it was like to *feel* different from the dominant, assimilated, majority. Even though they were grounded in extremely separate ideologies, they could still relate to the Jewish members at the Shaare Tefila Congregation. Watch how they interrogate Patricia Brannan and Deborah Garren and think about how their lived experiences exerted importance over their questioning.

Reviewing the Oral Argument of
Shaare Tefila Congregation v. Cobb

The US Supreme Court heard the oral argument for *Shaare Tefila Congregation v. Cobb* on Wednesday, February 25, 1987. The justices who heard the case included Chief Justice William H. Rehnquist and Associate Justices William J. Brennan Jr., Byron R. White, Thurgood Marshall, Harry A. Blackmun, Lewis F. Powell, Jr., John Paul Stevens, Sandra Day O'Connor, and Antonin Scalia. Proceedings began when Chief Justice Rehnquist called Patricia Brannan to the floor.

Brannan opened her argument by presenting the central issue at stake: whether a "complaint that alleges racially motivated discrimination and harassment against Jews may state a claim under Title 42 of the United States Code, Section 1982."[55] The complaint alleged that the respondents' defacement of Shaare Tefila was "racially motivated and hence covered by the statute."[56] Brannan described in detail the words and symbols the respondents had painted and their historical and ideological contexts.

After her assertions, the justices' interrogation commenced. Justice Stevens questioned Brannan about whether people who voted for the Civil Rights Act of 1866 at the time that it was passed—the members of the 39th Congress—thought that Jews were racially distinct. Brannan agreed that they likely did, but that this was not important to her argument. She maintained that if anyone viewed a group as racially distinct, and discriminated against them for that reason, then the group in question should be covered under the statute. Justice Stevens's argument echoed the allegation of Caroline Mitchell, the lawyer for Majid Al-Khazraji. He seemed to be wondering whether Brannan would choose to go that route, but she did not.

Other justices began to pose hypothetical situations and questions to Brannan. Justice Rehnquist inquired whether a German person would be covered if a "Frenchman" treated him differently than said Frenchman would treat another Frenchman.[57] Brannan responded negatively and said the principle for which she was arguing was narrower and would only cover *racially* motivated discrimination. When Justice Rehnquist asked what evidence would be necessary for this claim, Brannan indicated that it would include "statements and admissions of the defendants," and as evidence, she mentioned the neo-Nazi and KKK symbols and language painted by the respondents.[58] Brannan acknowledged that the plaintiffs had the burden of proof, but she asserted that the argument hinged on whether the defendants committed the act based on rac*ism* not on whether race, "in fact," exists in the case; here she cited Wilkinson's dissent in the Fourth Circuit Court of Appeals.

Justice Scalia returned to the example of the Frenchman and the German and pursued the position that perhaps discrimination against Germans *as Germans*—although not as a separate *race*—would also fall under the statute.[59] Brannan responded that it would be a fair assessment in regard to the legislative history and that it would lead to a reversal in this case as well as an affirmation of the *St. Francis College* case, but she emphatically wished to avoid "the issue of defining race to determine coverage."[60] She rejected any approach in which courts would attempt to determine that a particular group is, "in fact," racially distinct.

Then, Justice Rehnquist asked Brannan how she would respond to a potential example in which someone discriminated against people with brown eyes. Brannan replied that the statute might cover this type of case if the discrimination was racially motivated, and she argued that if the plaintiffs were motivated by racially recognized "facts," it could be proven as such. She asserted: "The charge should be on whether it is conduct that we understand as racial, as based on that person and their heritage and background and what they are in unchangeable ways—unlike, for instance religion—and that should be backed up in the evidence; and the plaintiff has the burden to show that it ties in historically or culturally with an understanding that is racial."[61] She noted, however, that it would be unlikely for the plaintiff to prevail in the hypothetical case regarding eye color discrimination.

Justice O'Connor wondered whether Brannan was asking the Court to equate racial discrimination with national origin discrimination, and Brannan responded negatively. Then, Justice Scalia inquired how Brannan would argue if the defendants *knew* that a group was not racially distinct but attacked it anyway. Brannan admitted, "if we could know completely what was in their minds, it would not be actionable."[62] Justice O'Connor next asked what in the legislative history would support her approach to the statute. Brannan deferred the question by repeatedly referring to two cases in which the Supreme Court examined the intent of the actors to determine the outcomes, *General Building Contractors v. Pennsylvania United Engineers* and *McDonald v. Santa Fe Trail Transportation* Co.[63] In *General Building Contractors*, the Commonwealth of Pennsylvania and Black workers brought an action against the union that was neutral on its face, but that administered a system that intentionally discriminated against Black workers based on their race. *Pennsylvania* cited section 1981 to make their claims and illustrated that the law needed to have discriminatory intent.[64] Not content with this diversion, Justice O'Connor repeated that she wanted to know if there was anything in the *legislative* history that would support attempting to be inside the mind of the discriminator. Brannan responded that the court had addressed the same issue in *McDonald* and reiterated that motivation is important to racially discriminatory intent. When Justice Scalia pushed her on this point, she noted that the Court has looked to intent in these two cases.

Justice Scalia then asked Brannan whether skin color would affect the ruling in cases such as the ones she had cited in making her argument about intent, and she replied that skin color is closely tied to race in US society. Continuing with Scalia's line of inquiry, Justice Marshall asked Brannan what she would argue if the defendants had painted swastikas on the synagogue on Lenox Avenue in Harlem, noting "there is not a white person within ten blocks."[65] When Brannan stated that she would make the same argument and that the congregants in that synagogue should be covered just as the Shaare Tefila congregants should be, Justice Marshall responded: "Well, you couldn't do it on race, could you?" and then interrupted Brannan's response to add: "But there are no Jews in that synagogue." He then stopped before continuing: "There are no white Jews, I would say." Brannan responded that it does not matter whether the Jews are Black or White "if the racial animus is there to support the cause of action."[66] Here, Justice Marshall first assumed that race primarily can be defined by the "color line." He refers not only to the long history in the United States, in which "race" typically means skin color but also to his own experience of being a constant racialized target.[67] Automatically, he then assumed that Jews can be only White, which was typical of the 1980s, and the assumption that judges in the two prior courts had made.

Justice White inquired whether Brannan would make the same argument if the defendants had just vandalized the synagogue without painting anything, such as swastikas. She conceded that it would be a more difficult case to make, in that instance, and that there would have to be some evidence that they committed the act based on race. "Here," she reasserted, "the character of what was painted was the strongest evidence."[68] Again, Justice White pushed Brannan on whether she would argue that at the time the Civil Rights Act of 1866 was passed Jews were "considered enough different to be covered by the statute."[69] When Brannan attempted to respond, starting with "We might . . . " Justice White interjected with the question: "You don't want to urge in this Court, I take it, that Jews are a different race?" She began with "No, not at all" and the justice interrupted her with "And you don't want to— you are not arguing that Congress thought Jews were a different race at the time they passed the statute?" Brannan stated: "there is some of evidence of that, but . . . what Congress was after was concerned about racial discrimination against anyone."[70]

Justice Scalia asked her whether it would be an error to read the statute and legislative history to say that Congress thought that Jews were a different race and that therefore the statute would cover it. Brannan replied that she did not think it would be an *error*, but that she "would certainly urge the Court to make clear that of course Jews or any other group *now* bringing a claim would not have to prove some racial distinctness," as the Fourth Circuit Court of Appeals had suggested in the majority opinion.[71] She emphasized that the "crux" of the Circuit Courts' error was to insist that the plaintiffs show that they are non-White or racially distinct, "although," Brannan noted, "it is unclear racially distinct from *whom*."[72] The Circuit Court, in this case, had implied that to be "White" is the norm, which is the prevailing assumption, not only in the United States, but also, in various ways, in the colonizing "West." How did Whiteness *become* the norm? This assumption is based on how and by whom race was constructed and who would want it to occur. To highlight how this operates, law scholar Martha Minow writes: "The attribution of difference hides the power of those who classify and of the institutional arrangements that enshrine one type of person as the norm, and then treat classifications of difference as inherent and natural while debasing those defined as different."[73] Here, a Foucauldian structure defines who has the ability to classify others on the basis of supposedly innate characteristics.[74]

Next, another justice inquired whether, in Brannan's argument, the respondents could be criminally prosecuted under the criminal counterpart of the statutes, which would include preventing the vandals from defacing their property. Brannan stated that she believed they could and noted that they were prosecuted under state law but only under statutes regarding the malicious destruction of property and not under any statutes that address the race-based civil rights violation that "was the most hurtful part of the conduct."[75] She explained: "It wasn't really getting the wall messed up that is offensive to the congregation."[76] The court noted that for criminal prosecution to be successful in this type of case, the burden of proof would be exceptionally high, since the plaintiffs' lawyer would have to prove what was in the defendants' minds. Brannan agreed that it would be "a question of fact" but that legitimate arguments could be made based, for instance, on the plaintiffs' depositions, given how they had answered the questions.[77]

The justices then compared the argument that Brannan made regarding the sections deriving from the Civil Rights Act of 1866 to Title VII of the Civil Rights Act of 1964, which applied to equal employment, and Title VIII sections of the Civil Rights Act of 1968, which pertained to the Fair Housing Act.[78] They expressed concern that perhaps Brannan's interpretation of the statutes cited in *Shaare Tefila* would overlap with the protection provided in Title VII and Title VIII.[79] Note that Title VII prohibits discrimination regarding "compensation, terms, conditions, or privileges of employment" on the basis of "race, color, religion, sex, or national origin," and that Title VIII "prohibits discrimination in the sale, rental and financing of dwellings based on race, color, religion, sex or national origin." Brannan argued that Title VIII also covered religious and gender-based discrimination, however, and she asserted that the Titles stand independently from section 1982 of the Civil Rights Act of 1866.

Justice Scalia asked Brannan again about racial motivation. He posed a hypothetical in which a landlord does not want to lease an apartment to a particular racial group because he believes that members of that group are "sloppy" and wondered if that would count as "racial motivation."[80] Brannan replied that it would and remarked: "it's those kinds of stereotyped generalizations about racial groups that have created the disabilities that Congress was trying to break in the 1866 Act."[81] Scalia complicated the hypothetical example by positing that the landlord thinks that all Frenchmen are sloppy but knows that French people are not a separate racial group. Or, he added, the group could be Puerto Ricans or Italians. Brannan responded that if it were not a racially based distinction (rather than a "national origin" distinction, in response to some of Justice O'Connor's questions), the case would not be covered, which Scalia said he found was a peculiar decision.[82] But Brannan urged Scalia to consider that in 1866 Congress was concerned with "creating situations in which the newly freed slaves could function in our society."[83] She noted: "It was really a deep concern with racial motivation as being something distinct and particularly odious in our society that was at the heart of their concern."[84] Scalia wondered if Brannan's approach covered only the "ill-educated discriminator,"[85] but Brannan countered that prejudice is a matter of ignorance rather than educational degrees. She pointed out: "I think that there are perhaps those in much more sophisticated places with a string of degrees who may be surprised to hear a congregation arguing before the Supreme Court that Jews are not a race."[86]

In her concluding statement to the Supreme Court, Brannan reiterated the problem with the Fourth Circuit Court's decision, as she understood it. She argued that the Fourth Circuit erroneously diverged from the Supreme Court's judgments in *McDonald* and *General Building Contractors* by adding a test in which plaintiffs must prove that they are "racially distinct." She stated: "It is unclear, first of all, what the [Fourth Circuit] Court [of Appeals] even meant by 'racially distinct.' Racially distinct from whom?"[87] Furthermore, Brannan noted, the Supreme Court even held that Whites who are victims of discrimination could bring a claim under sections 1981 and 1982 in *Sullivan* and *Tillman*.[88] Brannan continued:

> In terms, of course, of its language about the Jewish plaintiffs in Shaare Tefila being non-white, we think perhaps it goes without saying that it would be a completely inappropriate exercise for the district courts to undertake trying to figure out who is white and non-white in some objective, anthropological, or scientific test; that simply would not be an appropriate approach for the courts to take.[89]

Chief Justice Rehnquist thanked Patricia Brannan and then invited Deborah Garren to make her argument on behalf of the respondents.

Garren opened her argument by emphasizing Shaare Tefila's status as a "place of worship" and asserted that "inclusion of such a religious discrimination claim within the scope of this race discrimination statute" is incongruent with the purpose of the statute and with the Court's interpretation of it.[90] Furthermore, she asserted that determining a race discrimination statute on the basis of the "erroneous perceptions of discriminators" is not in keeping with the "purpose and language of the statute" as the court has previously interpreted it.[91]

Justice O'Connor responded to Garren by noting that legislative history includes references to "Gypsies and Chinese and Germans and so forth" such that Congress may have "intended to cover discrimination on the basis of a different version of what constitutes race."[92] Justice O'Connor also noted that President Andrew Johnson vetoed the statute, but his veto was overruled by Congress. President Johnson did not think that the federal government had the right to advocate for these groups to qualify for the same protections, although he did not specifically mention "Gypsies," Chinese, and Germans in his veto. He had advocated ardently for states' rights and vehemently opposed this first federal bill for civil rights.[93] Furthermore, Justice O'Connor maintained that the concept of "race" was conceptualized quite differently in 1866.

Garren seemed to evade her statement and instead asserted that she did not think Congress meant to define the statute on the basis of racist *intent*. Then, Justice O'Connor asked how Garren would respond to the argument in the companion case, *St. Francis College v. Al-Khazraji*, in which Caroline Mitchell argued that the Civil Rights Act of 1866 protects Majid Al-Khazraji, because "Arabs" were considered a race in 1866. Garren observed, however, that the petitioners in *Shaare Tefila* had not claimed either that Jews have a racial identity or that they are commonly identified as racially distinct. She acknowledged that although the legislative history may have included some references to Jewish people as members of a different race, it would be inappropriate to make this argument based on one legislator's comment. Here she was referring to Representative Dawson, in the 39th Congress. He had contended that "Jews were a race,"[94] and he noted: "It is the homogenous races which have controlled the world. The Jew, though without a country and every where the object of prejudice, yet maintains his physical and mental excellence even to this present day; and it is because he chiefly intermarries with his own race."[95] In this context, Dawson made the gross discriminatory stereotype that people of one "race" who intermarry will have increased or decreased capabilities based on particular qualities, in this case "physical and mental excellence," and draws on the philosemitic trope that Jews are smarter than other people.

Garren then went on to argue that the petitioners in no way adopted the argument of the companion case, and she thought a more appropriate approach would involve examining whether "particular groups" are commonly identified as "white" or "non-white" in the twentieth century.[96] To which Justice O'Connor noted that the Court included Whites within the protection of the act in *McDonald*, and asked Garren how, if it is unlawful to discriminate against *White* people, she could exclude Jews. Garren responded: "Jewish people would have a cause of action based on discrimination because they are white, if that was their contention in this case. They also do not contend that they are racially distinct from whites in any way. So, I would argue that they do not fall within a group that is protected by the statute."[97]

In response, Justice Powell noted that "the problem we have in the U.S. . . . when I say problem, perhaps it's a great asset of our country . . . is that we have so many races that over a period of many years that there have been a great number of intermarriages."[98] He then asked Garren how her theory would apply to intermarriage, to the descendants of a marriage between a White person and an Asian person, for example. Garren hesitated before stating that she is not trying to argue for scientific categories of race and that coverage from the statute would depend on whether a group is perceived as non-White. When the justice inquired whether her answer aligned her argument closely with that of the petitioners, she responded that it did not, because the logical conclusion of their argument would allow "homosexuals" or "handicapped individuals" to claim that they were discriminated against based on race just because the discriminator viewed them as a race.[99] Instead, Garren claimed that she aimed to realign the statute with twentieth-century social perceptions.

Justice Marshall then asked her where or in what book we should look to find the answer to how a person "part Scandinavian, part Indian, part South African, and part Japanese" would be classified.[100] Garren responded that a jury could determine whether someone was discriminated against because she or he is a member of a group commonly identified as "non-white." He then asked how the individual *became* identified as a non-White person, and Garren answered that one way would be by "immutable physical charac-teristics such as skin color."[101] He then interrupted her by stating: "I would like . . . to have seen you identify my father. He was white with blond hair and blue eyes."[102] Garren replied: "In that case, sir, I don't think he would have a cause of action for race discrimination." The justice responded: "Oh, but he did. He was a Negro." Here, Justice Marshall cited how the laws of hypo-descent constructed the race of his father. In line with this concept, Nadine Ehlers asserts: "there has been a belief that race is at once in plain sight and yet is potentially hidden. . . . This epistemological loop is a recurrent motif in American racial ideology. For while social discourse and legal measures have advanced that race is inevitably pronounced by the body, the fear has always been present that race may defy visibility."[103] Ehlers notes that people often imagine race can be seen because of how we define it, based on hypodescent or skin color or blood lineage, because that's what we *believe* it to be.

Justice Marshall continued: "I am trying to find where you—what do you do with Sammy Davis?"[104] Sammy Davis Jr., 1925–1990, was a singer, actor, dancer, vaudevillian, and comedian, who was Black and converted to Judaism. Laughter filled the Supreme Court. After it ended, Garren replied: "Sammy Davis might certainly have a cause of action for race discrimination. He would not have a cause of action based on his religion."[105]

Marshall paused, and then he said: "the people who did this act knew exactly what they were doing, and they knew exactly who they were aim-ing at, didn't they?"[106] Garren stopped, and then agreed that an "egregious wrong" had been committed.[107] "And should be punished," he replied. Garren concurred and claimed that there *was* already a remedy available. "What?" he asked. She told him that Michael Remer, who had instigated the vandalism, had been convicted of malicious destruction of property and convicted to the maximum sentence in the State of Maryland. Other criminal restitution was available under Maryland law, she stated, but the petitioners had never really wanted to bring state claims against them because they wanted to bring a federal lawsuit against them. She argued, however, that this could not be done under section 1982, because Congress gave no indication that federal jurisdiction would cover "individual discriminators' illogical and irrational perceptions of race."[108]

Justice Blackmun then posed another hypothetical example, supposing that Shaare Tefila had been a synagogue of Ethiopian Jews. Garren responded that it would be a different case, in which the synagogue could make allegations based on its members being predominantly Black, which she acknowledged would be covered by section 1982. Blackmun asked: "Black, not Jewish, then?"[109] Garren reminded him that the petitioners agreed that Jews are not racially distinct. So, Justice Marshall followed with: "Well, if they are black and Jewish?"[110] And then "If they painted swastikas they wouldn't have a cause of action because they are Jewish?"[111] She replied: "That's correct, Your Honor."[112] He countered, "You would have to take that position," and she agreed that "In order to take that position, I would have to. Yes, sir, I do."[113] The people listening in the courtroom laughed.[114]

Following this scenario, Garren gave a short speech about how the petitioners did not claim a racial identity and that the statute does not apply to all forms of bigotry, such as sex discrimination, religious discrimination, or national origin discrimination. Justice Blackmun inquired whether she applied the statute only to Blacks, and Garren said that she did not; further, he asked if "it were the yellow . . . the Chinese, you would say the statute is applicable?"[115] Blackmun's qualification of Chinese people as "yellow" highlights a prevalent White narrative at that time. Garren said that it would but went on to state that the statute was provided to protect newly freed enslaved peoples. The Court, she noted, had indicated that Blacks are protected and subsequently that Whites are also protected. She then critiqued Patricia Brannan's argument, in that Brannan had said she did not need to define what "racism" entails in her claim.[116]

In the next hypothetical case, Justice Stevens pointed out that over the years, and "it's still prevalent in some areas, there was prejudice against Jews. That was known in our society. There was a lot of anti-Semitism. How would you characterize that prejudice?"[117] He interrupted Garren's statement to say: "You wouldn't call it racial prejudice?" "Prejudice that is based on their religion," she asserted.[118] Stevens inquired: "Do you think it was based

entirely on their religion?" Garren responded: "That is the characteristic that
defines them. There is no racial characteristic that in fact defines people of the
Jewish faith. It is a religion."[119] Then he probed: "Do you think that would be
the proper characterization in Germany when it was so virulent?"[120] Garren
commented: "No, sir. But again that was the deviant perception of a couple
of organizations in the society that had run rampant. It wasn't a common perception in the society. They weren't commonly identified."[121] In response, he
queried whether Garren thought that the origin of the prejudice in this country
was "entirely religious." Garren responded that she does not think that she is
qualified to comment on that but stated: "I have every reason to believe that
religion in part motivated the prejudice, because that is what in fact defines
the group."[122]

Justice Scalia followed up by asking: "It didn't extend to Jews who were
atheists, nonbelievers? Do you really think that was the case?"[123] When
Garren expressed uncertainty, he continued: "I mean, do you think that the
prejudice that existed against Jews in this country was only against believing
Jews, and so long as the Jew said, I really no longer believe in the religious
tenets of Judaism, the prejudice no longer existed and that person would have
been able to get into all sort of country clubs and whatnot?" Garren hesitated
before she answered: "No, sir, but I do think that the discriminators define
the group by their religious beliefs. They may not know in each individual
instance whether that Jewish person follows his faith or not."[124]

He asked her if she wanted to use "modern concepts of taxonomy in order
to apply this statute," to which she responded: "I don't think I do. I am not
suggesting that you attempt to define racial categories in a taxonomical
fashion, or any kind of scientific way, because I do think there are incredible
difficulties with doing that."[125] When she reasserted that it should involve
the common perception of a group as non-White, Justice Scalia asked why it
would just be non-White, and what the term "non-White" means. He noted
that Germans would have been considered non-White as the statute was
interpreted in 1866. He also reminded Garren of the Know-Nothing movement and the nativism that prevailed at the time the Act was passed.[126] Garren
responded that it was a Reconstruction-era statute that emphasized the rights
of freed slaves but that the courts later extended it to Whites. Justice Marshall
inquired whether Garren thought the court should amend *McDonald* to say
that when "we said 'white people' we didn't mean Jews?"[127] Garren reiterated her position that Jews *who are White* could sue if they are discriminated
against as Whites and Jews *who are Black* could sue if they are discriminated
against as Black, but that Jews do not have a racial identity. In response,
Justice Marshall expressed: "Just because some Jews are white in complex-
ion, doesn't take away the rights of them as *Jews*."[128] Garren replied: "those
are rights against *religious* discrimination," and concluded: "I would say this

is religious discrimination and is not encompassed within the race discrimination statute."[129]

Justice Marshall rejected Garren's insistence that the vandalism consisted of *only* religious discrimination: "That's the only thing a swastika means . . . 'Death to the Jews,' that's what the swastika means."[130] Garren responded that she understood what the Nazis believed and that she did not think that these beliefs are common in our society. But he persisted that the swastika carries the same meaning regardless of *who* uses it. He continued: "It means that you should die," and then he thundered: "The word is Holocaust. The word is Holocaust. That's what the swastika means."[131] After pausing for several moments, Garren agreed that Jews have been subject to terrible discrimination, but she insisted that the statute does not apply to Jews in which a "defendant acted out of a misperception."[132] Justice Marshall then asked how the congregation members could use the law to protest the swastika painted on the synagogue. When Garren asserted that they should have pursued "these fellows" in the state court, the justice asked her what statute the state court had that said: "you shall not use swastikas?" Garren conceded that the state has no such statute, but that punitive damages such as common-law actions and criminal restitution in the form of state sentencing laws would address the issue.[133]

Justice Scalia asked Garren about her argument that the location of the graffiti—a synagogue—demonstrated that the discrimination was religious. He noted, however, that the defendants had just spray-painted a drugstore, which is not notably religious, and that they had painted the words "White Power" and "Arian Brotherhood" [sic].[134] Members in the courtroom laughed. Garren claimed: "no one has denied . . . that these defendants acted out of a belief that Jews are racially inferior and that the symbols they painted suggested that."[135] Justice Scalia responded by noting that just because the act occurred at the synagogue did not prove her argument. She reiterated that she was trying to make the point that it *is* religious discrimination because the court cannot apply a "misperception" scheme, which would mean that "all religious discrimination claims, national origin discrimination claims, and even some sex discrimination claims might come within this race discrimination statute."[136] Justice Scalia returned to the framers' intent, who may have thought that "Germans and Gypsies" were races, because by races they meant "a stock," and Garren replied that the petitioners have "stipulated that away here," that Jews are not "racially distinct," nor "commonly identified as such."[137] Scalia asked if it would be "within their power" to decide the case on that basis, to which Garren responded, "clearly it would be within your power," and, again, laughter ensued.[138]

Garren reiterated her argument that a more appropriate approach than "reaching back" to the late 1860s to figure out which groups were viewed as a race would be to examine the society now and to ask "what groups are commonly identified as non-white, with reference to what we all recognize as racial characteristics."[139] "Why not non-white?"[140] Justice Scalia asked, continuing, "What groups are identified as races?"[141] and, "What if we concluded that that theory of these people was scientifically foolish but not necessarily *socially* foolish? There are a lot of people who might use the term 'Jewish' to refer to what they think is a racial group, a stock."[142] Scalia noted that the congregation had *not* argued: "there is no general social perception that to be a Jew is only a religious thing."[143] Garren replied that the congregation did not claim that Jews are racially distinct either.

Justice Stevens asked if it was important to her case "that there be some well-defined categories of races?"[144] He said, "I imagine at one time, perhaps scientists might have thought there were five or six races, ten or twenty. Now, they seem to say there are three, is it, three races."[145] Apparently, he had not kept abreast of the UNESCO statement about race in 1950, which emphasized the social rather than the scientific realities of race. "What if," he said, "twenty years from now they really study this thing and determine there is only one race, that really the differences among the races are not scientifically scientific?"[146] His question coincides with Brannan's argument: that judges should not be making decisions about race, because what he was positing for the future had already occurred almost thirty years prior. Stevens then wondered whether the statute would have any relevance if "race" were not scientifically determined. Garren responded that anthropologists conceive of race in "reference to culture" and to "common perceptions in our society."[147] Stevens responded by stating: "Well, if you look at culture, I suppose a pretty strong argument could be made that the Jewish people have a very special culture of their own." Evading his point, Garren reiterated that Jews are commonly perceived as White. "What I am trying to get at is, how does one decide whether two people are in the same or different races?" Stevens asked. Faltering here, Garren said that "you look at the individual . . . and you evaluate whether that individual is identified as white or is identified as non-white in our society, in some sense."[148] Justice O'Connor inquired about the terms "Hispanics" and "Arabs," after some debate regarding a rejoinder question in which she had used the terms "Moslems" and "Arabs." Garren pointed out that "Moslems" is a religious term, and she concluded that those groups would be protected, "because in many instances individuals that are in those groups have dark skin, for example."[149] Garren hesitated slightly as she concluded her interaction with the justices by reminding the court of the state remedies available and asking the Court to uphold the lower court's dismissal of the synagogue's claim for desecration of a synagogue under section 1982.

Patricia Brannan gave a one-minute rebuttal argument on behalf of the petitioners, in which she focused on the "common knowledge" argument that Deborah Garren had made.[150] First, she stated, there was no mention of Shaare Tefila's position on commonness of the belief [that Jews are a racial group] in the court documents, because the lower court's Motion to Dismiss prevented the submission of further materials that Shaare Tefila had included in the record. Second, she argued, "some Gallup poll or test of the prevalence of the view really doesn't solve the problem."[151] Rather, "the facts of this case show that this kind of conduct occurs" and that it is "not unique to Shaare Tefila."[152] Furthermore, wherever the conduct occurs, regardless of how prevalent it is, "the harm is the same."[153] She concluded: "It is a harm based on racially motivated conduct, and it should be redressed under Section 1982."[154] The oral argument ended after Chief Justice Rehnquist stated: "Thank you, Ms. Brannan. The case is submitted."[155]

Religion- and Race-Based Analysis of the Supreme Court Argument

For the Supreme Court justices, because of the arguments that Patricia Brannan and Deborah Garren made, one of the central issues was how to situate Jewish identification legally in relation to the civil rights categories of "religion" and "race." During their presentations and engagement with the justices, assumptions regarding the justices' and the lawyers' understandings of these categories became apparent. For example, Justice Scalia's certitude that "belief" is evidence of "religion," and Garren's conviction that "race" is defined by skin color. These concepts were not only unquestioned components of American discourse in the 1980s; they still are, in the twenty-first century.

One of the ways in which the justices should have defined these categories was precedent, but the oral argument rarely examined precedent, it mainly relied on the prevailing socio-legal narratives during the 1980s.[156] The justices considered Jewish identification in relation to how they personally understood "religion" and "race," and how those understandings reflected their own viewpoints of legal history. Later in the oral argument, they addressed the history of Jewish marginalization in the United States.

Both Garren and Brannan had to appeal to the justices' conceptions of "religion" and "race," as shaped by their environment and social location. For Garren's argument to succeed, she had to prove that Jews are only a religious group and that they are not "commonly perceived" as a racial group. For Brannan to succeed, she had to convince the justices that Jews are not a race but that *some* people, such as the vandals, think that they are and treat them accordingly. Her assertion also invoked the vandals' actions in defacing the synagogue.

The justices questioned Brannan and Garren to understand the exact boundaries of their arguments. They posed various hypothetical examples with the aim of determining their soundness, and they also made some legitimate assumptions based on how the history of "religion" and "race" has been defined in the United States. For Justice Scalia, religion has to do with "belief," it's existential, and it's something that one can change. "Race" is determined by skin color, by hypodescent—as in Justice Marshall's father's case—and by "common perception."[157] It is fixed, permanent, and embodied. These assessments draw on the histories of these categories as colonial fixtures, based on their origins as embodiments of power.[158]

Deborah Garren's argument regarding Jewish identification relied on the prevailing American conception during the 1980s, evident in the perspectives of the lower court judges who dismissed the case on the basis that Jewish Americans are White. Her argument also assumed that a single narrative fully encompassed the different types of marginalization that Jewish Americans have faced. In her citation of "common perception," she relied on what Ian Haney López calls the "common knowledge" test, which was used in racial prerequisite cases.[159] This opinion, theoretically, should be the same opinion that any "common person" would have; in other words, the justices were not expected to be experts on race. Her assertion relied on the narrative about race in the 1980s, because, so the argument went, the "common person" knows what race is by living in the United States, in which a certain conception of race predominates. Garren's argument further necessitated that this "common person" could distinguish between someone who was White versus someone who was not White. This premise implies that "White" is something "common people" can see and that we can see it correctly because we know what physical characteristics make someone White or not White.[160]

In contrast to Garren, Patricia Brannan asserted that racial discrimination did occur, regardless of whether Jews are or are not "in fact" a race; she did not think that the courts should be deciding or defining the boundaries between "races" at all. Rather, race and racism were determined by examining cultural practices and histories of racial discourses. Brannan emphasized not only that Jewish Americans were not a "race" but also that the court should not engage in determining the boundaries or definitions of racial subcategories. In Brannan's argument, civil rights protection based on race equates with protection against ra*cism*, such that race need not be proven but rather only that discrimination based on *perceptions* of race be proven. Like Judge Wilkinson, in the Fourth Circuit Court of Appeals, the factual qualifications of race, for Brannan, were immaterial.

Brannan rejected the "common knowledge" test because not all racist actions follow dominant views of race and racial divisions and because White supremacist perceptions about race continued to inform identity-based crimes.[161] She requested that the court define racism in terms of the mental approach or the intention that informs how an individual operates when he or she commits a crime. In effect, Brannan aimed to move the court away from the "common knowledge" test toward a test still based on conception but one that allowed for *other* perceptions of racial differences besides the dominant one. Bruce Lincoln points out that not "all thought reflects, encodes, re-presents, or helps replicate the established structures of society, for society is far broader and more complex than its official structures and institutions alone."[162] Historical movements that espoused racism and subversive racial discourses, Brannan asserted, should significantly inform the court's views on racism.

A major strength of Brannan's argument was her emphasis on rac*ism* rather than on "proven" racial characteristics or "factual" racial distinction. This reasoning accounted for and required legal coverage for the variety of narratives that depict Jews as somehow "essentially" inferior. Whereas Garren's argument reified a trope prevalent in the 1980s—that Jews were White and a religious group—Brannan's argument allowed for protection against a wide variety of identification-based attacks on Jews.[163] Following Brannan's reasoning, the statute would cover anyone who committed a crime against Jewish Americans based on a supposed "quality" that *any* American might have associated with the category of "race." This reasoning implicitly deconstructs the normative perceptions affiliated with the category "race." Rather than assuming either that a factual definition of race and its subcategories existed or that Americans necessarily shared the very same ideas about race, Brannan's approach accounted for the diversity of views about Jews that could inform crimes committed against Jews.

Garren's argument required, in contrast, that Jews seeking legal protection prove that the prevailing understanding of Jewish identification is factually wrong. According to Garren, a judge could "look at" a person and determine her Whiteness. Garren grounded this argument on the premise that everyone "saw" race in the same way or that some universal code existed that allowed a person to know immediately how to categorize another person.

Garren asserted that Jews can be identified only as a religious group, and, correspondingly, that Jews were not, "in fact," a race. She did not provide reasoning for what specifically makes Jews "religious"; in other words, she did not describe religion and demonstrate how Jews fit that category. Instead, she simply noted: "that is the category that defines them."[164] Furthermore, Garren pointed to the synagogue, a religious building, as evidence that the vandalism attacked Jews for being members of a religious group and not for any other reason. The synagogue, in this case, stands for religion, since it serves a "religious" function, among others, as a space for prayer services. In Garren's argument, the larger legal category at stake is "religion," and the subcategory in question is "Judaism." Like the lower court judges, she examined not the content of the graffiti or the historical associations between it and

Ku Klux Klan or Nazi ideologies of Jewish racialized inferiority but the governing discourse of the 1980s that defined Jews, and how they have typically identified in courts as members of a religious group. Brannan's argument regarding Jewish identification, however, precluded any need to categorize Jews according to either religion or race. Rather, her approach focused on the incident itself and the narratives that informed the vandals' actions.

Let's consider the Supreme Court justices' perceptions and determinations regarding the Jewish American congregants who brought *Shaare Tefila*. They knew that the legal definition of race changes over time because the court questioned Brannan about whether the members of the 39th Congress *would have* categorized Jews as a race in 1866.[165] They also had *St. Francis College* in mind because they aimed to make a decision that would satisfy both sets of circumstances. So, they returned to the argument of Caroline Mitchell, Al-Khazraji's lawyer, in their questioning of both Patricia Brannan and Deborah Garren, asking what reasons the lawyers would have given for not reiterating Mitchell's claim that Iraqi Arab and Jewish Americans—then called "Hebrews"—would have been considered separate races in 1866 and 1871 when the 39th Congress passed the Civil Rights Acts. Neither Brannan nor Garren explicitly rejected the possibility that the argument could apply, but they both pointed out problems with that argument relative to Brannan's assertions. Brannan noted the problem of accepting the argument if it would mean that the court would then conclude that Jews are *legally* a race; and Garren maintained that Mitchell's argument would be relevant only if Brannan had argued that Jews *are* a race and should be protected for that reason.

Note the two "minority" justices' perceptions here. When Justice Marshall asked Deborah Garren how she would classify his father after describing his skin color and features, she stated that he would be considered White and would have no cause for action under the statute. In response, he retorted: "Oh, but he did. He was a Negro."[166] Such a classificatory conundrum recalled *Plessy v. Ferguson* (1896), in which a man traveling on a train appeared White but was legally Black. When he revealed his Black identification, he had to move to the "Negro" car on the train.[167] In referencing his father, Justice Marshall implied that although Shaare Tefila congregation members "look White," they *also* could have been the victims of race-based discrimination.

Justice Marshall's hypothetical example about the Harlem synagogue conveyed the complexity of contemporary narratives about race and the predominance of the Black/White distinction as the salient form of race. In his conversation with Patricia Brannan, he noted that "there are no Jews in that synagogue" before realizing that he had made a mistake based on the assumption that Jews are White. He corrected himself and stated: "There are no white Jews, I would say."[168] He posited that the vandals had defaced this synagogue in Harlem, and asked Brannan what argument she would make in that situation. When she explained that she would construct it in the same way, he replied, "Well, you couldn't do it on race, could you?"[169] His response revealed his initial assumption that the White/Black racial distinction trumped or negated the argument that antisemitism is also racism. This assumption reflects the dominant narrative of race in the United States, in which it refers specifically to Black and White people and to the relationship between them.

At the end of the oral argument, Justice Scalia questioned Deborah Garren's assertion that Jews are *only* a religious group. Recall that he had asked her whether Jews could get into "any country club" if they swore off their religious beliefs, and she had recognized that they could not, but she maintained that the discrimination in question pertained to belief. Her response acknowledged that someone could *be* a Jewish person without "follow[ing] his faith." This acknowledgment potentially undermined her argument because she agreed with Scalia that "religion" pertained to belief. If Judaism, as a religion, is *based* on belief—the dominant White Christian assumption in the United States—this basis supported Scalia's point that Jewish identification need not rely *only* on belief. It could, for instance, apply to a cultural, secular, or another identity that could be considered "racial" by the vandals.

Scalia's questioning highlighted the association of religion with belief as well as the problem of how to categorize "non-believing Jews" in relation to religion. It raises the issue of what "religious discrimination" entails. According to Scalia's logic, discrimination *not* based on belief must not be religious discrimination. If a nonbeliever is not religious, how should the court categorize nonbelieving Jews? The court shied away from Brannan's argument, which emphasizes perception, but at the same time seemed to define religion in terms of belief, also a state of mind that cannot be fully known by someone else, as Scalia pointed out in this example. Scalia implied that Jews who reject the tenets of the Jewish faith, on the one hand, remain Jewish and, on the other hand, would not remain within the bounds of the legal category of religion, as it has been defined. This example illustrates both that Scalia assumed that religion necessarily entails belief *and* that Jews faced discrimination for other, perhaps "racial" reasons.

When Jewish identifications surpassed the boundaries of belief, they no longer "fit" the ways religion was determined. As the justices struggled to make sense of the relationship between Jewish Americans and race, they also had to see beyond the ways that "race" had been defined in American history, because the assumption is that it is correlated with skin color. Jews, as a category of people, do not share a "skin color." So, neither Jews, in general, nor Jewish Americans, fit the somewhat arbitrary definitions used by imagined American discourse to describe groups of individuals in a socio-legal way.

The Supreme Court's Decision

After listening to the oral argument, the court made a unanimous decision in favor of *Shaare Tefila* on May 18, 1987. Justice Byron White wrote the ruling. In his tenure as Supreme Court justice from 1962 to 1993, Byron White had written 993 other opinions.

White served as Associate Justice his entire time on the Supreme Court, and he had a judicial perspective that was difficult to typify. In his younger years, White was a star student. He was twice valedictorian and a Rhodes scholar, and an American football player, who delayed his time at both Oxford University and law school at Yale University to play football for the National Football League, the Pittsburgh Pirates (later the Steelers), and the Detroit Lions. White was elected to the Football Hall of Fame in 1954. In World War II, he had wanted to enroll in the Marines, but because he was color-blind, he settled for working as an intelligence officer in the Navy, for which he earned two Bronze Stars. Back at law school, he graduated first in his class in 1946 and then served as a law clerk to Supreme Court Chief Justice Fred Vinson. Afterward, he moved back to Denver, Colorado, his home state, and practiced law for about fifteen years. He served as John F. Kennedy (JFK)'s Colorado state chair for JFK's 1960 campaign, then as US Deputy Attorney in 1961, and later as Associate Justice to the Supreme Court. As a justice, he was known for having an expansive view of government powers but also for judicial restraint. Notable cases include his dissents, like Justice Scalia, in *Miranda v. Arizona* (1966),[170] and in *Roe v. Wade* (1973), which gave women the right to have an abortion. He argued the latter was "an exercise in raw judicial power."[171]

In *Shaare Tefila*, White, on behalf of the court, reversed the opinion of the Court of Appeals to determine that "because Jews *today* are not thought to be members of a separate race, they cannot make out a claim of racial discrimination within the meaning of §1982."[172] The court had determined when the section was passed, it "intended to protect from discrimination identifiable classes of persons who are subjected to intentional discrimination solely because of their ancestry or ethnic characteristics."[173] White held: A charge of racial discrimination within the meaning of §1982 cannot be made out by alleging only that the defendants were motivated by racial animus. It is also necessary to allege that the animus was directed toward the kind of group that Congress intended to protect when it passed the statute."[174] He continued: "Jews can state a §1982 claim of racial discrimination since they were among the peoples considered to be distinct races and hence within the protection of the statute at the time it was passed."[175] White referred to the legislative history that informed the court's ruling in *St. Francis College* to note that "that Jews and Arabs were among the peoples *then* considered to be distinct races and hence within the protection of the statute. Jews are not foreclosed from stating a cause of action simply because the defendants are also part of what today is considered the Caucasian race."[176] White concluded: "The judgment of the Court of Appeals is therefore reversed, and the case is remanded for further proceedings consistent with this opinion."[177]

In the *St. Francis College v. Al-Khazraji* ruling, decided the same day, White referred to Representative Dawson, of the 39th Congress, who remarked that Jews, among other peoples whom he and other Congressional Representatives had discussed, including Arabs, Mexicans, Spanish, Blacks, and Mongolians, needed to be protected by the Civil Rights Act of 1866.[178]

The Supreme Court agreed with Mitchell's argument that emphasized legislative history. She based it, however, on dictionary definitions, which recorded the prevailing definitions of race close to the period of 1866.[179] This ruling accounts for the conception of race in 1866 but does *not* account for the underlying issue of racialization as a fluid concept.

CONCLUSION

In the *Shaare Tefila* oral argument, it is evident that Jewish identification does not neatly fit the available categories of legal protection—"religion" and "race"—as the court understood them. Throughout American history, *belief* has been central to the category of religion. Because Jews have experienced discrimination whether they were "religious" or not, the court concluded that religion did not encompass all the facets of Jewish identification. Neither did the court find that Jews fit the category of "race." In this regard, the prevailing American thinking about race describes it in terms of skin color, and particularly in terms of "colors" other than White.[180] Patricia Brannan emphasizes, in contrast, the existence of rac*ism* rather than the "actuality" of race apparent in the incident. Like Judge Wilkinson, she located the violation of *rights* in the rac*ism*, rather than in the identification of the members themselves.

This analysis of the Supreme Court's ruling on *Shaare Tefila* has underscored how it reflects the larger argument that concepts of "religion," "race," and here, specifically of Jewish identification, change over time. The judges' conclusions in the lower courts identified Jewish Americans as "White," whereas in the oral argument, the Supreme Court acknowledged the *history* of race-based discrimination against Jews. The disparate ruling in the Supreme Court versus the lower courts demonstrates the uncertainty of Jewish identification as it is legally categorized. Careful examination of the court proceedings reveals the contested nature of *Jewish* identification as a legal concept and the challenges that the judges faced in drawing on existent precedent regarding the categorization of Jews. The actions of the vandals, the argument for the congregation, and the justices' engagement with the legal assertions on both sides illuminate the multiple tropes that continue to inform and construct Jewish identifications.

NOTES

1. 481 U.S. 604 (1987).
2. Patricia Brannan, interview by author, Washington, DC, July 14, 2008.
3. See Marcia Graham Synott, "Anti-Semitism and American Universities: Did Quotas Follow the Jews?" in *Anti-Semitism in American History*, ed. David A. Gerber (Urbana: University of Illinois Press, 1986), 233–71.
4. In bringing the case to the Supreme Court, *Shaare Tefila* focused on section 1982 and excluded sections 1981 and 1985(3) from its claim.
5. See John Tehranian, *Whitewashed: America's Invisible Middle Eastern Minority* (New York: New York University Press, 2009).
6. Naturalization Act of 1870, Laws of 1870, ch. 254; 16 Stat. 254 (1870), codified at 1 Rev. Stat. Title XXX (1873).
7. Takao Ozawa v. United States, 260 U.S. 178 (1922).
8. Ian Haney Lopez, *White by Law: The Legal Construction of Race, Tenth Anniversary Edition* (New York: New York University Press, 2006), 5–6. *Ozawa v. United States* 260 U.S. 178 (1922).
9. Ian Haney Lopez, *White by Law: The Legal Construction of Race, Tenth Anniversary Edition* (New York: New York University Press, 2006), 4–5. Lopez describes the legal thinking about naturalization and Whiteness as culminating in 1909, explaining that six lower courts based their decision on common knowledge and seven others considered scientific evidence as the important factor.
10. Ian Haney Lopez, *White by Law: The Legal Construction of Race, Tenth Anniversary Edition* (New York: New York University Press, 2006), 5–6. *United States v. Bhagat Singh Thind* 261 U.S. 204 (1923).
11. Ian Haney Lopez, *White by Law: The Legal Construction of Race, Tenth Anniversary Edition* (New York: New York University Press, 2006), 65.
12. United States v. Bhagat Singh Thind, 261 U.S. 204, 209 (1923).
13. For more information, and to read a compelling piece on this issue, see John Tehranian, "Performing Whiteness: Naturalization Litigation and the Construction of Racial Identity in America" in *The Yale Law Journal* 109, no. 4 (Jan. 2000). For further work on the history of Arab-American identification and Whiteness in the United States, see Khaled Beydoun, "Between Muslim and White: The Legal Construction of Arab American Identity," in *New York University Annual Survey of American Law* 69, issue 1 (2013).
14. John Tehranian, "Performing Whiteness: Naturalization Litigation and the Construction of Racial Identity in America" in *Yale Law Journal* 109, no. 4 (Jan. 2000): 838. He cites *Ex Parte Mohriez* 54 F. Supp. 941 (D. Mass. 1944): 942.
15. Khaled A. Beydoun, "Faith in Whiteness: Free Exercise of Religion as Racial Expression," *Iowa Law Review* 105, no. 4 (May 2020): 1483.

16. Brief Amicus Curiae of the American-Arab Anti-Discrimination Committee in Support of Respondent Majid Ghaidan Al-Khazraji and Petitioners Shaare Tefila Congregation, et al., at 2, Shaare Tefila Congregation v. Cobb, 606 F.Supp. 1504 (D. Md. 1985) (No. R-84–880), *rev'd*, 107 S.Ct. 2019 (1987) in Philip Kurland and Gerhard Casper, *Landmark Briefs and Arguments of the Supreme Court of the United States: Constitutional Law, 1986 Term Supplement* (Frederick, MD: University Publications of America, Inc., 1988), 598.

17. Brief Amicus Curiae of the American-Arab Anti-Discrimination Committee in Support of Respondent Majid Ghaidan Al-Khazraji and Petitioners Shaare Tefila Congregation, et al., at 2, Shaare Tefila Congregation v. Cobb, 606 F.Supp. 1504 (D. Md. 1985) (No. R-84–880), *rev'd*, 107 S.Ct. 2019 (1987) in Philip Kurland and Gerhard Casper, *Landmark Briefs and Arguments of the Supreme Court of the United States: Constitutional Law, 1986 Term Supplement* (Frederick, MD: University Publications of America, Inc., 1988), 599.

18. Brief Amicus Curiae of the American-Arab Anti-Discrimination Committee in Support of Respondent Majid Ghaidan Al-Khazraji and Petitioners Shaare Tefila Congregation, et al., at 2, Shaare Tefila Congregation v. Cobb, 606 F.Supp. 1504 (D. Md. 1985) (No. R-84–880), *rev'd*, 107 S.Ct. 2019 (1987) in Philip Kurland and Gerhard Casper, *Landmark Briefs and Arguments of the Supreme Court of the United States: Constitutional Law, 1986 Term Supplement* (Frederick, MD: University Publications of America, Inc., 1988), 610.

19. Brief Amicus Curiae of the American-Arab Anti-Discrimination Committee in Support of Respondent Majid Ghaidan Al-Khazraji and Petitioners Shaare Tefila Congregation, et al., at 2, Shaare Tefila Congregation v. Cobb, 606 F.Supp. 1504 (D. Md. 1985) (No. R-84–880), *rev'd*, 107 S.Ct. 2019 (1987) in Philip Kurland and Gerhard Casper, *Landmark Briefs and Arguments of the Supreme Court of the United States: Constitutional Law, 1986 Term Supplement* (Frederick, MD: University Publications of America, Inc., 1988), 615.

20. Brief Amicus Curiae of the American-Arab Anti-Discrimination Committee in Support of Respondent Majid Ghaidan Al-Khazraji and Petitioners Shaare Tefila Congregation, et al., at 2, Shaare Tefila Congregation v. Cobb, 606 F.Supp. 1504 (D. Md. 1985) (No. R-84–880), *rev'd*, 107 S.Ct. 2019 (1987) in Philip Kurland and Gerhard Casper, *Landmark Briefs and Arguments of the Supreme Court of the United States: Constitutional Law, 1986 Term Supplement* (Frederick, MD: University Publications of America, Inc., 1988), 611.

21. Brief Amicus Curiae of the American-Arab Anti-Discrimination Committee in Support of Respondent Majid Ghaidan Al-Khazraji and Petitioners Shaare Tefila Congregation, et al., at 2, Shaare Tefila Congregation v. Cobb, 606 F.Supp. 1504 (D. Md. 1985) (No. R-84–880), *rev'd*, 107 S.Ct. 2019 (1987) in Philip Kurland and Gerhard Casper, *Landmark Briefs and Arguments of the Supreme Court of the United States: Constitutional Law, 1986 Term Supplement* (Frederick, MD: University Publications of America, Inc., 1988), 615.

22. Kevin Lipson, phone interview by author, May 20, 2009.

23. This is confirmed by my findings at the American Jewish Committee. I wrote to Charlotte Bonelli, the Director of the American Jewish Committee's Archive and

Records Center, and she responded with the suggestion that I search the digitized archives because the office was closed for an extended period due to COVID-19, which I had already done—finding three documents, but nothing of compelling interest. She responded a day later, telling me that her assistant, Deisree Guillermo, had been able to find a little bit more information about the case, which is copied here: "From 1986 October BOG Minutes:

REPORT OF THE NATIONAL LEGAL COMMITTEE Mr. NEVAS next asked Carl Koch to report on the activities of the National Legal Committee. Mr. KOCH stated that the Governors will soon be receiving the latest summary of the activities of the National Legal Committee. He referred to a specific case that the committee is currently debating — *Shaare Tefila Congregation vs. Cobb*. This case involves a Maryland congregation which is seeking damages from vandals who defaced their synagogue and were convicted of their crime. Instead of using existing state laws to support their claim, they are invoking the old Federal law which protects races from discrimination. The Legal Committee originally voted not to get involved in this case, since AJC has always maintained that Jewishness is not a distinct race, but this decision is now being reconsidered by the Committee since the case will be heard by the Supreme Court. (The Committee subsequently decided to intervene.) Bruce RAMER mentioned that the Shaare Tefila case and the Important issues involved would be discussed further at the meeting of the National Affairs Commission."

24. Naomi Wiener Cohen, *"Shaare Tefila Congregation v. Cobb*: A New Departure in American Jewish Defense?"* in *Jewish History* 3, no. 1 (1988): 100. Quoted from J. Sinensky and S. Freeman to National Legal Affairs Committee, Dec. 8, 1986, ADL.

25. Brief Amicus Curiae of the Anti-Defamation League of B'nai B'rith, et al., in Support of Respondent Majid Ghaidan Al-Khazraji and Petitioners Shaare Tefila Congregation, Shaare Tefila Congregation v. Cobb, 606 F.Supp. 1504 (D. Md. 1985) (No. R-84–880), *rev'd*, 107 S.Ct. 2019 (1987) in Philip Kurland and Gerhard Casper, *Landmark Briefs and Arguments of the Supreme Court of the United States: Constitutional Law, 1986 Term Supplement* (Frederick, MD: University Publications of America, Inc., 1988), 628.

26. Brief Amicus Curiae of the Anti-Defamation League of B'nai B'rith, et al., in Support of Respondent Majid Ghaidan Al-Khazraji and Petitioners Shaare Tefila Congregation, Shaare Tefila Congregation v. Cobb, 606 F.Supp. 1504 (D. Md. 1985) (No. R-84–880), *rev'd*, 107 S.Ct. 2019 (1987) in Philip Kurland and Gerhard Casper, *Landmark Briefs and Arguments of the Supreme Court of the United States: Constitutional Law, 1986 Term Supplement* (Frederick, MD: University Publications of America, Inc., 1988), 632.

27. Brief Amicus Curiae of the Anti-Defamation League of B'nai B'rith, et al., in Support of Respondent Majid Ghaidan Al-Khazraji and Petitioners Shaare Tefila Congregation, Shaare Tefila Congregation v. Cobb, 606 F.Supp. 1504 (D. Md. 1985) (No. R-84–880), *rev'd*, 107 S.Ct. 2019 (1987) in Philip Kurland and Gerhard Casper, *Landmark Briefs and Arguments of the Supreme Court of the United States: Constitutional Law, 1986 Term Supplement* (Frederick, MD: University Publications of America, Inc., 1988), 640.

28. Brief Amicus Curiae of the Anti-Defamation League of B'nai B'rith, et al., in Support of Respondent Majid Ghaidan Al-Khazraji and Petitioners Shaare Tefila Congregation, Shaare Tefila Congregation v. Cobb, 606 F.Supp. 1504 (D. Md. 1985) (No. R-84–880), *rev'd*, 107 S.Ct. 2019 (1987) in Philip Kurland and Gerhard Casper, *Landmark Briefs and Arguments of the Supreme Court of the United States: Constitutional Law, 1986 Term Supplement* (Frederick, MD: University Publications of America, Inc., 1988), 647.

29. Naomi Wiener Cohen, *"Shaare Tefila Congregation v. Cobb*: A New Departure in American Jewish Defense?" in *Jewish History* 3, No.1 (1988), 100; Quoted from M. Stern to Executive Committee, Apr. 4, 1986, *Shaare Tefila v. Cobb*/Internal Correspondence, AJCong; Minutes of Executive Committee, Apr. 14, 1986, AJCong.

30. Naomi Wiener Cohen, *"Shaare Tefila Congregation v. Cobb*: A New Departure in American Jewish Defense?" in *Jewish History* 3, No.1 (1988), 100; Memo by R. Krauss. June 30, 1986, *Shaare Tefila Congregation v. Cobb*/Internal Correspondence, AJCong; J. Chanes to NJCRAC Member Agencies, Oct. 7, 1986; *Shaare Tefila Congregation v. Cobb*/External Correspondence, AJCong.

31. Naomi Wiener Cohen, *"Shaare Tefila Congregation v. Cobb*: A New Departure in American Jewish Defense?" in *Jewish History* 3, No.1 (1988), 100; Memo by R. Krauss. June 30, 1986, *Shaare Tefila Congregation v. Cobb*/Internal Correspondence, AJCong; J. Chanes to NJCRAC Member Agencies, Oct. 7, 1986; *Shaare Tefila Congregation v. Cobb*/External Correspondence, AJCong.

32. Obituary for Majid Al-Khazraji Allen, 1933–2016, Koch Funeral Home, accessed February 24, 2021, kochfuneralhome.com/tribute/details/1352/Majid-Allan/obituary.html.

33. Obituary for Majid Al-Khazraji Allen, 1933–2016, Koch Funeral Home. Emilie Allan, Monday, January 16, 2017, "A Tribute to My Husband," accessed February 24, 2021, kochfuneralhome.com/tribute/details/1352/Majid-Allan/obituary.html.

34. Obituary for Majid Al-Khazraji Allen, 1933–2016, Koch Funeral Home. Emilie Allan, Monday, January 16, 2017, "A Tribute to My Husband," accessed February 24, 2021, kochfuneralhome.com/tribute/details/1352/Majid-Allan/obituary.html.

35. Obituary for Majid Al-Khazraji Allen, 1933–2016, Koch Funeral Home. Emilie Allan, Monday, January 16, 2017, "A Tribute to My Husband," accessed February 24, 2021, kochfuneralhome.com/tribute/details/1352/Majid-Allan/obituary.html.

36. Majid Ghaidan Al-khazraji, A/k/a Majid Al-khazraji Allen v. St. Francis College, et al., 784 F.2d 505 (3d Cir. 1986).

37. Majid Ghaidan Al-khazraji, A/k/a Majid Al-khazraji Allen v. St. Francis College, et al., 784 F.2d 505, 507 (3d Cir. 1986).

38. Majid Ghaidan Al-khazraji, A/k/a Majid Al-khazraji Allen v. St. Francis College, et al., 784 F.2d 505, 514 (3d Cir. 1986).

39. Judge Stapleton determined that the Supreme Court's decision in *Wilson v. Garcia* 471 U.S. 261 (1985) required the courts, in Al-Khazraji's case, to allow a longer time frame for his legal action.

40. St. Francis College v. Al-Khazraji 481 US 604 (1987).

41. "An act considering that baptisme of slaves doth not exempt them from bondage" (1667), Encyclopedia Virginia, Virginia Humanities, accessed March 11, 2022,

encyclopediavirginia.org/entries/an-act-declaring-that-baptisme-of-slaves-doth-not-exempt-them-from-bondage-1667/, *Transcription Source:* William Waller Hening, ed., The Statutes at Large; Being a Collection of All the Laws of Virginia from the First Session of the Legislature, in the Year 1619 (New York: R. & W. & G. Bartow, 1823), 2:260.

42. See particularly the introduction in David Sehat, *The Myth of American Religious Freedom* (New York: Oxford University Press, 2011), 1–10; Naomi Wiener Cohen, *Jews in Christian America: The Pursuit of Religious Equality* (New York: Oxford University Press, 1992).

43. See Stephen R. Haynes, *Noah's Curse: The Biblical Justification of American Slavery* (New York: Oxford University Press, 2002); David M. Goldenberg, *The Curse of Ham: Race and Slavery in Early Judaism, Christianity, and Islam* (Princeton, NJ: Princeton University Press, 2003);

44. See Ian Haney Lopez, *White by Law: The Legal Construction of Race, Tenth Anniversary Edition* (New York: New York University Press, 2006); John Tehranian, "Performing Whiteness: Naturalization Litigation and the Construction of Racial Identity in America" in *The Yale Law Journal* 109, no. 4 (Jan. 2000).

45. Major U.S. Immigration Laws, 1790–Present (March 2013) Fact Sheet, *Migration Policy Institute*, accessed February 25, 2021, www.migrationpolicy.org/research/timeline-1790. See also U.S. Immigration Timeline, Updated May 14, 2019, History.com, accessed February 25, 2021, www.history.com/topics/immigration/immigration-united-states-timeline.

46. Twelve and a half million Africans traveled on 35,000 ships operated by American and European slave traders; eleven million survived, which meant that more than one million perished during the horrific journey. See "Middle Passage," *Slavery and Remembrance: A Guide to Sites, Museums, and History*. United Nations Education, Scientific, and Cultural Organization, accessed February 25, 2021, slaveryandremembrance.org/articles/article/?id=A0032.

47. Thurgood Marshall, Oyez. Accessed February 25, 2021, www.oyez.org/justices/thurgood_marshall.

48. Thurgood Marshall, Oyez. Accessed February 25, 2021, www.oyez.org/justices/thurgood_marshall.

49. Thurgood Marshall, Oyez. Accessed February 25, 2021, www.oyez.org/justices/thurgood_marshall.

50. History.com Editors, "Thurgood Marshall," History, accessed February 25, 2021, www.history.com/topics/black-history/thurgood-marshall.

51. Thurgood Marshall, Oyez. Accessed February 25, 2021, www.oyez.org/justices/thurgood_marshall.

52. Biography.com Editors, "Antonin Scalia, Biography," The Biography.com website, www.biography.com/law-figure/antonin-scalia.

53. "Antonin Scalia." Oyez. Accessed February 25, 2021. www.oyez.org/justices/antonin_scalia

54. "Antonin Scalia." Oyez. Accessed February 25, 2021. www.oyez.org/justices/antonin_scalia

55. Oral argument at 673, Shaare Tefila Congregation v. Cobb, 606 F.Supp. 1504 (D. Md. 1985) (No. R-84–880), *rev'd*, 107 S.Ct. 2019 (1987), in *Landmark Briefs and Arguments of the Supreme Court of the United States: Constitutional Law, 1986 Term Supplement* (Frederick, MD: University Publications of America, Inc., 1988), 673.

56. Oral argument at 673, Shaare Tefila Congregation v. Cobb, 606 F.Supp. 1504 (D. Md. 1985) (No. R-84–880), *rev'd*, 107 S.Ct. 2019 (1987), in *Landmark Briefs and Arguments of the Supreme Court of the United States: Constitutional Law, 1986 Term Supplement* (Frederick, MD: University Publications of America, Inc., 1988), 673.

57. Oral argument at 675, Shaare Tefila Congregation v. Cobb, 606 F.Supp. 1504 (D. Md. 1985) (No. R-84–880), *rev'd*, 107 S.Ct. 2019 (1987), in *Landmark Briefs and Arguments of the Supreme Court of the United States: Constitutional Law, 1986 Term Supplement* (Frederick, MD: University Publications of America, Inc., 1988), 675.

58. Oral argument at 675, Shaare Tefila Congregation v. Cobb, 606 F.Supp. 1504 (D. Md. 1985) (No. R-84–880), *rev'd*, 107 S.Ct. 2019 (1987), in *Landmark Briefs and Arguments of the Supreme Court of the United States: Constitutional Law, 1986 Term Supplement* (Frederick, MD: University Publications of America, Inc., 1988), 675.

59. This line of questioning reveals the justices' intent to determine the distinction between discrimination based on race versus discrimination based on "national origin." The court had not previously applied section 1982 to cases of discrimination based on national origin.

60. Oral argument at 676, Shaare Tefila Congregation v. Cobb, 606 F.Supp. 1504 (D. Md. 1985) (No. R-84–880), *rev'd*, 107 S.Ct. 2019 (1987), in *Landmark Briefs and Arguments of the Supreme Court of the United States: Constitutional Law, 1986 Term Supplement* (Frederick, MD: University Publications of America, Inc., 1988), 676.

61. Oral argument at 678, Shaare Tefila Congregation v. Cobb, 606 F.Supp. 1504 (D. Md. 1985) (No. R-84–880), *rev'd*, 107 S.Ct. 2019 (1987), in *Landmark Briefs and Arguments of the Supreme Court of the United States: Constitutional Law, 1986 Term Supplement* (Frederick, MD: University Publications of America, Inc., 1988), 678.

62. Oral argument at 679, Shaare Tefila Congregation v. Cobb, 606 F.Supp. 1504 (D. Md. 1985) (No. R-84–880), *rev'd*, 107 S.Ct. 2019 (1987), in *Landmark Briefs and Arguments of the Supreme Court of the United States: Constitutional Law, 1986 Term Supplement* (Frederick, MD: University Publications of America, Inc., 1988), 679.

63. General Building Contractors v. Pennsylvania United Engineers, 458 U.S. 375 (1982); McDonald v. Santa Fe Trail Transportation Co., 427 U.S. 273 (1976).

64. For more, see General Bldg. Contractors Assn., Inc. v. Pennsylvania, 458 U.S. 375 (1982), Justia US Supreme Court, Volume 458, supreme.justia.com/cases/federal/us/458/375/

65. Oral argument at 681, Shaare Tefila Congregation v. Cobb, 606 F.Supp. 1504 (D. Md. 1985) (No. R-84–880), *rev'd*, 107 S.Ct. 2019 (1987), in *Landmark Briefs and Arguments of the Supreme Court of the United States: Constitutional Law, 1986 Term Supplement* (Frederick, MD: University Publications of America, Inc., 1988), 681.

66. Oral argument at 681, Shaare Tefila Congregation v. Cobb, 606 F.Supp. 1504 (D. Md. 1985) (No. R-84–880), *rev'd*, 107 S.Ct. 2019 (1987), in *Landmark Briefs and Arguments of the Supreme Court of the United States: Constitutional Law, 1986 Term Supplement* (Frederick, MD: University Publications of America, Inc., 1988), 681.

67. W. E. B. Du Bois, *The Souls of Black Folk* (New York: Barnes & Noble Classics, 2003 [1903]), 34. See Michael Omi and Howard Winant, *Racial Formation in the United States: From the 1960s to the 1990s, Second Edition* (New York: Routledge, 1994), 66.

68. Oral argument at 682, Shaare Tefila Congregation v. Cobb, 606 F.Supp. 1504 (D. Md. 1985) (No. R-84–880), *rev'd*, 107 S.Ct. 2019 (1987), in *Landmark Briefs and Arguments of the Supreme Court of the United States: Constitutional Law, 1986 Term Supplement* (Frederick, MD: University Publications of America, Inc., 1988), 682.

69. Oral argument at 682, Shaare Tefila Congregation v. Cobb, 606 F.Supp. 1504 (D. Md. 1985) (No. R-84–880), *rev'd*, 107 S.Ct. 2019 (1987), in *Landmark Briefs and Arguments of the Supreme Court of the United States: Constitutional Law, 1986 Term Supplement* (Frederick, MD: University Publications of America, Inc., 1988), 682.

70. Oral argument at 682, Shaare Tefila Congregation v. Cobb, 606 F.Supp. 1504 (D. Md. 1985) (No. R-84–880), *rev'd*, 107 S.Ct. 2019 (1987), in *Landmark Briefs and Arguments of the Supreme Court of the United States: Constitutional Law, 1986 Term Supplement* (Frederick, MD: University Publications of America, Inc., 1988), 682.

71. Oral argument at 682, Shaare Tefila Congregation v. Cobb, 606 F.Supp. 1504 (D. Md. 1985) (No. R-84–880), *rev'd*, 107 S.Ct. 2019 (1987), in *Landmark Briefs and Arguments of the Supreme Court of the United States: Constitutional Law, 1986 Term Supplement* (Frederick, MD: University Publications of America, Inc., 1988), 682.

72. Oral argument at 683, Shaare Tefila Congregation v. Cobb, 606 F.Supp. 1504 (D. Md. 1985) (No. R-84–880), *rev'd*, 107 S.Ct. 2019 (1987), in *Landmark Briefs and Arguments of the Supreme Court of the United States: Constitutional Law, 1986 Term Supplement* (Frederick, MD: University Publications of America, Inc., 1988), 683. (emphasis added). The court had assumed that "white" was/is the racial norm.

73. Martha Minow, *Making All the Difference: Inclusion, Exclusion, and American Law* (Ithaca, NY: Cornell University Press, 1990), 111.

74. See Michel Foucault, *Discipline and Punish: The Birth of the Prison*, trans. Alan Sheridan (New York: Vintage Books, 1995 [1977]).

75. Maryland state law did not include options for any further legal remedies.

76. Oral argument at 683, Shaare Tefila Congregation v. Cobb, 606 F.Supp. 1504 (D. Md. 1985) (No. R-84–880), *rev'd*, 107 S.Ct. 2019 (1987), in *Landmark Briefs and Arguments of the Supreme Court of the United States: Constitutional Law, 1986 Term Supplement* (Frederick, MD: University Publications of America, Inc., 1988), 683.

77. Oral argument at 683, Shaare Tefila Congregation v. Cobb, 606 F.Supp. 1504 (D. Md. 1985) (No. R-84–880), *rev'd*, 107 S.Ct. 2019 (1987), in *Landmark Briefs and Arguments of the Supreme Court of the United States: Constitutional Law, 1986 Term Supplement* (Frederick, MD: University Publications of America, Inc., 1988), 683.

78. Title VII of the Civil Rights Act of 1964 "prohibits discrimination by covered employers on the basis of race, color, religion, or national origin," and Title VIII sections of the Civil Rights Act of 1968 "prohibits discrimination in the sale, rental and financing of dwellings based on race, color, religion, sex or national origin."

79. Their concern stems from the issue of more recent acts providing protection not granted by a previous act—if the previous act were determined to grant the same protection, it would make the more recent acts irrelevant. Also, the implication is that

the older acts could not be interpreted to contain the same protections, since otherwise there would have been no need for the new acts.

80. Oral argument at 685, Shaare Tefila Congregation v. Cobb, 606 F.Supp. 1504 (D. Md. 1985) (No. R-84–880), *rev'd*, 107 S.Ct. 2019 (1987), in *Landmark Briefs and Arguments of the Supreme Court of the United States: Constitutional Law, 1986 Term Supplement* (Frederick, MD: University Publications of America, Inc., 1988), 685.

81. Oral argument at 685, Shaare Tefila Congregation v. Cobb, 606 F.Supp. 1504 (D. Md. 1985) (No. R-84–880), *rev'd*, 107 S.Ct. 2019 (1987), in *Landmark Briefs and Arguments of the Supreme Court of the United States: Constitutional Law, 1986 Term Supplement* (Frederick, MD: University Publications of America, Inc., 1988), 685.

82. It seems likely that Brannan thought that the statute should not cover this example, since it arguably refers to "national origin."

83. Oral argument at 686, Shaare Tefila Congregation v. Cobb, 606 F.Supp. 1504 (D. Md. 1985) (No. R-84–880), *rev'd*, 107 S.Ct. 2019 (1987), in *Landmark Briefs and Arguments of the Supreme Court of the United States: Constitutional Law, 1986 Term Supplement* (Frederick, MD: University Publications of America, Inc., 1988), 686.

84. Oral argument at 686, Shaare Tefila Congregation v. Cobb, 606 F.Supp. 1504 (D. Md. 1985) (No. R-84–880), *rev'd*, 107 S.Ct. 2019 (1987), in *Landmark Briefs and Arguments of the Supreme Court of the United States: Constitutional Law, 1986 Term Supplement* (Frederick, MD: University Publications of America, Inc., 1988), 686.

85. Oral argument at 686, Shaare Tefila Congregation v. Cobb, 606 F.Supp. 1504 (D. Md. 1985) (No. R-84–880), *rev'd*, 107 S.Ct. 2019 (1987), in *Landmark Briefs and Arguments of the Supreme Court of the United States: Constitutional Law, 1986 Term Supplement* (Frederick, MD: University Publications of America, Inc., 1988), 686.

86. Oral argument at 686, Shaare Tefila Congregation v. Cobb, 606 F.Supp. 1504 (D. Md. 1985) (No. R-84–880), *rev'd*, 107 S.Ct. 2019 (1987), in *Landmark Briefs and Arguments of the Supreme Court of the United States: Constitutional Law, 1986 Term Supplement* (Frederick, MD: University Publications of America, Inc., 1988), 686.

87. Ibid. Again the judges imply that "white" is the racial norm.

88. Sullivan v. Little Hunting Park, Inc., 396 U.S. 229 (1969), in which Paul E. Sullivan leased a house to a Black man, T. R. Freeman Jr., the latter was denied benefits at Little Hunting Park, which was for the benefit of the owners/renters. Sullivan won. Tillman v. Wheaton-Haven Recreation Assn., 410 U.S. 431 (1973), in which a Black couple, the Presses, bought a home from a White nonmember with the association, then attempted and were denied the ability to join it for racially discriminatory reasons. Tillman and the Presses won.

89. Oral argument at 68, Shaare Tefila Congregation v. Cobb, 606 F.Supp. 1504 (D. Md. 1985) (No. R-84–880), *rev'd*, 107 S.Ct. 2019 (1987), in *Landmark Briefs and Arguments of the Supreme Court of the United States: Constitutional Law, 1986 Term Supplement* (Frederick, MD: University Publications of America, Inc., 1988), 689. This is exactly what occurred in the cases covered by Ian Haney Lopez in this book *White by Law: The Legal Construction of Race, Tenth Anniversary Edition* (New York: New York University Press, 2006).

90. Oral argument at 687, Shaare Tefila Congregation v. Cobb, 606 F.Supp. 1504 (D. Md. 1985) (No. R-84–880), *rev'd*, 107 S.Ct. 2019 (1987), in *Landmark Briefs and*

Arguments of the Supreme Court of the United States: Constitutional Law, 1986 Term Supplement (Frederick, MD: University Publications of America, Inc., 1988), 687.

91. Oral argument at 687, Shaare Tefila Congregation v. Cobb, 606 F.Supp. 1504 (D. Md. 1985) (No. R-84–880), *rev'd*, 107 S.Ct. 2019 (1987), in *Landmark Briefs and Arguments of the Supreme Court of the United States: Constitutional Law, 1986 Term Supplement* (Frederick, MD: University Publications of America, Inc., 1988), 687.

92. Oral argument at 688, Shaare Tefila Congregation v. Cobb, 606 F.Supp. 1504 (D. Md. 1985) (No. R-84–880), *rev'd*, 107 S.Ct. 2019 (1987), in *Landmark Briefs and Arguments of the Supreme Court of the United States: Constitutional Law, 1986 Term Supplement* (Frederick, MD: University Publications of America, Inc., 1988), 688.

93. Andrew Johnson, Veto of the First Reconstruction Act, March 2, 1867, "America's Reconstruction: People and Politics After the Civil War," www.digitalhistory.uh .edu/exhibits/reconstruction/section4/section4_10veto.html

94. *Decision: St. Francis College v. Al-Khazraji*, 481 U.S. 604 (May 18, 1987) Philip Kurland and Gerhard Casper, *Landmark Briefs and Arguments of the Supreme Court of the United States: Constitutional Law, 1986 Term Supplement* (Frederick, MD: University Publications of America, Inc., 1988), 275.

95. *Decision: St. Francis College v. Al-Khazraji*, 481 U.S. 604 (decision date) Philip Kurland and Gerhard Casper, *Landmark Briefs and Arguments of the Supreme Court of the United States: Constitutional Law, 1986 Term Supplement* (Frederick, MD: University Publications of America, Inc., 1988), 275.

96. Oral argument at 689, Shaare Tefila Congregation v. Cobb, 606 F.Supp. 1504 (D. Md. 1985) (No. R-84–880), *rev'd*, 107 S.Ct. 2019 (1987), in *Landmark Briefs and Arguments of the Supreme Court of the United States: Constitutional Law, 1986 Term Supplement* (Frederick, MD: University Publications of America, Inc., 1988), 689.

97. Oral argument at 689, Shaare Tefila Congregation v. Cobb, 606 F.Supp. 1504 (D. Md. 1985) (No. R-84–880), *rev'd*, 107 S.Ct. 2019 (1987), in *Landmark Briefs and Arguments of the Supreme Court of the United States: Constitutional Law, 1986 Term Supplement* (Frederick, MD: University Publications of America, Inc., 1988), 689.

98. Oral argument at 689, Shaare Tefila Congregation v. Cobb, 606 F.Supp. 1504 (D. Md. 1985) (No. R-84–880), *rev'd*, 107 S.Ct. 2019 (1987), in *Landmark Briefs and Arguments of the Supreme Court of the United States: Constitutional Law, 1986 Term Supplement* (Frederick, MD: University Publications of America, Inc., 1988), 689.

99. Oral argument at 690, Shaare Tefila Congregation v. Cobb, 606 F.Supp. 1504 (D. Md. 1985) (No. R-84–880), *rev'd*, 107 S.Ct. 2019 (1987), in *Landmark Briefs and Arguments of the Supreme Court of the United States: Constitutional Law, 1986 Term Supplement* (Frederick, MD: University Publications of America, Inc., 1988), 690.

100. Oral argument at 691, Shaare Tefila Congregation v. Cobb, 606 F.Supp. 1504 (D. Md. 1985) (No. R-84–880), *rev'd*, 107 S.Ct. 2019 (1987), in *Landmark Briefs and Arguments of the Supreme Court of the United States: Constitutional Law, 1986 Term Supplement* (Frederick, MD: University Publications of America, Inc., 1988), 691.

101. Oral argument at 691, Shaare Tefila Congregation v. Cobb, 606 F.Supp. 1504 (D. Md. 1985) (No. R-84–880), *rev'd*, 107 S.Ct. 2019 (1987), in *Landmark Briefs and Arguments of the Supreme Court of the United States: Constitutional Law, 1986 Term Supplement* (Frederick, MD: University Publications of America, Inc., 1988), 691.

102. Oral argument at 691, Shaare Tefila Congregation v. Cobb, 606 F.Supp. 1504 (D. Md. 1985) (No. R-84–880), *rev'd*, 107 S.Ct. 2019 (1987), in *Landmark Briefs and Arguments of the Supreme Court of the United States: Constitutional Law, 1986 Term Supplement* (Frederick, MD: University Publications of America, Inc., 1988), 691.

103. Nadine Ehlers, *Racial Imperatives: Discipline, Performativity, and Struggles against Subjection* (Bloomington: Indiana University Press, 2012), 51.

104. Oral argument at 691, Shaare Tefila Congregation v. Cobb, 606 F.Supp. 1504 (D. Md. 1985) (No. R-84–880), *rev'd*, 107 S.Ct. 2019 (1987), in *Landmark Briefs and Arguments of the Supreme Court of the United States: Constitutional Law, 1986 Term Supplement* (Frederick, MD: University Publications of America, Inc., 1988), 691.

105. Oral argument at 691, Shaare Tefila Congregation v. Cobb, 606 F.Supp. 1504 (D. Md. 1985) (No. R-84–880), *rev'd*, 107 S.Ct. 2019 (1987), in *Landmark Briefs and Arguments of the Supreme Court of the United States: Constitutional Law, 1986 Term Supplement* (Frederick, MD: University Publications of America, Inc., 1988), 691.

106. Oral argument at 692, Shaare Tefila Congregation v. Cobb, 606 F.Supp. 1504 (D. Md. 1985) (No. R-84–880), *rev'd*, 107 S.Ct. 2019 (1987), in *Landmark Briefs and Arguments of the Supreme Court of the United States: Constitutional Law, 1986 Term Supplement* (Frederick, MD: University Publications of America, Inc., 1988), 692.

107. Oral argument at 692, Shaare Tefila Congregation v. Cobb, 606 F.Supp. 1504 (D. Md. 1985) (No. R-84–880), *rev'd*, 107 S.Ct. 2019 (1987), in *Landmark Briefs and Arguments of the Supreme Court of the United States: Constitutional Law, 1986 Term Supplement* (Frederick, MD: University Publications of America, Inc., 1988), 692.

108. Oral argument at 692, Shaare Tefila Congregation v. Cobb, 606 F.Supp. 1504 (D. Md. 1985) (No. R-84–880), *rev'd*, 107 S.Ct. 2019 (1987), in *Landmark Briefs and Arguments of the Supreme Court of the United States: Constitutional Law, 1986 Term Supplement* (Frederick, MD: University Publications of America, Inc., 1988), 692.

109. Oral argument at 693, Shaare Tefila Congregation v. Cobb, 606 F.Supp. 1504 (D. Md. 1985) (No. R-84–880), *rev'd*, 107 S.Ct. 2019 (1987), in *Landmark Briefs and Arguments of the Supreme Court of the United States: Constitutional Law, 1986 Term Supplement* (Frederick, MD: University Publications of America, Inc., 1988), 693.

110. Oral argument at 693, Shaare Tefila Congregation v. Cobb, 606 F.Supp. 1504 (D. Md. 1985) (No. R-84–880), *rev'd*, 107 S.Ct. 2019 (1987), in *Landmark Briefs and Arguments of the Supreme Court of the United States: Constitutional Law, 1986 Term Supplement* (Frederick, MD: University Publications of America, Inc., 1988), 693.

111. Oral argument at 693, Shaare Tefila Congregation v. Cobb, 606 F.Supp. 1504 (D. Md. 1985) (No. R-84–880), *rev'd*, 107 S.Ct. 2019 (1987), in *Landmark Briefs and Arguments of the Supreme Court of the United States: Constitutional Law, 1986 Term Supplement* (Frederick, MD: University Publications of America, Inc., 1988), 693.

112. Oral argument at 693, Shaare Tefila Congregation v. Cobb, 606 F.Supp. 1504 (D. Md. 1985) (No. R-84–880), *rev'd*, 107 S.Ct. 2019 (1987), in *Landmark Briefs and Arguments of the Supreme Court of the United States: Constitutional Law, 1986 Term Supplement* (Frederick, MD: University Publications of America, Inc., 1988), 693.

113. Oral argument at 693, Shaare Tefila Congregation v. Cobb, 606 F.Supp. 1504 (D. Md. 1985) (No. R-84–880), *rev'd*, 107 S.Ct. 2019 (1987), in *Landmark Briefs and*

Arguments of the Supreme Court of the United States: Constitutional Law, 1986 Term Supplement (Frederick, MD: University Publications of America, Inc., 1988), 693.

114. Oral argument at 693, Shaare Tefila Congregation v. Cobb, 606 F.Supp. 1504 (D. Md. 1985) (No. R-84–880), *rev'd*, 107 S.Ct. 2019 (1987), in *Landmark Briefs and Arguments of the Supreme Court of the United States: Constitutional Law, 1986 Term Supplement* (Frederick, MD: University Publications of America, Inc., 1988), 693.

115. Oral argument at 694, Shaare Tefila Congregation v. Cobb, 606 F.Supp. 1504 (D. Md. 1985) (No. R-84–880), *rev'd*, 107 S.Ct. 2019 (1987), in *Landmark Briefs and Arguments of the Supreme Court of the United States: Constitutional Law, 1986 Term Supplement* (Frederick, MD: University Publications of America, Inc., 1988), 694.

116. Oral argument at 694, Shaare Tefila Congregation v. Cobb, 606 F.Supp. 1504 (D. Md. 1985) (No. R-84–880), *rev'd*, 107 S.Ct. 2019 (1987), in *Landmark Briefs and Arguments of the Supreme Court of the United States: Constitutional Law, 1986 Term Supplement* (Frederick, MD: University Publications of America, Inc., 1988), 694.

117. Oral argument at 694, Shaare Tefila Congregation v. Cobb, 606 F.Supp. 1504 (D. Md. 1985) (No. R-84–880), *rev'd*, 107 S.Ct. 2019 (1987), in *Landmark Briefs and Arguments of the Supreme Court of the United States: Constitutional Law, 1986 Term Supplement* (Frederick, MD: University Publications of America, Inc., 1988), 694.

118. Oral argument at 694, Shaare Tefila Congregation v. Cobb, 606 F.Supp. 1504 (D. Md. 1985) (No. R-84–880), *rev'd*, 107 S.Ct. 2019 (1987), in *Landmark Briefs and Arguments of the Supreme Court of the United States: Constitutional Law, 1986 Term Supplement* (Frederick, MD: University Publications of America, Inc., 1988), 694.

119. Oral argument at 694, Shaare Tefila Congregation v. Cobb, 606 F.Supp. 1504 (D. Md. 1985) (No. R-84–880), *rev'd*, 107 S.Ct. 2019 (1987), in *Landmark Briefs and Arguments of the Supreme Court of the United States: Constitutional Law, 1986 Term Supplement* (Frederick, MD: University Publications of America, Inc., 1988), 694.

120. Oral argument at 694, Shaare Tefila Congregation v. Cobb, 606 F.Supp. 1504 (D. Md. 1985) (No. R-84–880), *rev'd*, 107 S.Ct. 2019 (1987), in *Landmark Briefs and Arguments of the Supreme Court of the United States: Constitutional Law, 1986 Term Supplement* (Frederick, MD: University Publications of America, Inc., 1988), 694.

121. Oral argument at 694, Shaare Tefila Congregation v. Cobb, 606 F.Supp. 1504 (D. Md. 1985) (No. R-84–880), *rev'd*, 107 S.Ct. 2019 (1987), in *Landmark Briefs and Arguments of the Supreme Court of the United States: Constitutional Law, 1986 Term Supplement* (Frederick, MD: University Publications of America, Inc., 1988), 694.

122. Oral argument at 695, Shaare Tefila Congregation v. Cobb, 606 F.Supp. 1504 (D. Md. 1985) (No. R-84–880), *rev'd*, 107 S.Ct. 2019 (1987), in *Landmark Briefs and Arguments of the Supreme Court of the United States: Constitutional Law, 1986 Term Supplement* (Frederick, MD: University Publications of America, Inc., 1988), 695.

123. Oral argument at 695, Shaare Tefila Congregation v. Cobb, 606 F.Supp. 1504 (D. Md. 1985) (No. R-84–880), *rev'd*, 107 S.Ct. 2019 (1987), in *Landmark Briefs and Arguments of the Supreme Court of the United States: Constitutional Law, 1986 Term Supplement* (Frederick, MD: University Publications of America, Inc., 1988), 695.

124. Oral argument at 695, Shaare Tefila Congregation v. Cobb, 606 F.Supp. 1504 (D. Md. 1985) (No. R-84–880), *rev'd*, 107 S.Ct. 2019 (1987), in *Landmark Briefs and*

Arguments of the Supreme Court of the United States: Constitutional Law, 1986 Term Supplement (Frederick, MD: University Publications of America, Inc., 1988), 695.

125. Oral argument at 695, Shaare Tefila Congregation v. Cobb, 606 F.Supp. 1504 (D. Md. 1985) (No. R-84–880), *rev'd*, 107 S.Ct. 2019 (1987), in *Landmark Briefs and Arguments of the Supreme Court of the United States: Constitutional Law, 1986 Term Supplement* (Frederick, MD: University Publications of America, Inc., 1988), 695.

126. Naomi W. Cohen writes about Jewish Americans: "Recognizing the vulnerability of a very small minority, non-Christion to boot, they never ceased to ponder whether a public stand on matters of church and state would in any way prompt an adverse reaction toward matters of Jewish security or comfort. Was it wise to risk public notice, let alone criticism, during the years of the Know-Nothing movement, or Henry Ford's anti-Semitic campaign, or Joe McCarthy's witch hunt? Indeed, in large measure, Jewish activity or inactivity on separationism is the inverse of the ebbs and flows of popular religious prejudice and American hypernationalism." See Naomi W. Cohen, *Jews in Christian America: The Pursuit of Religious Equality* (New York: Oxford, 1992), 8.

127. Oral argument at 696, Shaare Tefila Congregation v. Cobb, 606 F.Supp. 1504 (D. Md. 1985) (No. R-84–880), *rev'd*, 107 S.Ct. 2019 (1987), in *Landmark Briefs and Arguments of the Supreme Court of the United States: Constitutional Law, 1986 Term Supplement* (Frederick, MD: University Publications of America, Inc., 1988), 696.

128. Oral argument at 697, Shaare Tefila Congregation v. Cobb, 606 F.Supp. 1504 (D. Md. 1985) (No. R-84–880), *rev'd*, 107 S.Ct. 2019 (1987), in *Landmark Briefs and Arguments of the Supreme Court of the United States: Constitutional Law, 1986 Term Supplement* (Frederick, MD: University Publications of America, Inc., 1988), 697.

129. Oral argument at 697, Shaare Tefila Congregation v. Cobb, 606 F.Supp. 1504 (D. Md. 1985) (No. R-84–880), *rev'd*, 107 S.Ct. 2019 (1987), in *Landmark Briefs and Arguments of the Supreme Court of the United States: Constitutional Law, 1986 Term Supplement* (Frederick, MD: University Publications of America, Inc., 1988), 697. (emphasis added)

130. Oral argument at 697, Shaare Tefila Congregation v. Cobb, 606 F.Supp. 1504 (D. Md. 1985) (No. R-84–880), *rev'd*, 107 S.Ct. 2019 (1987), in *Landmark Briefs and Arguments of the Supreme Court of the United States: Constitutional Law, 1986 Term Supplement* (Frederick, MD: University Publications of America, Inc., 1988), 697.

131. Oral argument at 698, Shaare Tefila Congregation v. Cobb, 606 F.Supp. 1504 (D. Md. 1985) (No. R-84–880), *rev'd*, 107 S.Ct. 2019 (1987), in *Landmark Briefs and Arguments of the Supreme Court of the United States: Constitutional Law, 1986 Term Supplement* (Frederick, MD: University Publications of America, Inc., 1988), 698.

132. Oral argument at 698, Shaare Tefila Congregation v. Cobb, 606 F.Supp. 1504 (D. Md. 1985) (No. R-84–880), *rev'd*, 107 S.Ct. 2019 (1987), in *Landmark Briefs and Arguments of the Supreme Court of the United States: Constitutional Law, 1986 Term Supplement* (Frederick, MD: University Publications of America, Inc., 1988), 698.

133. Deborah Garren, phone interview by author, September 22, 2009.

134. Oral argument at 69, Shaare Tefila Congregation v. Cobb, 606 F.Supp. 1504 (D. Md. 1985) (No. R-84–880), *rev'd*, 107 S.Ct. 2019 (1987), in *Landmark Briefs and*

Arguments of the Supreme Court of the United States: Constitutional Law, 1986 Term Supplement (Frederick, MD: University Publications of America, Inc., 1988), 699.

135. Oral argument at 699, Shaare Tefila Congregation v. Cobb, 606 F.Supp. 1504 (D. Md. 1985) (No. R-84–880), *rev'd*, 107 S.Ct. 2019 (1987), in *Landmark Briefs and Arguments of the Supreme Court of the United States: Constitutional Law, 1986 Term Supplement* (Frederick, MD: University Publications of America, Inc., 1988), 699.

136. Oral argument at 699, Shaare Tefila Congregation v. Cobb, 606 F.Supp. 1504 (D. Md. 1985) (No. R-84–880), *rev'd*, 107 S.Ct. 2019 (1987), in *Landmark Briefs and Arguments of the Supreme Court of the United States: Constitutional Law, 1986 Term Supplement* (Frederick, MD: University Publications of America, Inc., 1988), 699.

137. Oral argument at 700, Shaare Tefila Congregation v. Cobb, 606 F.Supp. 1504 (D. Md. 1985) (No. R-84–880), *rev'd*, 107 S.Ct. 2019 (1987), in *Landmark Briefs and Arguments of the Supreme Court of the United States: Constitutional Law, 1986 Term Supplement* (Frederick, MD: University Publications of America, Inc., 1988), 700.

138. Oral argument at 700, Shaare Tefila Congregation v. Cobb, 606 F.Supp. 1504 (D. Md. 1985) (No. R-84–880), *rev'd*, 107 S.Ct. 2019 (1987), in *Landmark Briefs and Arguments of the Supreme Court of the United States: Constitutional Law, 1986 Term Supplement* (Frederick, MD: University Publications of America, Inc., 1988), 700.

139. Oral argument at 700, Shaare Tefila Congregation v. Cobb, 606 F.Supp. 1504 (D. Md. 1985) (No. R-84–880), *rev'd*, 107 S.Ct. 2019 (1987), in *Landmark Briefs and Arguments of the Supreme Court of the United States: Constitutional Law, 1986 Term Supplement* (Frederick, MD: University Publications of America, Inc., 1988), 700.

140. Oral argument at 700, Shaare Tefila Congregation v. Cobb, 606 F.Supp. 1504 (D. Md. 1985) (No. R-84–880), *rev'd*, 107 S.Ct. 2019 (1987), in *Landmark Briefs and Arguments of the Supreme Court of the United States: Constitutional Law, 1986 Term Supplement* (Frederick, MD: University Publications of America, Inc., 1988), 700.

141. Oral argument at 700–701, Shaare Tefila Congregation v. Cobb, 606 F.Supp. 1504 (D. Md. 1985) (No. R-84–880), *rev'd*, 107 S.Ct. 2019 (1987), in *Landmark Briefs and Arguments of the Supreme Court of the United States: Constitutional Law, 1986 Term Supplement* (Frederick, MD: University Publications of America, Inc., 1988), 700–701.

142. Oral argument at 701, Shaare Tefila Congregation v. Cobb, 606 F.Supp. 1504 (D. Md. 1985) (No. R-84–880), *rev'd*, 107 S.Ct. 2019 (1987), in *Landmark Briefs and Arguments of the Supreme Court of the United States: Constitutional Law, 1986 Term Supplement* (Frederick, MD: University Publications of America, Inc., 1988), 701.

143. Oral argument at 701, Shaare Tefila Congregation v. Cobb, 606 F.Supp. 1504 (D. Md. 1985) (No. R-84–880), *rev'd*, 107 S.Ct. 2019 (1987), in *Landmark Briefs and Arguments of the Supreme Court of the United States: Constitutional Law, 1986 Term Supplement* (Frederick, MD: University Publications of America, Inc., 1988), 701.

144. Oral argument at 701, Shaare Tefila Congregation v. Cobb, 606 F.Supp. 1504 (D. Md. 1985) (No. R-84–880), *rev'd*, 107 S.Ct. 2019 (1987), in *Landmark Briefs and Arguments of the Supreme Court of the United States: Constitutional Law, 1986 Term Supplement* (Frederick, MD: University Publications of America, Inc., 1988), 701.

145. Oral argument at 701, Shaare Tefila Congregation v. Cobb, 606 F.Supp. 1504 (D. Md. 1985) (No. R-84–880), *rev'd*, 107 S.Ct. 2019 (1987), in *Landmark Briefs and*

Arguments of the Supreme Court of the United States: Constitutional Law, 1986 Term Supplement (Frederick, MD: University Publications of America, Inc., 1988), 701.

146. Oral argument at 701, Shaare Tefila Congregation v. Cobb, 606 F.Supp. 1504 (D. Md. 1985) (No. R-84–880), *rev'd*, 107 S.Ct. 2019 (1987), in *Landmark Briefs and Arguments of the Supreme Court of the United States: Constitutional Law, 1986 Term Supplement* (Frederick, MD: University Publications of America, Inc., 1988), 701.

147. Oral argument at 701, Shaare Tefila Congregation v. Cobb, 606 F.Supp. 1504 (D. Md. 1985) (No. R-84–880), *rev'd*, 107 S.Ct. 2019 (1987), in *Landmark Briefs and Arguments of the Supreme Court of the United States: Constitutional Law, 1986 Term Supplement* (Frederick, MD: University Publications of America, Inc., 1988), 701.

148. Oral argument at 702, Shaare Tefila Congregation v. Cobb, 606 F.Supp. 1504 (D. Md. 1985) (No. R-84–880), *rev'd*, 107 S.Ct. 2019 (1987), in *Landmark Briefs and Arguments of the Supreme Court of the United States: Constitutional Law, 1986 Term Supplement* (Frederick, MD: University Publications of America, Inc., 1988), 702.

149. Oral argument at 702, Shaare Tefila Congregation v. Cobb, 606 F.Supp. 1504 (D. Md. 1985) (No. R-84–880), *rev'd*, 107 S.Ct. 2019 (1987), in *Landmark Briefs and Arguments of the Supreme Court of the United States: Constitutional Law, 1986 Term Supplement* (Frederick, MD: University Publications of America, Inc., 1988), 702.

150. See discussion about common perception in Ian Haney Lopez, *White by Law: The Legal Construction of Race, Tenth Anniversary Edition* (New York: New York University Press, 2006), 4–7, 45–47.

151. Oral argument at 703, Shaare Tefila Congregation v. Cobb, 606 F.Supp. 1504 (D. Md. 1985) (No. R-84–880), *rev'd*, 107 S.Ct. 2019 (1987), in *Landmark Briefs and Arguments of the Supreme Court of the United States: Constitutional Law, 1986 Term Supplement* (Frederick, MD: University Publications of America, Inc., 1988), 703.

152. Oral argument at 703, Shaare Tefila Congregation v. Cobb, 606 F.Supp. 1504 (D. Md. 1985) (No. R-84–880), *rev'd*, 107 S.Ct. 2019 (1987), in *Landmark Briefs and Arguments of the Supreme Court of the United States: Constitutional Law, 1986 Term Supplement* (Frederick, MD: University Publications of America, Inc., 1988), 703.

153. Oral argument at 703, Shaare Tefila Congregation v. Cobb, 606 F.Supp. 1504 (D. Md. 1985) (No. R-84–880), *rev'd*, 107 S.Ct. 2019 (1987), in *Landmark Briefs and Arguments of the Supreme Court of the United States: Constitutional Law, 1986 Term Supplement* (Frederick, MD: University Publications of America, Inc., 1988), 703.

154. Oral argument at 703, Shaare Tefila Congregation v. Cobb, 606 F.Supp. 1504 (D. Md. 1985) (No. R-84–880), *rev'd*, 107 S.Ct. 2019 (1987), in *Landmark Briefs and Arguments of the Supreme Court of the United States: Constitutional Law, 1986 Term Supplement* (Frederick, MD: University Publications of America, Inc., 1988), 703.

155. Oral argument at 703, Shaare Tefila Congregation v. Cobb, 606 F.Supp. 1504 (D. Md. 1985) (No. R-84–880), *rev'd*, 107 S.Ct. 2019 (1987), in *Landmark Briefs and Arguments of the Supreme Court of the United States: Constitutional Law, 1986 Term Supplement* (Frederick, MD: University Publications of America, Inc., 1988), 703.

156. Jennifer Grace Redmond notes, in her article about the two cases that the justices "accomplishes this expansion of Runyon without examining precedent or establishing a constitutional foundation." Jennifer Grace Redmond, "Redefining Race in *St. Francis College v. Al-Khazraji* and *Shaare Tefila Congregation v. Cobb*:

Using Dictionaries instead of the Thirteenth Amendment," *Vanderbilt Law Review* 42 (1989): 210.

157. Ian Haney Lopez argues: "In the Court's opinion, science had failed as an arbiter of human difference, and common knowledge was made into the touchstone of racial division." Ian Haney Lopez, *White by Law: The Legal Construction of Race, Tenth Anniversary Edition* (New York: New York University Press, 2006), 6.

158. See Daniel Dubuisson, *The Western Construction of Religion: Myths, Knowledge, and Ideology* trans. William Sayers (Baltimore, MD: Johns Hopkins University Press, 2007 [2003]), 1–6, particularly p. 3.; Irene Silverblatt, *Modern Inquisitions: Peru and the Colonial Origins of the Civilized World* (Durham, NC: Duke University Press, 2004), 17.

159. See Ian Haney Lopez, *White by Law: The Legal Construction of Race, Tenth Anniversary Edition* (New York: New York University Press, 2006), 66–72.

160. Garren's argument reflects Omi and Winant's assertion that race in the post–civil rights era is largely defined by the "color line." W. E. B. Du Bois, *The Souls of Black Folk* (New York: Barnes & Noble Classics, 2003 [1903]), 34. Michael Omi and Howard Winant, *Racial Formation in the United States: From the 1960s to the 1990s, Second Edition* (New York: Routledge, 1994), 66.

161. Haney Lopez asserts: "That common knowledge emerged as the only workable racial test shows that race is something which much be measured in terms of what people believe, that it is a socially mediated idea." See Haney Lopez, *White by Law*, 7.

162. Bruce Lincoln, *Discourse and the Construction of Society: Comparative Studies of Myth, Ritual, and Classification* (New York: Oxford University Press, 1989), 7.

163. For an argument for the necessity of reframing legal evaluations of racism to account for the racist content of the action rather than the racial "status" of the victim, see Linda A. Lacewell and Paul A. Shelowtiz, "Beyond a Black and White Reading of Sections 1981 and 1982: Shifting the Focus from Racial Status to Racial Acts," *University of Miami Law Review* 41 (1987): 823–54.

164. Oral argument at 694, Shaare Tefila Congregation v. Cobb, 606 F.Supp. 1504 (D. Md. 1985) (No. R-84–880), *rev'd*, 107 S.Ct. 2019 (1987), in *Landmark Briefs and Arguments of the Supreme Court of the United States: Constitutional Law, 1986 Term Supplement* (Frederick, MD: University Publications of America, Inc., 1988), 694.

165. Likewise, Martha Minow argues: "when asked whether Jews and Arabs are distinct races for the purposes of civil rights statutes, the Supreme Court in 1987 reasoned that objective, scientific sources, could not resolve this question, essentially acknowledging that racial identity is socially constructed." She refers to the *Shaare Tefila* and *Al-Khazraji* cases here. See Martha Minow, *Making All the Difference: Inclusion, Exclusion, and American Law* (Ithaca, NY: Cornell University Press, 1990), 55.

166. Oral argument at 691, Shaare Tefila Congregation v. Cobb, 606 F.Supp. 1504 (D. Md. 1985) (No. R-84–880), *rev'd*, 107 S.Ct. 2019 (1987), in *Landmark Briefs and Arguments of the Supreme Court of the United States: Constitutional Law, 1986 Term Supplement* (Frederick, MD: University Publications of America, Inc., 1988), 691.

167. Plessy v. Ferguson, 163 U.S. 537 (1896).

168. Oral argument at 681, Shaare Tefila Congregation v. Cobb, 606 F.Supp. 1504 (D. Md. 1985) (No. R-84–880), *rev'd*, 107 S.Ct. 2019 (1987), in *Landmark Briefs and Arguments of the Supreme Court of the United States: Constitutional Law, 1986 Term Supplement* (Frederick, MD: University Publications of America, Inc., 1988), 681.

169. Oral argument at 681, Shaare Tefila Congregation v. Cobb, 606 F.Supp. 1504 (D. Md. 1985) (No. R-84–880), *rev'd*, 107 S.Ct. 2019 (1987), in *Landmark Briefs and Arguments of the Supreme Court of the United States: Constitutional Law, 1986 Term Supplement* (Frederick, MD: University Publications of America, Inc., 1988), 681.

170. Miranda v. Arizona, 384 U.S. 436 (1966).

171. Roe v. Wade, 410 U.S. 113 (1973).

172. Shaare Tefila Congregation v. Cobb, 481 U.S. 615, 617 (1987), emphasis added.

173. 481 U.S. 615 (1987). For a discussion of the overlap between "religion" and "ethnicity" in civil rights protection, see Julie D. Arp, "The *Batson* Analysis and Religious Discrimination," *Oregon Law Review* 74 (1995): 721–39.

174. Shaare Tefila Congregation v. Cobb, 481 U.S. 615, 617 (1987).

175. Shaare Tefila Congregation v. Cobb, 481 U.S. 615, 617 (1987).

176. Shaare Tefila Congregation v. Cobb, 481 U.S. 615, 617–618 (1987), emphasis added. For an informative article on Congress's intent in passing the Civil Rights Act of 1866, see Cynthia Gail Smith, "*Patterson v. McLean Credit Union*: New Limitations on an Old Civil Rights Statute," *North Carolina Law Review* 68 (1990): 799–834. Shaare Tefila Congregation v. Cobb, 481 U.S. 615, 617–18 (1987).

177. Shaare Tefila Congregation v. Cobb, 481 U.S. 618 (1987).

178. St. Francis College v. Al-Khazraji College, 481 US 604, 612.

179. For a critique of the justices' ruling and of their rationale, see Jennifer Grace Redmond, "Redefining Race in *St. Francis College v. Al-Khazraji* and *Shaare Tefila Congregation v. Cobb*: Using Dictionaries instead of the Thirteenth Amendment," *Vanderbilt Law Review* 42 (1989): 209–31.

180. See Michael Omi and Howard Winant, *Racial Formation in the United States: From the 1960s to the 1990s, Second Edition* (New York: Routledge, 1994); and Irene Silverblatt, *Modern Inquisitions: Peru and the Colonial Origins of the Civilized World* (Durham, NC: Duke University Press, 2004).

Chapter Five

The Shaare Tefila Congregation
after the Supreme Court Decision

Shaare Tefila members were thrilled that they had won the Supreme Court case, but most of them did not know the reason for their success. Many congregation members diligently attempted to counter the idea that to be Jewish was to be "different" from other White people. It was not that they were not proud of their Jewish identities, but rather that the 1980s was an era in which complete assimilation to a *religious* identity was the ideal. Racially, the congregation members identified themselves legally as "White" in *Shaare Tefila*, and it was also the affiliation they adopted socially. One member, however, noted she was the only "open Jew" where she worked. The discordance between "White" and "open Jew" recalls Khaled Beydoun's distinction between Jewish Americans as "formally" versus "substantively" White.[1] When they could not disguise their Jewishness, they were often subject to antisemitic discrimination. This tension reflected the broader situation of most Jewish Americans in the 1980s, and still today. These Jews considered themselves "White" but many of them needed to conceal their Jewishness in various situations. Jewish locations sometimes disguised their Jewishness; hence, as mentioned earlier, often synagogues gave no indication that they *were* a synagogue.[2]

This chapter returns to the Shaare Tefila Congregation: the congregants first respond to the Supreme Court case, then to the case's return to the US Federal District Court of Maryland, and the last portion of the chapter recollects their embodied experiences as Jewish Americans who were impacted by the vandalism and the civil suit in different ways. It highlights five members' responses to those events and several of their distinct roles within the congregation. The chapter concludes by addressing Shaare Tefila Congregation as more than solely a defaced synagogue but one that has a full life beyond the defacement and the civil suit. These congregants' statements demonstrate the tenuous connection between available legal categories of civil rights protection, such as "religion" and "race," and Jewish identifications as they are lived and experienced.

With the Supreme Court's backing, the congregation could legally resolve this newly defined civil rights abuse in District Court. The initial plan was a trial, which required discovery, new depositions, a pre-trial order, and all the other necessary documents. New depositions required interviews with vandals, including the supposed ring-leader, Michael Remer. The congregation eventually decided to settle with Remer and the other defendants on the condition that their leaders, Rabbi Halpern, and President Shirley Altman, could speak with them in the courthouse and tell their legal story.[3] They sought not money or revenge, but an understanding from the vandals that what they had done was wrong and emotionally traumatic for the congregation, and by extension, for other Jews.

SHAARE TEFILA MEMBERS REACT TO
THE SUPREME COURT CASE

Because the Supreme Court hears arguments and then sometimes takes months to reach its decision, the congregation members who attended the session that February morning in 1987 left not knowing which side had won. Shirley Altman, Board of Trustees President at the time of the Supreme Court hearing and decision, dedicated her March 2, 1987, report to the board to reflect on the oral argument and the significance of the case. At the Trustees meeting, Altman recalled:

> The desecration hearing at the U.S. Supreme Court on Feb. 25, 1987, was a terrific experience, whether or not they find in our favor. I feel a great sense of personal satisfaction that I did not let this case die in committee. Using my prerogative as President, the lawyers were brought in to address the Congregation Board on July 1, 1985. The Board then passed a motion to proceed with the case through all appeals. I am grateful that we, as a group, saw fit to stand up for the right to petition for justice. I am very hopeful for a favorable decision.[4]

Altman's statement conveys the proactive stance she took to ensure that the board agreed to pursue the civil suit and the value she placed on seeking justice in response to the vandalism incident.

As noted, several Shaare Tefila members attended the Supreme Court oral argument, although not all the parties to the civil suit were there, nor were several congregation leaders. Adult members who did attend reported a deep sense of satisfaction with the experience of being present and with witnessing the legal process. They also expressed gratification that the congregation had pursued the case all the way to the highest court and for its eventual success there. Susan Goldsamt noted: "Now, as far as the Supreme Court was concerned, I was proud as can be. I mean, that's the way it should have been dealt with."[5] She took her two sons out of school to attend the Supreme Court hearing of Shaare Tefila's case; it was important to her that they witnessed this historic event. Goldsamt was surprised that more Shaare Tefila members had not attended or taken their children. She recalled that one other child was there, who was unrelated to them, and that her husband had brought him.[6]

Several congregants were adamant that bringing the civil suit was important to them not only because they presumed it would expand legal protections for Jewish Americans, but also for other groups targeted based on their racialization. Susan Goldsamt asserted:

> If they had said, it would only apply to Jews, I would have been extremely against it. But I can see the Chinese being discriminated against, and I can see the Hispanics being discriminated against, which is happening today. And it angers me incredibly. And they should have the same remedy that we have. And I don't think we did it just for religious bases.[7]

Note Goldsamt's vacillation between the socio-legal categories of "race" and "religion." Likewise, President Shirley Altman stated in the *Washington Jewish Week* that she "was 'dismayed at the court's finding because the intention of the suit was not just to protect Jewish religious interests, but to protect all religious and minority groups who are harassed by people because they consider them different. There should be protection in the federal court against this kind of harassment."[8] Clearly, although Shaare Tefila Congregation nearly lost their case because they were considered "formally white," according to government jurisdiction and most of the judges, they were not viewed as "substantively white," either by the vandals or by many other people who thought of themselves as influential members of US society.

The Supreme Court's eventual unanimous ruling almost three months later, on May 18, 1987, did not end the legal process, since a reverse and remand meant that the congregation had once again to pursue the civil suit against the vandals in the Federal District Court of Maryland. Neither did the ruling automatically require the vandals to pay the fine of three thousand dollars in compensatory damages that Shaare Tefila sought and had planned to donate to the Montgomery County Human Relations Commission. The Congregation had to begin again, with the knowledge that now they had the protection of Section 1982.

Several days after the decision, President Shirley Altman sent letters to the now-former executive director of the synagogue Marshall Levin,[9] to the law firm Hogan & Hartson, Patricia Brannan, and to Irvin Shapell of the Jewish Advocacy Center, thanking them for their dedication to the case. Altman wrote to Levin: "You should really be proud of the Supreme Court landmark decision in reinterpreting the 1866 Civil Rights Act. If it were not for your efforts at the outset of this case it could never have happened. The Jewish community as a whole owes a great deal of thanks to you."[10] In her letter to Shapell, Altman noted that the Supreme Court decision "will have far-reaching effects on the ability of the Jewish community and other groups to combat hate-motivated acts."[11] To Patricia Brannan, she wrote that the congregation was "very fortunate to have had the services of such a truly outstanding attorney as yourself. . . . You were outstanding in every phase of the case."[12]

Marshall Levin, arguably the driving force behind the decision to leave the graffiti temporarily on the synagogue walls, considered the significance of the congregation's actions ten years afterward. In a book chapter that he wrote on the case, Levin recalled:

> I believe that Shaare Tefila illustrates a congregation chosen, through no action of its own, to play an important role in history. The congregation certainly did not realize the significance of their decision about how to handle the incident until after they had taken action. We had a unique collection of people there at that time who were able to make innovative, against-the-current decisions and see them through. The congregation stayed together through the entire series of events which followed the incident. . . . Looking back now, it is gratifying to see that our actions, undertaken without any guarantee of success or long-term impact, changed the way that many communities deal with hate-motivated speech, violence, and vandalism.[13]

Levin was proud of how the Shaare Tefila members handled the case. Here, he emphasized that the synagogue members were committed to their response to the defacement, even as they were unaware of what relevance their decisions would have to other communities.

The case was widely covered in national and international news at the time, so other Jewish Americans would have been able to see the dedication of the congregation members to each other and the support of the community throughout the response to the incident.

Many Shaare Tefila members were committed to the civil suit as it was decided in the Federal District Court of Maryland in Baltimore on April 22, 1985; argued on November 5, 1985, and decided on March 7, 1986, in the Fourth Circuit Court of Appeals; and finally, about one year later, argued on February 25, 1987, and decided on May 18 by the US Supreme Court. Jewish American communities, many of them beset with hate speech, violence, and/or vandalism, would finally have a way to proceed if they chose to follow Shaare Tefila Congregation's example. Few White-perceived Jewish Americans did so, however, because they still did not want to distinguish themselves from other White people by seeking legal coverage for race-based civil rights abuses. The suit itself and the precedent it set were important, but the congregation's public stance made what was at the time an unprecedented statement about how one Jewish community responded to antisemitic vandalism.[14]

SHAARE TEFILA CONGREGATION V. COBB RETURNS TO THE US FEDERAL DISTRICT COURT

After the Supreme Court reversed and remanded the ruling of the District Court, it was again heard by the same judge, Norman P. Ramsey. Now, however, the Congregation had the backing of the Supreme Court, with the decision by Justice Byron White that had emphasized the significance of section 1982 in its decision. On March 31, 1988, Judge Ramsey ordered the plaintiffs and defendants to submit their proposed Pretrial Order.

On the previous Tuesday, Jeff Sprung, from Hogan & Hartson, had taken the deposition of William Randall Harris Jr., who continued to claim that Remer was primarily responsible for painting the symbols and slogans on the synagogue walls; however, on this Tuesday he said that he could not see clearly enough to know who did all the painting.[15] Patricia Brannan wrote to Rabbi Halpern on April 11, 1988, regarding the Pretrial Order.[16] She noted that Hogan & Hartson would proceed with the deposition of Remer and find out how many other defendants he cited; then the legal firm and the Congregation could decide whether to proceed against all the defendants.[17]

The depositions of Michael Remer and Dominic Queen were held at the law offices of Hogan & Hartson on June 21, 1988. Lawyer Steven P. Hollman asked the questions for the Congregation, James J. Nolan represented Defendant Remer, and Joseph M. Niland represented Defendant Queen. Remer seemed repentant at some points in his testimony, due to his increased sensitivity about the horrified responses to the vandalism expressed by his family and friends as well as members of the larger community, but not in others. He drew from his assertion, in his earlier deposition, that defacing the synagogue had been an act of rebellion.

In response to Hollman's question about how he learned to be more considerate, he lamented:

> I watched my family go through what I was going through as far as having to deal with the situation. I experienced that, learning how they were sensitive to the whole thing. My friends, I watched people go through changes because of

that particular situation. I've been at seminars dealing with sensitivity and I've been to meetings that deal with racism and I would say that my experience going through the years after that had happened, my experiences just living day-to-day showed me how much of an impact they would give.[18]

Certainly, at least part of him shifted during the aftermath of the defacement.

Regarding the vandalism to the synagogue, however, Remer stated: "To my recollection, it's not like it was an organized thing against the Jewish people. It just happened"; to which Hollman asked: "Do you agree that Jews were a special target of Nazism?" Remer replied: "Of nazism,[19] yes. But I don't think they were a special target of what was put on that wall." Hollman attempted to respond: "Well,—" And then Remer interrupted him: "I think that anyone was a target for that. It's quite obvious." Hollman intervened: "Can you explain what you mean by 'it was quite obvious?'" Remer explained: "All kinds of different slogans have been put on there other than nazi symbols. There is initials and KKK and groups like that—like the KKK are more well known for their anti-black ideologies other than their anti-Jewish ideologies, that I know of." Hollman responded: "Although you've recognized that the KKK is also an anti-Jewish organization, is that correct?" "Yes, I've recognized that," Remer replied. "And you've also recognized that a Star of David with an arrow through it could be an anti-Semitic slogan, is that correct?" "It could be, yes," agreed Remer.

Quite a few pages of the deposition entailed questions and answers between Hollman and Remer, in which Hollman asked about his understanding of White and national socialism.[20] Remer revealed that he had requested and received pamphlets from a number of organizations, such as the American Communist Party; the National Alliance, which was out of D.C.; the Ku Klux Klan; the Thunderbolt Magazine; NAAWP—the National Association for the Advancement of White People; and the Vanguard.[21] Nolan advised him not to answer when Hollman questioned him about his membership in any of these organizations between 1982 through 1988 because it's likely that Remer became even more radicalized while he was in prison during those years.[22] Remer stated, however, that he was not a member of any of them when the deposition took place on June 21, 1988.[23]

Upon request, he showed Hollman his tattoo, which had what Remer called "a stormtrooper swastika with 'SS' in the center."[24] When Hollman asked him what this meant, Remer said: "I have no idea. Schutzstaffel, whatever that means"; he also said he had it done eight or nine months ago.[25] When Hollman inquired: "What possessed you to have that put on your arm?" Remer replied: "I was in the Maryland House of Corrections.[26] . . . Within the prison structure there are certain insignias when you carry them you are affiliated with certain, inside the prison organizations, it's more of a protection move while you are there."[27] It is a widespread phenomenon that in prison White men can be *safer* when they identify with other White men based on their shared Whiteness. This usually takes extreme forms such as identifying with neo-Nazis, the Aryan Brotherhood,[28] or other White nationalist organizations.[29] Race-based "gangs" can further radicalize prisoners, making it even more difficult for them when they return to the free world. Hollman probed: "Is there any generally accepted significance to the swastika among these people?" Remer answered: "In prison, it symbolizes a unity amongst white people, yes." Hollman probed further: "Would that be exclusive of black people?" Remer responded: "In prison, yes." Then Hollman inquired: "Would that also be exclusive of Jewish people?" Remer said: "I don't know. I've never really ran across too many Jewish people in prison."[30] Since depositions are simply texts, it's impossible to know how he articulated this statement. Remer seems to have understood prison as a space without Jewish people. Either Jewish prisoners were hiding the fact that they were Jewish, or there were no Jewish prisoners at the prison where Remer was. If White-perceived Jewish Americans were housed at the Maryland House of Corrections, likely they would have hidden their Jewishness and passed as "formally" White. Secrecy functioned as a protective mechanism.

When Hollman asked him if he identified as a "white supremacist," Remer stated: "I'd like to object to that question, but I will answer it. No, I have never really thought that I was any [way] better than anyone else, as far as my color is concerned. White supremacy. I mean you mentioned white supremacy. I'm a pretty good artist."[31] Hollman followed the first question with another one: "How about as far as any other innate attributes?" To which Remer replied, "no."[32]

Remer may have quickly moved away from identifying with his potentially "superior" skin color to identifying with one of his abilities. It's not clear what he was thinking as he made this shift: was he intentionally shifting topics? Did he seriously imagine that his artistic ability could somehow replace his assertion of White supremacy? Recall that Remer's stepfather and stepbrothers are Jewish. Remer did not *choose* this family situation, but—likely, in part, because of his anger and emotional distance from them—it motivated what he narrated on the "screen" of the synagogue walls, a Jewish space.[33] This screen, perhaps, provided ample opportunity to demonstrate how he experienced his relationship with the Jews in his immediate family. He had mentioned that he was "a pretty good artist," so the white color of the synagogue made it easy for him to spray-paint exactly what he desired and how he felt about his situation. The synagogue walls could be the canvas on which he could project to the world his feelings about his family, and by extension, the same outlook toward the Jewish community more broadly.

After Remer's deposition, Shaare Tefila Congregation decided to move ahead with the Pretrial Order.[34] Judge Ramsey granted this motion, but the trial never occurred because the congregation decided to settle with the defendants, on the condition that the defendants meet with their leaders in the courthouse. This situation would afford Shaare Tefila Congregation a type of "narrative control."[35] Afterward, the defendants submitted letters of apology.[36] Finally, the Congregation signed a settlement with the defendants, after the Consent Injunction—a special court order that requires that a party refrain from certain acts—was brought by Hogan & Hartson.

The meeting with the defendants occurred in the US Federal District Courthouse in Baltimore. Some members of Shaare Tefila saw this resolution as a kind of restitution, a chance for them to tell their story. With Judge Ramsey's approval, the courtroom served as the epicenter of juridical space.[37] Legal decisions that emerge from these spaces have an unquestioned status . . . until a legal appeal potentially occurs. Discussing this restitution, Patricia Brannan explained in the *Washington Post* that the point of the lawsuit "was some kind of face-to-face encounter between the perpetrators and the leaders of the congregation. It was really a matter of having the court's affirmation that this *really was* a civil rights issue.'"[38] Note that this point ran directly counter to Judge Murnaghan's statement, in the Fourth Circuit Court of Appeals, when he noted that the defacement was *not* a civil rights issue.

Brannan recalled that she remembered talking about the meeting with Rabbi Halpern and President Shirley Altman as they drove up to the US Federal District Courthouse from Silver Spring.[39] Several of the vandals,[40] including Michael Remer, met with them at the courthouse. Brannan remembered that the settlement was very "structured" and "formal," one of the components important to the juridical space of the courtroom.[41] Each of the parties to the case met in different rooms to discuss before they proceeded with the conversation. She had no idea how it would proceed before it happened.[42]

When they all sat down, Rabbi Halpern showed them a series of large black-and-white photos of what they had painted, and he talked to them about what they meant.[43] He spoke about the spray-painted references to the Shoah, the horror that evoked for the Holocaust survivors in the congregation, and noted that he was one himself. Brannan recalled that they were very quiet, not at all defiant.[44] And from that point, she remembered, we "basically had a remarkable conversation about why they had done this and where they had gotten these awful slogans."[45] She noted that Rabbi Halpern "approached this not with animosity, but with a genuine belief that this conversation could have meaning."[46] Afterward, the vandals made various statements of regret about what they had painted. According to Brannan, they all wrote letters of apology, but only one of those letters, by Michael Remer, remains in the congregation's or the court's files.[47]

In his apology letter to the congregation, written on October 5, 1988,[48] Remer explained: "when the desecration of the synagogue was committed, it wasn't an act of sole anti-Semitism or hatred just against the Jewish people, it was just an outright act of hatred against everyone and everything."[49] Here, Remer relates to his responses in both depositions regarding the purpose of the defacement. In the letter, Remer acknowledged that he "didn't try to understand people's feelings and their values," but that he has "felt remorse for the last six years and . . . will feel remorse for the rest of . . . [his] life for the crime that . . . [he] committed bringing back memories and ideas of a situation that should have never, ever occurred, the holocaust [sic]."[50] Remer continued:

> My understanding of values and my appreciation for people's feelings and people's emotions are much clearer now and I would just like to say to every-one in the congregation and the community that I am very sorry for what I have done and I will never, ever indulge in such an activity again and I hope that my positive thoughts about that bad situation can spread around and throughout the world and anything like this can never happen again, not just with me, but with anyone else.[51]

This sentence and the last line of Remer's letter reflect his awareness that his deeds had an impact on the community, a larger sphere than the congregation alone. He followed that statement with: "I just hope that the congregation and the community will forgive me."[52] This declaration is exactly what the Shaare Tefila members wanted to hear.

After this meeting, another Consent Injunction was ordered by Judge Ramsey on December 21, 1988, and signed by Steven Hollman and by James Noland for Pierson & Pierson, attorneys for Michael Remer. It required that Michael Remer, and anyone associated with him, refrain from "harassing, threatening, insulting or intimidating" plaintiffs or other Jewish persons in the Washington, DC, metropolitan area, or trespassing on plaintiffs' or any other Jewish person's property in the DC area and otherwise interfering with their rights to practice their religion. It also stipulated that Remer, and others associated with him, are "permanently enjoined" from placing Nazi and Ku Klux Klan symbols or slogans on said property, and it ordered that Michael Remer sign the document within fifteen days.[53]

Steven Hollman then wrote to Rabbi Halpern on December 23, 1988, with a copy of Michael Remer's letter of apology and the consent injunction order. Hollman noted that Hogan & Hartson had sent a stipulation dismissing the lawsuit to Remer's attorneys, which would be filed with the court, and he enclosed—with his letter—an original copy of the Settlement Agreement and General Release of Claims. Hollman asked that the rabbi obtain the necessary signatures from the trustees, named plaintiffs, and the appropriate signature for the Congregation. Along with Patricia Brannan, he wished the rabbi and the congregation a "healthy and fulfilling" new year.[54]

This Settlement Agreement and General Release of Claims specified that the Shaare Tefila Congregation had asserted claims against Michael Remer, which initially had been in the lawsuit *Shaare Tefila Congregation v. Cobb* and was now pending as Civil Action No. R84-880 in the US District Court for the District of Maryland. It stated that the two parties, Shaare Tefila Congregation, and Michael David Remer, wished to resolve the controversies between them and settle the suit. Further, it lists Remer's agreements: the letter of apology, the consent injunction order, that he pay Aetna Casualty and Surety Company $300, and that he "remise, release, and forever discharge the Shaare Tefila Congregation" from any claim he had related to the *Shaare Tefila* suit. It also lists Shaare Tefila's agreements: that it will file a Stipulation of Dismissal with Prejudice and Order of Dismissal stating that it would bear its own costs and that it would release Michael David Remer from any claim related to *Shaare Tefila*. Both parties signed the settlement, finally concluding the case.

Shaare Tefila Members' Embodied Relationships to Shaare Tefila Congregation

During my first visit to Shaare Tefila, it seemed that synagogue members had not discussed the defacement and Supreme Court case as a community for many years. I inquired in interviews about whether that was correct and what the reasons might be. Then-President Maurice Potosky and longtime congregants Sid Schwartz, Milt, and Susan Goldsamt discussed the vandalism incident and the case with me, sitting in the finished basement of the building that I would learn later was donated by a synagogue member and former doctor. Potosky discussed the memory of it, saying: "The congregation today is not quite the same congregation. The bulk of the people who were there then have either passed on, [or] gone to other congregations. For those who remain, there's the memory. And there's not any significant impact other than noting that Shaare Tefila participated in a historic event, and that's about it."[55] He elaborated: "Whenever I have the opportunity, we play the tape [*Desecration in Darkness*, the video that the congregation made about the incident] and we discuss it. It appears primarily as a historical event from which almost everyone who is around today is removed."[56] Susan Goldsamt noted:

> Actually, I hadn't thought of this incident in years. In years. And it's a shame that we haven't. The only time that I did was when I had to write this grant proposal about why our building should be protected. . . . And it all came

bubbling up. And then it all came back to me. And it was powerful. . . . I think it's a point of pride, that we should be emphasizing in our congregation when we attract new members because it is something that not every congregation had the guts to do.[57]

In speaking with Sid Schwartz after the others had left, he commented to me on the impact of the case:

After the fact there was satisfaction with the way it was handled and certainly satisfaction with the outcome, and I think that has become a part of life today for a minority [of the congregation]. That you do have some recourse, which fifty years ago or sixty years ago we didn't have. So, I think that's a big change.[58]

He further explained that he viewed the case as part of a larger shift in Jewish American experiences within the dominant culture:

I don't see . . . [the case] as singularly significant. I think it's part of a pattern of events that have occurred over the last twenty, thirty, or forty years. . . . The case was part of a broader picture of civil liberties generally improving for minorities in general and Jewish people as well. . . . People today don't have to hide the fact that they're Jewish. They're more open. Right here on the street Orthodox people will walk around with their *kippahs* on their head and their *tallit* hanging out. . . . They're not bashful, nobody has to hide. When I grew up everybody was quiet, you want to maintain a low profile, you're always fearful that things that were happening might be because you were Jewish. It was very easy for people to say, well, that's because we're Jewish.[59]

This Jewish "coming out" experience has been very significant for the congregation members and for other Jewish Americans in terms of how they interact in their public and private lives.

Rabbi Jonah Layman, the congregation's rabbi since 1994, told me that the case is not part of the congregation's current identity. He noted:

It's rare that it comes up. Every now and then somebody will mention—will be reminded of it, but I haven't done any programming in the congregation about it, to remind people about that case, and in fact, some newer members aren't even aware of that history. It's not on our [current] website. It's not something we advertise, to say, you know, join Shaare Tefila because we laid the groundwork for the Supreme Court case. It's not part of our identity in any way.[60]

When asked about the effects of the case on the congregation, however, he commented that people who were involved at the time remember it with pride: "I think people are proud of it. I think certainly everyone in the congregation who knows of it is very proud of the work that went into it and . . .

of going all the way to the Supreme Court . . . nobody is ashamed of that."[61] Rabbi Layman stated that although the congregation does not discuss the case today, it is not purposefully avoided either. He explained:

> No, it's not on purpose. It's just the way it is. It was before I came, like ten years before I came to the congregation. And I don't even remember it coming up in my interview. . . . So I think it's just a matter of modesty on the part of the congregation. They don't show off to say: "Hey, we did this." And then nobody has advocated with me to say we should do some kind of programming about this, and I haven't thought to do it either.[62]

When I expressed surprise that nobody discusses the case these days, Rabbi Layman responded: "You know, it might go to part of the Jewish psyche, you don't want to try to make yourself too known. Even though we're very safe and secure in America as Jews, there could be just that part—I guess the people who were involved twenty years ago were more part of that generation, you know, don't make waves."[63] Rabbi Layman's point resembles Sid Schwartz's statement above—that people several decades ago felt less comfortable about displaying their Jewish identities than today—but Rabbi Layman additionally notes that worries of being "too known" may continue today.

Throughout conversations with former and current Shaare Tefila members, they made comments that revealed more about their views on and experiences of their Jewishness than my specific question on the topic elicited. The question was: "How would you describe the effects of the vandalism and the court cases on your own Jewish American identity?" Some of their reflections referred specifically to the vandalism and civil suit, but other memories related to their everyday participation at Shaare Tefila and meaningful moments, such as *bar* or *bat* mitzvah, the celebration of *hagim* (holidays), Sunday school, or taking part in morning and evening minyans. Their statements refer not to socio-legal categories of "religion" or "race," but to their own lived experiences.

The next paragraphs focus on how five congregants responded to the vandalism and the civil suit based on their embodied relationship to it and to the synagogue. For some members of Shaare Tefila, the vandalism incident and the decision to bring the civil suit *did* shift how they thought about and experienced being Jewish American. Among this group, several members told me that the congregation's response to the events of the vandalism particularly affected them. For example, Susan Goldsamt recalled:

> Well, as I said in the meeting, in the . . . Shabbes, it was very common to keep it quiet. Because you were afraid, oh, it will only draw more attention. We'll be a bigger target. You don't want to call attention to yourself, because you are different, and people have made you a target in the past. But it was time

to move forward. And I think from that point it really changed my feeling of identity. Um, as far as being someone who was different and had to blend in to somebody who is who she is, rather than, and not having to apologize for it. It doesn't mean I go out of my way to make things difficult for people, but I'm not backing down. So, that's—it was a very, very big thing.[64]

For Goldsamt, the board members' decision to display the defacement publicly and to pursue the case caused her to feel that she did not have to conceal her Jewish identification or to try to resemble non-Jews around her. To contextualize her experience in the language of race, she no longer tried to "pass" as non-Jewish, nor as the dominant religious group: White Christians. In writing her trailblazing article "Whiteness as Property," critical race theorist Cheryl Harris observes: "White identity conferred tangible and economically valuable benefits, and it was jealously guarded as a valued possession, allowed only to those who met a strict standard of proof."[65] Although Harris conceived all these benefits as accessible to anyone who appeared White, they did not all accord with Goldsamt's *experiences*. As a Jew, she felt different from other White people, who, in the United States at that time, were almost entirely Christian, or maybe who were not "religious," per se, but identified as Christian because their parents or grandparents were. For Goldsamt, to be considered a Jew was something different—something of which she was now proud. In John Tehranian's terms, she no longer had to "perform" Whiteness when that meant not being Jewish,[66] although, of course, she still received the benefits of Whiteness when others did not know that she was Jewish. So, the congregation's transformation of the dominant narrative in the wider Jewish community at the time, given the congregation's choice to publicize the situation, resulted in her personal transformation.

Not everyone I interviewed told me that the vandalism incident or the civil suit made a significant impact on their Jewish identity; in fact, many interviewees said that they do not think of the events often and that the events had not changed their sense of identity at all. For example, Bill Harkaway wrote:

I can't say it affected my relationship to Judaism. I grew up in New Hampshire, a place which was not heavily populated with Jews and [I] had friends of various religions. I also had occasion to face—and sometimes to fight with—some non-Jews who, for some unknown reason, didn't like me. I can't say I won all my fights, but I managed to survive. Sometimes I opened my friends' eyes to Judaism; sometimes not.[67]

For Harkaway, the incident was one among others in which his Jewish identification marked him as different from the norm, and it did not alter his sense of self or his relationship with non-Jews. In contrast with those fights, the vandalism was not as influential to him as the skirmishes for which he was a target when he was a child. It certainly impacted him, but perhaps it was not as challenging as it had been for Susan Goldsamt. Retrospectively, as a retired adult, it was the interactions as a kid that changed him more, because these memories likely made a much deeper impression on him.

Goldsamt's experience transformed her into a person who owned her Jewishness, who was more proud of it then than ever before. She recalled a previous incident of antisemitism at her workplace:

> I worked for a store named Julius and Garfinkle, which was not Jewish-owned, it was owned by the YWCA, and it was very prejudiced there. I was the first Jew. Well, the first open Jew. And I underwent a lot of discrimination there. For instance, my merchandise manager, every time there was something in Israel, he would come to me and say "what do you know? is it safe for us to go?" Now I was pregnant and he didn't know it and I was going to leave. . . . And I looked at him, and I said, "Well, Wendall, my spies haven't reported in to me this morning."[68]

In that setting, she was less powerful than her boss, both as an employee and as a woman. She may have seen the world through this lens previously and felt compromised. Her female, Jewish identity was pointedly significant then, but also when we talked: her confidence and determination were clear. She was, as she said, "not backing down."[69]

Harriet Steinhorn Roth (z"l) was a survivor of the Shoah and the principal of the Hebrew school at Shaare Tefila, which met three times a week. After reading my letter to the Shaare Tefila news bulletin, she contacted me and then graciously invited me to her house for lunch, so we could talk.[70] During the conversation, in her responses to nearly every question, she returned to her experiences during the Shoah, which she had not only lived through but spoke about many times at many schools in the Washington, DC, area. At one point, midway into the interview, she said something that struck me:

> My daughter is now fifty-six. . . . And, um, when she was about two years old, I remember being in her room, in her bedroom. And suddenly this thought entered my head. Because I hated with such passion all those Nazis that did what they did to us. Not what they did to me. Because I felt that whatever they did to me, I survived. I'm living. But to all those who did not. Not only that they suffered, but in spite of all of the suffering, they died, they didn't even let them live. And I hate them, and I spent so much time thinking about them, and you know, but it's hurting *me*, it's not hurting them. And from that moment on I said no, never, I will never think about it. And I wish that I could have gone to a psychiatrist and you know learned about that stuff sooner because it took me many years. And it was after that that I went back to college. I could not, feeling the way I felt, it was crippling me. Emotionally, mentally. And that's what helped me

overcome it. So, heal thyself. . . . I healed myself. And thank goodness for that. When I give my talks, people afterward come over [and say]—you don't talk with hatred or anger. [The reality is] I don't feel any hatred or anger anymore. I mean, I don't love them, I don't like them.[71]

Her realization that she was hurting *herself* enabled her to live in a new way, with a focus other than her hatred of Nazis. And with that focus, she could make her presentations to school children in a way that did not reiterate her anger, over and over. It was a transforming experience for her.

When asked about how the vandalism affected her experience of being Jewish in the United States, she responded:

Well, not only as a citizen of the U.S. but as a citizen of the world, of humanity, it affected me tremendously, because deep down I believe that people are good. The evil, I don't begin to understand how people can be so evil, to commit what I watched, what I saw. Never mind what they did to me, but what I saw, what they did to others. And of course, I am sure that had I not been tortured like all the others, had I not been treated like all the others that I might not have understood the enormity of what was being done. I still believed that people were good, and in fact, at the time that I was liberated, whenever I saw a good deed, whenever I saw people acting humanely and helping others, I would cry [for] joy. I was so touched, I was so happy—[to this . . .] day, I still feel the same way.[72]

Steinhorn Roth told me that she was a citizen of the *world*. The defacement seemed to cause her grief that went beyond her life as a Jewish American—as separate from other Jews internationally—grief that connected them with the long-held despair they felt due to the history of antisemitism globally, and to anti-Judaism in its many forms.[73] In the face of her own torture and, more so, that of others, she emphasized her universal humanity among other people; her sense of joy when people were kind and humane. The vandalism influenced her, yet she saw it through the lens of her experiences during the Shoah. Through that lens, she aimed to teach her students "tolerance"; what she felt most was that people are good, and so that's what she taught her students. The Shoah did not happen because of God, it happened because of *people*, she told me, to whom God gave the will to choose between good and evil.

Then, there was the synagogue's cantor, Gershon Levin (z"l). He had an important position at Shaare Tefila, and he likely felt very protective of the synagogue because he was so deeply connected with it. By 1982, he had already been the synagogue's cantor for a long time, since 1966. At the time of the desecration, he was in the midst of mourning for his father, who had passed away on October 13, 1982. Levin had traveled to Israel to sit *shiva*, a mourning period of seven days, with his family. He had been growing a beard for a month at that point and he was very depressed. Upon his return to Silver Spring, the Ritual Director told him about the vandalism. He had entered the synagogue from a different door, and he was "very shocked to learn that the back of the school was defaced with swastikas and the rest of the horrible drawings." "What made it worse," he noted, "was that our synagogue had Holocaust survivors."[74] When he wrote to me that he could not forget painting over that one place on the synagogue—with his son on his arm—perhaps the vandals had shaken something within him: the ability to defend it from attack.[75] This synagogue space was a part of what he held most dear. Perhaps he felt powerless against the vandals, who, even though younger than he was, nonetheless exercised dominance over him. Having his son with him, a child who was perhaps unaware of what they were doing, may have made that sense of powerlessness even more traumatic for him. Nevertheless, he wrote: "I am proud to be a Jew in a place where religion and our voice can be heard, where we can reach the highest court of the land."[76]

Marshall Levin likely wanted to make a name for himself and for Shaare Tefila Congregation, as a critical thinker relatively new to the congregation, and as an Executive Director who took charge in response to the defacement and who thought in legal terms about it. He knew that American law *should* have protected the synagogue members as Jewish Americans. Recall that he mentioned that the law had not protected the German Jews on *Kristallnacht*, which occurred over the course of two days—November 9 and 10, 1938— because the Nazis had revoked Jewish citizenship three years beforehand with the Nuremberg Laws. Since Jews in the United States *did* have citizenship rights, however, Levin expected US legal protection. He was young, and he believed that the law should be a force for justice. He saw himself as equal to other Americans and fought for the rights of the synagogue members on those terms. Levin approached the situation as a social justice–oriented academic and activist.

In the introduction to her book of the same name, Mari Matsuda writes: "*Where Is Your Body?* asks how it is that where we stand shapes what we see, what we believe, and what privileges and subordinations we experience."[77] She points beyond race or religion, or any other descriptors that might socially locate a person, including their gender, ability, and sexuality. Her work makes intersectionality apparent, for example in Black bodies who are women and differently abled; yet it also personalizes: it investigates one individual's experience of these factors, plus additional ones, such as facets of their childhood, or who they aspire to become.

How do the concepts that Matsuda identifies affect the way various synagogue members interpreted the vandalism? As she writes, "where they stand," their bodies in the spaces where they went, were affected by the vandalism in different ways.[78] The viewpoints of Susan Goldsamt, Bill Harkaway, Harriet

Steinhorn Roth, Gershon Levin, and Marshall Levin, among others, were
naturally varied. They might apply to their understanding of their role at the
synagogue, their age at the time, and their conception of what the vandalism
might mean with respect to other events, such as what else was happening to
them in that particular moment and what had happened to them in the past.
The defacement might also have unearthed deep-seated traumas, such as life
in Europe or under the Nazis during World War II. These embodied events
emerged as the congregation members described their experiences.

Although Matsuda writes about racialized Americans who are not "formally" White, as White-perceived Jewish Americans are, if we're careful, we
can apply her description to the way that many, especially older, generations
of Jewish Americans see themselves. She explains: "We are here in the particular sense of our personal genealogies because we are the children of survivors . . . we are the children of generations before us who refused to accept
the message of racial inferiority."[79] This directly informs Shirley Altman's
message: "We don't want to be considered a race, but as long as vandals
perceive us as being different, we should be protected by law. All atrocities
against Jews in the world have been committed by those who *perceive* us as
a race. We should have a ruling nationwide with the message that this will
not be tolerated."[80]

Further, Matsuda wants to "tap the source" of marginalized and racialized
people, which means that she wants to understand who they are as individuals and what they have internalized from their experiences. She applied this
concept to the example of Justice Thurgood Marshall's vision of reality
that is related to his experience as a Black man. "What I intend to suggest
is only that there is something about life on this side of the color line that
has theory-building potential. There is a reason," she noted, "that Thurgood
Marshall understands things not only about people of color, but also women,
poor people, homosexuals, the physically disabled, and other outsiders that
his colleagues, in all their intelligence, fail to understand."[81] Remember that
in the oral argument, he said that his father had blond hair and blue eyes, but
also that his father "was a Negro."[82] Here, he pointed out where Deborah
Garren had failed in her argument, namely by assuming that his father was
"White," because one of the American rationales for racial difference is the
historic "one-drop" rule.[83]

Surprisingly, even though he shares almost nothing else in common with
Justice Marshall—and as a constitutional originalist has no interest in other
forms of racialization or marginalization—in *Shaare Tefila*, Justice Scalia
understood the Jewish congregants' social location from his position as an
ethnic Italian member of the Supreme Court. Growing up in Queens, he
likely had friends who were Jews or at least knew them and likely viewed
them as another ethnic group. He seems to have drawn on his conception of

Italianness to conceive of Jews as not *just* a religion. As Scalia put it "the congregation had *not* argued: 'there is no general social perception that to be a Jew is only a religious thing.'"[84]

When Irvin Shapell and Kevin Lipson founded the Jewish Advocacy Center, they also tapped into the discrimination faced by "formally" White Jewish Americans, which enabled Shaare Tefila to win their civil suit. Shapell and Lipson believed it was important to seek protection from antisemitic vandalism even if it meant bringing to the forefront a race-based claim. Note that the Jewish American community had the time and the financial resources to bring the lawsuit, whereas other racially marginalized communities most likely did not have these options. For example, Irvin Shapell had the financial backing of his family, which allowed Shapell and Lipson to construct the Jewish Advocacy Center in the first place. Many other long-standing Jewish American organizations had begun as a response to antisemitic discrimination in the dominant Christian, White, American discourse;[85] but they had also emerged to solidify Jewish American philanthropy as a broader force.[86]

Where a body stands often relates to where that body goes. At least two of the Jewish places where Shaare Tefila members go are their houses and the synagogue. In the American context, synagogues might try to combine most of the components of Jewish life into one place. It serves as a space for prayer, a place of study, and a center of Jewish activity, and could possibly include such amenities as a nursery, a Hebrew school, a basketball court, or a swimming pool.[87] To many Jewish Americans, synagogues might be a place to meet friends, a refuge from the dominant Christian society, or, perhaps more extremely, a place of solidarity among imminently hostile neighbors.

Shaare Tefila members' Jewishness and the synagogue space they inhabited were integral to their stories and to the ways that they experienced their legal rights. After the vandalism, Shaare Tefila members found themselves in a challenging position. Although they experienced emotional distress because of the defacement, they lived at a time and in a place in which they felt two types of pressure: one was to erase the vandalism immediately and pretend to ignore it, and the other was to follow the dominant sentiment that it was not a particularly important issue. In other words, they may have been expected both to bear the pain of the event silently, and simultaneously to pretend that it was not ultimately significant.

As one might imagine, most Shaare Tefila members did not spend time during their everyday lives contemplating how Jewish Americans should be categorized as a legal entity. When I had asked what they thought of the legal ruling regarding Jewish identification and the categories of "religion" and "race," most of them did not know what the legal argument or the final decision stated. When I inquired further about these categories in relation to their own sense of identification, they responded in ways that made clear that they did not conceive of their identities in those terms, although they *did* understand the synagogue as a religious community.

Instead, they told me about their regular involvement with Shaare Tefila over the years. For example, former member Samuel Rensin, who was a teenager at the time of the defacement and the civil suit, recalled the importance of the welcoming environment that Shaare Tefila had sustained during his childhood there and of the congregation's rabbi and cantor to his personal development:

> It was a great sense of community. At the time we had a spectacular rabbi, Martin Halpern. Martin was just a warm great guy, and the cantor was a fellow named Gershon Levin. And I remember training for my *bar mitzvah* with these two guys, and I remember . . . growing up through some very formative years with those two individuals. They were unquestionably the heart and soul of that place. . . . The temple was a real place where you got more out of it than you put in, because it was made up of those kinds of people.[88]

Rensin's statement echoes the feelings that many other Shaare Tefila members expressed about the synagogue.

Similarly, Sid Schwartz told me about his participation in the daily *minyans* that the congregation held: "We have morning *minyan* seven days a week, and we have evening *minyans* too. It's one of the few synagogues here that can do it. It's dicey sometimes, but we do it. Wendy [the previous cantor] will come in and this morning we got up to nine. There's one guy who will call in the morning before he goes to work—do you need me to stop?"[89] In order to include portions of the daily prayer service and to allow a person in mourning to say *kaddish* for his or her deceased parent, which is a daily requirement for Jewish mourners, ten Jews must be present.[90] Schwartz's comment illustrates the dedication of a core group of Shaare Tefila members to *davening* (praying) daily and providing the opportunity for mourners to fulfill their obligation. Because few non-Orthodox synagogues in most parts of the United States can support a daily *minyan*, those that do offer a service to Jews outside of the congregation as well.[91]

One woman, who was not a member, lived up in Columbia, north of Silver Spring, and "she knew how to *daven*," Schwartz told me. She was very appreciative that she could stop on her way to work in the morning, and she sometimes led the service. On one morning in the summer, she was "up there with her tallit" leading the prayers, and this man came in, but he didn't "seem like he wanted to be there," Schwartz told me. "There was something about him that looked like he really wanted this place across the street . . . he looked Orthodox, and he wasn't from the area, so somebody said there's a synagogue on this street." "Somehow, just at that instant, Rabbi Layman happened to turn his head and saw him, and he connected, he understood it right away . . . he jumped up, and he walked over quickly and he escorted him out into the foyer, and he asked him, can I help you?" He told Rabbi Layman that he was looking for Southeast Hebrew Congregation, an Orthodox synagogue, and Layman, said, "Yeah . . . I thought you might be in the wrong place," and told him it was just down the street. Schwartz declared: "I wonder what this guy was thinking! Seeing a woman with a tallit, tefillin on . . . you know, those people would have real nightmares."[92]

Midway through my conversation with Sid Schwartz, someone came into the room where we were talking, and he said "hi" to him, which led Sid to tell me that the house we were currently sitting in was owned by a doctor whose wife had passed away, and that the doctor was now living in an assisted-living facility. Schwartz recalled him saying: "The housekeeper, she stays!" When I mentioned that it seemed very nice of him, Schwartz said that it was "characteristic of core members" of the Shaare Tefila Congregation. Clearly, these core members care deeply for each other and are also invested in the future of the synagogue.

CONCLUSION

In this chapter, Shaare Tefila Congregation members reflected on their embodied experiences of the defacement, the Supreme Court case, and its conclusion in the Federal District Court; it focuses on five members in particular and highlights several of their distinct roles within the congregation. Initially, the congregation had wanted to obtain a verdict, but in the end, they decided to meet with the vandals. At the Federal District Court in Baltimore, Michael Remer and the other vandals who heard Rabbi Halpern and Shirley Altman speak seemed to internalize the gravity of what they had done. After this significant dialogue, in which they expressed their regret, they wrote letters of apology. Through this exchange with the three vandals, the synagogue was able to tell their story, which granted Shaare Tefila the narrative control that they sought in the juridical space of the courtroom.[93] For synagogue members who had questioned the choices made by the Shaare Tefila Congregation Board of Trustees, the answer seemed clear: the risks had been worth it.

In response to more in-depth questions, some Shaare Tefila members were more affected or were affected in different ways by the vandalism and the civil suit that followed than others. Mari Matsuda's theoretical perspective provides a tool to "personalize" their relationship with the synagogue and analysis of "where they stand."[94] For example, Susan Goldsamt told me that living through the experience of vandalism was critical for her because she felt empowered by it as a Jewish American. She was not going to endure antisemitism directed at her anymore. Bill Harkaway, however, viewed the vandalism and the resulting civil suit in the Supreme Court, as less life-changing than other antisemitic experiences he had witnessed in the past, some of which had caused him bodily injury. Harriet Steinhorn Roth, Cantor Gershon Levin, and Marshall Levin all experienced the vandalism differently depending on their role in the synagogue.

Clearly, the synagogue was much more than a site of defacement. It was, and is, a space for Jewish study, prayer, friendship, and community; it is one small fraction of *Klal Yisrael* (the people of Israel) and more than simply a site of "religion" or "race." It has its own ever-changing life, with the individual lives of many people contributing to it. The experiences of each person constructed what came to be known as "Shaare Tefila Congregation"—each one contributing to the synagogue in their own way. These collective perceptions defined and continue to define the role of Jewish identification(s), and how they operated and operate at Shaare Tefila Congregation, both in terms of what that meant at the time of the vandalism, and what it means years later, to *be* Jewish Americans.

NOTES

1. Khaled Beydoun, "Faith in Whiteness: Free Exercise of Religion as Racial Expression" in *Iowa Law Review* 105, no. 4 (May 2020): 1487.

2. Shaare Tefila Congregation was one of those synagogues. See Rabbi Jonah Layman, email to author, April 23, 2022.

3. Elizabeth Mertz, "Consensus and Dissent in U.S. Legal Opinions: Narrative Structure and Social Voices" in *Disorderly Discourse*, ed. Charles Briggs (New York: Oxford University Press, 1996), 152.

4. Shaare Tefila Congregation Board of Trustees meeting minutes, March 2, 1987.

5. Susan Goldsamt, interview by author, Silver Spring, MD, July 7, 2008.

6. Michael Holmes, phone interview by author, July 2, 2009.

7. Susan Goldsamt, interview by author, Silver Spring, MD, July 7, 2008.

8. "Fighting for Protection under Racial Laws: Shaare Tefila to Petition Supreme Court" *Washington Jewish Week*, March 20, 1986, p. 6.

9. Levin had completed his term as executive director and had left the congregation for a new position.

10. Letter from Shirley Altman to Marshall Levin, dated May 25, 1987.

11. Letter from Shirley Altman to Irvin Shapell, dated May 25, 1987.

12. Letter from Shirley Altman to Patricia Brannan, dated May 25, 1987.

13. Levin, "Desecration in Darkness," in *The Price We Pay: The Case against Hate Speech, Hate Propaganda, and Pornography*, eds. Laura Lederer and Richard Delgado (New York, NY: Hill & Wang, 1995), 44.

14. According to Jewish Advocacy Center lawyer, Kevin Lipson, *Katzenbach v. McClung* (1964) had a much longer reach than *Shaare Tefila Congregation v. Cobb*. See "Katzenbach v. McClung." Oyez. Accessed March 4, 2021. www.oyez.org/cases/1964/543.

15. Deposition of William Randall Harris, Shaare Tefila Congregation v. Cobb, 606 F.Supp. 1504 (D. Md. 1985), *rev'd*, 107 S.Ct. 2019 (1987).

16. Patricia A. Brannan, letter to Rabbi Martin Halpern, April 11, 1988.

17. Patricia A. Brannan, letter to Rabbi Martin Halpern, April 11, 1988.

18. Deposition of Michael D. Remer at 29, Shaare Tefila Congregation v. Cobb, 606 F.Supp. 1504 (D. Md. 1985), *rev'd*, 107 S.Ct. 2019 (1987) (deposition of June 21, 1988).

19. Not capitalized in the original document.

20. Deposition of Michael D. Remer at 32–38, Shaare Tefila Congregation v. Cobb, 606 F.Supp. 1504 (D. Md. 1985), *rev'd*, 107 S.Ct. 2019 (1987) (deposition of June 21, 1988).

21. Deposition of Michael D. Remer at 35–36, Shaare Tefila Congregation v. Cobb, 606 F.Supp. 1504 (D. Md. 1985), *rev'd*, 107 S.Ct. 2019 (1987) (deposition of June 21, 1988).

22. See "White Supremacist Prison Gangs the United States," Anti-Defamation League, May 14, 2016. www.adl.org/resources/reports/white-supremacist-prison-gangs-united-states.

23. Deposition of Michael D. Remer at 38, Shaare Tefila Congregation v. Cobb, 606 F.Supp. 1504 (D. Md. 1985), *rev'd*, 107 S.Ct. 2019 (1987) (deposition of June 21, 1988).

24. Deposition of Michael D. Remer at 80–81, Shaare Tefila Congregation v. Cobb, 606 F.Supp. 1504 (D. Md. 1985), *rev'd*, 107 S.Ct. 2019 (1987) (deposition of June 21, 1988).

25. Deposition of Michael D. Remer at 81, Shaare Tefila Congregation v. Cobb, 606 F.Supp. 1504 (D. Md. 1985), *rev'd*, 107 S.Ct. 2019 (1987) (deposition of June 21, 1988).

26. See Alex DeMetrick, "Notoriously Dangerous Maryland House of Correction in Jessup Being Demolished," CBS Baltimore, January 17, 2014, baltimore.cbslocal.com/2014/01/17/md-house-of-correction-in-jessup-being-destroyed/.

27. Deposition of Michael D. Remer at 81, Shaare Tefila Congregation v. Cobb, 606 F.Supp. 1504 (D. Md. 1985), *rev'd*, 107 S.Ct. 2019 (1987) (deposition of June 21, 1988).

28. See, for example, "Aryan Brotherhood," SPLC, www.splcenter.org/fighting-hate/extremist-files/group/aryan-brotherhood; Jon Kelly, "Aryan Brotherhood of Texas: How did Neo-Nazi Prison Gangs Become So Powerful?" *BBC News Magazine*, April 4, 2013. www.bbc.com/news/magazine-22019433.

29. See, for example, Christopher Blackwell, "How Prison Turned My Childhood Friend into a Neo-Nazi," *The Marshall Project*, August 6, 2020. www

.themarshallproject.org/2020/08/06/how-prison-turned-my-childhood-friend-into-a -neo-nazi; Bevan Hurley, "Alaskan Neo-Nazi Prison Gang Members Guilty of Brutal Murder, Independent, May 3, 2022. www.independent.co.uk/news/world/americas /crime/alaska-neo-nazi-prison-gang-murder-b2070941.html; Neal Conan, "A Look Inside White Prison Gangs," *Talk of the Nation*, NPR, April 9, 2013, www.npr.org /2013/04/09/176681634/a-look-inside-white-supremacist-prison-gangs.

30. Deposition of Michael D. Remer at 82, Shaare Tefila Congregation v. Cobb, 606 F.Supp. 1504 (D. Md. 1985), *rev'd*, 107 S.Ct. 2019 (1987) (deposition of June 21, 1988).

31. Deposition of Michael D. Remer at 45, Shaare Tefila Congregation v. Cobb, 606 F.Supp. 1504 (D. Md. 1985), *rev'd*, 107 S.Ct. 2019 (1987) (deposition of June 21, 1988).

32. Deposition of Michael D. Remer at 45, Shaare Tefila Congregation v. Cobb, 606 F.Supp. 1504 (D. Md. 1985), *rev'd*, 107 S.Ct. 2019 (1987) (deposition of June 21, 1988).

33. Thanks to Dean Franco for pointing this out this to me.

34. On behalf of the congregation, Hogan and Hartson sought a class certification, which would mean that every individual member of the synagogue would be protected from any antisemitic action by the defendants. On July 5, Remer's lawyers, Nolan and Robert L. Pierson, responded, asserting that these antisemitic actions had only occurred on the night of November 1, 1982, and that therefore the congregation had no basis for their claim. For that reason, Judge Norman Ramsey denied the motion for certification of the plaintiff class on September 7, 1988. Next, Brannan, Hollman, and Jeffrey G. Schneider compiled a Motion to Compel Discovery, which they completed on September 8, 1988, and mailed to Remer's lawyers. In that motion, they requested that Remer disclose his membership in White supremacist organizations between 1982 and 1988. In response, his lawyers sent a Memorandum in Opposition to Motion to Compel Discovery, on September 19, 1988, claiming that the knowledge the congregation sought was not relevant to the outcome of the case. Judge Norman Ramsey denied the motion on September 22, 1988. On September 15, 1988, the plaintiffs and the defendants submitted the Pretrial Order. In addition, on that date, the congregation submitted a Motion for Leave to File Amended Complaint for the purpose of making some technical changes to their suit, including: dropping a named plaintiff, Marshall Levin, who was no longer employed by the congregation; reflecting that its venue of incorporation is the District of Columbia; dropping the count 42 U.S.C. §1981 as well as deleting the class action allegations pursuant to the Court's decision on September 7, 1988; reflecting that the action was brought by the Board of Trustees; and alleging that the "defendants' animus was directed towards the kind of group that Congress intended to protect in enacting 42 U.S.C. §1982, as recognized by the Supreme Court in *Shaare Tefila Congregation v. Cobb* . . . " Motion for the Leave to File Amended Complaint at 1–2, Shaare Tefila Congregation v. Cobb, 606 F.Supp. 1504 (D. Md. 1985) (No. R-84–880), *rev'd*, 107 S.Ct. 2019 (1987).

35. Elizabeth Mertz, "Consensus and Dissent in U.S. Legal Opinions: Narrative Structure and Social Voices" in *Disorderly Discourse*, ed. Charles Briggs (New York: Oxford University Press, 1996), 139–40.

36. Patricia Brannan, phone interview by author, February 21, 2018.

37. Patricia Ewick and Susan S. Silbey, *The Common Place of Law: Stories from Everyday Life* (Chicago: University of Chicago Press, 1998), 96–97.

38. Patricia Brannan in Merry Madway Eisenstadt, "Shaare Tefila Source of Hate Crime Precedent," *Washington Jewish Week*, Local News Section, 1 February 2001, 16 (emphasis added).

39. Patricia Brannan, telephone interview by author, February 21, 2018.

40. Patricia Brannan could not remember how many of the defendants were there. See Patricia Brannan, telephone interview by author, February 21, 2018.

41. Patricia Ewick and Susan S. Silbey, *The Common Place of Law: Stories from Everyday Life* (Chicago: University of Chicago Press, 1998), 96–97.

42. Patricia Brannan, telephone interview by author, March 23, 2021.

43. Patricia Brannan, telephone interview by author, February 21, 2018.

44. Patricia Brannan, telephone interview by author, February 21, 2018.

45. Patricia Brannan in Merry Madway Eisenstadt, "Shaare Tefila Source of Hate Crime Precedent," *Washington Jewish Week*, Local News Section, February 1, 2001, p. 16.

46. Patricia Brannan in Merry Madway Eisenstadt, "Shaare Tefila Source of Hate Crime Precedent," *Washington Jewish Week*, Local News Section, February 1, 2001, p. 16.

47. Patricia Brannan, telephone interview by author, February 21, 2018.

48. Michael D. Remer, letter "To the Members of Shaare Tefila Congregation," October 5, 1988.

49. Michael D. Remer, letter "To the Members of Shaare Tefila Congregation," October 5, 1988 (emphasis added).

50. Michael D. Remer, letter "To the Members of Shaare Tefila Congregation," October 5, 1988.

51. Michael D. Remer, letter "To the Members of Shaare Tefila Congregation," October 5, 1988.

52. Michael D. Remer, letter "To the Members of Shaare Tefila Congregation," October 5, 1988.

53. Consent Injunction at 2–3, Shaare Tefila Congregation v. Cobb, 606 F.Supp. 1504 (D. Md. 1985) (No. R84-880), *rev'd*, 107 S.Ct. 2019 (1987).

54. Steven P. Hollman, letter to Rabbi Martin S. Halpern, December 23, 1988.

55. Maurice Potosky, interview by author, Silver Spring, MD, July 7, 2008.

56. Maurice Potosky, interview by author, Silver Spring, MD, July 7, 2008.

57. Susan Goldsamt, interview by author, Silver Spring, MD, July 7, 2008.

58. Sid Schwartz, interview by author, Silver Spring, MD, July 7, 2008.

59. Sid Schwartz, interview by author, Silver Spring, MD, July 7, 2008.

60. Rabbi Jonah Layman, interview by author, Silver Spring, MD, August 17, 2009.

61. Rabbi Jonah Layman, interview by author, Silver Spring, MD, August 17, 2009.

62. Rabbi Jonah Layman, interview by author, Silver Spring, MD, August 17, 2009.

63. Rabbi Jonah Layman, interview by author, Silver Spring, MD, August 17, 2009.

64. Susan Goldsamt, interview by author, Silver Spring, MD, July 7, 2008.

65. Cheryl I. Harris, "Whiteness as Property" in *Critical Race Theory: The Key Writings that Formed the Movement*, eds. Kimberlé Crenshaw et al. (New York: The New Press, 1995), 280.

66. John Tehranian, "Performing Whiteness: Naturalization Litigation and the Construction of Racial Identity in America" in *Yale Law Journal* 109, no. 4 (Jan. 2000).

67. Bill Harkaway, email correspondence with author, received June 10, 2009.

68. Susan Goldsamt, interview by author, Silver Spring, MD, July 7, 2008.

69. Susan Goldsamt, interview by author, Silver Spring, MD, July 7, 2008.

70. Sadly, only snippets of our three-hour interview can be included here.

71. Harriet Steinhorn Roth, interview by author, Silver Spring, MD, August 17, 2009.

72. Harriet Steinhorn Roth, interview by author, Silver Spring, MD, August 17, 2009.

73. Shaare Tefila members did not want to feel separate from other groups, perhaps particularly the predominant White one. Naomi W. Cohen, *Jews in Christian America: The Pursuit of Religious Equality* (New York: Oxford, 1992), 5–6.

74. Cantor Gershon Levin, written responses to interview questions by author, submitted via email, August 26, 2009.

75. Cantor Gershon Levin, written responses to interview questions by author, submitted via email, August 26, 2009.

76. Cantor Gershon Levin, written responses to interview questions by author, submitted via email, August 26, 2009.

77. Shaare Tefila Congregation v. Cobb, 481 U.S. 615, 617 (1987). Mari Matsuda, *Where Is Your Body? And Other Essays on Race, Gender, and the Law* (Boston, MA: Beacon Press, 1996), xi.

78. Mari Matsuda, *Where Is Your Body? And Other Essays on Race, Gender, and the Law* (Boston, MA: Beacon Press, 1996), xi.

79. Mari Matsuda, *Where Is Your Body? And Other Essays on Race, Gender, and the Law* (Boston: Beacon Press, 1996), 26.

80. Shirley Altman in "Fighting for Protection under Racial Laws: Shaare Tefila to Petition Supreme Court" *Washington Jewish Week*, March 20, 1986, p. 6.

81. Mari Matsuda, *Where Is Your Body? And Other Essays on Race, Gender, and the Law* (Boston: Beacon Press, 1996), 26–27.

82. Oral argument at 691, Shaare Tefila Congregation v. Cobb, 606 F.Supp. 1504 (D. Md. 1985) (No. R-84-880), *rev'd*, 107 S.Ct. 2019 (1987), in *Landmark Briefs and Arguments of the Supreme Court of the United States: Constitutional Law, 1986 Term Supplement* (Frederick, MD: University Publications of America, Inc., 1988), 691.

83. Oral argument at 691, Shaare Tefila Congregation v. Cobb, 606 F.Supp. 1504 (D. Md. 1985) (No. R-84-880), *rev'd*, 107 S.Ct. 2019 (1987), in *Landmark Briefs and Arguments of the Supreme Court of the United States: Constitutional Law, 1986 Term Supplement* (Frederick, MD: University Publications of America, Inc., 1988), 691.

84. Oral argument at 701, Shaare Tefila Congregation v. Cobb, 606 F.Supp. 1504 (D. Md. 1985) (No. R-84-880), *rev'd*, 107 S.Ct. 2019 (1987), in *Landmark Briefs and Arguments of the Supreme Court of the United States: Constitutional Law, 1986 Term Supplement* (Frederick, MD: University Publications of America, Inc., 1988), 701.

85. See Stuart Svonkin, *Jews Against Prejudice: American Jews and The Fight for Civil Liberties* (New York: Columbia University Press, 1997).

86. See Lila Corwin Berman, *The American Jewish Philanthropic Complex: The History of a Multibillion-Dollar Institution* (Princeton, NJ: Princeton University Press, 2020).

87. See David Kaufman, *Shul with a Pool: The "Synagogue-Center" in American Jewish History* (Lebanon, NH: Brandeis University Press, 1999).

88. Samuel Rensin, phone interview by author, July 30, 2009.

89. Sid Schwartz, interview by author, Silver Spring, MD, July 7, 2008.

90. Most of whom are Conservative men and women, and Orthodox, who are mainly men.

91. Women who wish to say *kaddish* because they are in mourning often have difficulty finding a place to do so daily. Orthodox synagogues, where most daily *minyans* occur, do not count women in the required quorum of ten Jews. Also, many Orthodox synagogues actively discourage women from saying *kaddish*, since they do not consider it an obligation for women, according to *halacha* (Jewish law), and since women and men do not pray together due to concerns regarding modesty.

92. Sid Schwartz, interview by author, Silver Spring, MD, July 7, 2008.

93. See Jenna Gray-Hildenbrand's introduction and conclusion for courtrooms as active spaces of legal production. Jenna Gray-Hildenbrand, "Saving Religion from Ballardhoo: Metaphysical Religion, the Government, and the Creation of Religious Criminals" *Nova Religio* 27, no. 1 (August 2023), forthcoming.

94. Mari Matsuda, *Where Is Your Body? And Other Essays on Race, Gender, and the Law* (Boston, MA: Beacon Press, 1996), xi.

Conclusion

On Saturday, July 28, 2018, almost forty years after the vandalism at Shaare Tefila Congregation in Silver Spring, Maryland, Shaarey Tefila Congregation in Carmel, Indiana, was defaced with Nazi symbols. It consisted of two black swastikas with a red flag surrounding each of them, one with an iron cross on each side, spray-painted on different sides of a cement trash container behind the synagogue. This vandalism evoked a similar response to what had happened at Shaare Tefila Congregation. Because Shaarey Tefila Congregation allowed it to remain on the wall, an outpouring of local support followed. Like Shaare Tefila Congregation in 1982, the vandalism made local, national, and international news, and in part for that reason, Shaarey Tefila was able to open its doors on the following Monday to more than one thousand people who came to stand with them in opposition to it.[1]

People who spoke that night at Shaarey Tefila included members of other religiously, racially, and sexually marginalized communities: Hindu, Muslim, Sikh, Latinx, and LGBTQ+ groups, as well as Christian pastors, priests, and a representative from the Latter-Day Saints Church.[2] One Episcopal priest mentioned that, given the Christian history of doctrine, sermons, and texts that demeaned Jews, he felt an obligation to stand by these Jews when this sort of hateful action occurred. Some of the speakers pointedly mentioned that the State of Indiana does not have a hate crimes law, and a few of them encouraged the audience to write to their legislators about it.[3] Perhaps because the defacement was in the national news, state officials also called for the law to be changed. Indiana now *has* a hate crime law, which was passed the next year on April 3, 2019; but it fails to cover age, sex, or gender identity.[4]

Recall that the ADL had changed its policies in response to antisemitic vandalism when Shaare Tefila Congregation publicized the desecration of their synagogue in 1982. So, with the aid of the ADL, which offered $5,000 to anyone who could identify the perpetrator(s),[5] police caught them. Nolan Brewer, twenty, was charged with conspiracy to violate civil rights, which could imprison him for up to ten years, and his seventeen-year-old wife, K(i) yomi Brewer was charged with state criminal mischief and arson.[6]

Nolan Brewer subsequently said he had targeted the synagogue because it "was full of ethnic Jews."[7] He fashioned himself as a Nazi, thus, his statement referred to Jewish "blood lineage" and drew on European traditions of racializing Jews. Special Agent in Charge of the FBI's Indianapolis Division, Grant Mendenhall, responded to the situation stating: "Crimes such as this—fueled by hatred towards individuals based simply on their faith—will not be tolerated by the FBI and our law enforcement partners."[8] To him, faith was an obvious term that described Jewish Americans. It's another example of the Protestant norm that Jewish Americans had internalized. In a nutshell, these two comments about the Shaarey Tefila members illustrate two dramatically disparate tropes regarding Jewish identification, *both* that continue to claim meaning in the United States. Although section 1982 provides rights based on "race," Mendenhall conceived of Jews as a "faith," an exchangeable word for "religion" in the US context.

Nolan and K(i)yomi Brewer had been in contact with White supremacist groups prior to the defacement. They often spent hours reading articles on Breitbart and the Nazi website Stormfront, and they had become members of Identity Evropa.[9] They conversed on a website called Discord, and they spoke with a person named "Asbestos Peter," who persuaded them to vandalize Shaarey Tefila. The Brewers traveled fifty miles to the synagogue from their house after buying supplies at Walmart the day before, including red and black spray paint, Gatorade bottles, aluminum foil, Drano cleaner, rubber gloves, Styrofoam plates, and bandanas. They had intended to break in and burn down the synagogue but became anxious when they saw the security cameras.[10] At his workplace, Nolan Brewer tried to convince his co-workers that Adolf Hitler's views were correct and justified the Nazis' treatment of Jewish people. After the vandalism, he bragged to them about what he had done.[11]

Due to the legal outcome in *Shaare Tefila Congregation v. Cobb*, the FBI and the Carmel Police Department were able to indict Nolan Brewer on September 12, 2018 based on the "Conspiracy to Violate Rights," 18 U.S.C. 241(a). Justice Byron White's decision allowed them to cite section 1982, which White had emphasized in his ruling for *Shaare Tefila*. Brewer pled guilty on May 21, 2019, before US Federal District Court Judge Tanya Walton Pratt, and was sentenced to three years in prison, ordered to pay both a $1,000 fine and $700 to the synagogue for damages.[12] K(i)yomi Brewer[13] was charged as an adult in Hamilton County and pled guilty to committing arson, but received probation and no jail time.[14]

At the community response to Shaarey Tefila's vandalism, which was held at the synagogue on Monday, July 30, 2018, Alia Amin from the Muslim

Alliance of Indiana told the audience almost exactly what Marshall Levin had said in 1982 when he had encouraged Maurice Potosky and Rabbi Halpern to let the graffiti remain for the community to see: "it's a crime against the community."[15] Amin told those assembled that this "act, while aimed at our Jewish sisters and brothers, is really an attack on all of us."[16] Shaare Tefila's leaders were not sure whether the public would be behind them in the 1980s; they took a risk. But in 2018, almost forty years later, Shaarey Tefila could be much more confident of local support.

Shaare Tefila Congregation v. Cobb was an important case in that it paved the way, both legally and socially, for other synagogues to respond to racist and antisemitic vandalism. Even if leaders of other synagogues did not know about the civil suit specifically, the case had sociological implications within synagogue communities that began to shift Jewish American perspectives about synagogue defacement. The fact that Shaare Tefila Congregation left the vandalism on its walls led other defaced synagogues to be more willing to let the public see *their* maligned walls. Other synagogues could then come to rely more readily on their community for support as they dealt with their experiences of grief, anger, and anxiety.

Shaare Tefila marked a turning point in which judges attempted to determine whether Jews are legally defined as a "religion" or a "race." As noted above, Justice White decided not to identify Jews in the contemporary moment, but to examine the way Jews were viewed in the past, during the time preceding the Civil Rights Act of 1866. The Court followed Caroline Mitchell's argument: she had argued that Al-Khazraji would have been considered a different "race" in 1866, as an "Arab." The Court decided similarly about the Shaare Tefila Congregation, whose members would have been considered "Hebrews."

Kevin Lipson noted: "I think that in American Jewish legal history, it is almost of singular significance. I cannot think of another case that elevates Jewish identity as a federal issue. This case does . . . I'm thinking more as a lawyer, you know? But I think from a cultural and a Jewish cultural and an American Jewish historical perspective, I think it is of singular significance."[17]

Two other cases, which also used *Shaare Tefila* as precedent, focus on judges' decisions about how to classify Jewish people and, in doing so, emphasize the ingrained socio-legal qualities of "religion" and "race."[18] The cases highlight other ways in which the statutes that undergird *Shaare Tefila* could be used with the potential of attaining similar ends. In one of them, a Latino converted to Judaism, and in the other one, a Jewish American man converted to Christianity. These cases highlight the complexity with which dominant European and then American powers historically constructed "religion" and "race" as *separate* categories and then the Founding Fathers wrote them, separately, into US law. Their underlying feature, however, is

206 Conclusion

that they are "co-constituted categories." They are, in Henry Goldschmidt's words: "wholly dependent on each other for their social existence and symbolic meanings."[19]

In these two cases, the socio-legal terms: Latino, Hasidic Jewish, and Baptist Christian, are unquestionably used as descriptors here. Not that to do so is *wrong*, necessarily, but the judges overlooked the way they are *constructed* in relation to the concepts of "religion" and "race." Again, it's important to recall how these terms operate as part of White, Christian dominant discourse.

The first case occurred on April 9, 1997 *Singer v. Denver School District*, in which Yishai Singer, a Latino man who converted to Judaism, claimed that he was forced to leave his position as a high school teacher due to the principal, Edward Cordova's, repeated harassment regarding his Hasidic religious practices, beliefs, and clothing.[20] Among other legal claims, Singer brought Section 1981 and 1983 claims, and he cited *Shaare Tefila*, among other cases, to assert that he was targeted due to his Jewish identity. Senior United States District Judge John L. Kane Jr. decided the case and found in favor of the Denver School District for many reasons, but, specifically, for an especially notable one: Kane determined that Cordova discriminated against Singer for "religious" reasons, not "racial" ones, so section 1981—drawn from the Shaare Tefila case—would not apply in Singer's case.[21] According to Kane, Singer's religious beliefs, practices, and clothing constitute "religious" practices. "Religion," as noted elsewhere in this book, was produced by Christian leaders as a category, and one that is based primarily on "belief." Most Jewish Americans have internalized Protestant American dominant discourse, viewing *themselves* as a "religion." But Singer did not "blend in"; he did not fit the "modern," "Western" image that most Jewish American immigrants attempted to relinquish when they reached American shores. Legal scholar William Kaplowitz points out that Hasidic Jews are subject to "normative stereotypes" internalized by Jewish Americans because they do not assimilate or conform to the social norms of *Jewish* assimilation in the United States.[22] To adopt Tehranian's terms, Singer's "performance" does not resemble assimilationist Jewish identification, so he is not performing "Whiteness" as the majority of Jews do, who are then perceived as White.[23]

In the second case, *Bonadona v. Louisiana College*,[24] Judge Mark Hornsby first gave a recommendation and it was decided on August 28, 2019, by another judge.[25] Joshua Bonadona appealed the case to the Fifth Circuit Court of Appeals, but he and President Brewer settled it out of court. Bonadona was raised Jewish,[26] but he converted to Christianity while he was a student at Louisiana College. He had played football there, made it clear to the team that he was Christian, and often led them in prayer before the games. Bonadona had gone on to train as a football coach and had quit his job at

Southeast Missouri State University when Coach Justin Charles offered him a position at his alumni institution. Charles assured him that President Rick Brewer signing off on the position was just a formality. Turned out it was not, because, according to Charles, Brewer was opposed to hiring him because of his 'Jewish descent.'"[27] When Bonadona asked what that meant, Charles "stated that Dr. Brewer refused to approve his hiring because of what Dr. Brewer called his 'Jewish blood.'"[28] Brewer's apparent description of Bonadona's "Jewish blood" draws from a long history in Europe, beginning with the *limpieza de sangre* (purity of blood) laws in Spain. The refusal, in Bonadona's case, was not due to his *religious* beliefs, according to Judge Hornsby, since Bonadona is a member of the "Baptist faith."[29] Bonadona filed a charge of discrimination with the Equal Employment Opportunity Commission, stating that he had been discriminated against because of his "race (Caucasian-Jewish)," in violation of Title VII of the Civil Rights Act of 1964, which prohibits discrimination by employers "on the basis of race, color, religion, sex, or national origin,"[30] which Judge Hornsby granted, and listed *St. Francis College v. Al-Khazraji* (protection under section 1981), and *Shaare Tefila Congregation v. Cobb* (protection under section 1982), as well as *T.E. v. Pine Bush Central School District*[31] (protection under Title VI) in his complaint to the court. Although President Brewer denied the statement, his purported assessment that Joshua Bonadona had Jewish blood resembled Nolan Brewer's reason for targeting Shaarey Tefila synagogue because it was "full of ethnic Jews." Here we have someone who spray-painted Nazi flags on a synagogue making the same claim as the president of a college. As Patricia Brannan mentioned in the Supreme Court, White supremacy does not depend on one's degree of education.

The first case illustrates the significance of thinly drawn distinctions between "religion" and "race," in which Singer could not win. The second case highlights dominant anti-Jewish tropes, such as the concept of "Jewish blood," meaning that somehow Bonadona is inherently Jewish even though he is a believing Christian. In the initial ruling, Judge Hornsby determined that Bonadona be granted race-based protection under Title VII, however, Judge Kane did *not* grant Singer race-based protection under section 1981.

As we can see from these two cases, Jewish racialization continues in the US courts, and likewise, it also pervades political and social situations. Incidents of racist antisemitic vandalism and violence occur increasingly in the United States. The vast majority of them occur at the hands of White supremacists. Two situations help to clarify.

Whiteness proponent and former US President Donald Trump commented that "there were good people on both sides" of the "Unite the Right" Charlottesville rally on August 13, 2017. The rally consisted of self-identified members of the alt-right, neo-Confederates, neo-fascists, White nationalists, neo-Nazis, Klansmen, and many other right-wing militias. On college campuses, White nationalist presence has ebbed and flowed, except—of course— at historically Black colleges and universities. But it has always been present.[32] These White nationalists noted Trump's response and then made their presence more explicit. David Nirenberg told Emma Green, a journalist for *The Atlantic*, that he had recently talked to a group of college students: "At the end of the . . . talk, I said, 'I wouldn't rush from all this material to thinking that this anti-Semitism is as dangerous as its early 20th-century predecessor,'" but "Seeing the images of the Virginia protest, I must admit, I kind of felt otherwise. . . . It certainly made me feel that books and ideas that I had treated as very marginal in our society are not as marginal as I might have hoped."[33]

A year later, a mass shooting, killing eleven Jews and wounding seven, including law enforcement, occurred at the Tree of Life Synagogue in the Squirrel Hill neighborhood of Pittsburgh, Pennsylvania on October 27, 2018.[34] On a website called Gab, the shooter[35] had posted antisemitic and anti-immigrant statements about HIAS (formerly the Hebrew Immigrant Aid Society), regarding Central American migrant "caravans" and other immigrants.[36] Often on Shabbat mornings, first a few people gather at the synagogue, and then more of them trickle in as the service progresses toward the central ritual of the Torah reading. Because the perpetrator arrived early, he killed the most dedicated. One Shoah survivor, Judah Samet, arrived minutes after the shooting, was warned about it, and then left the scene.[37]

Anti-Jewish violence and graffiti point to a broader sentiment in the United States: as White people in the United States decrease in number, due to both an actual and imagined increase in immigrants—who, in their minds, must be brown or black—White supremacists believe that they need to take a stand to ensure that this country stays "White." Jews, in effect, represent the ancestral Other of Western thought, the longest-standing targeted, marginalized—and in most times and places—minority community.

This book has explored how courts judge Jewish Americans; why they do not *fit* into the socio-legal categories of "race" or "religion" in the United States; how those categories configure Jewish legal identification in the United States, and why we should step back, observe their construction, and consider them both products of the same hierarchy. Given the White, Christian, male background of most judges, many of them failed to see beyond the legal boundaries of "religion" and "race" in *Shaare Tefila Congregation v. Cobb* and other cases in which "racialization" of Jewish Americans is in question. The judges may not have recognized the social construction of "religion" and "race," *who* constructed them, and that it furthered the objectives of those who conceived it—sometimes consciously and sometimes unconsciously— of hierarchy and control.

Further, *Judging Jewish Identity in the United States* has looked to Daniel I. Rubin's HebCrit and the importance he places on Jewish stories. Why are Jewish stories so important? In terms of court cases, they are significant because they tell the embodied experiences of Jews seeking justice. Although "formally" White Jewish Americans may be economically middle- to upper-class, that perceived Whiteness immediately changes when their synagogue is defaced. They are not "substantively" White since they are not socially perceived as White once their Jewishness is known.[38] These narratives provide meaning to the case. In considering their lived and embodied experiences, their social location becomes easier to comprehend.

What this book has done is expand the legal discussion of race to include Jewish Americans and to emphasize the role of race in Jewish American legal history. It has focused on *Shaare Tefila Congregation v. Cobb* and its significance to the Jewish American narrative. It illustrates how Jewishness is defined according to the external categories of "religion" and "race," given the embodied experiences of its members, both individually and collectively. This case has led to other ones, in which Jewish Americans claim racialization for different reasons related to their Jewishness, and it has highlighted important components of those cases too. While not a landmark case, *Shaare Tefila Congregation v. Cobb* marks a significant moment in Jewish American history.

NOTES

1. For local news, see Crystal Hill, "Indiana Man Sentenced to Federal Prison for Vandalism at Carmel Synagogue," *IndyStar*, May 21, 2019, accessed April 18, 2021, www.indystar.com/story/news/crime/2019/05/21/carmel-synagogue-vandalism-indiana-man-nolan-brewer-sentenced-federal-prison/3758040002/. For national news, see Ewan Palmer, "Indiana Man Who 'Openly Identified With Nazism' Traveled 50 Miles to Set Fire to Synagogue with Homemade Napalm," *Newsweek*, May 22, 2019, accessed April 18, 2021, www.newsweek.com/indianapolis-nazi-vandalized-synagogue-swastikas-shaarey-tefilla-1432648. For international news, see Marcy Oster, "Indiana Man Gets 3-Year Prison Sentence for Nazi Graffiti on Synagogue," *Times of Israel*, May 23, 2019, accessed April 18, 2021, www.timesofisrael.com/indiana-man-gets-3-year-prison-sentence-for-nazi-graffiti-on-synagogue/.

2. Video of the event in response to the vandalism of Shaarey Tefila included in: Carol Kuruvilla, "Indiana Synagogue Vandalized with Nazi Symbols Receives Outpouring of Support," *Huffington Post*, July 30, 2018. www.huffpost.com/entry/indiana-synagogue-vandalized-with-nazi-symbols-receives-outpouring-of-support_n_5b5f8282e4b0b15aba9bf1f6.

3. Kellie Hwang, "Here's How Indiana's Proposed Hate Crime Bills Would Compare to Other States,'" *IndyStar*, January 10, 2019. www.indystar.com/story/

news/2019/01/10/how-gender-identity-protection-hate-crime-laws-looks-throughout
-u-s/2515931002/ Hwang notes that Senate Bill 12 would have allowed "judges to
consider a stricter sentence if a person or group was harmed based on their race, religion, and/or gender identity." But including "gender identity," according to Speaker
of the House Brian Bosma, would prevent any such bill from passing in the State. In
January 2019, Indiana Representative Greg Steuerwald filed House Bill 1093, which
passed July 1, 2019. It does not list any specific protected groups, rather it's at the
judge's discretion to apply harsher sentencing, due to a person or group's "real or
perceived characteristic, trait, belief, practice, or association, or other attribute the
court chooses to consider." Significantly, the application of the law depends on the
judge's *discretion*. The hate crimes statute in Utah, which like Indiana's proposed bill
is not specific, only criminalizes an act with "intent to intimidate or terrorize another
person," and has not been enforced in the twenty years that the law has been in effect.
Even though the law exists, it does not mean that judges use it.

4. Rick Callahan, "Indiana Governor Signs Hate Crimes Measure into Law," AP
News, April 3, 2019, accessed April 18, 2021, apnews.com/article/939de847d4cf4d4
086048b0c74170496.

5. WTHR.com staff, "20-Year-Old and Co-Conspirator Charged in Carmel Synagogue Vandalism," 13 WTHR, accessed April 18, 2021, www.wthr.com/article/news
/local/20-year-old-and-co-conspirator-charged-carmel-synagogue-vandalism/531
-a96f5165-5213-4b12-91a9-43aa9764e6cf.

6. K(i)yomi Brewer's name was spelled differently in various newspaper articles.

7. "Synagogue Attacker Gets Three Years in Federal Prison," United States Attorney's Office, Southern District of Indiana, United States Department of Justice, May
22, 2019. accessed April 18, 2021, www.justice.gov/usao-sdin/pr/synagogue-attacker
-gets-three-years-federal-prison.

8. "Synagogue Attacker Gets Three Years in Federal Prison," United States Attorney's Office, Southern District of Indiana, United States Department of Justice, May
22, 2019, accessed April 20, 2021.www.justice.gov/usao-sdin/pr/synagogue-attacker
-gets-three-years-federal-prison. Emphasis added.

9. Claudia Koerner, "An Indiana Man Who Vandalized a Synagogue With Nazi
Symbols Admitted How Far-Right Figures Radicalized Him," *Buzzfeed News*, May
26, 2019, www.buzzfeednews.com/article/claudiakoerner/indiana-man-vandalized
-synagogue-nazi-symbols-radicalized.

10. Courtney Crown, "Cloverdale Man Sentenced to Three Years in Prison for Hate
Crime Against Carmel Synagogue," Fox59, Updated 10:52, May 21, 2019, fox59.
com/2019/05/21/cloverdale-man-sentenced-to-3-years-in-prison-for-hate-crime-
against-carmel-synagogue/.

11. "Synagogue Attacker Gets Three Years in Federal Prison," United States Attorney's Office, Southern District of Indiana, United States Department of Justice, May
22, 2019, accessed April 18, 2021, www.justice.gov/usao-sdin/pr/synagogue-attacker
-gets-three-years-federal-prison.

12. "Synagogue Attacker Gets Three Years in Federal Prison: Morgan County
Man Convicted on Federal Hate Crime Charges," May 22, 2019, The United States

Attorney's Office Southern District of Indiana, www.justice.gov/usao-sdin/pr/
synagogue-attacker-gets-three-years-federal-prison.

13. Reporters spell her name in different ways.

14. Crystal Hill, "Indiana Man Sentenced to Federal Prison for Vandalism at Carmel Synagogue," *Indianapolis Star*, Updated 6:13 pm, May 22, 2019, www.indystar
.com/story/news/crime/2019/05/21/carmel-synagogue-vandalism-indiana-man-nolan
-brewer-sentenced-federal-prison/3758040002/.

15. Marshall Levin, interview by author, New York, NY, June 10, 2008.

16. Video of the event in response to the vandalism of Shaarey Tefila included
in: Carol Kuruvilla, "Indiana Synagogue Vandalized with Nazi Symbols Receives
Outpouring of Support," *Huffington Post*, July 30, 2018. www.huffpost.com/entry/
indiana-synagogue-vandalized-with-nazi-symbols-receives-outpouring-of-support_n
_5b5f8282e4b0b15aba9bf1f6.

17. Kevin Lipson, phone interview by author, May 20, 2009.

18. "Jewish" is in parentheses here because Joshua Bonadona identifies himself as
a Christian.

19. Henry Goldschmidt, *Race and Religion among the Chosen Peoples of Crown
Heights* (New Brunswick, NJ: Rutgers University Press, 2006), 26.

20. Singer v. Denver School District, 959 F. Supp. 1325 (D. Colo. 1997). law.justia.
com/cases/federal/district-courts/FSupp/959/1325/2367644/.

21. Singer v. Denver School District, 959 F. Supp. 1325 (D. Colo. 1997). law.justia.
com/cases/federal/district-courts/FSupp/959/1325/2367644/.

22. William Kaplowitz, "We Need Inquire Further: Normative Stereotypes, Hasidic
Jews, and the Civil Rights Act of 1866," *Mich. J. Race and L.* 357, no. 12 (2007):
541, 560–64.

23. John Tehranian, "Performing Whiteness: Naturalization Litigation and the
Construction of Racial Identity in America" in *Yale Law Journal* 109, no. 4 (Jan.
2000): 817–48.

24. Bonadona v. Louisiana College, No. 18-cv-0224, (W.D. La. July 13, 2018).

25. Judge Dee D. Drell.

26. Amended complaint at 2, Bonadona v. Louisiana College, No. 18-cv-0224,
(W.D. La. July 13, 2018) (emphasis added).

27. Bonadona v. Louisiana College, No. 18-cv-0224, slip op. at 4 (W.D. La. July
13, 2018).

28. Bonadona v. Louisiana College, No. 18-cv-0224, slip op. at 10 (W.D. La. July
13, 2018).

29. Bonadona v. Louisiana College, No. 18-cv-0224, slip op. at 5 (W.D. La. July
13, 2018) (emphasis added).

30. Bonadona v. Louisiana College, No. 18-cv-0224, slip op. at 14 (W.D. La. July
13, 2018). See also Christina Dumitrescu and Richard Scharlat, "Tackling 'Race' Discrimination: A Jewish Baptist Seeks Protection Under Title VII," *JDSupra*, accessed
June 9, 2022, www.jdsupra.com/legalnews/tackling-race-discrimination-a-jewish
-13557/.

31. T.E. v. Pine Bush Central School District, 58 F.Supp. 3d 332 (S.D. New
York 2014).

32. See, for instance, Doe v. University of Michigan 721 F. Supp. 852 (E.D. Mich. 1989).

33. Emma Green, "Why the Charlottesville Marchers Were Obsessed with Jews," *The Atlantic*, August 15, 2017.

34. See Nicole Chavez, Emanuella Grinberg, and Elliott C. McLaughlin, "Pittsburgh Synagogue Gunman Said He Wanted All Jews to Die, Criminal Complaint Says, CNN, October 18, 2018. www.cnn.com/2018/10/28/us/pittsburgh-synagogue-shooting/index.html.

35. Names are not included so as not to give the shooters fame.

36. Dara Lind, "The Conspiracy Theory that Led to the Pittsburgh Synagogue Shooting Explained," Vox, October 29, 2018. www.vox.com/2018/10/29/18037580/pittsburgh-shooter-anti-semitism-racist-jewish-caravan.

37. Kelly Frazier, "Holocaust Survivor Dodges Tree of Life Synagogue Shooting by 4 Minutes," World Religion News, October 31, 2018, www.worldreligionnews.com/religion-news/holocaust-survivor-dodges-tree-life-synagogue-shooting-4-minutes.

38. Khaled Beydoun, "Faith in Whiteness: Free Exercise of Religion as Racial Expression" in *Iowa Law Review* 105, no. 4 (May 2020): 1487.

Bibliography

Aberth, John. 2010. *From the Brink of the Apocalypse: Confronting Famine, War, Plague, and Death in the Later Middle Ages*. London: Routledge.

Abrams, Robert. 1982. "President, Har Tzeon-Agudath Achim," November 2, 1982. Private Collection of Shaare Tefila Congregation.

"'An Act Declaring That Baptisme of Slaves Doth Not Exempt Them from Bondage' (1667)." 2020. In *Encyclopedia Virginia*. encyclopediavirginia.org/entries/an-act-declaring-that-baptisme-of-slaves-doth-not-exempt-them-from-bondage-1667/.

Alcoff, Linda Martín. 2006. *Visible Identities: Race, Gender, and the Self*. New York: Oxford University Press.

Alexander, Michelle. 2010. *The New Jim Crow: Mass Incarceration in the Age of Colorblindness*. New York: The New Press.

Al-Khazraji v. St. Francis College 784 F.2d 505. 1986. Third Circuit Court of Appeals.

Allen, Emilie. n.d. "Obituary for Majid Al-Khazraji Allen, 1933–2016." Koch Funeral Home. Accessed February 25, 2021. kochfuneralhome.com/tribute/details /1352/Majid-Allan/obituary.html.

Altman, Shirley. 2009. Phone interview.

Alvarado, Marcie. 1991. "The Trail of Michael D. Remer: Ocean City Robbery Suspect Linked to Several Other Crimes." *Maryland County Dispatch*, August 30, 1991.

American Jewish Committee. "1986 Board of Governer Minutes." 1986.

"Anti-Jewish Discrimination in American Hotels Declines Sharply." n.d. *Jewish Telegraphic Agency* (blog). Accessed June 21, 2022. www.jta.org/archive/anti -jewish-discrimination-in-american-hotels-declines-sharply.

Antler, Joyce. 2018. *Jewish Radical Feminism: Voices from the Women's Liberation Movement*. New York: New York University Press.

"Antonin Scalia." n.d. Oyez. Accessed June 22, 2022. www.oyez.org/justices/antonin _scalia.

"Antonin Scalia, Biography." n.d. Biography.Com. Accessed February 26, 2021. www .biography.com/law-figure/antonin-scalia.

"Application for a 1983 Solomon Schecter Award: United Synagogue of America, Presented by Shaare Tefila Congregation: 11120 Lockwood Drive, Silver Spring, Maryland 20901, Category: Unique Programs, 5." n.d.

Arabia, Steve. 1984. "Congregants Sue Over Defaced Synagogue." *Montgomery County Sentinel*, March 9, 1984.

Arp, Julie D. 1995. "The Batson Analysis and Religious Discrimination." *Oregon Law Review* 74: 721–39.

"Aryan Brotherhood." n.d. Southern Poverty Law Center. Accessed June 16, 2022. www.splcenter.org/fighting-hate/extremist-files/group/aryan-brotherhood.

Asad, Talal. 1993. *Genealogies of Religion: Discipline and Reasons of Power in Christianity and Islam*. Johns Hopkins University Press.

"The Association of Religion Data Archives | Maps & Reports." 1980. Report 1980. www.thearda.com/rcms2010/rcms2010a.asp?U=24031&T=county&S=Name&Y=1980.

———. 1990. Report 1990. www.thearda.com/rcms2010/rcms2010a.asp?U=24031&T=county&S=Name&Y=1990.

Avanzato, Joseph. 1987. "Section 1982 and Discrimination Against Jews: Shaare Tefila Congregation v. Cobb." *American University Law Review* 37 (1): 225–58.

The Bar Association of Montgomery County, MD Newsletter. 2016. "The Honorable Rosalyn B. Bell, Date of Death: August 17, 2016," The Bar Association of Montgomery County," October 16, 2016, sec. vol. 64, no. 4.

Batnitzky, Leora. 2011. *How Judaism Became a Religion: An Introduction to Modern Jewish Thought*. Princeton, NJ: Princeton University Press.

Bauer, Laura, Dave Helling, and Brian Burnes. 2014. "Man with History of Anti-Semitism Jailed in Fatal Shooting of Three at Johnson County Jewish Centers." *The Kansas City Star*, April 13, 2014. www.kansascity.com/news/local/article344979/Man-with-history-of-anti-Semitism-jailed-in-fatal-shooting-of-three-at-Johnson-County-Jewish-centers.html.

Baum, Bruce. 2006. *The Rise and Fall of the Caucasian Race: A Political History of Racial Identity*. New York: New York University Press.

Beckerman, Gal. 2010. "How a Quest to Save Soviet Jews Changed the World." *All Things Considered, National Public Radio*. www.npr.org/templates/story/story.php?storyId=130936993.

Benedictow, Ole Jorgen. 2018. *The Black Death, 1336–1353: The Complete History*. Woodbridge, UK: Boydell Press.

Berkowitz, Francine. 2017. By Mara Cherkasky and Sarah Shoenfeld. Petworth Public Library.

Berman, Lila Corwin. 2020. *The American Jewish Philanthropic Complex: The History of a Multibillion-Dollar Institution*. Princeton, NJ: Princeton University Press.

Bernier, Francois. 2000. "A New Division of Earth." In *The Idea of Race*, edited by Robert Bernasconi and Tommy L. Lott. Indianapolis, IN: Hackett Publishing Company.

Bernstein, David. 1990. "The Supreme Court and Civil Rights, 1886–1908." *The Yale Law Journal*, 725–44. doi.org/10.2307/796668.

Beydoun, Khaled. 2013. "Between Muslim and White: The Legal Construction of Arab American Identity." *New York University Annual Summary of American Law* 69 (1).

———. 2020. "Faith in Whiteness: Free Exercise of Religion as Racial Expression." *Iowa Law Review* 105 (4): 1475–1536.

Biale, David. 1986. *Power and Powerlessness in Jewish History*. New York: Schocken.

———. 2007. *Blood and Belief: The Circulation of a Symbol Between Jews and Christians*. Berkeley, CA: University of California Press.

Biale, David, Michael Galchinsky, and Susannah Heschel, eds. 1998. *Insider/ Outsider: American Jews and Multiculturalism*. Berkeley, CA: University of California Press.

"Bias." n.d. Law.Com Legal Dictionary. Accessed June 16, 2022. dictionary.law.com /Default.aspx?selected=61.

Blair, Leonardo. 2019. "Alleged Synagogue Shooter John Ernest Was a Regular Churchgoer Who Blamed Jews for Killing Jesus." *The Christian Post*, May 2, 2019. www.christianpost.com.

Blumenbach, Johann Friedrich. 2000. "On the Natural Variety of Mankind." In *The Idea of Race*. Indianapolis, IN: Hackett.

Bonadona v. Louisiana College. 2019. U.S. District Court Western District of Louisiana Alexandria Division.

Bonadona v. Lousiana College. 2018. U.S. District Court of Western District of Louisiana Alexandria Division.

Bowman Esq., Forest J. 2007. "The History of the United States District Court for the Southern District of West Virginia." West Virginia Law Review. www.wvsd .uscourts.gov/pdfs/historysdwv.pdf.

Boyarin, Daniel. 2004. *Border Lines: The Partition of Judaeo-Christianity*. Philadelphia: University of Pennsylvania Press.

Boyarin, Jonathan. 1997. *Thinking in Jewish*. Chicago: University of Chicago Press.

Boyarin, Jonathan, and Daniel Boyarin. 2008. *Jews and Other Differences: The New Jewish Cultural Studies*. Minneapolis, MN: University of Minnesota Press.

Brannan, Patricia. 2008. Washington D.C.

———. 2018. Phone interview.

———. 2021a. Phone interview.

———. 2021b. Email received.

Brannan, Patricia A. 1988. "To Rabbi Martin Halpern," April 11, 1988.

Brodkin, Karen. 2004. *How Jews Became White Folks and What That Says About Race in America*. New Brunswick, NJ: Rutgers University Press.

Budinsky v. Corning Glass Works 425 F.Supp. 786. 1977. U.S. District Court, Western District Court of Pennsylvania.

Callahan, Rick. 2019. "Indiana Governor Signs Hate Crimes Measure into Law." *AP News*, April 3, 2019. www.apnews.com.

"Cantwell v. Connecticut." n.d. Oyez. Accessed August 18, 2021. www.oyez.org/ cases/1940-1955/310us296.

Cantwell v. Connecticut 310 U.S. 296. 1940. U.S. Supreme Court.

Caplan, Marvin. 1988. "Shepherd Park." In *Washington at Home: An Illustrated History Neighborhoods in the Nation's Capital*, edited by Kathryn Smith. Northridge, CA: Windsor Press. www.culturaltourismdc.org/portal/web/portal%20 /neighbors-incorporated-site-african-american-heritage-trail.

Carbado, Devon W., and Mitu Gulati. 2013. *Acting White: Rethinking Race in "Post-Racial America."* New York: Oxford University Press.

Carter Jr., William M. 2007. "Race, Rights, and The Thirteenth Amendment: Defining the Badges and Incidents of Slavery." *U.C. Davis Law Review* 40 (April).

Cervantes, Erika. 2019. "Suspect Said Synagogue Shooting Was to 'Defend Country,' Unsealed Search Warrant Says." *NBC San Diego*, June 16, 2019. www.nbcsandiego.com.

Chappell, David L. 2007. "Did Racists Create the Suburban Nation?" *Reviews in American History* 35 (1): 89–97. doi.org/10.1353/rah.2007.0004.

Chasnoff, Joel. 1982. "Montgomery-Howard Counties District 1A, Judiciary Committee, House of Delegates," November 3, 1982. Private Collection of Shaare Tefila Congregation.

"Circuit Split." n.d. LII / Legal Information Institute. Accessed June 5, 2022. www.law.cornell.edu/wex/circuit_split.

City New Service. 2019. "Suspected Poway Synagogue Shooter Charged with Murder, Hate Crimes." *Fox 5 San Diego*, October 3, 2019. www.fox5sandiego.com.

"Civil Rights Act of 1871, Exhibits, History of the Federal Judiciary." n.d. Federal Judicial Center. Accessed March 29, 2021. www.fjc.gov/history/timeline/civil-rights-act-1871.

Cohen, Jeremy. 1982. *The Friars and the Jews: The Evolution of Medieval Anti-Judaism*. Ithaca, NY: Cornell University Press.

Cohen, Naomi Wiener. 1988. "Shaare Tefila Congregation v. Cobb: A New Departure in American Jewish Defense?" *Jewish History* 3 (1). doi.org/10.1007/BF01667350.

———. 1992. *Jews in Christian America: The Pursuit of Religious Equality*. New York: Oxford University Press.

Conan, Neil. 2013. "A Look Inside White Supremacist Prison Gangs." *NPR*, April 9, 2013, sec. National. www.npr.org/2013/04/09/176681634/a-look-inside-white-supremacist-prison-gangs.

"COUNTRY CLUBS ADOPT INTEGRATION POLICIES." n.d. Greensboro News and Record. Accessed June 21, 2022. greensboro.com/country-clubs-adopt-integration-policies/article_f8b227bd-fa59–5c02-b177-50a83f1bed70.html.

Cover, Robert. 1993. "Nomos and Narrative." In *Narrative, Violence, and the Law: The Essays of Robert Cover*, edited by Martha Minow, Michael Ryan, and Austin Sarat. Ann Arbor, MI: University of Michigan Press.

Cowan, Jill. 2019. "What to Know About the Poway Synagogue Shooting." *The New York Times*, April 29, 2019. www.nytimes.com.

Crown, Courtney. 2019. "Cloverdale Man Sentenced to Three Years in Prison for Hate Crime Against Carmel Synagogue." *Fox59*, May 21, 2019. www.fox59.com.

Cunningham, David. 2014. *Klansville, U.S.A.: The Rise and Fall of the Civil Rights Era Ku Klux Klan*. New York: Oxford University Press.

Dale, Maryclaire. 1999. "Longtime Judge Kenneth K. Hall Dies at 81." *Charleston Gazette*, July 9, 1999, sec. A.

Darian-Smith, Eve. 2010. *Religion, Race, and Rights: Landmarks in the History of Modern Anglo-American Law*. Oxford, UK: Hart Publishing.

Darwin, Charles. 2000. "The Descent of Man." In *The Idea of Race*, edited by Robert Bernasconi and Tommy L. Lott. Indianapolis, IN: Hackett.

Dawidowicz, Lucy S. 1982. "A Century of Jewish History, 1881–1981: The View from America." *American Jewish Yearbook*, Special Articles, 82.

Dean, Alan P. 1984. "HRC to Be Recipient in Synagogue Lawsuit." Montgomery County Government.

Demaske, Chris. 2009. "Village of Skokie v. Nationalist Socialist Party of America (Ill) (1978)." In *The First Amendment Encyclopedia*. www.mtsu.edu/first-amendment.

DeMetrick, Alex. n.d. "Notoriously Dangerous Md. House Of Correction In Jessup Being Demolished—CBS Baltimore." Accessed June 16, 2022. baltimore.cbslocal .com/2014/01/17/md-house-of-correction-in-jessup-being-destroyed/.

"Demise of the Jewish Club." 2009. *Golfweek* (blog). June 22, 2009. golfweek.usato day.com/2009/06/22/demise-jewish-club/.

Des Rosiers, Natalie, and Steven Bittle. 2004. "Introduction." In *What Is a Crime? Defining Criminal Conduct in Contemporary Society*, edited by Law Commission of Canada. Vancouver, British Columbia: University of British Columbia Press.

"'Desecration in Darkness: A Community Fights Back, A Historic Documentary Film' Press Release." 1985.

Di Lisi, Richard A. 1989. "Justice White Mixes More than Just Color to Create a New Shade of Racial Protection." *Case Western Reserve Law Review* 39: 1343–70.

Diner, Hasia R. 2006. *The Jews of the United States, 1654 to 2000*. University of California Press.

Doe v. University of Michigan 721 F. Supp. 852. 1989. U.S. District Court for the Eastern District of Michigan.

Dollinger, Marc. 2018. *Black Power, Jewish Politics: Reinventing the Alliance in the 1960s*. Waltham, MA: Brandeis University Press.

DuBois, William Edward Burghardt. 1994. *The Souls of Black Folk*. New York: Dover Publications.

Dubuisson, Daniel. 2003. *The Western Construction of Christianity: Myths, Knowledge, and Ideology*. Translated by William Sayers. Baltimore, MD: Johns Hopkins University Press.

Dumitrescu, Christina, and Richard Scharlat. n.d. "Tackling 'Race' Discrimination: A Jewish Baptist Seeks Protection Under Title VII." *JD Supra*. Accessed June 16, 2022. www.jdsupra.com/legalnews/tackling-race-discrimination-a-jewish-13557/.

Editors, History com. n.d. "The Settlement of Maryland." History. Accessed June 16, 2022. www.history.com/this-day-in-history/the-settlement-of-maryland.

Eisen, Arnold M. 1983. *The Chosen People in America: A Study in Jewish Religious Ideology*. Bloomington: Indiana University Press.

Eisenstadt, Merry Madway. 2001a. "Golden Anniversary Shaare Tefila Celebrates 50 Years of Touching Lives." *Washington Jewish Week*, February 1, 2001.

———. 2001b. "Shaare Tefila Source of Hate Crime Precedent." *Washington Jewish Week*, February 1, 2001, sec. Local.

Entine, Jon. 2007. *Abraham's Children: Race, Identity, and the DNA of the Chosen People*. New York: Grand Central Publishing.

"Everson v. Board of Education of the Township of Ewing." n.d. Oyez. Accessed August 18, 2021. www.oyez.org/cases/1940-1955/330us1.

Everson v. Board of Education of the Township of Ewing 330 U.S. 1. 1947. U.S. Supreme Court.

Ewick, Patricia, and Susan S. Silbey. 1998. *The Common Place of Law: Stories from Everyday Life*. University of Chicago Press.

Faigman, David L. 2007. "Factfinding in Constitutional Cases." In *How Law Knows*, edited by Austin Sarat, Lawrence Douglas, and Martha Merrill Umphrey. The Amherst Series in Law, Jurisprudence, and Social Thought. Stanford, CA: Stanford University Press.

Fattal, Isabel. 2018. "A Brief History of Anti-Semitic Violence in America." *The Atlantic*, October 28, 2018. www.theatlantic.com/politics/archive/2018/10/brief -history-anti-semitic-violence-america/574228/.

Feagin, Joe R. 2010. *The White Racial Frame: Centuries of Racial Framing and Counter-Framing*. New York: Routledge.

Federal Bureau of Investigations. n.d. "Hate Crime Definition." FBI.Gov. Accessed August 18, 2010. www.fbi.gov/ucr/cius_04/offenses_reported/hate_crime/index .html.

Fetzer, Philip L. 1993. "'Reverse Discrimination': The Political Use of Language." *UCLA National Black Law Journal* 12 (3).

Fichte, Johann Gottlieb. 1995. "A State Within a State (1793)." In *The Jew in the Modern World: A Documentary History Second Edition*, edited by Paul R. Mendes-Flohr and Yehuda Reinharz, Second, 309. New York: Oxford University Press.

Fishbein, Leslie. 2018. "Marc Dollinger: Black Power, Jewish Politics: Reinventing the Alliance in the 1960s." *Contemporary Jewry* 38 (3). doi.org/10.1007/ s12397-018-9275-4.

"Former Shaare Tefila Congregation Website." n.d. Accessed April 22, 2010. www .shaaretefila.org/page/history.

Foucault, Michel. 1995. *Discipline and Punish: The Birth of a Prison*. Translated by Alan Sheridan. Trans. Alan Sheridan. New York: Vintage Books.

Frazier, Kelly. 2018. "Holocaust Survivor Dodges Tree of Life Synagogue Shooting by 4 Minutes." World Religion News. October 31, 2018. www.worldreligionnews .com/religion-news/holocaust-survivor-dodges-tree-life-synagogue-shooting-4 -minutes.

"Free Exercise Clause." n.d. LII / Legal Information Institute. Accessed June 6, 2021. www.law.cornell.edu/wex/free_exercise_clause.

Funkenstein, Amos. 1993. *Perceptions of Jewish History*. Berkeley, CA: University of California Press.

Galvan, Ana. 2020. "How Prison Turned My Childhood Friend Into a Neo-Nazi." *The Marshall Project*, August 7, 2020. www.themarshallproject.org/2020/08/06/how -prison-turned-my-childhood-friend-into-a-neo-nazi.

Garren, Deborah. 2009. Phone interview.

General Building Contractors v. Pennsylvania United Engineers 458 U.S. 375. 1982. U.S. Supreme Court.

Gerstenfeld, Phyllis B. 2004. *Hate Crimes: Causes, Controls, and Controversies.* Thousand Oaks, CA: Sage Publications.

Gillespie, Nick. 2021. "Would the ACLU Still Defend the Nazis' Right to March in Skokie?" *Reason: Free Minds and Free Markets*, January 2021. reason.com/2020/12/20/would-the-aclu-still-defend-nazis-right-to-march-in-skokie/.

Glauz-Todrank, Annalise E. 2014a. "Judging and Protecting Jewish Identity in Shaare Tefila Congregation v. Cobb." In *Who Is a Jew?: Reflections on History, Religion, and Culture*, edited by Leonard J. Greenspoon. West Lafayette, IN: Purdue University Press.

———. 2014b. "'Race Thinking' and Rights Making." *Critical Research on Religion* 2 (2): 191–94.

———. 2020. "Jewish Critical Race Theory and Jewish 'Religionization' in Shaare Tefila Congregationv. Cobb." In *Judaism, Race, and Ethics: Conversations and Questions*, edited by Jonathan K. Crane, 304. Dimyonot. University Park, PA: Pennsylvania State University Press.

Glenn, Evelyn Nakano. 2009. *Shades of Difference: Why Skin Color Matters.* Stanford, CA: Stanford University Press.

Gold, Ali, and Michael Watkins. 2019. "Suspect in Jersey City Linked to Black Hebrew Israelite Group." *New York Times*, December 11, 2019. www.nytimes.com/2019/12/11/nyregion/jersey-city-shooting.html.

Goldberg, David Theo. 2000. "Racial Knowledge." In *Theories of Race and Racism: A Reader*, edited by Les Back and John Solomos. London: Routledge.

Goldberg, Jeremy. n.d. "Shaare Tefila Congregation, Through The Lens, Photographic Histories." Jeremy Goldberg's Washington. Accessed December 20, 2020. www.jhsgw.org/exhibitions/online/goldberg/photographs/shaare-tefila.

Goldsamt, Milton. 2008. Silver Spring, MD.

Goldsamt, Susan. 2008. Silver Spring, MD.

Goldschmidt, Henry. 2006. *Race and Religion among the Chosen Peoples of Crown Heights.* New Brunswick, NJ: Rutgers University Press.

Goldstein, Eric L. 2006. *The Price of Whiteness: Jews, Race, and American Identity.* Princeton, NJ: Princeton University Press.

Goluboff, Risa L. 2001. "The Thirteenth Amendment and the Lost Origins of Civil Rights." *Duke Law Journal* 50: 1609–85. doi.org/10.2307/1373044.

Gordon, Sarah Barringer. 2010. "Malnak v. Yogi: The New Age and The New Law." In *Law and Religion: Cases in Context*, edited by Leslie C. Griffin. Austin, TX: Aspen Publishers.

Gotanda, Neil. 1995. "A Critique of 'Our Constitution Is Color-Blind.'" In *Critical Race Theory: The Key Writings That Formed the Movement*, edited by Kimberle Crenshaw, Neil Gotanda, Gary Peller, and Kendall Thomas, 258–253. New York City, NY: New Press.

Gray-Hildenbrand, Jenna. 2023. "Saving Religion from Ballardhoo: Metaphysical Religion, the Government, and the Creation of Religious Criminals." *Nova Religio* 27 (1).

Green, Emma. 2017. "Why the Charlottesville Marchers Were Obsessed with Jews." *The Atlantic*, August 15, 2017.

Green, Judy. 1982. "High School Kids Kick the Klan." *Montgomery County Sentinel*, November 11, 1982.

Griffin v. Breckenridge 403 U.S. 88. 1971. U.S. Supreme Court.

Gross, Ariela J. 2008. *What Blood Won't Tell: A History of Race on Trial in America*. Cambridge, MA: Harvard University Press.

Gualtieri, Sarah. 2001. "Becoming White: Race, Religion, and the Foundations of Syrian/Lebanese Ethnicity in the United States." *Journal of American Ethnic History* 20: 29–58.

"Guard Killed During Shooting at Holocaust Museum." 2009. News. CNN. June 10, 2009. www.cnn.com/2009/CRIME/06/10/museum.shooting/.

Guillermoprieto, Alma. 1982. "23-Year-Old Charged in Desecration of Synagogue in Montgomery County." *The Washington Post*, November 16, 1982.

Halpern, Martin S. 1986. "To Judge David L. Cahoon, Montgomery County Circuit Court, Judicial Center, Rockville, Maryland," April 15, 1986.

———. Unknown. "The Desecration of a Synagogue." Unnamed.

Harkaway, Bill. 2009a. Email received.

———. 2009b. "With author," June 10, 2009.

———. 2009c. Bethesda, MD.

Harris, Cheryl I. 1995. "Whiteness as Property." In *Critical Race Theory: The Key Writings That Formed the Movement*, edited by Kimberle Crenshaw, Neil Gotanda, Gary Peller, and Kendall Thomas. New York: The New Press.

Hattam, Victoria. 2007. *In the Shadow of Race: Jews, Latinos, and Immigrant Politics in the United States*. Chicago, IL: University of Chicago Press.

Heng, Geraldine. 2018. *The Invention of Race in the European Middle Ages*. New York: Cambridge University Press.

Herberg, Will. 1960. *Protestant, Catholic, Jew: An Essay in American Religious Sociology*. New York: Anchor Books.

Herbold, Hilary. 1994. "Never a Level Playing Field: Blacks and the GI Bill." *The Journal of Blacks in Higher Education*, no. 6: 104–8. doi.org/10.2307/2962479.

Hill, Crystal. 2019. "Indiana Man Sentenced to Federal Prison for Vandalism at Carmel Synagogue." *IndyStar*, May 21, 2019. www.indystar.com.

Himmelstein, Drew. 2015. "One in Six American Jews Are Converts and Nine Other Findings in Pew Study." *The Jewish News of Northern California*, March 15, 2015. jweekly.com.

"Historical Census." n.d. Planning. Accessed June 20, 2022. planning.maryland.gov/MSDC/Pages/default.aspx.

"History." n.d. Shaare Tefila. Accessed April 22, 2010. www.shaaretefila.org/page/history.

"History of Federal Voting Rights Laws." 2017. The United States Department of Justice. July 28, 2017. www.justice.gov/crt/history-federal-voting-rights-laws.

Hoffman, Jordan. 2020. "Film Explores Why a Jewish Former ACLU Head Defended Nazis' Right to Free Speech." *Times of Israel*, October 2, 2020. www.timesofisrael.com/film-explores-why-a-jewish-former-aclu-head-defended-nazis-right-to-free-speech/.

Hoffman, Sharona. 2004. "Is There a Place for 'Race' as a Legal Concept?" *Arizona State Law Journal* 26: 1093–1159.

Hollman, Steven P. 1988. "To Rabbi Martin D. Halpern," December 23, 1988. Private Collection of Shaare Tefila Congregation.

Holmes, Michael. 2009. Phone interview.

Hurd v. Hodge 334 U.S. 24. 1948. U.S. Supreme Court.

Hurley, Bevan. 2022. "Alaskan Neo-Nazi Prison Gang Members Guilty of Brutal Murder." *The Independent*, May 3, 2022, sec. News. www.independent.co.uk/news /world/americas/crime/alaska-neo-nazi-prison-gang-murder-b2070941.html.

Hwang, Kellie. 2019. "Here's How Indiana's Proposed Hate Crime Bills Would Compare to Other States.'" *IndyStar*, January 10, 2019. www.indystar.com.

Hyer, Marjorie. 1982a. "Jewish Leader Seeks Action on Vandalism." *Washington Post*, November 4, 1982, Final edition, sec. B.

———. 1982b. "KKK, Desecration Strengthen Resolve to Combat Bigotry." *Washington Post*, November 6, 1982.

Idel, Moshe. 1995. *Hasidism: Between Ecstasy and Magic*. Albany, NY: State University of New York Press.

Jacobson, Matthew Frye. 1998. *Whiteness of a Different Color: European Immigrants and the Alchemy of Race*. Cambridge, MA: Harvard University Press.

Johnson, Andrew. 1867. "Veto of the First Reconstruction Act." America's Reconstruction: People and Politics After the Civil War. March 2, 1867. www .digitalhistory.uh.edu/exhibits/reconstruction/section4/section4_10veto.html.

Jones v. Alfred H. Mayer Co. 392 U.S. 409. 1968. U.S. Supreme Court.

Jossi, Frank. 1983. "Symposium Focuses County's Attention on Racial Violence." *Montgomery Count Sentinel*, October 28, 1983.

JTA. 2015. "Kansas City JCC Shooter Sentenced to Death." *The Jerusalem Post*, November 11, 2015. www.jpost.com/Diaspora/Kansas-City-JCC-shooter -sentenced-to-death-432637.

JTA, and Jenny Schwartz. 2018. "The Radical Jewish Feminists, and Why They Never Spoke of Their Jewish Identities." *HaAretz*, August 12, 2018. www.haaretz .com/life/the-radical-jewish-feminists-and-why-they-never-spoke-of-their-jewish -identities-1.6724970.

Kaczorowski, Robert J. 1989. "The Enforcement of the Civil Rights Act of 1866: A Legislative History in Light of Runyon v. McCrary." *The Yale Law Journal* 98: 565–95. doi.org/10.2307/796630.

KALB. 2020. "LC Settles Civil Suit Filed by Former Player, Coaching Candidate," January 28, 2020. www.kalb.com.

Kaplan, Janice L. 1982. "Halpern Sees Good from Evil in Reaction to Synagogue Vandalism." *Washington Jewish Week*, November 1982.

Kaplowitz, William. 2007. "We Need Inquire Further: Normative Stereotypes, Hasidic Jews, and the Civil Rights Act of 1866." *Michigan Journal of Race and Law* 357.

Karabel, Jerome. 2005. *The Chosen: The Hidden History of Admission and Exclusion at Harvard, Yale, and Princeton*. Boston: Houghton Mifflin.

Katzenbach v. McClung 379 U.S. 294. 1964. U.S. Supreme Court.

Katznelson, Ira. 2005. *When Affirmative Action Was White: An Untold History of Racial Inequality in Twentieth-Century America.* W. W. Norton & Company.

Kaufman, David. 1999. *Shul with a Pool: The "Synagogue-Center" in American Jewish History.* Lebanon, NH: Brandeis University Press.

Kelly, Jacques. 2000. "Balto. Jurist Murnaghan Dies at 80." *Baltimore Sun*, September 1, 2000. www.baltimoresun.com/news/bs-xpm-2000-09-01-0009010211-story .html.

Kelly, Jon. 2013. "Aryan Brotherhood of Texas: How Did Neo-Nazi Prison Gangs Become so Powerful?" *BBC News*, April 4, 2013, sec. Magazine. www.bbc.com/ news/magazine-22019433.

Kernan, Michael. 1982. "The Specter of Anti-Semitism, The Unending Web of Fear." *Washington Post*, December 1, 1982, Final edition, sec. Style.

Kessler, Gary. 2007. *Studying Religion: An Introduction Through Cases.* Third. New York: McGraw Hill.

Kimmel, Ross M. 1974. "'Chapter IV: Freedom or Bondage' in Blacks before the Law in Colonial Maryland." Unknown. Maryland State Archives.

Knott, Kim. 2015. *The Location of Religion: A Spatial Analysis.* London: Routledge. doi.org/10.4324/9781315652641.

Koerner, Claudia. 2019. "An Indiana Man Who Vandalized a Synagogue With Nazi Symbols Admitted How Far-Right Figures Radicalized Him." *Buzzfeed News Inc.*, May 26, 2019. www.buzzfeednews.com.

Korzenik, Emily. 1992. "Letter to the Editor." *New York Times*, November 5, 1992. www.nytimes.com/1992/11/05/opinion/l-remember-moses-married-a -midianite-563692.html.

Kramer, Sidney. 1982. "Anti-Semitic Acts at Shaare Tefila, B'nai Israel." Private Collection of Shaare Tefila Congregation.

Krysan, M., and S. Moberg. 2016. "Trends in Racial Attitudes." University of Illinois Institute of Public Affairs. August 26, 2016. igpa.uillinois.edu/programs/ racial-attitudes.

Kurland, Philip, and Gerhard Casper. 1988. *Landmark Briefs and Arguments of the Supreme Court of the United States: Constitutional Law, 1986 Term Supplement.* Frederick, Maryland: University Publications of America, Inc.

Kuruvilla, Carol. 2018. "Indiana Synagogue Vandalized with Nazi Symbols Receives Outpouring of Support." *Huffington Post*, July 30, 2018. www.huffpost.com/entry /indiana-synagogue-vandalized-with-nazi-symbols-receives-outpouring-of-support _n_5b5f8282e4b0b15aba9bf1f6.

Lacewell, Linda A., and Paul A. Shelowitz. 1987. "Beyond a Black and White Reading of Sections 1981 and 1982—Shifting the Focus from Racial Status to Racial Acts | Office of Justice Programs." *University of Miami Law Review*, no. 41: 823–54.

Landsberg, Brian K. 1992. "Race and the Rehnquist Court." *Tulane Law Review* 66: 1267–1340.

Layman, Jonah. 2008. Phone call.

———. 2009. Silver Spring, MD.

———. 2022. Email received.

Learmonth, Susan. 1982. "Neighbors, Inc.," November 9, 1982. Private Collection of Shaare Tefila Congregation.

"Legal Challenges to Racially Restrictive Covenants." n.d. Mapping Segregation in Washington D.C. Accessed January 5, 2021. mappingsegregationdc.org/index.htm l#mapping.

Levin, Gershon. 2009a. "To Author," August 26, 2009.

———. 2009b. Written responses to questions prepared by author.

Levin, Marshall. 1982. "Chief of Police Bernard Cooke," November 22, 1982. Private Collection of Shaare Tefila Congregation.

———. 1995. "Desecration in Darkness." In *The Price We Pay: The Case against Racist Speech, Hate Propaganda, and Pornography*, edited by Laura J. Lederer and Richard Delgado. New York: Hill & Wang.

———. 2008. New York City, NY.

Levitt, Laura. 2008. "Other Moderns, Other Jews: Revisiting Jewish Secularism in America." In *Secularisms*, edited by Janet R. Jakobsen and Ann Pellegrini. Durham, NC: Duke University Press.

Light, Caroline E. 2014. *That Pride of Race and Character: The Roots of Jewish Benevolence in The Jim Crow South*. New York: New York University Press.

Lincoln, Bruce. 1989. *Discourse and the Construction of Society: Comparative Studies of Myth, Ritual, and Classification*. New York: Oxford University Press.

Lind, Dara. 2018. "The Conspiracy Theory That Led to the Pittsburgh Synagogue Shooting, Explained." *Vox*, October 29, 2018. www.vox.com/2018/10/29/18037580 /pittsburgh-shooter-anti-semitism-racist-jewish-caravan.

Lipson, Kevin. 2009. Phone interview.

———. 2021. Phone interview.

Lopez, Ian Haney. 2006. *White by Law: The Legal Construction of Race*. Tenth Anniversary. New York: New York University Press.

Lopez v. Sears, Roebuck and Co. 493 F.Supp. 801. 1980. U.S. District Court for the District of Maryland.

Mahone v. Waddle 564 F.2d 1018. 1977. Third Circuit Court of Appeals.

"Major U.S. Immigration Laws, 1790-Present (March 2013) Fact Sheet." 2013. Migration Policy Institute. March 2013. www.migrationpolicy.org/research/ timeline-1790.

Maltz, Judy. 2015. "One, Two, Three, Four—We Opened Up the Iron Door." *HaAretz*, February 3, 2015. www.haaretz.com/st/c/prod/eng/25yrs_russ_img/.

Manzanares v. Safeway Stores, Inc. 593 F.2d 968. n.d. Tenth Circuit Court of Appeals.

"Mapping Segregation DC." n.d. Accessed June 16, 2022. mappingsegregationdc.or g/index.html#mapping.

"Maps, Restricted Housing and Racial Change, 1940–1970, Prologue DC." n.d. Mapping Segregation DC. Accessed January 5, 2021. www.mappingsegregationdc .org/#maps.

Marco DeFunis Jr. v. Odegaard 416 U.S. 312. 1974. U.S. Supreme Court.

Marcus, Kenneth L. 2006. "The Most Important Right We Think We Have but Don't—Freedom from Religious Discrimination in Education." *Nevada Law Journal* 7: 171–81.

Marlowe v. Fisher Body. 1973, F.2d 489 1057. 6th Cir.

Marlowe v. Fisher Body 489 F.2d 1057. n.d. 1973.

Martinez v. Hazelton Research Animals, Inc. 430 F.Supp. 186. 1977. U.S. District Court for the District of Maryland.

Martire, Gregory, and Ruth Clark. 1982. *Anti-Semitism in the United States: A Study of Prejudice in the 1980s*. New York: Praeger.

"Maryland Manual Online: A Guide to Maryland and Its Government." n.d. State and Government Document. Msa.Maryland.Gov/Msa/Mdmanual/36loc/Mo/Former/Html/Msa02719.Html.

Matsuda, Mari. 1996. *Where Is Your Body? And Other Essays about Race, Gender, and the Law*. Boston: Beacon Press.

Matsuda, Mari J. 1993. "Public Responses to Racist Speech: Considering the Victim's Story." In *Words That Wound: Critical Race Theory, Assaultive Speech, and the First Amendment*, edited by Mari J. Matsuda, Charles R. Lawrence III, Richard Delgado, and Kimberlé Williams Crenshaw. Boulder, CO: Westview Press.

Mazur, Eric Michael. 2004. *The Americanization of Religious Minorities: Confronting the Constitutional Order*. Johns Hopkins University Press.

McDonald v. Santa Fe Trail Transportation Co. 427 U.S. 273. 1976. U.S. Supreme Court.

McLaughlin, Nicole, Emanuella Chavez, and Eliott C Grinberg. 2018. "Pittsburgh Synagogue Gunman Said He Wanted All Jews to Die, Criminal Complaint Says." *CNN*, October 28, 2018. www.cnn.com/2018/10/28/us/pittsburgh-synagogue-shooting/index.html.

Meier, Ryan, and Jacqueline Canzoneri. 2019. "Judges of the Fourth Circuit—Hon. J. Harvie Wilkinson III." *Wake Forest Law Review*, January. wakeforestlawreview.com/2019/01/honorable-j-harvie-wilkinson-iii/.

Mertz, Elizabeth. 1996. "Consensus and Dissent in U.S. Legal Opinions: Narrative Structure and Social Voices." In *Disorderly Discourse*, edited by Charles Briggs. New York: Oxford University Press.

"Middle Passage." n.d. United Nations Education, Scientific, and Cultural Organization. Slavery and Remembrance: A Guide to Sites, Museums, and History. Accessed February 25, 2021. slaveryandremembrance.org/articles/article/?id=A0032.

Minow, Martha. 1990. *Making All The Difference: Inclusion, Exclusion, and American Law*. Ithaca, NY: Cornell University Press.

Miranda v. Arizona 384 U.S. 436. 1966. U.S. Supreme Court.

Montgomery County Sentinel. 1982a. "Vandalism," November 4, 1982.

———. 1982b. "Six Arrested in Defacing," November 25, 1982, sec. B.

———. 1982c. "Hate: Council Adopts Penalties for Racial Violence," December 2, 1982.

———. 1983a. "Man Convicted in Defacement," June 23, 1983.

———. 1983b. "Vandal Sentenced for Graffiti," August 19, 1983.

———. 1983c. "Vandals Sentenced for Graffiti," August 19, 1983.

———. 1984. "Hughes Stresses Program to Combat Racial Violence," February 3, 1984.

———. 1985. "Two Youths Charged with Vandalizing Gaithersburg Temple," April 18, 1985.

Mosse, George L. 1978. *Toward the Final Solution: A History of European Racism.* New York: Howard Fertig.

Muhammad, Khalil Gibran. 2019. *The Condemnation of Blackness: Race, Crime, and the Making of Modern Urban America.* Cambridge, MA: Harvard University Press.

Nadler, Allen. 1999. *The Faith of the Mithnagdim: Rabbinic Responses to Hasidic Rapture.* Baltimore, MD: Johns Hopkins University Press.

Nee, Dermot A. 1982. "Industrial and Commercial Land Developers and Consultants." Private Collection of the Shaare Tefila Congregation.

"Next Stop . . . Riggs Park." 2016. Wordpress. December 8, 2016. nextstopriggs. wordpress.com/2016/12/08/tbt-riggs-parks-jewish-community-roots/.

New York Times. 1964. "60% Drop in Anti-Jewish Bias Since 1957 Noted in Hotel Study," January 31, 1964, sec. Archives. www.nytimes.com/1964/01/31/archives /60-drop-in-antijewish-bias-since-1957-noted-in-hotel-study.html.

Nirenberg, David. 2013. *Anti-Judaism: The Western Tradition.* New York: W.W. Norton and Company.

———. 2014. *Neighboring Faiths: Christianity, Islam, and Judaism in the Middle Ages and Today.* Chicago: University of Chicago Press.

Nittle, Nadra Kareem. 2020. "How the Black Codes Limited African American Progress After the Civil War." HISTORY. October 1, 2020. www.history.com/news /black-codes-reconstruction-slavery.

"Not So Grand: Discrimination at the Hotels—Museum of the White Mountains." n.d. Accessed June 21, 2022. www.plymouth.edu/mwm/exhibitions/the-grand -hotels-of-the-white-mountains-online-exhibition/not-so-grand/.

Noymer, Andrew. 2007. "Contesting the Cause and Severity of the Black Death: A Review Essay." *Population and Development Review* 33 (3): 616–27.

"The Nuremberg Laws: Law for the Protection of German Blood and German Honor." n.d. Jewish Virtual Library. Accessed June 17, 2022. www.jewishvirtuallibrary.org/ law-for-the-protection-of-german-blood-and-german-honor.

"The Nuremberg Laws: The Reich Citizenship Law." n.d. Jewish Virtual Library. Accessed June 17, 2022. www.jewishvirtuallibrary.org/the-reich-citizenship-law.

"OMB DIRECTIVE 15: RACE AND ETHNIC STANDARDS FOR FEDERAL STATISTICS AND ADMINISTRATIVE REPORTING." 1977. May 12, 1977. won der.cdc.gov/wonder/help/populations/bridged-race/directive15.html.

Omi, Michael, and Howard Winant. 1994. *Racial Formation in the United States from the 1960 to the 1990s.* New York: Routledge University Press.

Oster, Marcy. 2019. "Indiana Man Gets 3-Year Prison Sentence for Nazi Graffiti on Synagogue." *Times of Israel,* May 23, 2019. www.timesofisrael.com.

"Overview of Hate Crime." n.d. National Institute of Justice. Accessed September 6, 2021. nij.ojp.gov/topics/articles/overview-hate-crime.

Painter, Nell Irvin. 2010. *The History of White People.* New York: W.W. Norton and Co.

Palmer, Ewan. 2019. "Indiana Man Who 'Openly Identified With Nazism' Traveled 50 Miles to Set Fire to Synagogue with Homemade Napalm." *Newsweek*, May 22, 2019. www.newsweek.com.

Parker, Wendy. 1987. "Synagogue Can Seek Damages for Hate Act, High Court Rules." *Montgomery County Sentinel*, May 21, 1987.

Pianko, Noam. 2015. *Jewish Peoplehood: An American Innovation*. Rutgers University Press.

Plessy v. Ferguson 163 U.S. 537. 1896. U.S. Supreme Court.

"Poor People's Campaign." 2020. In *Encyclopaedia Britannica*. www.britannica.com /topic/Poor-Peoples-March.

Potosky, Maurice. 2008. Silver Spring, MD.

Powell, Cedric Merlin. 2019. "How Race-Neutral Rulings by the Supreme Court Perpetuate Inequalities." Scholars Strategy Network. August 8, 2019. scholars.org/ contribution/how-race-neutral-rulings-supreme-court-perpetuate-inequalities.

Proctor, Robert N., and Robert Proctor. 1988. *Racial Hygiene: Medicine Under the Nazis*. Harvard University Press.

Ramirez, Margaret, and Ameet Sachdev. 2011. "Jerold S. Solovy, 1930–2011." *Chicago Tribune*, January 19, 2011. www.chicagotribune.com/lifestyles/ct-xpm -2011-01-19-ct-met-solovy-obit-0120-20110119-story.html.

Redmond, Jennifer Grace. 1989. "Redefining Race in St. Francis College v. Al-Khazraji and Shaare Tefila Congregation v. Cobb: Using Dictionaries Instead of the Thirteenth Amendment." *Vanderbilt Law Review* 42: 209–31.

Regents of the University of California v. Bakke 438 U.S. 265. 1978. U.S. Supreme Court.

Rensin, Samuel. 2009. Phone interview.

Roe v. Wade 410 U.S. 113. 1973. U.S. Supreme Court.

Roediger, David. 2005. *Working Toward Whiteness: How America's Immigrants Became White, The Strange Journey from Ellis Island to the Suburbs*. New York: Basic Books.

Rosa, Jonathan. 2019. *Looking Like a Language, Sounding Like a Race*. Oxford University Press.

Rosen, Larry. 2006. "Making the Rounds." Orthodox Union. August 2, 2006. www.ou .org/life/inspiration/making_the_rounds/.

Rosenberg, George, and Micha Lev. 1984. *Desecration in Darkness: A Community Fights Back*. The Rosenberg and Issembert Production Company.

Roth, Harriet Steinhorn. 2009. Silver Spring, MD.

Rubin, Daniel Ian. 2020. "HebCrit: A New Dimension of Critical Race Theory." *Social Identities* 26 (4): 499–514. doi.org/10.1080/13504630.2020.1773778.

———. 2021. *The Jewish Struggle in the 21st Century: Conflict, Positionality, and Multiculturalism*. BRILL.

Sales, Ben. 2017. "How the Six Day War Changed American Jews." *The Times of Israel*, May 17, 2017. www.timesofisrael.com/how-the-six-day-war-changed -american-jews/.

Sanua, Marianne R. 2000. "Jewish College Fraternities in the United States, 1895–1968: An Overview." *Journal of American Ethnic History* 19 (2): 3–42.

Sarna, Jonathan D., and David G. Dalin. 1997. *Religion and State in the American Jewish Experience*. Notre Dame, IN: University of Notre Dame Press.

Schere, Daniel. 2017. "Researchers Look at Where Jews and Blacks Weren't Allowed to Go." *Washington Jewish Week*, May 10, 2017.

Schnader. 2009. "Former Managing Partner of Schnader's Washington Office Honored by the American Association of Jewish Lawyers and Jurists." Schnader: The Higher Calling of Law. December 3, 2009. www.schnader.com/event/former -managing-partner-of-schnaders-washington-office-honored-by-the-american -association-of-jewish-lawyers-and-jurists/.

Schneider, Lisa. 1982. "New Anti-Hate Laws in Montgomery County." *Washington Jewish Week*, December 9, 1982.

Scholem, Gershom. 1974. *Major Trends in Jewish Mysticism*. New York: Schocken.

Schraub, David. 2019. "White Jews: An Intersectional Approach." *AJS Review* 43 (2). doi.org/10.1017/S0364009419000461.

Schwartz, Sid. 2008. Silver Spring, MD.

Sehat, David. 2011. *The Myth of American Religious Freedom*. New York: Oxford University Press.

"Shaare Tefila Congregation Board of Trustees Meeting Minutes." 1985.

"Shaare Tefila Congregation Board of Trustees Meeting Minutes." 1984.

———. 1987.

Shaare Tefila Congregation v. Cobb 481 U.S. 615. 1987. U.S. Supreme Court.

Shaare Tefila Congregation v. Cobb 606 F.Supp. 1504. 1985. District of Maryland.

Shaare Tefila Congregation v. Cobb 785 F.2d 523. 1986. Fourth Circuit Court of Appeals.

Shapell, Irvin. 1983. "(Speech)." Shaare Tefila Congregation, January 7.

———. 2009. Phone interview.

Sharp, Edward F. 1992. "To Rabbi Martin Halpern," September 29, 1992.

Shelley v. Kramer 334 U.S. 1. 1948. U.S. Supreme Court.

Silberstein, Laurence J., ed. 2000. *Mapping Jewish Identities*. New York: New York University Press.

Silverblatt, Irene. 2004. *Modern Inquisitions: Peru and the Colonial Origins of the Civilized World*. Durham, NC: Duke University Press.

Singer, Carl. 2017. "The G.I. Bill—The Great, The Bad, and The Ugly." Jewish War Veterans of the United States of America. December 14, 2017. www.jwv.org.

Singer v. Denver School District 959 F.Supp. 1325. 1997. U.S. District Court for the District of Colorado.

"Slaying the Dragon of Debt: Fiscal Policies from the 1970s to the Present: 1980–82 Early 1980s Recession." n.d. Regional Oral History Office, The Bancroft Library, University of California, Berkeley. Accessed January 31, 2021. bancroft.berkeley. edu/ROHO/projects/debt/1980srecession.html.

Smith, Cynthia Gail. 1990. "Patterson v. McLean Credit Union: New Limitations on an Old Civil Rights Statute." *North Carolina Law Review* 68: 799–834.

Soni, Varun. 2005. "Freedom from Subordination: Race, Religion, and the Struggle for Sacrament." *Temple Political and Civil Rights Law Review* 15 (33).

Spetner, Lee. n.d. "A History of Young Israel Shomrai Emunah Genesis of a Washington Synagogue." Young Israel Shomrai Emunah of Greater Washington. Accessed December 18, 2020. wp.yise.org/about/.

St. Francis College v. Al-Khazraji 481 U.S. 604. 1987. U.S. Supreme Court.

"State Action Requirement." n.d. LII / Legal Information Institute. Accessed August 18, 2021. www.law.cornell.edu/wex/state_action_requirement.

State of Maryland v. Michael David Remer. 1983. Circuit Court for Montgomery County.

A Statement of the United States Commission on Civil Rights, ed. 1983. *Intimidation and Violence: Racial and Religious Bigotry*. Clearinghouse Publication 77.

Stern, Gerald M. 2008. *The Buffalo Creek Disaster: How the Survivors of One of The Worst Disasters in Coal-Mining History—And Won*. New York: Vintage Books.

Stiefel, Barry L. 2014. *Jewish Sanctuary in the Atlantic World: A Social and Architectural History*. Columbia, SC: University of South Carolina Press.

Stolzenberg, Nomi Maya. 2011. "Righting the Relationship Between Race and Religion in Law." *Oxford Journal of Legal Studies* 31 (3): 583–602. doi. org/10.1093/ojls/gqr014.

"Story Map Journal." n.d. Mapping Segregation in Washington D.C. Accessed January 5, 2021. www.arcgis.com/apps/MapJournal/index.html?appid=58c3e0088 1374a7b8acddade025ade64.

"Strict Scrutiny." n.d. LII / Legal Information Institute. Accessed June 16, 2022. www .law.cornell.edu/wex/strict_scrutiny.

Sullivan v. Little Hunting Park, Inc. 396 U.S. 229. 1969. U.S. Supreme Court.

"Summary Judgement Definition." n.d. Legal Information Institute, Cornell Law School. Accessed February 26, 2021. www.law.cornell.edu/wex/summary _judgment.

Svonkin, Stuart. 1997. *Jews Against Prejudice: American Jews and The Fight for Civil Liberties*. New York: Columbia University Press.

Synott, Marcia Graham. 1986. "Anti-Semitism and American Universities: Did Quotas Follow the Jews?" In *Anti-Semitism in American History*, edited by David A. Gerber, 233–71. Urbana, IL: University of Illinois Press.

Takao Ozawa v. United States 260 U.S.178. 1922. U.S. Supreme Court.

Tamanaha, Brian Z. 2001. *A General Jurisprudence of Law and Society*. New York City, NY: Oxford University Press.

T.E. v. Pine Bush Central School District 58 F.Supp. 3d 322. n.d. U.S. District Court for the Southern District of New York.

Tehranian, John. 2000. "Performing Whiteness: Naturalization Litigation and the Construction of Racial Identity in American." *The Yale Law Journal* 109 (4): 817–48. doi.org/10.2307/797505.

———. 2009. *Whitewashed: America's Invisible Middle Eastern Minority*. New York: New York University Press.

Teller, Bess. 2008. Silver Spring, MD.

Teller, Jack. 2009. Silver Spring,MD.

Tessman, Lisa. 2001. "Jewish Racializations: Revealing the Contingency of Whiteness." In *Jewish Locations: Traversing Racialized Landscapes*, edited by Lisa Tessman and Bat-Ami Bar On, 131–45. Rowman & Littlefield.

Thompson, Joseph. 2019. "The GI Bill Should've Been Race Neutral, Politicos Made Sure It Wasn't." MilitaryTimes. November 9, 2019. www.militarytimes.com.

"Thurgood Marshall." n.d. Oyez. Accessed February 25, 2021. www.oyez.org/justices /thurgood_marshall.

"Thurgood Marshall, History." n.d. History.Com. Accessed February 26, 2021. www .history.com/topics/black-history/thurgood-marshall.

Tillich, Paul. 1957. *Dynamics of Faith*. New York: Harper and Row.

Tillman v. Wheaton-Haven Recreation Assn. 410 U.S. 431. 1973. U.S. Supreme Court.

Tsesis, Alexander. 2006. "A Civil Rights Approach: Achieving Revolutionary Abolitionism through the Thirteenth Amendment." *U.C. Davis Law Review* 39: 1773–1849.

United States v. Bhagat Singh Thind 261 U.S. 204. 1923. U.S. Supreme Court.

U.S. Attorney's Office, Southern District of Indiana. 2019. "Synagogue Attacker Gets Three Years in Federal Prison." United States Department of Justice. May 22, 2019. www.justice.gov/usao-sdin/pr/synagogue-attacker-gets-three-years-federal -prison.

"U.S. Immigration Timeline." 2019. History.Com. May 14, 2019. www.history.com/ topics/immigration/immigration-united-states-timeline.

Vesey, Tom. 1984. "Synagogue in Md. Files Rights Suit in Defacement Case." *Washington Post*, March 4, 1984.

Wagschal, Brenda. 1992. "To Debbie Stern," September 25, 1992. Private Collection of Shaare Tefila Congregation.

Wald v. International Brotherhood of Teamsters 104 U.S. 503. 1983. U.S. Supreme Court.

Waldron, Thomas W. 1982a. "Police Charge Two Men in Vandalism." *Montgomery County Sentinel*, November 18, 1982.

———. 1982b. "Lawyers Offer Help for Victims of Hate." *Montgomery County Sentinel*, December 30, 1982.

Ward, Christian. 1982. "KKK, Anti-KKK Groups Head for Confrontation." *Montgomery County Sentinel*, November 4, 1982.

Ward, Christian, and Dana Allen. 1982. "The Klan in Montgomery: A Special Report." *Montgomery County Sentinel*, November 11, 1982.

Washington Jewish Week. 1982a. "Synagogue Defaced as Board Meets Inside," November 4, 1982.

———. 1982b. "Interfaith Service," November 11, 1982.

———. 1982c. "Publicity Led to Arrest," November 18, 1982.

———. 1986. "Fighting for Protection under Racial Laws: Shaare Tefila to Petition Supreme Court," March 20, 1986.

Washington Post. 1982. "Cross Burnings, Anti-Semitic Incidents Increase in Montgomery," November 22, 1982.

Weisman, Donald. 1982. "United Synagogue of America: Seaboard Region." Private Collection of the Shaare Tefila Congregation.

Wheeler, Sharae. n.d. "DeFunis v. Odegaard: Another Kind of 'Jewish Problem' - Seattle Civil Rights and Labor History Project." Accessed December 23, 2021. dep ts.washington.edu/civilr/DeFunis.htm.

"White Supremacist Prison Gangs in the United States." 2016. April 14, 2016. www .adl.org/resources/reports/white-supremacist-prison-gangs-united-states.

"Who's Who." n.d. Young Israel Shomrai Emunah of Greater Washington. Accessed December 29, 2020. wp.yise.org/about/whos-who/.

Wiener, Jason. 2018. "Judges of the Fourth Circuit—Hon. Francis D. Murnaghan Jr." *Wake Forest Law Review*, October. wakeforestlawreview.com/2018/10/ judges-of-the-fourth-circuit-hon-francis-d-murnaghan-jr/.

Wilkinson III, P. Harvie. 1997. *One Nation Indivisible: How Ethnic Separatism Threatens America*. New York: Basic Books.

Witte Jr., John, and Joel A. Nichols. 2016. *Religion and the American Constitutional Experiment*. Fourth. New York: Oxford University Press.

Wolf, KB, trans. 2008. "Sentencia-Estatuto de Toledo, 1449." canilup.googlepages. com.

Wright, Jacob L., and Tamara Eskenazi. n.d. "Contrasting Pictures of Intermarriage in Ruth and Nehemiah." TheTorah.Com: A Historical and Contextual Approach. the-torah.com/contrasting-pictures-of-intermarriage-in-ruth-and-nehemiah/.

WTHR.com Staff. 2018. "20-Year-Old and Co-Conspirator Charged in Carmel Synagogue Vandalism." *13 WTHR*, August 17, 2018. www.wthr.com/article/news /local/20-year-old-and-co-conspirator-charged-carmel-synagogue-vandalism/531 -a96f5165-5213-4b12-91a9-43aa9764e6cf.

Wuthnow, Robert. 1988. *The Restructuring of American Religion: Society and Faith since World War II*. Princeton, NJ: Princeton University Press.

Zogby, James J. 1982. "Anti-American Discrimination Committee." Private Collection of Shaare Tefila Congregation.

Zweigenhaft, Richard L., and G. William Domhoff. 1982. *Jews in the Protestant Establishment*. New York: Praeger Special Studies.

Index

About the Author

Annalise E. Glauz-Todrank is assistant professor in the Department for the Study of Religions at Wake Forest University. Her scholarship focuses on the intersections of religion, race, and law in the configuration of Jewish identification, particularly in the modern period. She investigates how these socially constructed categories become normalized, instantiate institutional inequalities, and shape conceptions of the self and the other. Previously, she taught at Wesleyan University and the University of California, Santa Barbara, where she received her PhD in 2010; her BA is from Hampshire College. Her articles and chapters have appeared in numerous publications. This is her first book.